Yale Historical Publications
Miscellany, 102

The Shaping of Southern Politics
Suffrage Restriction and the Establishment of the One-Party South, 1880-1910

J. Morgan Kousser

New Haven and London, Yale University Press

1974

Published with assistance from the Mary Cady Tew
Memorial Fund.

Library of Congress catalog card number: 73-86905
International standard book number: 0-300-01696-4

Designed by John O. C. McCrillis
and set in Baskerville type.
Printed in the United States of America by
The Murray Printing Co., Forge Village, Mass.

Published in Great Britain, Europe, and Africa by
Yale University Press, Ltd., London.
Distributed in Latin America by Kaiman & Polon,
Inc., New York City; in Australasia and Southeast
Asia by John Wiley & Sons Australasia Pty. Ltd.,
Sydney; in India by UBS Publishers' Distributors Pvt.,
Ltd., Delhi; in Japan by John Weatherhill, Inc., Tokyo.

Contents

List of Tables

List of Figures

Preface

"The South," V. O. Key, Jr., noted in 1949, "really has no political parties." Although Southerners voted overwhelmingly for Democratic candidates in national elections in the first half of the twentieth century, the internal politics of their states was in most cases utterly disorganized. Key found the Southern Democratic party of that era "merely a holding-company for a congeries of transient squabbling factions, most of which fail by far to meet the standards of permanence, cohesiveness, and responsibility that characterize the political party." The combination of partyless politics with the notorious political apathy of the region's white citizenry, the widespread disfranchisement of the blacks, and the malapportionment of the state legislatures produced a static political system where irresponsible rural demagogues competed in issueless campaigns.[1]

While upper-class groups found it easy to block change, it was virtually impossible for lower-class citizens to sustain a political organization long enough to use the government to fulfill their needs. Urban groups were usually politically impotent, but politicians from the "black belt" farming areas, as the Negro-majority counties were called, wielded power totally out of proportion to their counties' populations. Inequities, intolerance of dissent, racial discrimination, and extremes of wealth and poverty flourished as nowhere else in America. Shackled by a political system that largely prevented even minimal, gradualist responses to its grave socioeconomic problems, the South had to wait for national forces—the courts, Northern immigration, civil rights and social welfare laws—to compel it to begin again the process of social and political reconstruction.

This book is an attempt to explain the origins of the political system Key described. A complex topic with wide ramifications, it has received less attention than it deserves. As Sheldon Hackney remarked in a recent review article, "One of the unsolved, even unposed riddles of twentieth-century southern politics is why a two-party system did not

1. *Southern Politics in State and Nation,* pp. 16, 303–310.

develop after disfranchisement."[2] The solution to this riddle, I suggest, lies not in the period after disfranchisement and the establishment of the direct, statewide white primary, but in a study of the movements which sought to bring about those electoral changes. If so, then questions about the genesis of the electoral changes are important to political scientists and historians investigating not only the nineteenth century but also the twentieth.

I have attempted in this book to cover in detail the movements for suffrage restriction in each of the eleven ex-Confederate states. I have also treated intensively the changes in Northern opinion toward suffrage and the South, the identity and objectives of the restrictionists and their opponents, and the purposes and efficacy of the particular alterations in the political rules. My interpretation of the change from the post-Reconstruction Southern political system to the twentieth-century system rests on a thorough analysis of election statistics using a technique heretofore rarely used by historians—Leo Goodman's ecological regression method.[3] By employing Goodman's method, I have been able to obtain estimates of the percentages of blacks and whites who voted for each candidate, as well as the proportion who did not vote, in every presidential and gubernatorial election and in many primaries and referenda in the South from 1880 to 1910. For most of these elections, these are the first estimates based on a relatively sophisticated statistical procedure that have ever been made. These statistics allow the most firmly based answers that we have so far to such questions as: to what extent did blacks and whites, respectively, favor the Populists? What percentage of voters from each party favored disfranchisement in the various referenda? To what extent did the massive declines in votes turnout represent only the disfranchisement of blacks? To what extent did whites also stop voting?

The ecological regression technique is central to this book in two ways. First, it allows a direct confrontation with the gravest problem

2. *"Origins of the New South* in Retrospect," Journal of Southern History 38(1972): 205. After skeptically examining several possible explanations, Hackney suggests that "It may be that a homogeneity of economic interests and culture among whites was the real perpetrator of the Solid South." Thus, while praising C. Vann Woodward's *Origins of the New South,* Hackney seeks to replace its emphasis on class conflict with a consensus version of Southern history.

3. For an exposition of this methodology, see my "Ecological Regression and the Analysis of Past Politics," *"Journal of Interdisciplinary History* (1973) : 237–262.

facing political historians who have to analyze aggregate data, the so-called "ecological fallacy." To state the problem briefly as it arises in the study of elections: it is fallacious to estimate the way individuals voted if all one has is voting totals at the precinct or county level. As I explain more fully in my article on the subject, ecological regression was developed precisely to deal with the ecological fallacy. It is therefore usually preferable to techniques using correlation or shaded maps, the more familiar methods of analyzing relationships between variables. Second, it turns out that to run tests on the data using Goodman's technique, one must closely analyze data from all counties. Such close analysis often uncovers little-noticed trends, and it forces one to explain why the behavior of certain counties deviated from either their past behavior or from the statewide pattern of voting in a certain election. In perusing the data from elections in Florida, for example, I discovered that only a few of the black-majority counties deviated from the typical pattern of statewide Florida voting behavior in the early 1880s, but that the number of such deviant counties increased steadily during the decade. As a consequence, I was not only forced to offer an explanation of the Florida trend, but I was also alerted to the possibility that similar trends existed elsewhere. Carefully employed, then, the ecological regression technique can lead to new hypotheses as well as provide answers to the questions with which the historian begins.

A further advantage of ecological regression is the convenience of the form of the estimates it produces. Every political observer is used to reading survey results which give the percentages of such and such a candidate. Ecological regression estimates are in the same form. Although the statistical procedures used in obtaining both survey and ecological regression estimates of population behavior are seldom perfectly straightforward, the estimates themselves can be presented in a clear, simple manner. It is possible, therefore, to relegate most technical matters to footnotes and appendixes and to keep methodological intrusions in the text to a minimum; I have attempted to do so in this book. One need not be an initiate in the rites of statistics to understand my analysis of Southern politics.

In addition to analyzing election statistics and the crucial roll calls on disfranchisement and related matters in all of the key legislative and constitutional convention sessions, I have read extensively in published and unpublished sources, including legislative and convention journals and minutes, newspapers, M.A. and Ph.D. theses, and, of course, published books and articles. My examination of the extensive collections of private papers has been limited to the considerable information contained in scholarly writings on Southern history in this period. Given the state of scholarship in the field, it seemed that a large investment in the study of election statistics would earn greater dividends than further investigation of manuscript sources, which have already been extensively mined. I have attempted to cross-check the validity of any single historian's account by comparing it with other secondary analyses and with newspapers and published government documents. A close comparison of this study with other secondary works will demonstrate that I have not accepted others' interpretations of primary sources or other data uncritically.

I could not have completed a task as extensive as writing this book without the assistance, often far beyond what I have any right to expect, of many people. The Historical Data Archives of the Inter-University Consortium for Political Research provided me with the election returns on which this book is primarily based. The staffs of the Yale and Caltech libraries greatly facilitated my work by making available numerous and sometimes obscure books, theses, and other documents. The state librarians of nine Southern states forwarded data to me on wealth statistics which I could not have otherwise obtained. The computer centers at Yale and Caltech provided programming assistance and granted essential computer time. The Research Committee of the Humanities and Social Sciences Division at Caltech gave me funds so that my undergraduate research assistant, Bruce Bennett, could help me finish the computations. The secretaries in the division, Joy Hansen, Margaret Robison, Malvine Baer, Edith Taylor, and Connie Viancour, typed most of the preliminary drafts, and all of the final draft.

Several of my then fellow students at Yale gave me helpful comments, especially Jim Green, John McCarthy, and Cam Walker. I also profited from the remarks of Professors Howard Lamar and Douglas Rae during my dissertation colloquium, and from the comments of Professor Michael Holt on the completed dissertation. Three of my colleagues at Caltech, Robert H. Bates, Lance J. Davis, and Daniel J. Kevles, read much of the preliminary drafts, and provided encouragement as well as useful suggestions. Edward Tripp of Yale University Press saw within a too-flawed manuscript the germ of a better one, and encouraged and guided me in the elimination of at least some of those flaws. My copy editor at Yale Press, Nancy Paxton, has a passion for clarity which has, hopefully, overmatched my penchant for obscure constructions. Parts of the book have appeared in different form in *The Political Science Quarterly*, whose editor, Demetrios Caraley, provided several helpful comments.

Like all of his other students, I owe a great debt to C. Vann Woodward. His work provided the stimulus and inspiration for this book, he read and commented on an earlier draft and led me to new insights as well as saved me from errors. Naturally, neither he nor any of the others who read parts of the present work should be held responsible for the mistakes and inadequacies which remain.

Finally, my wife, Sally Ward Kousser, assisted with computations and proofreading, read and criticized the innumerable versions of various sections, and supported me when the burdens of Southern politics seemed least bearable.

Introduction

The first historians of suffrage restriction were the contemporary victors in the struggle. Southern Democrats of the late nineteenth century skillfully purveyed several false but lingering myths about their era. According to their distorted scenario, the North, finally realizing the uselessness and malevolence of the Reconstruction attempt to exalt black over white, resolved in 1877 to allow the Southern whites to control their own region. Paternalistic leaders then set about to heal racial and economic cleavages and construct a New South by introducing industry into the agrarian society. Some Negroes continued to vote freely while others lapsed into apathy, content to allow the "better sort" of white men to guide politics. When some temporarily misguided whites betrayed their race by opposing the party of their fathers and appealing for the corrupt Negro vote, the vast majority of white men united to end the threat. They first rejected the Populists in elections and then proceeded, with commendable speed and unanimity of purpose, to disfranchise the ex-slaves. This movement to purify the ballot box merely ratified the natural dominance of the superior over the inferior race. The various means of restriction did not matter much; what counted was the commitment to deny the franchise to the unfit in a legal, constitutional manner. Afterwards, the South settled down to racial peace and economic prosperity that was broken only after half a century (their later white Southern counterparts would say), by Communists, outside agitators, and hypocritical Yankees.[1]

Easily condemned in the 1970s as racist and self-serving, this explanation of suffrage restriction did satisfy an earlier America that was even more suffused with racism and anxious to conceal from itself the paradox of brutal inequities in a "democratic" country. But few

1. This sketch is a composite drawn from numerous speeches and articles. See, e.g., John B. Knox's presidential address in *Offic. Proc. Con. Con. Ala., 1901*, pp. 7–16; Thomas W. Hardwick, speech at Georgia Democratic State Convention, 1906, quoted in *Atlanta Constitution*, Sept. 5, 1906; Sen. Ben Tillman, speech in S.C. Constitutional Convention *J. Proc.* (1895), pp. 443–472; Gov. Charles B. Aycock's inaugural address, printed in N.C. Legis. *Pub. Doc. 1901*, vol. 1, doc. la; Sen. James F. George's speech, printed in *Cong. Rec.*, 51st Cong., 2nd sess., appendix, pp. 46–96.

historians or political scientists have attempted to replace the contemporary legend with a nonracist, nonpartisan, yet comprehensive view. While considerably more objective and often more sophisticated, recent analysts have usually focused on a few states, a few crucial events, or a relatively brief period. In narrowing their focus and thereby excluding important data, these historians have missed the benefits to be gained by systematically comparing the experiences of all eleven of the ex-Confederate states. Relying chiefly on such traditional sources of information as newspapers and paper collections, they have paid less attention to the most crucial type of data for the study of democratic politics—election returns. Some have also seriously misinterpreted the evidence they did scrutinize. It is hardly surprising, therefore, that no modern explanation for the alterations that occurred in Southern politics at the turn of the century commands general assent. It is time to replace the earlier mythic tale with a new, systematic, general analysis of political change in the South from 1877 to 1910.

Many historians have viewed the South as "solid" after 1877.[2] Focusing on the fact that the Democratic party carried every ex-Confederate state in the presidential elections from 1880 to 1920, these scholars have belittled the Southern Republicans of the era as impotent and interpreted the Independent and Populist movements as little more than factional fights within the Democratic party. For instance, Oscar Handlin states that "after 1876, the South was solidly Democratic. . . . Republican efforts to maintain a foothold below the Mason-Dixon line were half-hearted and ineffectual. . . . The only effective dissent came from among the Democrats."[3] By reading the characteristics of the twentieth-century Southern political structure back into the pre-disfranchisement[4] era, historians holding this view

2. Samuel Eliot Morison and Henry Steele Commager are able to speak of the South as "solid" in the midst of the Populist revolt. See their *Growth of the American Republic* 2: 334, 338; and, similarly, Philip E. Converse, "Change in the American Electorate," in Angus Campbell and Philip E. Converse, eds., *The Human Meaning of Social Change*, p. 307.

3. *The History of the United States*, 2 : 72. Similarly, Richard M. Current, T. Harry Williams, and Frank Freidel state in *American History: A Survey*, p. 470, that after 1877, the Democratic party was "the only party in the [South]. . . ."

4. The terms "disfranchisement," "suffrage restriction," "suffrage limitation," and similar variants will be used interchangeably in this book to avoid more repetition of the same phrase than necessary. As employed here, none of the terms implies an absolute, unequivocal provision which bans a discrete category of persons from the ballot box. No Southern state passed such a law after 1868. Instead, the laws made the economic and social costs of voting so high

dismiss too easily the national Republican party's post-1877 commitment to protecting the political rights of its Southern followers, underestimate the residual power of the Southern GOP in the late nineteenth century, and disregard the transformation of Southern politics that took place about the turn of the century.

Assuming that Southern politics did retain a good deal of vigor after 1877, what forces sapped that energy? Why did party competition and voting turnout decline so sharply throughout the South? Key set forth probably the most general explanation: "The evolution of suffrage restrictions differed from state to state, and for some, perhaps even for all, southern states, the thesis could be argued plausibly that formal disfranchisement measures did not lie at the bottom of the decimation of the southern electorate. They, rather, recorded a *fait accompli* brought about, or destined to be brought about, by more fundamental political processes" (*Southern Politics*, p. 533). In other words, the core of Key's thesis is that modifications in suffrage laws merely formalized changes produced by such extralegal forces as violence, intimidation, the growing hegemony of a socioeconomic elite, and the decline in party competition, a decline Key apparently believed came about for reasons not directly connected with suffrage restriction.

To a degree, Key's fait accompli hypothesis merely states a tautology: any statute passed by any legislative body reflects the structure of power at the time. If blacks and other advocates of widespread political participation had not been somewhat suppressed already, the disfranchisers could not have pushed their laws through the assemblies.

But Key went beyond the obvious to argue that in Texas and, by implication, throughout the South, "Negroes [had] been disfranchised . . . and the electoral abdication of a substantial part of the white population signed and sealed" before the major law limiting the electorate was passed (p. 535). In making this contention, Key reflected a more general belief shared by many other political scientists that electoral laws play a minimal role in shaping the political system. For example, the authors of twenty pages of entries under "Voting" and "Political Participation" in the recent *International Encyclopedia of the Social Sciences* include only two paragraphs on franchise laws. Nor are

---

that they discouraged many qualified electors from voting and allowed administrators to discriminate between voters with roughly the same legal qualifications.

such laws considered among the "determinants of party systems" by the *Encyclopedia*'s expert on political parties.[5]

Political scientists who do investigate the impact of voting statutes usually concentrate on the *extension* of the suffrage, while ignoring the process of franchise *contraction* in their theories.[6] Most would probably still accept Tocqueville's view, at least as applied to "democracies":

When a nation modifies the elective qualification, it may easily be foreseen that sooner or later that qualification will be entirely abolished. There is no more invariable rule in the history of society: the further electoral rights are extended, the greater is the need of extending them, for after each concession the strength of the democracy increases, and its demands increase with its strength. . . . no stop can be made short of universal suffrage.[7]

5. See Herbert McCloskey, "Political Participation," in Sills, *International Encyclopedia of the Social Sciences*, 22 : 252–265; Donald E. Stokes, "Voting," in ibid., 16 : 387–395; Harry Eckstein, "Parties, Political: Party Systems," in ibid., 11 : 436–452. For a similar treatment, see Seymour Martin Lipset, *Political Man*, chap. 6, "Voting in Western Democracies: Who Votes and Who Doesn't," pp. 183–229. Of course, there are exceptions to this prevailing view. Kelley et al. argued that the extension of registration laws in the early twentieth century sliced American voting turnout. Rusk argued that the amount of ticket-splitting from 1876 to 1908 varied inversely with the ease of marking the ballot for a straight party slate. See Stanley Kelley, Jr., Richard E. Ayres, and William G. Bowen, "Voting: Putting First Things First," *American Political Science Review* 61 (1967) : 359–379; Jerrold G. Rusk, "The Effect of the Australian Ballot Reform on Split Ticket Voting," ibid. 64 (1970) : 1220–1238.

6. See, for example, Stein Rokkan, "The Comparative Study of Political Participation," in Charles F. Cnudde and Deane E. Neubauer, eds., *Empirical Democratic Theory*, pp. 333–369; Rokkan, "Electoral Mobilization, Party Competition, and National Integration," in Joseph LaPalombara and Myron Weiner, eds., *Political Parties and Political Development*, pp. 241–266; Lipset and Rokkan, "Cleavage Structures, Party Systems, and Voter Alignments: An Introduction," in Lipset and Rokkan, eds., *Party Systems and Voter Alignments*, pp. 1–66; Roy C. Macridis, "Introduction," in Macridis, ed., *Political Parties*, pp. 9–13; Lipset, "Party Systems and the Representation of Social Groups," in ibid., p. 41; Gabriel A. Almond, "Political Systems and Political Change," *American Behavioral Scientist* 6 (1963) : 3–10; Sidney Verba, "Conclusion: Comparative Political Culture," in Lucian W. Pye and Sidney Verba, eds., *Political Culture and Political Development*, pp. 512–560; Lipset, *Political Man*, pp. 79–80; Lipset, "Some Social Requisites of Democracy: Economic Development and Political Legitimacy," *American Political Science Review* 53 (1959) : 86–91; Joseph LaPalombara and Myron Weiner, "The Origin and Development of Political Parties" and "The Impact of Parties Upon Political Development," in LaPalombara and Weiner, eds., *Political Parties and Political Development*, pp. 3–42, 399–435; Eric Nordlinger, "Political Development: Time Sequences and Rates of Change," in Nordlinger, ed., *Politics and Society*, pp. 329–347; Bendix and Rokkan, "The Extension of Citizenship to the Lower Classes," in Reinhard Bendix, ed., *Nation-Building and Citizenship*, pp. 74–104. For a fuller discussion of political science theories relevant here, see my dissertation, "The Shaping of Southern Politics: Suffrage Restriction and the Establishment of the One-Party South, 1880–1910" (Ph.D. diss., Yale Univ., 1971), pp. 1–14.

7. Alexis de Tocqueville, *Democracy in America* (New York: Schocken Books, 1961), 1 : 50.

Despite such reasoning, we shall see in the following pages that changes in electoral laws and procedures did in themselves have very substantial impacts on both the scope of political participation and the mode of political activity in the South.[8] The analysis I will present in this book not only shows that the fait accompli thesis as Key originally stated it ought to be abandoned, but also implies that political theory needs to be altered to take account of the fact that election laws can be and have been employed to limit the suffrage, restrict political choice, and, therefore, restructure the political system.

If procedural changes were indeed the most fundamental factors in the metamorphosis of Southern politics, then the crucial issues become the identity and motivation of the disfranchisers and their opponents. Perhaps the most widely accepted explanation among historians is that lower-class whites and politicians who relied chiefly on support from that stratum fostered restrictions on suffrage in order to exclude Negroes from voting. For instance, Hampton M. Jarrell asserted that "egalitarians in the class struggle were most extreme in their opposition to Negro participation in politics." An American history textbook declared that "the white masses demanded the disfranchisement of the Negro." Other historians have contended that the "agrarians," "white farmers," "small-farmer leaders," or disenchanted former Populists, angry at "Bourbon" control of the Negro vote, led or at least initiated

---

For similar, more recent statements, see V. O. Key, Jr., *Politics, Parties, and Pressure Groups*, p. 623; Giuseppe Di Palma, *Apathy and Participation*, p. 117; Richard Claude, *The Supreme Court and the Electoral Process*, pp. 254–256; Franklin Johnson, *The Development of State Legislation Concerning the Free Negro*, p. 44; Lipset, "Party Systems," p. 41; Rokkan, "Electoral Mobilization," pp. 244, 256–259; Rokkan, "Comparative Study," pp. 338–339, 348–358; Lipset and Rokkan, "Cleavage Structures," pp. 5, 26–30. Samuel P. Huntington, *Political Order in Changing Societies*, p. 431, states that "tendencies toward the rapid expansion of political participation. . . inhere in a two-party system."

8. A similar controversy seems to be developing now among political scientists over the effect of the Australian ballot on split-ticket voting and related changes in the nineteenth century "political universe." See W. Dean Burnham, "The Changing Shape of the American Political Universe," *American Political Science Review*, 59 (1965), pp. 7–28; Rusk, "Australian Ballot"; an exchange between Rusk and Burnham in *ibid.*, 65 (1971), pp. 1149–1157; Converse, "American Electorate"; and Burnham, "Theory and Voting Research: Some Reflections on Converse's 'Change in the American Electorate' " (unpublished manuscript, M. I. T., 1973), a copy of which Professor Burnham was kind enough to send me. In his article (pp. 297–299), Converse has discussed in a general way the effects of the Australian ballot and personal registration laws on electoral participation. He sees the nationwide decline in turnout at the turn of the century as an "unintended consequence" of these "reforms." His comments appear to be directed primarily, but not exclusively, at the Northern experience.

the movements to limit the electorate. The "rich whites" or "black belt planters" merely "acquiesced" in the campaigns.[9]

Two other theories relate political competition to electoral limitation. According to the first, the 1890s taught all whites the danger of allowing blacks to hold the balance of power when whites split over political issues. Therefore, all the whites collaborated to expel the Negroes from the electorate. V. O. Key put forth another view. Reasoning that any faction in power feared that the "outs" would appeal to the Negro to regain office, Key argued that the "ins," whether "Bourbon" or "radical" in each state, promoted laws to expunge black voters from the lists.[10]

All these hypotheses presuppose that the sole target of the restrictive movements was the black voter. The sizable decline in white turnout and the limitation of the whites' effective range of choice to a single party are treated as either coincidences, unintended consequences of Negro disfranchisement, or the result of other factors such as the decline in the national Republican party's interest in carrying the South.[11]

On the other hand, what we shall call the "black belt thesis" portrays suffrage restriction as a movement by predominantly upper-class whites from Negro-majority counties to secure their power against both blacks and lower-class whites. The plantation elite's reasons for wanting to

9. Hampton M. Jarrell, *Wade Hampton and the Negro*, p. xi; Richard B. Morris and William Greenleaf, *USA: The History of a Nation*, 2 : 36. See my "Shaping of Southern Politics,' 'pp. 34–63, for a full discussion of theories concerning the identity and motives of the disfranchisers and the attitude of upper- and lower-class whites toward Negro suffrage. The "acquiescence" theory is enunciated in Current et. al. *American History*, pp. 470–471; John S. Ezell, *The South since 1865*, p. 177; T. Harry Williams, "An Analysis of Some Reconstruction Attitudes," *Journal of Southern History* 12 (1946): 485; Thomas B. Clark and Albert D. Kirwin, *The South since Appomattox*, p. 74; John D. Stark, *Damned Upcountryman*, p. 29; and Allie Bayne Windham Webb, "A History of Negro Voting in Louisiana, 1877–1906" (Ph.D. diss., Louisiana State Univ., 1962), pp. iv–v. The disenchanted Populists appear in three works by C. Vann Woodward, *Tom Watson, Agrarian Rebel*, pp. 370–382; *Origins of the New South*, pp. 322–323; and *The Strange Career of Jim Crow*, pp. 60–64, 80–81, 89–90; as well as in such works as Horace Mann Bond's *Negro Education in Alabama*, p. 165; and Ezell's *South since 1865*, p. 173. It must be noted that Woodward puts less stress on the Populist than the Democratic role in disfranchisement. See his "The Ghost of Populism Walks Again," *N. Y. Times Magazine* (June 4, 1972), p. 66.

10. Dewey W. Grantham, Jr., *The Democratic South*, p. 40; Monroe Lee Billington, *The American South*, p. 224; Key, *Southern Politics*, pp. 542–550.

11. Paul Lewinson apparently believed that the lower class white leaders were so myopic they failed to see that poll taxes and literacy tests would discourage white as well as black voting. See his *Race, Class, and Party*, p. 97.

disfranchise blacks were obvious. The end of Negro voting would solidify their control over their tenants and free them from having to deal with elected or appointed black officials—a type of contact almost all Southern whites found distasteful. The reasons for disfranchising whites are less obvious. Traditional enmity between lowland (black belt) and hill country (white county) whites fed on malapportionment (in favor of the black belt), of legislatures, of party conventions, and of taxes, and on the rich rural whites' desire to keep taxes low in the face of urban and up-country demands for increased public services.[12] The easiest way for the black belt leaders to avoid conflict over these issues was to reduce the power of the white counties by disfranchising the poor whites who largely populated them.

Historians have slighted another possible but obviously potent motive for disfranchisement—partisanship. As we shall see, the vast majority of the members of opposition parties fought against the restrictive laws, while virtually all the disfranchisers were Democrats. Excluding Negroes from politics did have partisan as well as racial consequences: it deprived any anti-Democratic group of the hope of attracting the votes of those most persecuted by the political and economic status quo. Moreover, many of the laws that disfranchised blacks worked nearly as potently against lower-class whites. In case the white underclass in large numbers threatened to join any party opposed to the Democrats, suffrage laws could be enforced tightly enough to put down the challenge.

Contemporary Democrats sometimes even admitted to partisan

12. Malcolm C. McMillan, *Constitutional Development in Alabama, 1798–1901*, pp. 251, 268–269, 322; Key, *Southern Politics*, pp. 544–548. Key, of course, stressed the role of the black belt in twentieth-century Southern politics throughout his book. See, e.g. pp. 5–6. On traditional enmity, see McMillan, p. 251, 322; William Alexander Mabry, "The Disfranchisement of the Negro in the South" (Ph.D. diss., Duke Univ., 1933), p. 360; *Chicasaw* (Mississippi) *Messenger*, quoted in *Jackson Clarion-Ledger*, March 14, 1889, quoted in Vernon Lane Wharton, *The Negro in Mississippi, 1865–1890*, p. 207; J. S. McNeilly, "History of the Measures Submitted to the Committee on the Elective Franchise, Apportionment, and Elections in the Mississippi Constitutional Convention of 1890," Mississippi Historical Society, *Publications* 6 (1902): 133; Hallie Farmer, *Legislative Apportionment*, pp. 10–13; James A. Tinsley, "The Progressive Movement in Texas" (Ph.D. diss. Univ. of Wisconsin, 1953), pp. 91–92; Nelson M. Blake, *William Mahone of Virginia*, pp. 188–189; Joseph Flake Steelman, "The Progressive Era in North Carolina, 1884–1917" (Ph.D. diss., Univ. of North Carolina, 1955), pp. 8, 119–120, 485–491; William Ivy Hair, *Bourbonism and Agrarian Protest*, pp. 119–126.

motives. For example, Thomas J. Semmes, one of the South's most prominent lawyers and a leading delegate to three of his state's constitutional conventions, affirmed that the 1898 Louisiana constitution, which sharply restricted the franchise, "is the work of a Democratic convention. . . . It has been stated in some quarters that we have been actuated to a certain extent by party spirit. What of it? What is the State? It is the Democratic party. [Applause] . . . Whenever there were political questions involved, of course, we looked to the interests of the party, because they are the interests of the State."[13]

While many historians and political scientists have agreed that the procedural changes were important, there has been no consensus on the goals and efficacy of particular measures. Thus, the most recent work on the Australian or secret ballot pictures it as a "major reform issue . . . part of the general reforming spirit of the age"; whereas Southern Populists and Republicans attacked the secret ballot laws passed in their states as partisan attempts to disfranchise illiterate opponents of the Democratic party. Although a knowledgeable political observer stated 70 years ago that the poll tax had proven "the most effective instrumentality of Negro disfranchisement," V. O. Key believed that "the poll tax has had little or no bearing on Negro disfranchisement." Finally, historians and contemporaries have viewed the direct statewide primary as, variously, a "progressive reform," a potent device for disfranchising Negroes, and a technique for preserving the Democratic party's supremacy.[14]

This cacophony of opinions expressed by participants in the political ferment after 1877 and by scholars studying the period both suggests and serves as an introduction to the central questions to be addressed in this book:

What formed the Southern political system that operated in the first half of the twentieth century? Was it a product of the Civil War and Reconstruction, or did it take shape later? Was it an unintended con-

13. La. Con. Con. *Journal* (1898), p. 374. See also a speech quoted by the *New Orleans Daily Picayune*, March 17, 1898, in which Semmes identified the Democratic party with Christ, "the fatherhood of God and the brotherhood of man," and "the success of civilization."

14. See L. E. Fredman, *The Australian Ballot*, pp. ix-x. J. S. McNeilly ("History of the Measures," p. 316) refuted by Key, *Southern Politics*, p. 618. The various views are represented by Arthur S. Link, "The Progressive Movement in the South, 1870–1914," *North Carolina Historical Review* 23 (1946): 188; Clark and Kirwin, *South since Appomattox*, p. 109; Thomas J. Jarvis, quoted in *Raleigh* (N.C.) *News and Observer*, February 12, 1899.

sequence of a movement by lower-class whites to expel the Negro from politics? Or did a political and economic elite consciously seek to destroy party competition and widespread political participation—the bare requisites of a democratic political system?

Did the late nineteenth- and early twentieth-century laws and constitutional amendments restricting the suffrage merely give legal form to conditions already brought about by other forces? Or were those legal changes themselves the most significant forces molding the new political structure?

What were the objectives of the changes that Southerners made in the rules of the political game, and how effective were those procedural alterations in accomplishing their goals?

To state the questions in the most general manner: How important were the turn-of-the-century restrictions on suffrage and the legalization of the white Democratic primary in the transition from a competitive democratic political system to a structure that severely limited political choice and inhibited mass political involvement? Did disfranchisement and the primary shape twentieth-century Southern politics?

1

Southern Politics from Reconstruction
to Restriction: An Overview

Twentieth-century Southern politics did not spring full-grown from the heads of those who negotiated the Compromise of 1877. What followed after Reconstruction was a period of transition, uncertainty, fluctuation that ended only with the restriction of the suffrage and the consequent stifling of anti-Democratic political parties. During the period from 1877 through the last decade of the century, the possibility remained that the Northern Republicans, because of a residue of humanitarianism left over from the antislavery and Reconstruction struggles, or merely for party advantage, would pass new national election bills, or even, white Southerners feared, pass civil rights acts. Moreover, since not all ambitious white politicians had yet been taught the absolute necessity of confining quarrels within the Democratic party, serious candidates continued to campaign under Republican, Independent, and Populist party labels. Then, too, blacks who had learned the techniques of politics during Reconstruction did not immediately turn to other, less dangerous pursuits. Many of the leaders continued to hold office, to trade the still substantial Negro vote for favors for the race or for themselves, and even continued to influence legislation.

This chapter will identify the dynamic elements in the structure of Southern politics during this period and outline the principal political events. Its purposes are to revise some standard views about the era; to show how the logic of the political situation first encouraged those damaged by the status quo to join the opposition to the Democrats, and then led the Democrats, in response, to restrict the suffrage; and to set the context for later chapters on the methods of disfranchisement and the identity and motives of the restrictionists.

THE POST-RECONSTRUCTION SOUTHERN POLITICAL SCENE

The gross election statistics may help to dispel the myth of Southern solidity and clarify impressionistic notions of the transformation in the political structure. Table 1.1 presents the percentages of total adult males voting for each party as well as the overall turnout in presidential races from 1872 to 1908 in the South, and it compares these figures to percentages for the rest of the states. Approximately equal proportions

Table 1.1. Turnout and Proportion of Adult Males Voting for Each Party in the South and Non-South in Presidential Elections, 1872–1908.

Election	Democrat	Republican	Other	Turnout
		SOUTH		
1872	23.35	26.87	0	50.24
1876	38.73	26.70	0	64.94
1880	36.88	23.76	2.90	63.55
1884	37.20	25.70	0.34	62.84
1888	37.94	23.08	1.47	62.49
1892	33.87	14.58	9.71	58.16
1896	33.33	19.83	3.00	56.16
1900	26.54	15.35	1.22	43.10
1904	18.95	8.31	1.35	28.62
1908	19.44	9.58	1.15	30.18
		NON-SOUTH		
1872	21.83	28.36	0.18	50.37
1876	31.88	32.95	0.84	65.67
1880	33.70	37.80	2.64	74.14
1884	33.11	35.77	2.39	71.24
1888	33.42	36.62	2.66	72.69
1892	30.56	32.94	6.83	70.35
1896	32.65	40.82	1.95	75.42
1900	31.00	39.04	2.00	72.05
1904	22.35	38.73	3.97	65.05
1908	26.21	34.89	3.58	64.68

SOURCE: All calculations are my own, based on interpolations from census data and election returns from W. Dean Burnham, *Presidential Ballots 1836–1892* (Baltimore, Md.: Johns Hopkins Univ. Press, 1955), and Edgar E. Robinson, *The Presidential Vote, 1896–1932* (Stanford, Ca.: Stanford Univ. Press, 1934).

NOTE: Because the 1870 census was notoriously inadequate, the percentages for the 1872 and 1876 elections have been computed on the basis of the 1880 population figures. The estimates of turnout are consequently low for these elections.

of citizens in each section voted in the elections during the seventies. In the next four races, Northern turnout topped Southern by only 10 to 12 percent, despite the enactment of various disfranchising laws (especially between 1888 and 1892), extensive fraud and violence, and weaker party competition in the South. In 1896, the heated contest inflated Yankee participation rates, while the collapse of Populism produced a lull below the Potomac. That Southern lull became permanent with the passage of harshly restrictive laws in several more states around the turn of the century. Though participation fell off in the North, too, the percentage of Northern turnout more than doubled that in the South in 1904, and similar gaps separated the sections through midcentury.[1]

The table also shows the decline of opposition to the Democrats in the South. During the eighties, one of every four potential voters managed to have his ticket recorded for the Republicans. (Fewer than four in ten were Democrats.) The vitality of the Dixie GOP during this decade has been underrated. During the nineties, the passage of strong measures limiting the suffrage in six of the eleven states, in addition to the confusion of party allegiances as the Populists rose and fell, cut the percentage casting ballots for anti-Democratic candidates by a third. That percentage declined by another third from 1900 to 1904 as more states restricted voting, and as opposition electors who remained eligible drifted into apathy when disfranchisement reduced their parties' chances of winning.

The statistics for the three decades demonstrate the length of time required for the shift from the Reconstruction system of stiff party competition and high voter interest to the twentieth-century system of the solid, apathetic South. They also establish prima facie a case for the efficacy of the restrictive election statutes. But to understand how events unfolded and why the structure developed as it did, we must view the changing political condition of the South in more detail.

If the term "solid South" had gained currency by 1880, it signified

1. I used presidential figures in this discussion because governor's contests occurred in different years from state to state, and because the attraction of different candidates varied so much. The statistics from state-level races essentially confirm the findings presented in the text. In fact, they generally make the metamorphosis of the Southern political system even clearer. The GOP and the Populists were stronger in the eighties and nineties in many cases in the struggles for the statehouses than for the White House. Moreover, turnout often dropped off more precipitously in the series of gubernatorial races than in those for the presidency.

only that the Democrats carried each ex-Confederate state in that year's presidential election, not that opposition had been extinguished among voters of either race. Although violence and intimidation were the ultimate means of keeping Negro and white dissenters out of power, their effectiveness has been overrated. Nor did the Negro's economic dependence totally undermine his political independence, as some historians have stated. Staughton Lynd, for example, has written that since it lacked "an economic substratum, manhood suffrage [for blacks] was inevitably artificial," and that although Negroes continued to vote in large numbers after 1877, "rarely did they vote independently." Yet, as the Southern Redeemers often found to their chagrin, it was not as easy to control black votes as they had hoped.[2]

Table 1.2 contains estimates of voting by race in the 1880 presidential election. It indicates that a majority of the Negro adult males voted in that contest in every Southern state except two—Mississippi, where violence was extraordinarily thorough, and Georgia, which had adopted a cumulative poll tax. Not only did they vote. A majority of the black votes in ten states were actually counted for the Republican party, to which the Negroes overwhelmingly adhered. Moreover, a majority of the whites appear to have voted in every state except Louisiana, and there electoral chicanery in the black belt river parishes undoubtedly swelled my estimate of black participation and correspondingly diminished the estimate for whites.[3]

2. Staughton Lynd, "Introduction," in *Reconstruction*, p. 8. John R. Lynch, the last black congressman from Mississippi, told his House colleagues in 1882 that Negroes "have bravely refused to surrender their honest convictions, even upon the altar of their personal necessities. They have said to those upon whom they were dependent, you may deprive me for the time being of the opportunity of making an honest living. You may take the bread out of the mouths of my hungry and dependent families. You may close the schoolhouse door in the face of my children. Yes, more, you may take that which no man can give—my life. But my manhood, my principles, you cannot have." Quoted in U.S. House of Representatives, Committee on House Administration, Subcommittee on Elections, *Contested Elections in the First, Second, Third, Fourth, and Fifth Districts of the State of Mississippi*, 89th Cong., 1st Sess. (Washington, D. C.: G.P.O. 1965), p. 49. On the naïve hopes of the Redeemers, see Allen W. Trelease, *White Terror*, pp. xl—xli. On Negro activism, see, e.g., William Warren Rogers and Robert David Ward, "Jack Turnerism: A Political Phenomenon of the Deep South," *Journal of Negro History* 57 (1972): 313–332.

3. Some historians have claimed that blacks generally voted Democratic in the South during this period. See, e.g., Ezell, *The South since 1865*, p. 177; Paul M. Gaston, *The New South Creed*, pp. 132–133. Contemporaries disagreed. "We all know," said Alabama Congressman William C. Oates, "that nine-tenths of the Negroes are Republicans, and that when they vote at all it will be, with few exceptions the Republican ticket." Quoted in *Congressional Record*, 51st Cong., 1st Sess., p. 6724. For similar statements see *Pine Bluff* (Ark.) *Weekly Com-*

Table 1.2. The Unsolid South: Estimates of Voting, by Race, in the
1880 Presidential Election.

State	% Democratic	% Republican	% Other	% Not Voting
		WHITES		
Alabama	47	9	0	41
Arkansas	40	14	0	46
Florida	70	10	0	20
Georgia	49	7	0	44
Louisiana	31	5	0	64
Mississippi	55	12	0	33
North Carolina	58	21	0	21
South Carolina	86	11	0	4
Tennessee	41	24	2	33
Texas	48	4	7	41
Virginia	47	3	14	35
		NEGROES		
Alabama	25	34	0	41
Arkansas	21	49	0	30
Florida	19	69	0	12
Georgia	11	28	0	61
Louisiana	30	27	0	44
Mississippi	16	18	0	66
North Carolina	17	67	0	17
South Carolina	31	37	0	30
Tennessee	37	54	0	8
Texas	19	49	4	28
Virginia	2	58	6	35

mercial, Nov. 9, 1890; *Jacksonville Florida Times-Union,* Sept. 20, Oct. 12, 1890; William Pledger, quoted in Olive Hall Shadgett, *The Republican Party in Georgia, from Reconstruction through 1900,* p. 118; John R. Lynch, quoted in *Knoxville* (Tenn.) *Journal,* Feb. 20, 1890; Richard Nelson, quoted in Lawrence Delbert Rice, *The Negro in Texas, 1874–1900,* p. 35; and numerous statements by Rep. James Phelan (D., Tenn.) and others in *L. B. Eaton, Contestant, vs. James Phelan, Contestee: Contested Election Case from the Tenth Congressional District of Tennessee,* 51st Cong. (Washington, D. C.: R. O. Polkinhorn, n.d.), pp. 5, 58–92. Because voting behavior in East Tennessee varied so much from the other two sections, estimates of black and white voting in Tennessee throughout this book were computed by section (East Tennessee and the rest), then weighted and summed to get a statewide estimate. Many of the North Carolina and Virginia estimates below were computed by dividing each state into two groups of counties—those above and those below 30 percent Negro. In each case where separate estimates were made for various groups of counties, inspection of relevant regression diagrams had shown that single straight lines did not describe the data well. Inspections of the diagrams for the grouped data as well as comparisons of the percentages of variance explained by each method led to using the grouped data estimates. For a fuller discussion of the methodological points, see my "Ecological Regression and the Analysis of Past Politics," *Journal of Interdisciplinary History* 4 (1973): 237–262.

The key Democratic appeal was simple racism, and accordingly, the bulwark of Democratic strength lay in the counties composed of a majority or a near-majority of Negroes. In the 1884 North Carolina gubernatorial election, for example, the Democrats received 53.7 percent of the estimated white votes in counties below 30 percent Negro, but 92.4 percent in the counties above 30 percent black.

The black belt had been the center of slavery and the slaveholding aristocracy. It was in these most fertile areas of the South that the contrast between white dominance and black submission, white wealth and black poverty, white education and enforced black ignorance had been most striking before the War. The vestiges of the antebellum ideology and social structure—the unqualified belief in the innate inferiority or even inhumanness of the Negro, the contradictory impulses to violence and paternalism, the acceptance of the hegemony of a tiny white elite—retained their greatest strength after the War among whites in these counties. It was here, too, that Reconstruction came closest to social revolution, as the black masses with a few white allies took over many of the local offices. After Reconstruction, political arrangements in the black belt took several forms. Whites in some counties adopted the "first Mississippi plan," driving most blacks from politics by violence and intimidation. In others, whites appointed as local election officials by the state governments made elections a farce by manipulating the returns or by paying blacks not to vote for opposition parties. Elsewhere, whites and blacks negotiated "fusion" agreements dividing the offices along racial lines, or they continued the Reconstruction struggle, with each side winning some political battles and losing others.[4] These settlements were neither mutually exclusive nor permanent. Intimidation and ballot box chicanery might go hand in hand. Violence might suddenly put an end to years of fairly peaceful political competition. And the possibility always existed that a party which hoped to attract Negroes would win control of the state or federal governments and promote fair and peaceful elections.

The affluent whites who dominated the black counties had the most to lose if a party based on blacks, upland whites, or an alliance of the

4. Wharton, *The Negro in Mississippi*, pp. 157–215; George B. Tindall, *South Carolina Negroes, 1877–1900*, pp. 62–64. For details on how two fusion arrangements began and how they worked, see *Pine Bluff* (Ark.) *Weekly Commercial*, April 6, Aug. 10, 1890; *Congressional Record*, 50th Cong., 1st Sess., pp. 3564–3565.

two groups won control of a state. A government dependent on black votes would have to appoint some Negroes to office in the predominantly black areas and make it possible for them to elect a few of their fellows to other offices. The black belt whites would then have to pay taxes to Negro collectors, argue cases before Negro juries and judges, apply to a Negro legislator for favors. All these actions would be inescapable symbolic reminders of the dominance of a race that all Southern whites believed inferior. In addition, many of the Negro officials would no doubt *be* inferior to their white counterparts, for most whites seem to have thought that money spent on Negro education only made them more "uppity." (As the slogan went, "To educate a 'nigger' is to spoil a good field hand.") Caucasians who lived in counties with few Negroes, whatever the degree of their racial prejudice, did not have to fear having black officials rule them. But as long as Negroes retained the potential to bargain for office, the black belt whites had to fear Negro domination.

The methods that the Democrats had employed to end Reconstruction had not caused either turnout or opposition to cease by 1880. It was true that the Republican label had lost popularity in the South, especially the Deep South. Most white Republicans had been converted or coerced into the Democratic party, leaving blacks and ex-Unionist, hill-country whites in control of the GOP. Continued coercion, widespread Democratic fraud at the polls, poll taxes in Georgia and Virginia (before 1882), the registration and the eight-box law (after 1881) in South Carolina, and Rutherford Hayes's naïve attempt to convert Southern aristocrats further stultified attempts to reorganize Southern Republicanism.[5]

Nonetheless, efforts to create a winning opposition party did not cease. As upper-class Redeemers cut back government expenditures, absconded with a good deal of the budgeted public money, prevented mountain whites from electing their own local officials, and instituted policies strikingly favorable to big Northern-owned businesses, many whites began to doubt the virtues of Redemption. According to most historians of the period, moreover, small farmers continually suffered from deflation, the lien system and its tendency to promote overproduc-

5. See below, chapters 2 and 3, for an explanation of how the poll tax, registration, eight-box, secret ballot, and other restrictive devices worked.

tion and inhibit crop diversification, and a regressive, malapportioned, and often dishonestly administered state and local tax system.[6]

Most important, the logic of the political system itself encouraged party opposition to Democratic control. Kill, intimidate, defraud dissenters though they might, the Democrats had not yet succeeded in equating political opposition with treason. The presence of a large potential Negro vote, which was for the most part alienated from the established order, tempted any enemy of those in power to bolt the Democrats. As a Negro newspaper in Little Rock noted in 1883, "The greatest danger that threatens [D]emocratic supremacy in the south is that the 'out faction' always gravitates toward the Negro and secures his aid to route [*sic*] the 'ins'." Finally, besides being rewarded with local office, bolters might expect patronage and other assistance from the national Republican organization.[7] Until the sanctions against defection became too strong, until the blacks were disfranchised, until the GOP no longer needed Southern votes, political conditions fed the Independent and Populist movements.

Though the national Republican commitment to protect the former white Unionist and the former slave wavered, it did help stimulate revolt against the Dixie Democrats. A large proportion of the GOP leaders in the late nineteenth century had shared in the efforts to free the slaves, put down the Rebellion, and reconstruct the South on the basis of legal equality between masters and freedmen.[8] That Republican

6. Alex M. Arnett, *The Populist Movement in Georgia*, pp. 33–36; Woodward, *Origins of the New South*, pp. 1–22, 51–74, 85–86, 175–188; Steelman, "The Progressive Era in North Carolina," p. 66; Francis Clay Elkins, "The Agricultural Wheel in Arkansas, 1882–1890" (Ph.D. diss., Syracuse Univ., 1943), p. 96. On the scandalous misreporting of real and personal property values under one leading Redeemer regime, see *Columbia* (S.C.) *Daily Register*, May 5, 6, 14, June 3, 1881.

7. *Little Rock Weekly Mansion*, July 21, 1883, quoted in Donald Norton Brown, "Southern Attitudes toward Negro Voting in the Bourbon Period, 1877–1890" (Ph.D. diss., Univ. of Oklahoma, 1960), p. 73. On factionalism and defection, see also Claude H. Nolen, *The Negro's Image in the South*, p. 73; Charles Chilton Pearson, *The Readjuster Movement in Virginia*, pp. 75–76. On patronage, see Willie D. Halsell, "James R. Chalmers and 'Mahoneism' in Mississippi," *Journal of Southern History* 10 (1944): 37–58; Vincent P. DeSantis, *Republicans Face the Southern Question*, pp. 153–154.

8. The standard works on Northern Republican attitudes toward the South in this period are DeSantis, *Republicans Face the Southern Question* and Stanley P. Hirshson, *Farewell to the Bloody Shirt*. Both are harsher toward the Republicans' racial policies and more lenient toward the Democrats than either party deserves. For treatment of the Republicans, see Frederick H. Gillett, *George Frisbie Hoar*, pp. 1–34; Louis A. Coolidge, *An Old-Fashioned*

leaders took part in the antislavery and Reconstruction movements reflected for most a certain amount of egalitarianism and a consequent denial of the justification for racial oppression. Their actions also solidified these commitments—it was awkward for one who had defended Reconstruction before the electorate in the sixties and seventies to condemn similar policies later. Other Republicans found the conditions of Southern elections so outrageous that they joined in the effort to guarantee "a free ballot and a fair count." The typical Republican atrocity stories about the South were not mere campaign gimmicks; many GOP politicians were genuinely horrified by the facts of Southern political life. To be sure, no important national figure embodied racial radicalism of the Stevens or Sumner stripe, but then few ever had. Yet the postwar Republican party did usually combine an appeal to those business interests that desired government protection and subsidies with a recognition of the need for active federal intervention to guard at least some of the rights of the Southern black man.[9] As one of the most stalwart defenders of Republican humanitarianism, William E. Chandler, wrote to another conservator of that tradition, Congressman Thomas B. Reed:

Senator, Orville H. Platt (New York, G. P. Putnam's Sons, 1910), pp. 4–54; Louis J. Lang, comp. and ed., *The Autobiography of Thomas Collier Platt*, p. 7; Richard E. Welch, *George Frisbie Hoar and the Half-Breed Republicans*, pp. 5–27.

9. Sen. William M. Stewart's tergiversations during the Force Bill debates in 1890 exemplify how difficult it was for a Reconstructionist to abandon his stand later. See *Congressional Record*, 51st Cong., 2nd Sess., pp. 678–683, 1707–1713. The moderate view of Reconstruction held by late nineteenth century Republicans is outlined in William E. Chandler, "Our Southern Masters," *The Forum* 5 (1888): 508–520; James G. Blaine, "Ought the Negro Be Disfranchised? Ought He to Have Been Enfranchised?", *North American Review* 128 (1879): 225–231; Lang, *Platt*, p. 70. For the effect of exposure to Southern election practices on otherwise conservative Republicans, see Daniel J. Crofts, "The Blair Bill and the Elections Bill: The Congressional Aftermath to Reconstruction" (Ph.D. diss., Yale Univ., 1968), pp. 238–239; Dorothy Ganfield Fowler, *John Coit Spooner, Defender of Presidents*, pp. 133–138; *Congressional Record*, 50th Cong., 1st Sess., pp. 7826, 8523, 9001. For the "appeal to business," see Leon Burr Richardson, *William E. Chandler, Republican*, pp. 414–415; Richard E. Welch, Jr., "The Federal Elections Bill of 1890: Postscripts and Prelude," *Journal of American History* 52 (1965): 516–518; Gillett, *George Frisbie Hoar*, p. 280; William E. Chandler, "National Control of Elections," *The Forum* 9 (1890): 705–718. The GOP also paid some attention to civil rights for Northern Negroes. On the passage of public accommodations bills in 18 Northern states from 1884 to 1897, see Johnson, *Development of State Legislation Concerning the Free Negro*, pp. 30–35. Cf. the analysis of Republican policies presented here with C. Vann Woodward, "The Political Legacy of Reconstruction," in *The Burden of Southern History*, pp. 89–108.

A Republican can believe in tariff reduction or even free trade and yet properly adhere to the party. But he cannot fail to advocate the Fifteenth Amendment . . . and yet be a Republican . . . . So it is the duty of all Republicans to push on in all endeavors . . . to enforce the Fifteenth Amendment . . . . Failing to do this, the party . . . dishonorably dies.[10]

Nowhere was the contradiction between Republican and Democratic attitudes on Reconstruction, universal manhood suffrage, and racism better demonstrated than in the debates on the Lodge Elections Bill in 1890. To Democrats, North and South, Reconstruction represented an unconstitutional interference with the rights of the states, an era of outrageous fraud and corruption, an attempt, in the nature of things bound to fail, to impose Negro domination on the superior white race. The Fifteenth Amendment had been at best "a very unwise and mischievous error," and at worst an "indefensible political crime" which in any case plunged the South into violent racial conflicts. According to Representative Allen D. Candler (D., Georgia), the ballot had been "thrust" upon the Negro, "when he was utterly and totally unprepared for it. He regards it as a bauble, a plaything, an article of merchandise. He regards election day as a public holiday. He goes to the polls as he goes to the circus or to a public execution—as a frolic." Ninety percent of the Negroes, charged Senator Pugh of Alabama, were still "wholly illiterate and incapable of counting or casting their votes with any will, understanding, or comprehension of the objects, value, benefits, duties or responsibilities of suffrage or citizenship." It was fortunate, therefore, that "a large majority of them have the good sense to voluntarily abstain from all participation in conventions and political meetings." Yet at the same time that they denied suppressing the Negro vote through force and fraud, Democrats warned that any attempt by the federal government to guarantee fair elections in the South would lead to "Negro supremacy" as well as "revolution and the destruction of our Constitution and system of

10. Chandler to Reed, quoted in DeSantis, *Republicans Face*, pp. 205–206. Similarly, see Chandler, *The National Election Laws, Their Repeal by the Democratic Party* (Concord, New Hampshire: n.p., 1894, reprint of Senate speech of Feb. 5, 1894); George F. Hoar, "The Fate of the Election Bill," *The Forum* 11 (1891): 127–128. Marriott Brosius, in *Congressional Record*, 51st Cong., 1st sess., p. 6706; E. S. Williams in ibid., p. 6720; Joseph Dolph, in ibid., 51st Cong., 2nd sess., p. 520. Of course, not every Republican believed Negro suffrage so central to the party's identity. But that commitment did remain in the mainstream of Republicanism until at least the mid-1890s.

government." The Democrats appealed to Northern businessmen who had investments or customers in the South to assist them in preventing a return to Reconstruction.[11]

Republican speechmakers countered their party adversaries at every point. Although he acknowledged the presence of some mercenary men in the Southern Reconstruction governments, Daniel Kerr of Iowa still lauded those regimes for laying the groundwork of more recent Southern prosperity through their policies, especially their establishment of public schools. Jonathan Rowell of Illinois added that Negroes had to be enfranchised in the sixties for their own "self-defense," to prevent their relapse into a "subject class" and to enable them to develop into full-fledged, independent citizens. Besides, unlike the traitorous Democrats, the black man had fought for the Union "upon a hundred fields of battle . . . with a loyalty that never was excelled." "Can we forget," asked Marriott Brosius of Pennsylvania, that "in the darkest hour of the night of our trial . . . we made our covenant with him,

11. Quotations from speeches by Rep. William C. Oates (D., Alabama), in *Congressional Record*, 51st Cong, 1st sess., pp. 6863–6865, and *Boston Daily Globe*, Dec. 21, 1888; Senator James N. Pugh (D., Alabama) in *Congressional Record*, 51st Cong., 2nd sess., p. 76; and Rep. Candler in ibid., p. 6703. In a less guarded moment, Oates admitted that "nine-tenths of the Negroes are Republicans, and in some localities, all. . . ." (quoted in *Memphis Daily Appeal*, Dec. 5, 1888). For the Democrats' view of Reconstruction and examples of ·the extreme racism of both Northern and Southern Democrats, see ibid., 51st Cong., 1st sess., pp. 6715–6720, 6761–6763, 6765–6768, 6776–6779, 6806–6810, 6863–6865, appendix pp. 411, 562–564, and ibid., 51st Cong., 2nd sess., pp. 50–55, 1412, 1614–1616. For the "Negro supremacy" argument, see Amos J. Cummings (D., New York), in ibid., 51st Cong. 1st sess., p. 6680; Silas Hare (D., Texas), in ibid., p. 6812. For similar comments from other Northern and Southern Democrats, see ibid., pp. 6505, 6601, 6603, 6672–6675. (In the statements quoted here and throughout the rest of this book, the world "Negro" has been capitalized, in accord with modern usage.) Three U.S. senators, six congressmen, and four other Southern Democrats collaborated to produce *Why the Solid South? Or, Reconstruction and Its Results* (Baltimore, Md.: R. H. Woodward & Co., 1890). Dedicated "To The Business Men of the North," this propagandistic work portrayed the horrors of corrupt rule by carpetbaggers, scalawags, and ignorant Negroes during Reconstruction in an attempt to stop passage of the Lodge bill. Several chapters of the book were entered into the *Congressional Record* during the 1890 debates. There is little evidence that their appeal succeeded. Every Democrat in both houses of Congress opposed the bill anyway. Only two Northern Republicans broke ranks in the House, and they seem to have done so for other reasons. Only one non-western Republican, Senator Don Cameron of Pennsylvania, deserted the party on the crucial vote, and he clearly traded this vote for Democratic assistance in hushing up an investigation into his silver speculations. Crofts, "Blair Bill," pp. 233–234, 339, 340; Edward Arthur White, "The Republican Party in National Politics, 1888–1891" (Ph.D. diss., Univ. of Wisconsin, 1941), pp. 392–492.

sealed with his blood and ours and witnessed by heaven, that when the war was over and the nation saved he should enter into the enjoyment of the blessings and glories of citizenship? How are we fulfilling our covenant?" The reactionary post-Reconstruction governments of the South had instituted "new forms of servitude" for the Negroes, and "the policy of repression of the black men led to oppression of all laboring men, black and white." Yet the sacrifice of "free government . . . to get pure pure government by the Whites" had given the South neither. Witness, several Republicans pointed out, the recent extensive defalcations of Southern state treasurers.[12]

The triumph of reactionary regimes, Republicans charged, had also fertilized the seeds of reactionary political theory. Branding the increasingly influential view that suffrage was a privilege rather than a right as a doctrine foreign to "our form of popular government," Nils P. Haugen of Wisconsin countered with the declaration that universal manhood suffrage was "the cornerstone of our liberties." "Why are we to ignore the rights of a man because God made him black?" asked Iowa Congressman David B. Henderson. "The members of the colored race," the midwesterner continued, "have the same instincts, the same great impulses as ourselves." So strong did the current of humanitarianism still run within the party of Lincoln that it moved even the stolid William McKinley to a peroration:

This question will not rest until justice is done, and the consciences of the American people will not be permitted to slumber until this great constitutional right, the equality of the suffrage, equality of opportunity, freedom of political action and political thought, shall not be the mere cold formalities of constitutional enactment as now, but a living birthright which the poor-

12. Kerr in *Congressional Record*, 51st Cong., 1st sess., p. 6724; Rowell in ibid., p. 6556; Spooner in ibid., 2nd sess., p. 729; Hiscock in ibid., p. 857. Then see Edward P. Allen (R., Michigan) in ibid., p. 6799; Brosius in ibid., p. 6707; J. P. Dolliver (R., Iowa) in ibid., p. 6861; Louis E. McComas (R., Maryland) in ibid., pp. 6677–6678; Henry L. Morey (R., Ohio) in ibid., pp. 6897–6899; H. C. Lodge (R., Massachusetts), in ibid., p. 6543; E. S. Williams (R., Ohio) in ibid., p. 6721. In addition Benjamin Harrison's Annual Messages to Congress contained perhaps the last strong presidential defences of Negro rights until Harry Truman's time. See James D. Richardson, *A Compilation of the Messages and Papers of the Presidents, 1789–1897* (Washington, D. C.: G.P.O., 1900), 9: 56, 127–129, 331–332. Republican concern with Negro rights is also evidenced in the Senate debates on the Elections Bill. See *Congressional Record*, 51st Cong., 2nd sess., for example, Stewart (R., Nevada), ibid., pp. 679–680; Spooner (R., Wisconsin), ibid., p. 729; Hiscock (R., New York), ibid., p. 857; Dolph (R., Oregon), ibid., p. 520; Higgins (R., Delaware), ibid., pp. 763–772.

est and the humblest, white or black, native-born or naturalized citizen, may confidently enjoy, and which the richest and most powerful dare not deny . . . . It is our supreme duty to enforce the Constitution and laws of the United States.[13]

Even the humor of the debates harked back to the Civil War and Reconstruction era and clearly distinguished the antislavery lineage of the Republicans from the proslavery ancestry of the Democrats. When a Virginia Democratic congressman argued that he had been a friend to Negroes since he drew sustenance from a black wetnurse, Nils P. Haugen rejoined:

His obligations to the colored race the gentleman desires us to understand he fulfilled when at an early period of his existence he kindly condescended to receive the nourishment so essential to an infant statesman and constitutional lawyer from his dear colored nurse. It is not the first time that the "dear old black mammy" has been called into requisition on that side of the chamber. God only knows how many Democratic statesmen the dear old lady is responsible for. [Laughter on the Republican side.] We simply ask you, gentlemen, that you extend that same consideration to her brothers, her sons, and her uncles that you professedly and confessedly have for the "old mammy," her sisters, her daughters, and her aunts.[14]

Such small witticisms sounded more like Thad Stevens than Teddy Roosevelt.

The tight political battle in the North bolstered the idealistic Republican impulse not to leave the South to the mercy of the Democrats. A letter from William E. Chandler to James G. Blaine best illuminates the GOP dilemmas and policy after Reconstruction:

The situation is bad in New York and Pennsylvania. It is important to carry the House, for the next presidential election depends on it. We cannot carry as many seats in the North as two years ago. We must increase our Southern representation by ten to twenty. That depends upon the Republican support of the Democratic revolt in the South and the overthrow of the Bourbons there . . . . Our straight Republican and Carpetbag and

13. Haugen in ibid., 51st Cong., 1st sess., pp. 6592–6594; Henderson in ibid., p. 6686; McKinley in ibid., p. 6934; similarly, see Bishop W. Perkins (R., Kansas) in ibid., pp. 6934–6935; Robert M. LaFollette (R., Wisconsin) in ibid., appendix, pp. 467–469; and F. T. Greenhalge (R., Massachusetts) in ibid., pp. 6694–6695. That McKinley's florid speech seems bedewed with unconscious irony when exposed in the light of his later actions as president only proves how much the Republican party changed during the 1890s.

14. Ibid., p. 6592.

Negro governments cannot be revived. Without the aid of independent
Democrats we cannot carry enough seats there to save the next presidential
fight.[15]

Northern Republicans fluctuated between two Southern strategies:
the first envisaged men interested in rapid, federally encouraged expansion of Southern industry flocking to the banner of the party of the
protective tariff and internal improvements subsidies; the second,
never so precisely defined, counted on adding lower-class whites to
the party's Negro base by stressing such positive themes as fair elections and the improvement of public services, and such Democratic
foibles as corruption and boss rule. In 1876, Hayes chose the first,
conservative path, and Presidents McKinley, Theodore Roosevelt, and
Taft later resurrected essentially the same alliance with the "best
people."[16] From 1880 to 1896, however, the GOP usually backed
leaders who appealed to the enemies of the Southern upper class.

The bankruptcy of the Compromise of 1877 had been made clear to
Republicans by their 1878 congressional defeats in the South and by
the 1879 Senate investigation of Southern elections. Though Garfield
never enunciated a definite Southern policy, his assassination brought
to power the most vociferous critic of Hayes's genteel strategy. William
E. Chandler functioned as Arthur's unofficial Minister for Southern
Affairs as well as his naval chief. As the two statements quoted previously make clear, the New Hampshire Republican exemplified the
combination of realism and idealism that motivated the Republican
Southern policy between the administrations of Hayes and McKinley.
His practical experience included managing Grant's presidential
campaigns in 1868 and 1872, as well as Hayes's successful efforts to
carry Florida, South Carolina, and Louisiana after the 1876 election.
At the same time, Chandler was sincerely dedicated to protecting the
civil rights of the freedman, and he was forever denouncing Southern

15. William A. Robinson, *Thomas B. Reed, Parliamentarian* (New York: Dodd, Mead and Co.,
1930), p. 236; Woodward, *Burden of Southern History*, pp. 96–98; DeSantis, *Republicans Face
the Southern Question*, pp. 11–12. Chandler to Blaine, Oct. 2, 1882, quoted in Richardson,
Chandler, p. 346.

16. DeSantis, *Republicans Face the Southern Question*, pp. 73–74, 132; Theodore Roosevelt,
"The Progressive Party and the Colored Man," *The Outlook* 101 (1912): 909–912; William
Howard Taft, *The South and the National Government* (reprint of speech of Dec. 7, 1908, n.p.,
n.d.); Hugh C. Bailey, *Liberalism in the New South, Southern Social Reformers and the Progressive
Movement*, pp. 189–199.

white oppression of Negroes. His wide correspondence with Southern Republicans and his cordial relationship with Arthur insured closer attention to Southern affairs from 1882 to 1884 than in any administration from Grant's to Wilson's.[17]

Historians have often noted that the Independent movements stood for diverse economic programs. In Tennessee, the administration-endorsed Republicans opposed reducing the state's obligations to its bondholders, while in Virginia they favored the Readjusters. In Alabama, Texas, South Carolina, Louisiana, and Mississippi, the Greenback party received national and local Republican support; in North Carolina, the antiprohibitionists; in Florida, those opposed to the Disston land giveaway; in Arkansas, the Agricultural Wheel, an organization which later fused with the Farmers' Alliance. In Georgia and in many districts throughout the rest of the states the GOP simply allied with anyone who ran as an "Independent" against the Democrats.[18]

But the administration's policy was not so opportunistic or illogical as it is sometimes represented.[19] Every significant Independent candidate supported a "free vote and a fair count," a slogan that they applied to black as well as white ballots. The anti-Redeemers also pledged full support for public education, a necessity if the Southern poor, including the blacks, were to rise.[20] Moreover, nearly every Independent appealed openly for Negro votes, thereby legitimizing the race's participation in politics, sanctioning biracial political

17. *United States Senate Report No. 855*, 45th Cong., 1st sess.; Hirshson, *Farewell*, pp. 49–53, 93–98; Welch, *Hoar*, pp. 81–82; Vincent P. DeSantis, "President Garfield and the Solid South," *North Carolina Historical Review* 36 (1959): 442–465; DeSantis, *Republicans Face*, pp. 167–168; Richardson, *Chandler*.

18. Woodward, *Origins*, pp. 100–103; William Ivy Hair, *Bourbonism and Agrarian Protest*, pp. 70–72; Steelman, "Progressive Era in North Carolina," pp. 11–12; Edward C. Williamson, "Independentism; A Challenge to the Florida Democracy of 1884," *Florida Historical Quarterly* 27 (1948): 131–156; Shadgett, *Republican Party in Georgia*, pp. 62–73.

19. Woodward, *Origins*, pp. 105–106.

20. Chandler to Blaine, quoted in Richardson, *Chandler*, p. 346; DeSantis, *Republicans Face*, pp. 162–163; Clifton Paisley, "The Political Wheelers and Arkansas' Election of 1888," *Arkansas Historical Quarterly* 25 (1966): 5; David Y. Thomas, *Arkansas and Its People, A History, 1541–1930*, pp. 223–225; Allen J. Going, *Bourbon Democracy In Alabama, 1874–1890*, pp. 52, 57–59; John B. Clark, *Populism in Alabama*, pp. 25–28; Edward C. Williamson, "Independentism," pp. 131–156; Ernest William Winkler, *Platforms of Political Parties in Texas*, pp. 181, 200, 257, 261, 275, 282; Lawrence Delbert Rice, *The Negro in Texas, 1874–1900*, pp. 53–67; Pearson, *Readjuster Movement*, pp. 142–147.

alliances, and accustoming many white leaders to politicking in the black community.[21] Like the Populists who followed them, the Independents and Republicans derided Democratic charges that their apostasy from the "white man's party" would lead to "Negro domination." As the Virginia Readjuster William Mahone put it, the black issue "is employed as a mere scare-crow to excite prejudice and fear, in the hope of diverting the white working-man from casting his ballot for the candidate he honestly prefers." Thus, the party policy promised additional congressional and electoral votes for the national GOP, political equality and education for the blacks, office for any white Southern Democrat disgruntled by a factional dispute, and a two-party system for the South as a whole.[22]

Only the local politicians' hopes were fully realized. The Democrats lost power temporarily in two states, Tennessee and Virginia, but maintained it everywhere else. In some places they falsified returns, in others they bought votes, elsewhere they prevailed by murder and intimidation. In Virginia the 1883 Readjuster defeat was widely attributed to the fact that Democrats murdered several Negroes three days before the election and then plastered the state with handbills rumoring a Readjuster-inspired black uprising. Mississippi newspapers testified that mules had developed a taste for ballot boxes in Independent precincts, while in Louisiana composing fictional election returns approached the status of a popular art form. Everywhere the ruling oligarchy stressed the threat of Negro domination and of a return to Reconstruction and the consequent necessity of solid support for the "white man's party."[23]

21. Wharton, *The Negro in Mississippi*, pp. 201–205; James Harris Fain, "The Political Disfranchisement of the Negro in Arkansas" (M.A. thesis, University of Arkansas, 1961), p. 28; John William Graves, "Negro Disfranchisement in Arkansas," *Arkansas Historical Quarterly* 26 (1967): 206–208; Francis Roberts, "William Manning Lowe and the Greenback Party in Alabama," *Alabama Review* 5 (1952): 100–121; *Charleston News and Courier*, Jan. 4, 23, 1882; Pearson, *Readjuster Movement*, pp. 127–128, 131.

22. Mahone is quoted in Nelson M. Blake, *William Mahone of Virginia*, p. 246. Writing in New York in 1884, the Negro editor T. Thomas Fortune counseled his Southern brothers to support the Independents in state and local contests. See his *Black and White*, pp. 126–127. On the presence of disgruntled Democrats in the ranks of Independent movements, see *Little Rock Daily Democrat*, June 11, 1886, quoted in Elkins, "Agricultural Wheel in Arkansas," pp. 140–141; Willie D. Halsell, "Democratic Dissensions in Mississippi, 1878–1882," *Journal of Mississippi History* 2 (1940): 135.

23. For an excellent recent account of the Virginia episode, see Walter T. Calhoun, "The Danville Riot and Its Repercussions on the Virginia Election of 1883," in *Studies in the*

The assaults on the Democratic party came closer to success than some historians realize. As table 1.3 shows, the fusion efforts in governor's races failed very badly only in South Carolina, where the registration and eight-box law cut illiterates out of the electorate. Elsewhere, the Independents and Republicans garnered from a little less than a third to more than half of the votes. In seven of the eleven states, at least 40 percent of the voters opposed the ruling party, and in six of these states more than 60 percent of the potential voters participated. Given absolute Democratic control of the ballot boxes and their avowed willingness to fabricate returns in many black belt areas (particularly in Alabama and the river parishes in Louisiana), the opposition did remarkably well.[24]

Table 1.3. The High Points of Independent or Republican Political Strength in Gubernatorial Elections during the 1880s.

State	Year	Opposition Party Label	% of Those Voting Supporting Independents or Republicans	% Turnout
Alabama	1882	Independent	31.6	49.2
Arkansas	1888	Fusion	45.9	75.5
Florida	1884	Independent	46.5	79.4
Georgia	1880	Independent	35.1	56.7
Louisiana	1884	Republican	32.9	57.5
Mississippi	1881	Independent	40.2	50.8
North Carolina	1880	Republican	48.7	80.6
South Carolina	1882	Greenback	21.0	56.8
Tennessee	1884	Republican	48.7	71.7
Texas	1882	Greenback	40.5	61.6
Virginia	1881	Readjuster	52.8	62.3

History of the South, 1875–1922 (Greenville, North Carolina: East Carolina College Press, 1966), pp. 25–51. On other states, see Wharton, *Negro in Mississippi*, p. 205; Hair, *Bourbonism*, pp. 112–117; Going, *Bourbon Democracy in Alabama*, p. 31; Pearson, *Readjuster Movement*, pp. 75–76. For an extensive and persuasive picture of election methods in Louisiana, see *Congressional Record*, 50th Cong., 1st sess., pp. 3564–3565, 7819–7829, 7865–7881.

24. The *Selma* (Alabama) *Times*, Dec. 6, 1895, commented: "The *Times* is one of those papers that does not believe it is any harm to rob or appropriate the vote of an illiterate Negro. . . . The first law of nature, self preservation, gives us the right to do anything to keep our race and civilization from being wiped off the face of the earth." Quoted in Malcolm Cook McMillan, *Constitutional Development in Alabama, 1798–1901*, p. 225. The common Louisiana aphorism that "a dead darkey always makes a good Democrat" reflects the conduct of elections in that state. Quoted in Hair, *Bourbonism*, p. 115.

Table 1.4. Estimated Voting by Party and Race in Key Gubernatorial
Contests, 1880s.

| State | Year | % of Adult White Males | | | % of Adult Negro Males | | |
		Demo-cratic	Republican or Indepen-dent	No Vote	Demo-cratic	Republican or Indepen-dent	No Vote
Alabama	1882	43	18	39	36	16	48
Arkansas*a*	1888	49	29	22	23	46	30
Florida	1884	55	18	26	28	61	13
Georgia	1880	36	28	36	45	12	44
Louisiana	1884	56	24	20	29	22	48
Mississippi	1881	57	16	26	13	25	61
North Carolina	1880	46	27	27	35	58	9
South Carolina	1882	47	9	44	21	9	70
Tennessee	1884	38	31	28	25	42	33
Texas	1882	44	18	38	10	62	28
Virginia	1881	44	26	30	11	49	43

*a*Two deviant counties were deleted in making Arkansas estimate, because of evident tampering with returns.

Table 1.4 exhibits estimates of voting patterns separated by race in the same elections. Blacks gave the bulk of their votes to the opposition in at least seven of the states. In three of the others, the white leadership in counties with high proportions of Negroes probably tampered with the returns. A split in the Georgia Democratic convention resulted in a confused situation in which both candidates claimed to be Independents as well as Democrats. The racism of the more genuine Independent, Thomas M. Norwood, was widely known, and his opponent, with the help of the ex-Republican Joe Brown, courted the Negro vote openly and fervently.[25] Though the ruling party attracted large proportions of whites, from a sixth to a third of the white adult males bolted the "white man's party" in every state except South Carolina. Even the white South lacked solidarity.

Not only were the electors not unanimous, a large percentage of them still voted. After the turn of the century six or seven of every ten eligible Southerners neglected to vote. In the 1880s, however, about 75 percent of the white males over twenty-one years old turned out in

25. Mrs. Rebecca Latimer Felton, *My Memoirs of Georgia Politics*, pp. 273–274, 307.

six of the states, and 60 percent in four of the remaining ones. A majority of the black men participated—or were counted as participating—in elections in nine of the eleven commonwealths.

In sum, Southern politics in the eighties exhibited a fluidity and freedom unknown after disfranchisement. Politicians attempted to build up stable, continuous parties—a necessity if the voter's decision is to be rational. Both parties competed for votes among men of both races. And if the opposition could only guarantee a fair ballot count, it had a chance to carry several states—thus the bitter struggle over the Lodge fair elections bill.[26]

SOUTHERN POLITICS IN THE NINETIES: CHALLENGE AND RESPONSE

The 1890s witnessed the greatest political turmoil in the nation since Reconstruction. The political stalemate that had prevented decisive federal action in the seventies and eighties broke in the Fifty-first Congress (1889–91) when the Republicans gained slight majorities in both houses of Congress. A massive shift in the 1890 election swept in a 147-seat Democratic majority. The deepening depression and the Populist revolt, however, unmade the Democrats as quickly as those events had made them: the GOP enjoyed a 140-seat edge in the 1895–96 House and maintained a majority until the Bull Moose split of 1912.

To return to the last years of the century, the Republicans in 1888 won firm control of both branches of congress and the presidency for the first time in fourteen years. After rewriting the rules of procedure in the House to prohibit minority disruption of the legislative process, the GOP passed a higher tariff, an antitrust bill, and a currency expansion measure. Despite one of the bitterest filibusters in United States history and a campaign of distortion and vilification perhaps unparalleled in the annals of American legislation, the party of Lincoln almost managed to pass the Lodge Elections Bill.[27] A mild piece of legislation, the much-maligned "Force Bill" would have extended the federal supervisory act of 1870, which by 1890 covered 34 Southern and 129 Northern cities, to every congressional district in which 100 citizens petitioned

26. Hirshson, *Farewell*, pp. 205–206; Crofts, "Blair Bill," pp. 238–239.

27. White, "Republican Party," p. 368. The two best narratives on the Elections Bill are White, "Republican Party," pp. 367–504, and Crofts, "Blair Bill," pp. 221–355. See also John R. Lambert, *Arthur Pue Gorman*, pp. 160–161; Welch, "Federal Elections Bill," pp. 511–526; *Congressional Record*, 51st Cong., 2nd sess. (Senate), Jan. 20–22, 1891, shows the Democrats' desperate tactical maneuvering.

to have the law go into effect. By requiring supervision of all phases of registration and voting in national elections, and in effect nullifying certain practices and laws that facilitated fraud and disfranchisement, the bill's authors sought to attain two chief ends: "publicity" of all election procedures, and "honest elections." Although it passed the House, where only two Republicans joined the Democrats in opposition, the bill was displaced from the Senate calendar on a surprise procedural motion by one vote. Only the defection of the representatives of the silver mine owners, the strongest single economic interest group of the period, defeated the bill in the Senate.[28]

Despite the mildness of the Lodge bill, the Democrats were correct in fearing its possible consequences. Had it been enacted and enforced (and had the Southern states not passed disfranchising laws), the bill would have increased the number of Southern Republicans and Populists in Congress and focused attention on the malodorous Southern election practices. These exposures and the increased strength in Congress of Southerners opposed to the Democratic party might well have led Congress to pass stronger legislation, which would have added further to the erosion of Democratic power, and so on and on. As the radical Republican Harrison Kelley of Kansas noted during the House discussion, the Lodge bill itself was too weak to guarantee fair elections, but it might be the step "that will finally bring the crisis that will bring the remedy." To the Democrats, therefore, the bill was a Pandora's box.[29]

28. *Congressional Record*, 51st Cong., 1st sess., pp. 6538, 6551, 6561, 6674, 6849, 6868; ibid., 2nd sess., pp. 713, 855–856; Daniel Walker Hollis, "The Force Bill of 1890" (M.A. thesis, Columbia Univ., 1947), pp. 43–46; Robert A. Horn, "National Control of Congressional Elections" (Ph.D. diss., Princeton Univ., 1942), pp. 260–265; Crofts, "Blair Bill," p. 269. The connection between the 1870 and 1890 laws was dramatized by the key role John I. Davenport, elections supervisor in New York City, played in drafting the "Lodge Bill." See *Congressional Record*, 51st Cong., 2nd sess., pp. 253–254, 471–474, 500, 515, 713–716. The silverites' opposition to the Lodge bill obviously represented an overt or tacit agreement to trade votes for Democratic help on silver purchase measures. Six months before the crucial roll call in the Senate, a key Democratic congressman, Roger Q. Mills of Texas, predicted that "the help Democratic Senators rendered the silver Republicans will induce the latter to reciprocate" on the Lodge bill. *Alexandria* (Virginia) *Gazette and Virginia Advertiser*, June 18, 1890, quoted in *Congressional Record*, 51st Cong., 1st sess., p. 6685. See also George H. Mayer, *The Republican Party, 1854–1964*, pp. 229–230; Fred Wellborn, "The Influence of the Silver-Republican Senators, 1889–1891," *Mississippi Valley Historical Review* 14 (1928): 462–480; *Dallas Morning News*, Jan. 27, 1891; Hirshson, *Farewell*, p. 233; Fowler, *Spooner*, pp. 157–158. The crucial votes are given in *Congressional Record*, 51st Cong., 2nd sess., pp. 912–913, 1324, 1740.

29. Many Republicans stated at the time that they thought the bill exceedingly—several

The Lodge bill's narrow defeat and the Democrats' 1894 repeal of the remaining federal election statutes disheartened the proponents of national control of congressional elections. By 1896, the GOP national platform had dropped its earlier demand for legislative and executive actions to guarantee a free ballot and a fair count in the South.[30]

Among the other factors in the final Republican capitulation to the Southern oligarchy was the fact that not only death but the overwhelming Republican defeats in 1890 and 1892 eliminated many leaders who had participated, though not always fervently, in the party's campaigns for human rights. James G. Blaine, John Sherman, Benjamin Harrison, John J. Ingalls, Henry W. Blair, George F. Edmunds, William E. Chandler, Thomas B. Reed, and many others either died or left elective office during the nineties. In their places rose younger men to whom abolition and Reconstruction seemed irrelevant, merely picturesque, or even evil. To the new generation of Republican leaders, domestic politics consisted almost entirely of the promotion and/or regulation of business.[31] Those elder Republicans who continued to occupy important political positions after the turn of the century—Speaker Joe Cannon and Senators William B. Allison and Nelson W. Aldrich, for instance—abandoned the cause of Negro rights, which they apparently had not believed in very deeply anyway. Southern atrocity stories no longer seemed popular with Northern voters.

---

said excessively—mild. See, e.g., *Congressional Record*, 51st Cong., 1st sess., pp. 6544, 6554, 6602, 6721, 6929; Shelby Moore Cullom, *Fifty Years of Public Service* (Chicago, Ill.: A. C. McClurg and Co., 1911), p. 255. Democrats disagreed. Sen. Wilkinson Call of Florida called it "the most important bill that has ever been presented in the history of the legislation of this country," *Congressional Record*, 51st Cong., 2nd session, p. 804. Rep. Charles F. Crisp of Georgia denounced it as "the most outrageous and iniquitous measure ever brought before Congress for passage." Crofts, "Blair Bill," p. 262. See also *Congressional Record*, 51st Cong., 1st sess., pp. 6884–6885 where Kelley likened the Lodge bill to the fugitive slave law, inviting the next speaker, Charles H. Turner (D., New York), to refer to the Kansan as "this new John Brown." For another view, see Stewart (R., Nevada) in ibid., 2nd sess., pp. 678–683.

30. George Frisbie Hoar, *Autobiography of Seventy Years*, pp. 157–158; Charles C. Cook, "The Penning of the Negro," in American Negro Academy, *The Negro and the Elective Franchise* (Washington, D.C.: The Academy, 1905), pp. 25–27.

31. Richardson, *Chandler*, pp. 414–445; Sen. John C. Spooner to James S. Clarkson, April 16, 1893, quoted in Hirshson, *Farewell*, p. 249; speech by Elihu Root to Union League Club in New York City, cited in *Harper's Weekly* 47 (1903): 306–307; Mayer, *Republican Party*, p. 215; Welch, *Hoar*, pp. 145–162. The response of Northern newspapers to a Southern disfranchisement law further indicates the changes in the GOP after 1890. See *Springfield* (Massachusetts) *Republican*, *Philadelphia Times*, and *Philadelphia Press*, quoted in *Mobile* (Alabama) *Daily Register*, February 26, March 2, 4, 1893.

Then, too, the depression and the labor troubles of the 1890s focused attention on economic problems. Bankruptcies, unemployment, and strikes seemed more immediate to the Northern electorate and politicians than the increasing oppression of white and, particularly, of Negro Republicans in the South.

Quite as weighty was the fact that the reaction against the party in power at the low point of the economic downturn created a stable national Republican majority. After 1894, the GOP did not need to carry a single Southern congressional district to control the federal government. To increase its majority by seeking Southern Negro votes risked alienating Northern racists. Moreover, pushing a broad range of programs, as the GOP found out in the Fifty-first Congress, endangered all of them; for the opposition might gather enemies of each separate bill into a coalition antagonistic to all the proposed laws. The Republicans might, therefore, lose on the tariff and other financial policies as well as the question of intervening in the South.[32]

Most important, the Southern Democrats outflanked the forces pushing for possible federal election legislation by substituting legal for fraudulent control of the polls. As the *Jackson* (Mississippi) *Clarion-Ledger* noted at the time, one of the chief purposes of the Mississippi constitutional convention of 1890 was to "render [the Election Bill] largely nugatory" by expelling illiterates from the electorate.[33] When Senators George F. Hoar and John C. Spooner and New York Election Supervisor John I. Davenport were drawing up what became the "Lodge bill" at the end of the eighties, only Georgia and South Carolina had passed effective laws restricting the suffrage. By 1896, when the GOP regained national power, Florida, Tennessee, Arkansas, Alabama, and Virginia had adopted secret ballots and/or poll taxes; Mississippi and South Carolina had held dramatic disfranchising conventions. By 1903, every Southern state had enacted legislation limiting the vote. No longer would a Lodge bill guarantee fair elections by allowing federal

32. DeSantis, *Republicans Face*, pp. 213–214. For the Democrats' harangues on the Force Bill in the 1892 presidential campaign, see George Harrison Knoles, *The Presidential Campaign and Election of 1892* (Stanford, California: Stanford Univ. Press, 1942), pp. 81, 144–145, 162, 169, 174; Hoke Smith, "The Disastrous Effects of a Force Bill," *The Forum* 13 (1892): 686–692.

33. One of the chief reasons Albion W. Tourgée pushed a radically stronger alternative to Lodge's measure in 1890 was his understanding of the potency of legal disfranchisement and fear of the probability of its spread. See Tourgée to Thomas B. Reed, n.d. (1890), in Tourgée papers, Chautauqua County Historical Society, Westfield, N. Y.. *Jackson Clarion-Ledger*, Aug. 7, 1890, quoted in Mabry, "Disfranchisement of the Negro," p. 123. Similarly, see Wharton, *Negro in Mississippi*, p. 208.

supervisors to observe the registration of voters and guard against fraud at the polls.[34] For even if the supervisors managed to guarantee impartial administrative practices in registration—a difficult task, since registration took place at myriads of different places and times—a large portion of the Negroes and lower-class whites would be disfranchised by the literacy and poll tax qualifications. Fair administration would probably result in a smaller number of white voters rather than a larger number of Negroes, since registrars would have to offer real "understanding" tests to all illiterates. If so, federal intervention would diminish the chances of opposition parties in the South, not increase them. In such circumstances Republicans might well feel it was not worth the trouble to prohibit racial and political discrimination in voting. Republicans who believed the South still worthy of consideration turned increasingly to the reduction of Southern representation under the provisions of the Fourteenth Amendment as a means of forcing those states to loosen their suffrage qualifications.[35]

In the South itself, two major developments dominated the political stage in the century's last decade: Populism and suffrage restriction. The continual debility of the Southern economy inspired several agricultural protest organizations—the Wheel and the Brothers of Freedom in Arkansas, and the Farmers' Alliance in Texas.[36] These groups fused

34. On the drafting of the Elections Bill, see Hoar, *Autobiography*, pp. 151–153. Republicans realized that laws like the 1890 Lodge bill would have no effect on states such as Mississippi which had legally limited their suffrage. See Senators George F. Hoar (R., Massachusetts) in *Congressional Record*, 51st Cong., 2nd sess., pp. 503, 867; John C. Spooner (R., Wisconsin) in ibid., p. 728; Sen. Henry M. Teller (R., Colorado) in ibid., p. 894; Sen. Evarts (R., New York) in ibid., p. 1363; Rep. Henry Cabot Lodge, in ibid., 51st Cong., 1st sess,. p. 6544; and Andrew C. McLaughlin, "Mississippi and the Negro Question," *The Atlantic Monthly* 70 (1892) : 828–837. And one Southern Republican, Congressman Hamilton G. Ewart of North Carolina, predicted that passage of the Lodge bill would invite Democrats to pass legal disfranchisement measures. The threat alone proved sufficient. See *Congressional Record*, 51st Cong., 1st sess., p. 6690.

35. *Congressional Record*, 56th Cong., 2nd sess., pp. 517–521, 553–559, 590–619, 647–669, 707–748; ibid., appendix, pp. 67–75, 153; *House Report No. 2130*, 56th Cong., 2nd sess., pp. 121–146; *Congressional Record*, 59th Cong., 1st sess,, pp. 3885–3894; Ala. Con. Con. *Proceedings* (1901), vol. 3, pp. 2856, 2866; *The Independent* 52 (1900): 1876, 1935–1936; ibid., 55 (1903): 3008–3010; James W. Garner, "The Fourteenth Amendment and Southern Representation," *South Atlantic Quarterly* 4 (1905): 209–216; Edgar Gardner Murphy, "Shall the Fourteenth Amendment Be Enforced?" *North American Review* 180 (1905): 109–133; Richard B. Sherman, "The Harding Administration and the Negro: An Opportunity Lost," *Journal of Negro History* 49 (1964): 163; August Meier, *Negro Thought in America, 1880–1915*, p. 111.

36. Many of the factual statements about Southern Populism will be drawn, without further citation, from John D. Hicks, *The Populist Revolt*, and Woodward, *Origins*, pp. 175–290.

in the late eighties, and spirited organizers expanded the membership rolls until local units existed in nearly every Southern community.

At first, the Alliance, as the fused clubs became known, acted as a simple agricultural interest group, encompassing large as well as small farmers, Democrats as well as Independents, Greenbackers, and Republicans. In fact, many opportunistic Democratic politicians joined the Alliance just as they might join the Masons, the Confederate Veterans, or the Baptist church. Nonetheless, it was inevitable that many of the Alliance men would split with the Democrats. Several points in the Alliance program, particularly the subtreasury and anti-trust laws, required a strong, active federal government. But the national Democratic party traditionally stood for a weak central government, laissez-faire, and "no class legislation." As long as Grover Cleveland, David B. Hill, John G. Carlisle, August Belmont, and their followers dictated national party policy, backers of the Alliance's "Ocala platform" could not attain their goals within the Democratic party.[37]

The prospect of electoral and monetary support from the Republicans and Independents must also have tempted agrarians to leave the Democrats. The "Jeffersonian Democrats" in Alabama flirted with the protective tariff and received large contributions from Northern Republicans. In Virginia, according to one scholar, three-fourths of the Populist votes came from men who had theretofore supported the GOP. In fact, throughout the South in the nineties, a large number of those opposed to the dominant party rallied around the Populists, who provided not merely an economic, but more important a *political* alternative to the Democrats.[38]

The Alliance brought forward new, self-confident leaders whose power base existed independently of the Democratic party. Since they had not risen through the ranks of the party, they did not feel the same

37. Sheldon Hackney, *Populism to Progressivism in Alabama*, p. 55; Steelman, "Progressive Era in North Carolina," pp. 25–26; C. Vann Woodward, *Tom Watson, Agrarian Rebel*, pp. 136, 161–164.

38. Knoles, *Election of 1892*, p. 194; William Warren Rogers, *The One-Gallused Rebellion*, pp. 278–280; DeSantis, *Republicans Face*, pp. 230–248; William Du Bose Sheldon, *Populism in the Old Dominion*, p. 103; Albert B. Moore, *History of Alabama and Her People*, 1: 722; Edward C. Williamson, "The Era of the Democratic Country Leader: Florida Politics, 1877–1893" (Ph. D. diss., Univ. of Pennsylvania, 1954), pp. 310–315; Arnett, *The Populist Movement in Georgia*, p. 22; Hair, *Bourbonism*, pp. 228–233; *Pine Bluff* (Arkansas) *Weekly Commercial*, Sept. 18, 1892.

loyalty to it as the regulars. Furthermore, the men who finally split with the party tended to occupy less established social positions in their communities than their Democratic counterparts; therefore, they lost less from the social ostracism that resulted from party defection.[39]

Finally, unlike the denizens of the black belts, Alliance men outside the areas of concentrated Negro population felt less constrained to maintain white unity; local Negroes were simply not numerous enough to dominate politics. Consequently, while Alliance members in counties with large proportions of Negroes generally refused to leave the party of white supremacy, those in the hill country readily followed their leaders into Populism.[40]

Though the Populist insurgency copied some of the programs of the Greenback-Independent movement, though third-party men from the eighties often ended up in the Populist camp, though both political revolts attempted to weld the discontented of both races into a winning coalition, there were some important distinctions between Independent-ism and Populism. In the first place, the Alliance was much stronger than the old Granger organizations which had formed the nucleus of Greenbackism. The Populists, therefore, had a broader base of white support than their predecessors. The Populists also boasted a more elaborate economic and political ideology than the Independents. Like the Democrats, the Independents usually threw together a mélange of diverse appeals in an attempt to construct a jerry-built but successful coalition. Neither group in the 1880s seemed to prize a consistent philosophy. The Populists, on the other hand, evolved a broad and roughly consistent political theory in a much more self-conscious fashion.[41]

On the surface, too, the Populists seemed to have a better entrée to black voters, for the Colored Alliance claimed (exaggeratedly) a million members. Many Populists, therefore, felt that they could circumvent

39. On the social pressures to stay in the Democratic party, see William J. Cooper, Jr., *The Conservative Regime*, pp. 35, 71; Hair, *Bourbonism*, pp. 247–248. On the class composition of the Populists, see Roscoe C. Martin, *The People's Party in Texas*, pp. 60–65; Hackney, *Populism to Progressivism in Alabama*, pp. 23–31, 336–342; Rogers, *One-Gallused Rebellion*, p. 238.

40. Edwin Aubera Ford, "Louisiana Politics and the Constitutional Convention of 1898" (M.A. thesis, Louisiana State Univ., 1955), p. 21.

41. On the flow of Independent and Greenback ideas and voters into the Populist party, see Martin, *People's Party in Texas*, p. 72; Williamson, "Independentism," p. 156; J. E. Dovell, *Florida: Historic, Dramatic, Contemporary*, 2: 650; Hair, *Bourbonism*, pp. 214, 220, 231. On Populist ideology, see Norman Pollack, *The Populist Mind*, pp. 169–330.

the Negro politicians, whom they believed corrupt, by direct economic appeals to Negro farmers. But the tactic of identifying Negro and white agriculturalists as covictims of the same economic system ignored the fact that Negroes were often more concerned with social and political than with economic discrimination. In any case, Populists offered no panaceas for sharecroppers. And although some Negro politicos were no doubt venal, their influence was nonetheless real. Ignoring them sometimes provoked reprisals. Only when Populists conciliated local and state Negro politicians were they able to unify black voters in their cause.[42]

The Populists might also have noticed the increasing Democratic control of black belt counties during the 1880s.[43] Whereas the Democrats' opponents in the early eighties could count on heavy majorities in nearly every predominantly Negro country in Arkansas, Florida, North Carolina, Tennessee, Texas, and Virginia, and in many such counties in the other states, the dominant party by the end of the eighties had silenced opposition in most counties with heavy concentrations of Negroes. Only in North Carolina, Virginia, and in a few counties in Texas and Louisiana could the People's Party hope to gain substantial votes in the black belts. Even more crucial, Democrats could overcome white-county Populist majorities by illegally padding their majorities in the predominantly Negro areas.

Democrats countered Populist economic appeals with the old litany perfected during the Independent campaigns: if whites split, they warned, the Negroes would hold the balance of power. Blacks would then demand offices, favorable laws, appropriations, and ultimately social equality. The South would undergo another Reconstruction. Like the Independents before them, the Populists derided such pro-

42. On Populist economic appeals to blacks, see Tom Watson, "The Negro Question in the South," in Pollack, *Populist Mind,* pp. 367–372; Rice, *Negro in Texas,* pp. 68–85; Shadgett, *Republican Party in Georgia,* pp. 110–117; Moore, *History of Alabama,* p. 736; C. Vann Woodward, "Tom Watson and the Negro," *Journal of Southern History* 4 (1938): 23–24. For relations with Negro politicos, see Joseph Matt Brittain, "Negro Suffrage and Politics in Alabama Since 1870" (Ph.D. diss., Indiana Univ., 1958), pp. 105–111; Robert J. Saunders, "Southern Populists and the Negro, 1893–1895," *Journal of Negro History* 54 (1969): 257; Arnett, *Populist Movement in Georgia,* pp. 153, 183; Clarence A. Bacote, "The Negro in Georgia Politics, 1880–1908" (Ph.D. diss., Univ. of Chicago, 1955), pp. 214–223; Tom Watson, speech in 1896 Populist convention in Georgia, quoted in *Atlanta Constitution,* Aug. 12, 1906; Martin, *People's Party in Texas,* pp. 93–99.

43. The Republicans did. See, e.g., *Congressional Record,* 51st Cong., 1st sess., pp. 6786–6787.

positions as bogies conjured up to mislead and frighten white voters.[44] Both sides were partly correct. Certainly the Democrats played on the racism inbred in virtually every white Southerner to cloud over other issues and thereby maintain their control. On the other hand, in localities where Negro political strength was important, blacks did demand and obtain patronage, protection of their political and civil rights, larger funds for governmental programs servicing Negroes, and finally the right to representation by men of their own race—a right that implied a broad, though not necessarily social, equality.[45]

The Democrats' employment of white supremacy rhetoric may have been cynical. While chiding opponents for endangering the racial hierarchy, they often secretly courted black voters. Nonetheless, they undoubtedly internalized their campaign cries, so intertwining the Democratic party with the idea of white domination in their own minds that partisanship and racism became indistinguishable. For example, the official Democratic organ in Louisiana, the *Baton Rouge Daily Advocate*, referred to the Populists as "the most dangerous and insidious foe of white supremacy" and said of the Republican party that "the Africanization of the state was its cardinal doctrine." Constantly referring to the Democrats as " the party of the white man," it considered the fusion between Populists, Republicans, and sugar planters "a grave menace to our civilization." Conversely, the *Pine Bluff* (Arkansas) *Commercial* appealed to white Democrats to pass the poll tax in order to disfranchise blacks because "the most dangerous foe to democracy [the party] is the Negro. . . . The Negro is an uncontrollable objector to our ticket." A threat to the political establishment was a threat to the

44. The Democratic race-baiting appears in Sheldon, *Populism in the Old Dominion*, pp. 85–86; Woodward, *Burden of Southern History*, pp. 150–151; Thomas, *Arkansas*, p. 241; Williamson, "Era of the Democratic Country Leader," p. 311; Bacote, "Negro in Georgia," pp. 174–175; Mabry, "Disfranchisement of the Negro," pp. 286–292. For the Populist response, see William H. Skaggs, *The Southern Oligarchy*, pp. 60–61; Woodward, "Tom Watson and the Negro," pp. 26–28; *Raleigh* (North Carolina) *Caucasian*, March 12, 1896, quoted in Robert F. Durden, *The Climax of Populism*, p. 11.

45. Josephus Daniels, *Editor in Politics*, p. 285; John William Graves, "The Arkansas Negro and Segregation, 1890–1903" (M.A. thesis, Univ. of Arkansas, 1967), pp. 12–21, 71–90; Horace Mann Bond, *Negro Education in Alabama*, pp. 138–140; Rice, *Negro in Texas*, pp. 86–112; Shadgett, *Republican Party in Georgia*, pp. 109–117; Blake, *Mahone*, pp. 191–192; Brittain, "Negro in Alabama Politics," p. 115; Saunders, "Southern Populists and the Negro," pp. 254–256; *Baton Rouge Daily Advocate*, Feb. 4, 9, 18, 1896; Joseph L. Morrison, *Josephus Daniels Says* . . . , pp. 93–94; Steelman, "Progressive Era in North Carolina," pp. 49–53, 126; William J. Simmons, *Men of Mark*, pp. 501–502.

racial establishment, and vice versa. Only such rationalizations could
have saved thousands of politicians from consciousness of their own
self-serving hypocrisy. Few men could live with such an image of themselves.[46]

This equation of the Democratic party with white paramountcy
carried with it the implication that Negro domination threatened until
all partisan opposition was eliminated. Not only black, but potential
white dissent had to be eradicated. From such thinking arose violence,
intimidation, gerrymandering, fraud, and curtailment of the suffrage.
Even after almost every Negro ceased voting, Democrats instantly
charged any partisan adversary with racial treason. The expression
"white man's party" became popular dogma.[47]

Not satisfied that the cry of white supremacy would save them, the
Democrats also co-opted Populist issues and rhetoric. By the mid-
nineties, no stump speech in the South was complete without blasts
at the railroads, the trusts, Wall Street, the gold bugs, the saloonkeepers,
or some similarly evil "Interest." Political machines likewise became
objects of universal denunciation, even by organization stalwarts.
Conservatives appropriated the Populists' call for fair elections under

46. On "secret courting of blacks," see Charles Grayson Summersell, "The Alabama
Governor's Race in 1892," *The Alabama Review*, 8 (1955): 25; Arnett, *Populist Movement in
Georgia*, p. 183; Bacote, "Negro in Georgia," pp. 175–179, 215–223. For the fusion of Democratic partisanship and racism, see *Advocate*, Jan. 3, 9, 1896. According to William A. Mabry,
The Negro in North Carolina Politics since Reconstruction, pp. 29–30, the cry of white supremacy
was the chief issue which kept the Democrats together and the "Bourbons" in power in the
last quarter of the nineteenth century. A similar situation prevailed in Alabama, Mississippi,
and Tennessee. See Going, *Bourbon Democracy in Alabama*, p. 31; Wharton, *Negro in Mississippi*, p.
205; Verton M. Queener, "The East Tennessee Republican Party, 1900–1914," in *East Tennessee Historical Society's Publications* 22 (1950): 118; and then see *Pine Bluff Weekly Commercial*,
July 17, 1892. The context makes clear that the reference to "democracy" is to the Democratic
party.

47. Hackney, *Populism to Progressivism*, p. 47; unnamed Texas congressman, quoted in
Stanley L. Jones, *The Presidential Election of 1896*, pp. 195–196; Skaggs, *Southern Oligarchy*, pp.
109, 118; Hair, *Bourbonism*, pp. 75–78. Virginia Democrats charged that the 1905 Republican
candidate for governor favored miscegenation, and they race-baited extensively against the
lily-white Republican Bascom Slemp in a 1910 congressional campaign. See Guy B. Hathorn,
"The Political Career of C. Bascom Slemp" (Ph.D. diss., Duke Univ., 1950), pp. 33–35, 63.
Josephus Daniels charged that a GOP victory in North Carolina in 1908 would mean a return
to "nigger rule." See David Charles Roller, "The Republican Party in North Carolina, 1900–
1916" (Ph.D. diss., Duke Univ., 1965), p. 170. Although at the time only 1 percent of the
Negroes were registered to vote, the *Montgomery* (Alabama) *Daily Advertiser* in October 1902,
reprinted the bitterly racist 1874 address of the chairman of the Alabama Democratic Executive committee under the headline "White Supremacy the Keynote of Campaign of 1902 as
in that of 1874," *Advertiser*, Oct. 23, 1902.

the Australian ballot system and employed that system to disfranchise many potential converts to the People's Party.[48] The "horny-handed sons of toil" began to receive rhetorical attention once reserved for Confederate soldiers and Southern industrial magnates. The state Democratic party which could not boast of a leading farmer-turned-politician (or vice versa) during the nineties was poor indeed. The fusion behind Bryan in 1896 was only the last and most effective device to pull agrarians into the Democratic party.

If fraud, racism, and co-optation failed to quash the opposition, there was always disfranchisement. In the eighties and early nineties, Democrats developed a panoply of restrictive measures—registration and multiple-box laws, the poll tax, the Australian ballot, and the educational qualification. Each state became in effect a laboratory for testing one device or another. Indeed, the cross-fertilization and coordination between the movements to restrict the suffrage in the Southern states amounted to a public conspiracy.[49] Since newspapers

48. On the co-optation, see Sheldon, *Populism in the Old Dominion*, pp. 85–86, 140–142; Allen J. Going, "Critical Months in Alabama Politics, 1895–1896," *Alabama Review* 5 (1952): 273; Jones, *Presidential Election of 1896*, pp. 195–196; Thomas, *Arkansas*, 1: 223–225, 239, 248–252; Graves, "Arkansas Negro," pp. 65–67; Williamson, "Era of the Democratic Country Leader," pp. 306–307; Kathryn T. Abbey, "Florida Versus the Principles of Populism," *Journal of Southern History* 4 (1938): 465–468; Samuel Proctor, *Napoleon Bonaparte Broward*, pp. 60–62; Hair, *Bourbonism*, p. 239; Mabry, "Disfranchisement of the Negro," pp. 262, 285; Steelman, "Progressive Era in North Carolina," pp. 21–25, 123–125, 127–128, 165–167; Francis Butler Simkins, *Pitchfork Ben Tillman*, pp. 204–206, 265. See the denunciation of "machines" by Hal Flood, number two man in the Tom Martin organization, quoted in Burton Ira Kaufman, "Henry De La Warr Flood: A Case Study of Organization Politics in an Era of Reform" (Ph.D. diss., Rice Univ., 1966), p. 100. The Populist party platform, adopted at Omaha in July 1892, endorsed the secret ballot as a means of guaranteeing a free ballot and a fair count. Hicks, *Populist Revolt*, p. 443.

49. For evidence that Democrats in various states conspired with those in others and that the leaders of disfranchisement were cognizant of developments throughout the South, see Daniels, *Editor in Politics*, pp. 324, 374–380; Lambert, *Gorman*, p. 347; John B. Knox's Presidential Address and the Suffrage Committee's report in Ala. Con. Con. *Proceedings* (1901), pp. 7–17, 1256; McMillan, *Constitutional Development in Alabama*, pp. 272–275, 280, 346; Stephen B. Weeks, "The History of Negro Suffrage," *Political Science Quarterly* 9 (1894): 696; *Florida Times-Union*, April 24, 1889, Sept. 4, 17, 20, Oct. 13, Nov. 5, 20, 1890; *Pine Bluff Weekly Commercial*, Aug. 24, Oct. 26, 1890, Aug. 28, 1892; *Little Rock Arkansas Gazette*, March 3, 1891; Bacote, "Negro in Georgia," pp. 412–413; *New Orleans Daily Picayune*, Dec. 12, 14, 1897, Feb. 6, 9, 15–20, Mar. 9, 1898; Mabry, "Disfranchisement of the Negro," pp. 113, 123, 143, 300, 304; *Charleston News and Courier*, Oct. 10, 1894; *Nashville Daily American*, Jan. 12, Feb. 20, March 9, 1889; Charles K. Chamberlain, "Alexander Watkins Terrell, Citizen, Statesman" (Ph.D. diss., Univ. of Texas, 1956), pp. 238–239; John Goode's Presidential Address, in Va. Con. Con. *Proceedings* (1901), pp. 20–21.

reprinted comments from their counterparts throughout the South, since politicians could often get firsthand information about the effect of laws through personal friends or through associates in Congress, and since state libraries traded lawbooks, any successful law could easily be copied. Thus, Florida copied South Carolina's eight-box scheme, and Alabama and Florida borrowed from Tennessee's secret ballot law; Tennessee, Arkansas, Florida, and Mississippi followed Georgia's example in enacting a poll tax. There was a slight pause after the first enactment of any particular mechanism, perhaps to test the reaction of Northerners and the state's own electors. When Congress did not intervene, and when voters did not rise up against the disfranchisers, legislators in other states felt free to write similar laws.

Though Mississippi's constitutional disfranchisement certainly impressed contemporaries as the most permanent and effective solution, politicians in the early nineties hesitated to follow Mississippi's lead. One reason was that calling conventions or passing amendments usually required two-thirds majorities in the legislatures, as well as majorities in referenda and in constitutional conventions. Moreover, in a time of political upheaval, few groups with strong interests in any aspect of the status quo dared to invite constitutional change. Many Democrats feared Populists might poll sufficient strength in such conventions to alter other sections of the constitutions; conservatives in South Carolina feared the Tillmanites would permanently enshrine the Dispensary system in the fundamental law; reformers feared that the railroads would destroy utility commissions; where no commission yet existed, railroad men feared reformers might create one.[50] Only after the Democrats had gained secure majorities did they call disfranchisement conventions, and then only in five states.

Tables 1.5 and 1.6 demonstrate the efficacy of even simple disfranchising devices in cutting the strength of opposition to the Democrats. At the height of Populist or Republican strength in gubernatorial elections in each Southern state, the opposing parties were

50. McMillan, *Constitutional Development in Alabama*, pp. 229–230, 249–250; Hackney, *Populism to Progressivism*, pp. 150–153; H. E. Poindexter, "From Copy-Desk to Congress, The Pre-Congressional Career of Carter Glass (Ph.D. diss., Univ. of Virginia, 1955), pp. 198–199, 216–217, 271; *New Orleans Times-Democrat*, May 27, 1894, quoted in Mabry, "Disfranchisement of the Negro," p. 209; Ralph Clipman McDanel, *The Virginia Constitutional Convention of 1901–02*, p. 10; George B. Tindall, "The Campaign for the Disfranchisement of Negroes in South Carolina," *Journal of Southern History* 15 (1949) : 226–227.

Table 1.5. The Opposition at Its Crest in the 1890s: Populist or Republican Percentage and Turnout in Key Gubernatorial Races.

State	Year	Party	% Populist or Republican of Those Voting	% Turnout
Group 1[a]				
Arkansas	1896	Republican	25.3	48.7
Florida	1892	Populist	21.3	38.9
Georgia	1894	Populist	44.0	49.6
Mississippi	1895	Populist	27.2	20.8
South Carolina	1894	Independent	30.4	22.3
Tennessee	1896	Republican	46.8	70.5
Group 2[b]				
Alabama	1892	Populist	47.6	70.5
Louisiana	1896	Fusion	43.7	69.9
North Carolina	1896	Republican	46.5	85.4
Texas	1896	Fusion	44.4	85.6
Virginia	1893	Populist	40.8	54.3

[a]Group 1 is composed of states which adopted effective disfranchising statutes before 1894.
[b]Group 2 is composed of states which did not adopt effective disfranchising laws before 1894.

unable to garner a majority of the recorded votes. (The Populists were, however, undoubtedly counted out in the Louisiana and Alabama elections shown in the tables.)[51] The opposition was virtually crushed in four of the six states that adopted restrictive statutes before 1894; in none of the four did the chief opposition party poll one-third of the votes. Less than a majority of the potential electors went to the polls in five of these six states. Low turnout appears to have correlated with Populist defeat.

In states which had restricted the vote, the opposition party survived suffrage restriction only where it had exceptionally strong white support. In Georgia, where the poll tax had long discouraged Negroes from

51. Rogers, *One-Gallused Rebellion*, pp. 221–228. Robert McKee, black belt newspaper editor and astute political observer, admitted privately in 1892 that "excluding Negro votes, or stuffed ballots, as you please, [the Populist] candidate unquestionably has a large majority," quoted in Hackney, *Populism to Progressivism*, p. 23. The *Shreveport* (Louisiana) *Evening Judge*, Dec. 15, 1895, quoted in Hair, *Bourbonism*, p. 260, announced: "It is the religious duty of Democrats to rob Populists and Republicans of their votes whenever and wherever the opportunity presents itself and any failure to do so will be a violation of the true Louisiana Democratic teaching. The Populists and Republicans are our legitimate political prey. Rob them! You bet! What are we here for!"

voting, where the Republicans had been so weak since 1872 that whites had almost ceased to fear a return to Reconstruction, and where the Populists produced their most astute leader, Tom Watson, the People's Party did relatively well. The Peach State was the one polity where the Populists prospered despite a minority voter turnout. The mountaineer Republicans of Tennessee also continued to vote despite that state's adoption of a poll tax in 1890. In these two and other states, it is evident that the poll tax requirement was quietly relaxed or that parties raised money to pay the taxes of large numbers of their followers during fervent campaigns.[52]

Table 1.6. Estimated Voting Patterns, by Race, in Key Gubernatorial
Contests during the 1890s.

State	Year	Chief Opposition Party	White				Black			
			Democrat	Republican	Populist	No Vote	Democrat	Republican	Populist	No Vote
Group 1[a]										
Arkansas	1896	Republican	37	15	12	40	21	5	0	75
Florida	1892	Populist	43	0	17	41	11	0	0	89
Georgia	1894	Populist	35	0	34	31	23	0	15	62
Mississippi	1895	Populist	35	0	19	45	0	0	0	100
South Carolina	1894	Independent	22	0	11	67	12	0	5	84
Tennessee[b]	1896	Republican	42	45	3	10	24	−4[c]	5	74
Group 2[d]										
Alabama	1892	Populist	27	0	53	20	49	0	14	36
Louisiana	1896	Fusion	22	58	0	21	62	7	0	31
North Carolina	1896	Republican	45	31	9	15	20	59	8	13
Texas	1896	Fusion	48	34	0	18	47	50	0	3
Virginia	1893	Populist	40	0	11	47	19	0	46	35

[a]States which restricted suffrage before first Populist Party election.

[b]Tennessee estimates computed by sections, North Carolina and Virginia by splitting the state into counties above and below 30 percent Negro. Estimates in table are weighted sums of the separate estimates.

[c]For an explanation of estimates outside the 0–100% limits, see my "Ecological Regression" article.

[d]States which restricted suffrage after first Populist Party election.

52. Many Southern voters probably had their poll taxes paid for them by political organizations. The best scholarly evidence of this practice is for Virginia elections, on which see DeSantis, *Republicans Face the Southern Question*, p. 153; Hathorn, "C. Bascom Slemp," p. 43; Andrew Buni, *The Negro in Virginia Politics, 1902–1965*, p. 31. For proof that Tennessee

Table 1.6 shows that the most accurate estimate is that at least 60 percent of the adult male Negroes in each of the states in Group 1 failed to vote in the decade's hottest elections. The five states that did not restrict the franchise prior to the mid-1890s present quite a different picture. In none of these states did the chief opposition party fail to gather 40 percent of the voters. A majority of the adult males of each state voted in the elections cited. In two of the five states turnout reached astronomical proportions, by twentieth-century standards, as 85 percent of those eligible voted. Estimated Negro turnout and party preferences in the states in group 1 provide a striking contrast with those in group 2. In the former, less than 40 percent of the blacks voted; in the latter, at least 64 percent. In the first group, the Democrats carried the recorded black vote by at least two to one except in Georgia, where the old party won by a five to three margin. In the second, group, the majority of blacks supported the dissenters, except in Louisiana and Alabama, where black belt ballot fraud had become a vocation.

The degree to which disfranchising laws adversely affected dissenting parties becomes even clearer when we compare the nineties with the preceding decade in Southern politics. Whereas the Democrats lost governors' races in two states during the eighties, they lost only one in the next decade. In the 1880s, Independents or Republicans had polled at least 40 percent of the votes in seven states; in the 1890s, in six states. Independents scored at least 30 percent of the vote in ten states, Populists or Republicans in only eight. In the 1880s at least 49 percent of the voters participated in the key gubernatorial elections in each ex-Confederate state; in the 1890s, four states fell below that mark. Despite increased economic grievances, a better organization, and a more coherent ideology, the Populists were, on the whole, somewhat less successful politically than the Independents.[53]

The fact that franchise limitation was one of the chief reasons for Populist failure becomes unmistakable when we focus on three states. In Florida, Arkansas, and Mississippi the Independents had gained over 40 percent of the votes; the Populists won less than 30 percent in each state. In the key contests in the 1880s, overall turnout rates varied from

Republicans paid poll taxes for their followers in the 1896 contest and allegations that the tax requirements were relaxed in several East Tennessee counties, see below, chapter 5.

53. Cf. Monroe Lee Billington, *The American South*, pp. 211, 224.

50.8 percent in Mississippi to 79.4 percent in Florida; the range in the nineties was from 20.9 percent to 48.7 percent. From 39 percent to 87 percent of the Negroes are estimated to have voted in these three states in the Independent campaigns; from 0 percent to 25 percent in the Populist elections. Thus, the strong opposition movements in these three states in the eighties faded after the Democrats restricted the suffrage. The lesson must have been clear to politicians elsewhere.

2

Techniques of Abridging the Right to Vote: Fraud, Registration, and Literacy Tests

If election regulations shaped the Southern political system, then it is important to know how each operated, why particular types of laws were enacted at certain times, and how effective each was in re-forming the polity. Moreover, were the proponents conscious of the effects of all the various types of electoral laws, or were disfranchisement and the decline of opposition parties, in some cases, merely unintended consequences of legal changes proposed for other purposes? Since registration, residency, the secret ballot, the educational qualification, and the direct primary were not confined to the South, nor particular to the early part of this century, an examination of such mechanisms has quite general significance. Though the next two chapters focus primarily on methods of restriction in the South, they will also briefly suggest parallels with election legislation outside the South and with legislation in other time periods. Was Southern disfranchisement only the most blatant aspect of a nationwide impulse?

The Limitations of Fraud

Those who sought to prune the Southern electorate were hampered by various constitutional restrictions. The Fifteenth Amendment prohibited overt discrimination on the basis of race, color, or previous condition of servitude. The Fourteenth threatened reduction of representation in Congress and the Electoral College proportionate to the number of adult males disfranchised for any reason other than crime or participation in rebellion.[1] Aside from explicit Prohibitions, rapid and defiant Southern action to excise Republican electors from the body politic risked a change in the national and Republican mood that

1. Republicans repeatedly moved to reduce Southern representation because of disfranchisement. See *Congressional Record*, 51st Cong., 2nd sess., pp. 360–361; ibid., 59th Cong., 1st sess., pp. 3885–3894; Sherman, "The Harding Administration and the Negro," pp. 151–168.

would precipitate a return to Reconstruction.[2] The disfranchisers were, therefore, forced to contrive devious means to accomplish their purposes. Less subtle techniques could be employed only after national political conditions ruled out either a renewal of Reconstruction or a strict constructionist interpretation of the postwar amendments.[3]

At first, the Democrats relied primarily on laws and practices that decreased the influence of opposition voters but did not actually prohibit them from exercising the franchise. Some states vested the right to name local officials in governors or legislatures, a procedure which guaranteed that white Democrats would rule even in Republican areas. Other states devised ingenious gerrymanders or set bonds for local officials so high that no one except the agents of the economic elite could afford to serve.[4]

The stuffing of Southern ballot boxes became a national scandal. Senator Samuel D. McEnery of Louisiana stated that his state's 1882 election law "was intended to make it the duty of the governor to treat the law as a formality and count in the Democrats."[5] As governor

2. Louisiana governor Murphy J. Foster declared that the 1879 constitutional convention in that state did not enact suffrage limitations because they "dread[ed] renewed federal complications and interferences from which we had just escaped." See *New Orleans Daily Picayune*, Jan. 4, 1898, and a similar statement by Congressman Charles J. Boatner in the same newspaper, Jan. 6, 1898. Alabama, Tennessee, and Mississippi took no severe action because of the same fears. See McMillan, *Constitutional Development*, pp. 201, 217; Joshua W. Caldwell, *Studies in the Constitutional History of Tennessee* (Cincinnati: The Robert Clarke Co., 1907), pp. 314–315; Frank Johnston, "The Public Services of Senator James Z. George," *Publications of the Mississippi Historical Society* 8 (1904): 209–210. These fears were well grounded at least as late as 1875. See Grant's message to Congress asking Congress to overturn the 1874 Arkansas constitution for depriving minorities of their rights, in Richardson, *Messages and Papers*, 7: 319.

3. Some historians have so confused the time sequence of minor and major changes in election laws as to destroy any broad distinctions between the pre- and post-disfranchisement epochs in Southern politics. Paul Lewinson, for instance, indiscriminately mingles laws passed in the 1870s to disfranchise the few people who committed petty crimes with such major restrictive devices, passed thirty years later, as the literacy and property qualifications. See his *Race, Class and Party*, p. 81.

4. Charles E. Wynes, *Race Relations in Virginia, 1870–1902*, p. 13; Going, *Bourbon Democracy*, pp. 33–34; Frenise A. Logan, *The Negro in North Carolina, 1876–1894*, p. 9. On gerrymandering, see James Welch Patton, "The Republican Party in South Carolina, 1876–1895," in Green, ed., *Essays in Southern History*, pp. 102–104; Buni, *Negro in Virginia Politics*, p. 2; Mabry, *Negro in North Carolina Politics*, pp. 19–20; McMillan, *Constitutional Development*, pp. 221–223. On the bonding maneuver, see Going, *Bourbon Democracy*, pp. 33–34; *Jacksonville Florida Times-Union*, March 24, 1889; Rice, *Negro in Texas*, pp. 88–89.

5. During the debates on the Lodge Elections Bill in 1890, Rep. Julius Caesar Burrows

from 1879 to 1888, McEnery proved a dutiful servant of the legislative will. Democrats in South Carolina and Florida loaded the boxes with tissue ballots and extra-small tickets nicknamed "little jokers." When counters discovered that the number of ballots surpassed the number of voters, they put all the ballots back in the box and, blindfolded, withdrew and discarded a number of the thicker, larger GOP tickets equal to the excess. William A. Anderson, author of the chief Virginia election statute during this period, admitted that Virginia elections were "crimes against popular government and treason against liberty." A delegate to the 1901 Alabama constitutional convention reported that "any time it was necessary the black belt could put in ten, fifteen, twenty or thirty thousand Negro votes." A leader of the 1890 Mississippi convention declared that "it is no secret that there has not been a full vote and a fair count in Mississippi since 1875."[6]

Such flagrant chicanery eroded popular confidence in government, supplied grist for Republican campaign mills, and kept alive national GOP hopes that they could regain power in the South if only they could obtain a fair count. The Democrats therefore turned increasingly to methods that actually struck voters from the lists.

REGISTRATION AND QUASI-LITERACY TESTS

One effective device was to require periodic voter registration. Even where administered impartially, these laws have had a significant negative effect on turnout. As early as 1910, Ray Stannard Baker stated that registration and secret ballot laws together eliminated "hundreds of thousands of voters" in the Northern states. More recently, statutes making several months' residency in a state and an election district a prerequisite for voting reportedly disfranchised 4 million Americans in

---

remarked: "I firmly believe that if we were to strike out every word in this bill and insert three of the Ten Commandments: Thou shalt not steal; Thou shalt not bear false witness; Thou shalt not kill—the whole Democratic party would declare it an assault upon the South, subversive of the Constitution, and an infringement of the reserved rights of the States." *Congressional Record*, 51st Cong., 1st Sess., p. 6787. For McEnery's admission, see *New Orleans Daily Picayune*, Feb. 30, 1898.

6. *Charleston News and Courier*, Dec. 18, 1880; *Report of the Republican State Executive Committee of Florida to the Republicans of the State Upon the Election Held November 2, 1880* (Washington, D.C.: National Republican Publishing Co., 1881), pp. 24–25. Anderson quoted in Herman L. Horn, "The Growth and Development of the Democratic Party in Virginia Since 1890" (Ph.D. diss., Duke Univ., 1949), pp. 47–48. For delegates' remarks see Ala. Con. Con. *Proceedings* (1901), vol. 3, p. 3373, and Wharton, *Negro in Mississippi*, p. 206.

1950, 5 million in 1954, 8 million in 1960, and 6 million in 1968. In many places in the South in 1972, according to John Lewis, director of the Voter Education Project, registration boards dominated by "party hacks . . . set up rules and regulations and other barriers to the ballot which make it impossible for poor people and working people to register with ease." Southern states in the late nineteenth century usually required one or two years residency in the state and up to a year in the county. Even in the North it sometimes appears obvious that the intent of these laws was to disfranchise. A 1917 Indiana law, for example, required the applicant for registration to specify the material out of which his house was built, the full name of his nearest neighbor, and other matters equally relevant to the exercise of the franchise.[7]

The key disfranchising features of the Southern registration laws were the amount of discretion granted to the registrars, the specificity of the information required of the registrant, the times and places set for registration, and the requirement that a voter bring his registration certificate to the polling place. According to the North Carolina law of 1889, for instance, registrars, appointed indirectly by the Democratic legislature, could require that a voter prove "as near as may be" his "age, occupation, place of birth and place of residency . . . by such testimony, under oath, as may be satisfactory to the registrar." Black men born into slavery were often ignorant of their exact ages; streets in Negro areas often had no names, houses no numbers. Democrats employed this law to deny the vote to white and black Republicans and Populists in the early 1890s. Registration officials in Florida merely erased Republican names and then refused to meet with the voters so that they could re-register. Alabama, after 1892, allowed voters to register only in May, the busiest time of the year for farmers. The practice of closing registration before candidates were even nominated

7. Ray Stannard Baker, "Negro Suffrage in a Democracy," *The Atlantic* 106 (1910): 613. Similarly, see Stanley Kelley, Jr., Richard E. Ayres, and William G. Bowen, "Registration and Voting: Putting First Things First," *American Political Science Review* 61 (1967): 374; Chilton W. Williamson, *American Suffrage from Property to Democracy*, pp. 272–277; and Joseph P. Harris, *Registration of Voters in the United States*, pp. 65–106. Post-1950 statistics are taken from President's Commission on Registration and Voting Participation, *Report* (Washington, D.C.: G.P.O., 1963), p. 13; and *New York Times*, Nov. 17. 1968, p. 10-E. Lewis is quoted in *Los Angeles Times*, Nov. 4, 1972, pp. I-16, 17. For the late nineteenth-century Southern laws, see Ralph Wardlaw, "Negro Suffrage in Georgia, 1867–1930," *Bulletin of the University of Georgia* (Athens, Georgia: Univ. of Georgia Press, 1932), p. 37; N.C. *Acts* (1899), pp. 341–343; Miss. Con. Con. *Journal* (1890) pp. 229–230. For the Indiana statute, see Harris, *Registration of Voters*, p. 87.

obviously put relatively uninterested and unorganized voters at a disadvantage. The county machine could always remind its followers of the closing date for registration, but it neglected those voters outside the dominant political structure, or even prevented them from registering. Several states also required the voter to bring his easily misplaced registration certificate with him to the polls; otherwise, he could not vote.[8]

How much impact the registration laws had upon the electorate depended on their administration. If registrars throughout a state decided to keep the voting lists short, the effect could be quite spectacular. The federal district attorney for South Carolina, Samuel Melton, estimated that the registration section of the 1882 election law disfranchised 75 percent of the Palmetto State's Negro voters. The task of calculating the potency of such laws is complicated by the fact that only one state, Louisiana, published statewide registration figures for the period before 1900. The registration figures there were as fictional as the election returns: in 1897, the registration of white adult males exceeded 100 percent. Nonetheless, it is instructive to observe the effect of the 1896 Louisiana registration law on the electorate. On January 1, 1897, 103.2 percent of the white and 95.6 percent of the Negro adult males appeared on the rolls. By January 1, 1898, voters were required to have registered anew. Despite the fact that the constitutional qualifications for voting remained the same during both periods, only 46.6 percent of the whites and 9.5 percent of the blacks were listed at the later date. The law as administered reduced white registration by nearly 60 percent and Negro by 90 percent.[9]

8. N.C. *Acts* (1889), ch. 287, sections 3, 12, quoted in Logan, *Negro in North Carolina*, pp. 58–59. For a similar law in Mississippi, see Wharton, *Negro in Mississippi*, pp. 199–200. For proof that North Carolina Democratic boss, Furnifold Simmons, coordinated the administrative discrimination against his opposition, see Simmons to Marmaduke J. Hawkins, cited in Steelman, "The Progressive Era in North Carolina," p. 36, n. 11. The Fusion legislature's 1895 election law reversed the Democratic law's presumption that a voter (at least a Populist or Republican voter) was not registered unless he could prove it. See Helen G. Edmonds, *The Negro and Fusion Politics in North Carolina*, pp. 70–74. For the registration procedure in Florida, see *Report of the Republican State Executive Committee*, pp. 11–13. For the effect of the Alabama law, see Ala. Con. Con. *Proceedings* (1901), Vol. 3, pp. 3284–3285. On the importance of the closing date for registration, see Allen M. Shinn, Jr., "A Note on Voter Registration and Turnout in Texas, 1960–1970," *Journal of Politics* 33 (1971): 1120–1129. For registration certificates, see S. C. *Acts* (1881–1882), pp. 1110–1126; Ala. *Acts* (1892–1893), pp. 837–851; Tenn. *Acts* (1889), pp. 414–420.

9. Samuel Melton to Benjamin Brewster, Dec. 20, 1882, quoted in Cooper, *The Conservative Regime*, p. 216. Registration figures, by race, are given in the La. Con. Con. *Journal* (1898),

Undoubtedly, the effect was less dramatic in most instances. And since the technique relied upon discriminatory administration, a change in the control of the state government might reverse the direction of discrimination in voter registration. Federal regulation of registration, a feature of the Lodge Elections Bill of 1890, might eliminate it entirely. Registration laws were most efficiently used—as in South Carolina, Louisiana, and North Carolina—to cut the electorate immediately before a referendum on constitutional disfranchisement.[10]

Two states, South Carolina in 1882 and Florida in 1889, adopted eight-box laws; the latter state's action copied the former's. North Carolina instituted a multi-box law in time for the 1900 referendum on the disfranchisement amendment. These bureaucratic monstrosities extended the practice existing in several Southern states of maintaining separate ballot boxes for state and federal elections. The two-box system had been used to keep federal election supervisors who were observing congressional elections from discovering frauds in state contests. Under the eight-box laws, separate ballots for president, congressman, governor, state senator, etc., were supposed to be deposited in the proper boxes; if the ballots were distributed otherwise, they were not counted. Boxes were constantly shifted to prevent a literate voter from arranging the tickets of an uneducated friend in the correct order before he entered the voting place. Illiterates could ask the election judges to read the names on the boxes, but since all election officials were appointed by the Democratic governor, it is doubtful that Republicans got much assistance in voting. Since 55 percent of the adult male Negroes in South Carolina, 53 percent in North Carolina, and 39 percent in Florida were classed as illiterates as late as 1900, the effect of these de facto literacy tests was quite appreciable.[11]

---

insert opposite p. 42.

10. Crofts, "Blair Bill," pp. 252–254. The technique of requiring a new registration before a crucial election has been used recently, e.g., in the Mississippi elections of 1971. See *Los Angeles Times*, Jan. 2, 1972, p. G-5.

11. S.C. *Acts* (1881–82), pp. 1117–1118; Fla. *Acts* (1889), pp. 101–102. For the similarity of the two acts, compare sec. 29 of the South Carolina law with sec. 25 of the Florida law. For North Carolina, see N.C. *Acts* (1899), sec. 26–28, p. 670; N.C. *Acts* (Adjourned Sess., 1900), sec. 35, pp. 36–37. See also *Miller* vs. *Elliot*, in Chester H. Rowell, comp., *Digest of Contested Election Cases, 1789–1901*, pp. 461–464; James Owen Knauss, "The Growth of Florida's Election Laws." *Florida Historical Quarterly* 5 (1926): 10. Illiteracy rates from *Twelfth Census of the United States, 1900* (Washington, D.C.: G. P. O., 1901), vol. I, *Population*, part I, table 68, pp. 910–911.

Rarely included in discussions of disfranchisement, the secret ballot was a far subtler device than the multiple-box laws. The most recent historian of the "Australian system," although he notes its use as a literacy test in Louisiana, pictures it as a "major reform issue . . . part of the general reforming spirit of the age." Spokesmen for the lower strata in society—in England, the Chartists; and in America, the Populists, Terence Powderly of the Knights of Labor, and Henry George—argued that the secret ballot would prevent employers from dictating the votes of their workers. Upper-class reformers such as Henry Cabot Lodge and Richard Henry Dana III felt it would decrease corruption, encourage independent voting, and bring more of the "best men" into politics. With such backing, the new method of voting could be presented as an instrument of "reform" both above and below the Mason-Dixon line.[12]

Until 1888, political parties printed and distributed the ballots in each of the United States. Besides discouraging split-ticket voting and encouraging strong party organizations—just making sure all potential voters had ballots must have necessitated meticulous campaigning at the grass roots—the party ballot insured illiterates the right to vote. Nevertheless, reformers, who were more concerned with eliminating fraud than safeguarding the rights of illiterates, instituted the secret ballot in eight Southern and 30 non-Southern states between 1888 and 1900.[13]

The publicly printed ticket required the voter, sometimes without any aid from anyone, to scurry quickly through a maze of names of candidates running for everything from presidential elector to county court clerk, a list which was often arranged by office rather than party.

12. L. E. Fredman, *The Australian Ballot*, pp. ix–x, 4, 33, 36–41, 57–63. Loren P. Beth, in *The Development of the American Constitution, 1877–1917*, p. 113, states that "the poor" were disfranchised before the late 1880s by "the lack of a secret ballot, which tended to intimidate the frightened or halfhearted." Philip E. Converse believes the decline in turnout, North and South, resulting from the secret ballot and personal registration laws an "unintended consequence" or "side effect" of the desire by the "forces of good government" to eliminate "gross overtones of fraud in American elections." See his "Change in the American Electorate," in Campbell and Converse, *The Human Meaning of Social Change*, pp. 297–299. For a similar interpretation of the secret ballot's effect throughout the world, see Stein Rokkan, *Citizens, Elections, Parties* (New York: David McKay Co., 1970), pp. 35–36, 152–54. For the "reform" appeal see *Nashville Daily American*, April 5, 1889; *Little Rock Arkansas Gazette*, March 1, 1891; Joseph B. Bishop, "The Secret Ballot in Thirty-Five States," *The Forum* 2 (1892): 589–598.
13. Spencer D. Albright, *The American Ballot*, pp. 23–29.

He then had to mark an "X" by the names of the candidates for whom he wished to vote, or, in some states, mark through or erase those he opposed. Such a task demanded not merely literacy, but fluency in the English language. An ingenious lawmaker could make voting all but impossible. Florida totally abolished party designations on its ballot. A Populist or Republican who wished to vote for his presidential electors had to count down five, ten, or fifteen unfamiliar names before starting to mark. Voters in one Virginia congressional district in 1894 confronted a ballot printed in the German Fraktur script.[14]

The extent to which a desire to eliminate the "ignorant" or the "unfit" from the electorate motivated Northern ballot reformers, and the effect of such "reforms" of the political process outside the South deserves more attention from scholars than it has received. Although the *Nation* noted in 1889 that "in the discussions concerning the Australian system, a great deal has been said about the illiterate voter," historians have said little about him since then.[15]

There is evidence that the desire to reduce the electorate played a significant part in Northern adoption of the Australian system.[16] The magazine editor George Gunton, speaking primarily of the North, declared that "so obvious is the evil of ignorant voting that more stringent naturalization laws are being demanded, because too many of our foreign-born citizens vote ignorantly. It is to remedy this that the Australian ballot system has been adopted in so many states." The secret ballot's purpose, he said, was "to eliminate the ignorant, illiterate voters."[17] Eight states outside the limits of the Confederacy prohibited

14. Eldon C. Evans, *A History of the Australian Ballot System in the United States*, p. 43; Philip Loring Allen. "The Multifarous Australian Ballot," *North American Review* 191 (1910): 608–609.

15. See the anonymous article, "Successful Ballot Laws," *The Nation* 49 (1889) : 304. Analysts of the Australian system share the common mugwump prejudices against illiterates. For example, Harris, *Registration of Voters*, p. 158, says that "it is doubtful whether the loss of a vote of a person too illiterate or ignorant to mark [a secret ballot] is a public loss." Similarly, see Evans, *Australian Ballot System* pp. 42–43. Converse in "American Electorate" (p. 300), points out patronizingly that the secret ballot discourages vote-selling even by "benighted subpopulations . . . so cognitively vague about politics as to be indifferent to what vote they cast, and too inarticulate or subservient to create any public scandal if by chance the solicitation is resented."

16. On the desirability of disfranchising non-English speaking immigrants see an article by that mirror of American mugwump attitudes, James Bryce, "Thoughts on the Negro Problem," *North American Review* 153 (1891): 656.

17. Gunton quoted in *Review of Reviews* 6 (1892–93): 448. Similarly, see J. J. McCook,

election officials from assisting illiterates. About one of every four white males of voting age in the United States in 1900 had been born abroad, two-thirds of these in non-English-speaking countries. We do not know what proportion of the foreign-born citizens were literate in English, for the census counted as literate anyone who said he could read at all in any language.[18] It seems probable, therefore, that many immigrants did not have a sufficient command of English to complete their ballots unassisted. And it would be strange indeed if the same politicians who distributed campaign literature in a wide variety of languages had overlooked the effect of an intricate English ballot on the foreign-born voters.

Although existing evidence of the intent of the Northern ballot reformers is only circumstantial and suggestive, there is little question that the secret ballot was adopted in the South primarily to purge the electorate of illiterates. The president of the Alabama State Senate supported his state's Australian ballot law, he said, because under it, "the ignorant are practically disfranchised." The "father of Georgia disfranchisement" included the Australian ballot system in a list of the most effective ways of eliminating Negroes from politics. Tennessee Democrats beat down GOP attempts to allow election officials to aid the unlettered or print party initials after each candidate's name.[19]

"Venal Voting: Methods and Remedies," *The Forum* 14 (1892): 159–177; Bishop, "Ballot in Thirty-Five States," pp. 597–598; *Springfield* (Massachusetts) *Republican*, quoted in *Jacksonville Florida Times-Union*, April 17, 1889; *The Outlook* 116 (1901) 329–330.

18. Evans, *Australian Ballot System*, p. 53. See, for example, New York *Laws* (1890), pp. 482–487; New Jersey *Acts* (1890), pp. 361–402. The *New York Sun*, quoted in Evans, *Australian Ballot System*, p. 25, thought that the New York law, by making it more difficult to vote, would gradually disfranchise many New Yorkers. Racist Democrats in Maryland, which is usually classified as a Northern state, passed a secret ballot act in 1901 in an attempt to disfranchise black Republicans. See Margaret Law Callcott, *The Negro In Maryland Politics, 1870–1912*, pp. 102–114. Census data from U. S. Bureau of the Census, *Abstract of the Twelfth Census of the United States, 1900* (Washington, D.C.: G.P.O., 1904), Table 22, p. 19; table 59, p. 77; table 61, pp. 79–81; U.S. Bureau of the Census, *Thirteenth Census of the United States, 1910* (Washington, D.C.: G.P.O., 1913), vol. I, p. 1185.

19. George Washington Cable, "The Southern Struggle for Pure Government," a pamphlet (Boston, Mass.: Samuel Usher, 1890), p. 21; *New Orleans Daily Picayune*, Dec. 3, 1897; *Macon* (Georgia) *Telegraph*, quoted in *Mobile* (Alabama) *Daily Register*, Jan. 31, 1893; Memorial from the "Ballot Reform League," in La. *Senate Journal* (1894), pp. 319–320. Alabama Senate president quoted in McMillan, *Constitutional Development*, p. 225; Thomas W. Hardwick, quoted in I. A. Newby, *The Development of Segregationist Thought*, p. 99. The *Atlanta Constitution*, Sept. 4, 1906, designated Hardwick the father of disfranchisement in Georgia. Governor Tyler told the Virginia legislature that his state's ballot law "virtually disfranchised

Although officials could help illiterates in other Southern states that passed secret ballot laws in this period, many unschooled people, especially black Republicans and other opponents of the Democratic party, probably hesitated to expose their ignorance or did not trust the partisan election officials to instruct them correctly. Thus, a Democratic campaign song in Arkansas in 1892 included this stanza:

> The Australian Ballot works like a charm,
> It makes them think and scratch,
> And when a Negro gets a ballot
> He has certainly got his match.[20]

Many voters who persisted marked their ballots incorrectly. Virginia Governor J. Hoge Tyler stated that "thousands of defective or improperly marked ballots have been thrown out in every election since the [secret ballot] law was enacted—in many instances as many as one-third or one-half of the ballots deposited." By 1895, eight of the eleven ex-Confederate states had adopted secret ballot laws covering at least the large centers of population. Only Georgia and South Carolina, protected by the poll tax and eight-box laws, respectively, and North Carolina, then enjoying a Populist-Republican majority in the legislature, held out.[21]

Table 2.1 suggests the effect that the secret ballot and other literacy tests might have had on the South. In seven states the majority of black adult males were classed as illiterate in 1900. In two, nearly a fifth of the whites could not read. Moreover, many whom the census classified as "literate" certainly could not read a complex ballot or a typical clause in the state or national constitution. As the census bureau warned, "The 'literate' population in the report should be understood as including all persons who have had even the slightest amount of schooling,

---

many." Va. *House Journal* (1897–98), pp. 39–40. Tennessee events appear in Tenn. *Senate Journal* (extra sess., 1890), pp. 57–59. Florida's 1895 law contained identical provisions. Fla. *Acts* (1895), pp. 56–86. Louisiana in 1896 also prohibited assistance to illiterates. *New Orleans Daily Picayune*, June 15, 1896.

20. Walter A. Watson, a proponent of disfranchisement, admitted that when the secret ballot was introduced "great numbers of our white people were too sensitive to go to the polls, because they had to ask a judge of election or constable to fix their ticket." Va. Con. Con. *Proceedings* (1901–1902), p. 3070. The song is quoted in John William Graves, "Negro Disfranchisement in Arkansas," pp. 212–213.

21. Tyler, in Va. *House Journal* (1897–98), pp. 39–40; Albright, *American Ballot*, pp. 23–29.

Table 2.1. Percentage of Adult Males Who Were Illiterate, by Race, 1900.

State	White	Negro
Alabama	13.6	59.5
Arkansas	10.4	44.8
Florida	8.4	39.4
Georgia	11.7	56.4
Louisiana	18.0	61.3
Mississippi	8.2	53.2
North Carolina	18.8	53.1
South Carolina	12.2	54.7
Tennessee	14.0	47.6
Texas	8.6	45.1
Virginia	12.1	52.5

while the illiterate represent persons who have had no schooling whatever."[22]

But since many illiterates undoubtedly quit voting for other reasons, the statistics on illiteracy do not constitute a fair test of the effect of the secret ballot or other literacy qualifications. A better method of weighing the impact of the Australian system is to look at actual election returns. The electorates of Arkansas, Alabama, and Louisiana had not been limited by poll taxes, registration laws, or other devices before their legislatures authorized the use of the secret ballot. It is possible to measure the effect of the new ballot, therefore, by comparing turnout in the elections before and after its passage.[23] Table 2.2 gives the estimated

Table 2.2. Effect of the Secret Ballot: Estimates of Turnout, by Race, before and after Passage of Secret Ballot Laws in Three States.

State	Election	White	Negro
Alabama	1892 Governor	80	64
	1896 Governor	68	49
Arkansas	1890 Governor	75	71
	1892 Governor	67	38
Louisiana	1896 Governor (April)	79	69
	1896 President (November)	51	24

22. U.S. Bureau of the Census, *Thirteenth Census*, vol. I, *Population*, p. 1185. The same definition applied in 1900.

23. Unfortunately, such comparisons also reflect the power of registration laws passed at the same time in Alabama and Arkansas. Registration procedures in these states, however, do not seem to have been very stringent. The Louisiana registration law did not take effect until January 1, 1897.

turnout by race in each of the three pairs of elections. The decline in participation varied from 8 percent to 28 percent of the white adult males, and from 15 percent to 45 percent of the Negro adult males.

No other explanation accounts for such large declines in turnout. In Alabama and Arkansas both the first and second elections shown in the table were hotly contested by strong candidates with active party organizations. In each state, the Populists and Republicans repeatedly denounced the secret ballot laws as attempts to disfranchise and defraud the voters. After the bitter April 1896 campaign for governor in Louisiana, leading Democrats stated that unless a secret ballot law were passed, McKinley would carry the state in November. One Louisiana Republican concluded that the Australian system had disfranchised 50 percent of the Negro males, a figure not far from my estimate.[24] Comparisons of elections before and after institution of the secret ballot, then, indicate that it was quite a potent method of restricting the suffrage, especially among the poorly educated Negroes.

LITERACY AND PROPERTY REQUIREMENTS

At the time the Fifteenth Amendment was being considered in Congress, Senator Henry Wilson of Massachusetts proposed a version prohibiting discrimination on the basis of race, color, creed, nativity, property, or education. The Senate passed this broad guarantee of universal male suffrage, but a complicated and seemingly capricious process of haggling between the two houses reduced the amendment to a curb on disfranchisement on the grounds of race, color, or previous condition of servitude only.[25] Had the Wilson amendment passed, it is difficult to see what permanent means of suffrage limitation those who

24. On the elections and the secret ballot law in Alabama, see Hackney, *Populism to Progressivism*, pp. 37–40, 89–107, and chapter 5, below. On Arkansas, see Graves, "Arkansas Negro," pp. 45–57, as well as chapter 5, below. The anonymous prediction is quoted in *New Orleans Daily Picayune*, June 20, 1896. On the elections, see chapter 6, below. For GOP reaction see Walter J. Suthon to William McKinley, July 16, 1897, cited in Philip D. Uzee, "Republican Politics in Louisiana, 1877–1900" (Ph.D. diss., Louisiana State Univ., 1950), p. 174.

25. Leslie Fishel, "The North and the Negro, 1865–1900" (Ph.D. diss., Harvard Univ., 1953), pp. 119–121; James G. Blaine, *Twenty Years of Congress*, 2: 416–417; Richard P. Hallowell, *Why the Negro Was Enfranchised* (Boston, Mass.: George H. Ellis Co., 1903), pp. 13–14; John M. Matthews, *Legislative and Judicial History of the 15th Amendment* (Baltimore, Maryland: Johns Hopkins Univ. Press, 1909), pp. 49–50, 58, 76–77, 79–86; William Gillette, *The Right to Vote* (Baltimore, Md.: Johns Hopkins Univ. Press, 1965), pp. 46–78; Hans L. Trefousse, *The Radical Republicans: Lincoln's Vanguard for Racial Justice* (New York: Alfred A. Knopf, 1969) pp. 416–418.

wished to eliminate poor and uneducated groups from the electorate could have employed.

Literacy and property tests were not confined to the South. Between 1889 and 1913, nine states outside the South made the ability to read English a qualification for voting, and Rhode Island required voters to pay at least $1 in taxes.[26] Writing in the prestigious *North American Review*, a prominent University of Michigan geologist denounced "the communistic principle of universal and equal suffrage." Disfranchising those who lacked "the highest qualification of intelligence and virtue," he went on,

is not injustice to those who surrender control; it is justice to those who have a right to the best government; it is justice to those whom nature and education have fitted to administer best government. This is not oppression of the masses by a selected few; it is the best protection of the masses from all political evils; the best guidance of the masses toward the blessings of higher national and individual prosperity.[27]

Other Northerners supported state or national literacy tests to reduce the influence of immigrants or Negroes and expel the "bosses" and "demagogues" who allegedly benefited from the votes of these groups. Many Northern Democrats and Mugwumps publicly approved Southern suffrage restriction. Southern disfranchisers, in turn, justified their qualifications on the grounds that they were merely following Yankee examples.[28]

Seven ex-Confederate states adopted literacy qualifications from 1890

26. John B. Phillips, "Educational Qualifications of Voters," *University of Colorado Studies* (1906), pp. 55–62; Albert J. McCulloch, *Suffrage and Its Problems*, pp. 54–58.

27. Alexander Winchell, "The Experiment of Universal Suffrage," *North American Review* 136 (1883): 119–134.

28. Phillips, "Educational Qualifications," p. 57; McCulloch, *Suffrage*, pp. 133–157, 171; J. J. McCook, "Venal Voting," pp. 171–176; John R. Commons, *Races and Immigrants in America*, pp. 183, 195; Walter C. Hamm, "The Three Phases of Colored Suffrage," *North American Review* 168 (1899): 285–296; President Andrew D. White of Cornell, in Isabel C. Barrows, ed., *First Mohonk Conference on the Negro Question, June 4, 5, 6, 1890*, p. 120. Several Republicans in Congress strongly pushed a literacy test for immigrants. See John Higham, *Strangers in the Land*, pp. 101–105, 128–129. For Northern approval of Southern disfranchisement, see Rayford W. Logan, *The Betrayal of the Negro*, pp. 291–292; John J. Clancy, Jr., "A Mugwump on Minorities," *Journal of Negro History* 51 (1966): 178–182; Crofts, "Blair Bill," pp. 320–321; Rev. A. D. Mayo, in Barrows, *First Mohonk Conference*, p. 47. For Southern justification, see Edward McCrady, Jr., *The Registration of Electors*, a pamphlet; *New Orleans Daily Picayune*, March 9, 12, 1898; Rep. Andrew F. Fox (D., Mississippi) in *Congressional Record*, 56th Cong., 2nd sess., appendix, p. 75.

to 1908. Under the provisions of these plans, the potential voter had to read a section of the state or federal constitution to qualify, and in Virginia he also had to convince a registrar that he understood what he had read. In each of the seven states except Mississippi and North Carolina, an illiterate could qualify if he owned a certain amount of assessed property, usually $300 worth. Administered fairly, these provisions would certainly have disfranchised a majority of the potential Negro voters in 1900, and perhaps as many as 30 percent to 40 percent of the whites in some states.

Those whites faced with the extinction of their political rights under a franchise based on literacy or property naturally balked at the innovation. Fearing that lower-class white Democrats and Populists might join with Republicans to defeat the educational and property qualifications in conventions and referenda, the restrictionists invented three types of escape clauses: the understanding clause, the grandfather clause, and the fighting grandfather clause. The understanding clause allowed an illiterate to register if he could understand a section of the state constitution which was read to him and explain it to the registrar's satisfaction. In some states, the registrar had to pass judgment also on the man's "good character"—a rather awesome task for a minor civil servant. Men could register under the grandfather clause if they could have voted in 1867 (before Southern Negroes were allowed to) or if they were descendants of 1867 voters.[29] The fighting grandfather clause allowed the registration of anyone who had fought for the Union or Confederacy, or had fought in any other United States war, and his descendants.[30]

29. See the Mississippi Farmers' Alliance Memorial against education and property tests, and resolutions against such qualifications offered by Alliance leader Frank Burkitt, in Miss. Con. Con. *Journal* (1890), pp. 50–51, 79, 109. On white county insistence on the escape clauses and the disfranchisers' fear of defeat unless the clauses were inserted, see Mabry, "Disfranchisement of the Negro," p. 425, and his *Negro in North Carolina Politics*, p. 59; Wythe W. Holt, Jr., "The Virginia Constitutional Convention of 1901–1902: A Reform Movement Which Lacked Substance," *Virginia Magazine of History and Biography* 76 (1968): 87, 95–96; *Congressional Record*, 51st Cong., 2nd sess., pp. 734–735; Ala. Con. Con. *Proceedings* (1901), vol. 3, p. 2932. The "good character" qualifications originated in federal naturalization laws, which allowed foreigners to become citizens only when they could show they were persons of good character who understood the duties of citizenship. Disfranchisers argued that their phrases were as constitutional as the law from which they were lifted. See Ala. Con. Con. *Proceedings* (1901), vol. 2, p. 2714; vol. 3, p. 2829; U.S. Senator John T. Morgan (D., Ala.), in *Congressional Record*, 56th Cong., 1st sess., p. 675. The grandfather clause was apparently inspired by the Massachusetts constitution of 1857, which instituted a literacy test but exempted those qualified to vote at the time. McCrady, *Registration of Electors*, pp. 10–11.

30. It is no wonder that students often think the grandfather clause was a device to dis-

The escape clauses were obviously tailored for racial and partisan discrimination. When asked whether Christ could register under the good character clause, a leader of the Alabama convention replied, "That would depend entirely on which way he was going to vote." Carter Glass admitted the intent of the delegates to the Virginia constitutional convention: "Discrimination! Why, that is precisely what we propose; that, exactly, is what this convention was elected for." In Alabama, registrars were carefully selected to carry out the "spirit of the Constitution, which looks to the registration of all white men not convicted of crime, and only a few Negroes." Thus, the discrimination which had long occurred in counting the ballots was to be set back one stage. Registrars instead of election supervisors would now do the dirty work.[31]

Moreover, many Negroes would not even attempt to register, for, as a Virginia disfranchiser pointed out, Negroes "believe that they will have a hostile examination put upon them by the white man, and they believe that that will be a preventive to their exercising the right of suffrage, and they will not apply for registration."[32]

Surprisingly enough, the escape clauses seem to have had a similar effect on white registration. As spokesmen for the lower strata of whites had predicted, poor, illiterate men were often too humiliated to register under these provisions. A knowledgeable Mississippian, Frank Johnston, could find only about a dozen whites in the state's largest county in 1902 who were "willing to expose their illiteracy publicly" by qualifying through the understanding clause. Ten years earlier, only 1,084 whites (and 1,058 Negroes) in the whole state had registered under that section of the constitution.[33] Neighboring Louisiana had a similar experience

---

franchise Negroes directly, instead of to enfranchise otherwise unqualified whites, for even reputable historians sometimes misrepresent the clause's purpose. See, for example, Bernard Weisberger, *The New Industrial Society* (New York: John Wiley & Sons, Inc., 1969) p. 86; Beth, *Development of the American Constitution*, p. 111.

31. Alabama leader quoted in Hackney, *Populism to Progressivism*, p. 253, Carter Glass in Va. Con. Con. *Proceedings* (1901–02), pp. 3076–3077. Similarly, Alfred P. Thom, a delegate to that convention, commented, "I expect the examination with which the black man will be confronted, to be inspired by the same spirit that inspires every man upon this floor and in this convention . . . I would not expect for the white man a rigid examination," p. 2972. See also Governor William D. Jelks to Senator John T. Morgan, Jan. 10, 1902, quoted in Hackney, *Populism to Progressivism*, p. 208. Virginia acted similarly. See Horn, "Democratic Party in Virginia," p. 91, and *New Market* (Virginia) *Spirit of the Valley*, Oct. 11, 1901, quoted in ibid. p. 96.

32. Va. Con. Con. *Proceedings* (1901–02), p. 2973.

33. Ala. Con. Con. *Proceedings* (1901), vol. 3, pp. 2899–2911; U.S. Senator J. L. M. Irby

with the grandfather clause. Although about a quarter of the registrants were listed as qualifying under that provision, a contemporary political scientist revealed that these numbers were "greatly swelled" by educated whites who wished to give the grandfather clause "an air of respectability for those who could register under no other." Similarly, a delegate to the Alabama constitutional convention wrote in 1904 that "no man can deny that thousand[s] of unworthy white men are excluded from the suffrage," by the 1901 constitution's provisions.[34] These figures on registration under the escape clauses—the only ones available—suggest that the disfranchisers may not have expected whites to take advantage of these loopholes, that the clauses were simply window dressing to get the restrictive suffrage plans adopted. The fact that the exemption clauses for illiterate and propertyless whites were temporary, except in Mississippi, strengthens this contention. Whites who failed to register within a period ranging from three years in South Carolina to seven in Georgia would have to meet literacy or property qualifications.

It is exceedingly difficult to measure the effect of the literacy tests and their exemptions precisely, for only Louisiana published official registration figures both before and after it adopted its new constitution. In addition, the registration figures may reflect voter apathy engendered by the decline in party competition. Men who did not expect to vote may not have bothered to register. There was, however, a good deal of pressure on whites to get their names on the lists in the years immediately following the amendments, because an illiterate who acted within the time limit would be registered permanently; otherwise, he would be disfranchised until he learned to read.[35]

Table 2.3 presents the fragmentary official and unofficial registration figures which I have been able to locate in published sources and

in South Carolina's constitutional convention, quoted in Mabry, "Disfranchisement of the Negro," p. 186; Frank Johnston, "Suffrage and Reconstruction in Mississippi," *Publications of the Mississippi Historical Society* 6 (1902): 229. Senator John Sharp Williams (D., Mississippi) made a similar statement in *Congressional Record*, 56th Cong., 2nd sess., appendix, pp. 78–79. For the registration statistics, see James H. Stone, "A Note on Voter Registration under the Mississippi Understanding Clause, 1892," *Journal of Southern History* 38 (1972): 293–296.

34. J. L. Warren Woodville, "Suffrage Limitation in Louisiana," *Political Science Quarterly* 21 (1906): 188; James Weatherly to Hilary A. Herbert, Dec. 31, 1904, quoted in David Alan Harris, "Racists and Reformers: A Study of Progressivism in Alabama, 1896–1911" (Ph.D. diss., Univ. of North Carolina, 1967), p. 188.

35. McMillan, *Constitutional Development*, p. 353.

Table 2.3. Impact of Changes in Constitutional Suffrage Requirements on Voter Registration.

		Year	% Whites Registered	% Negroes Registered	% All Registered
(1)	Alabama	1902	74.8	1.3	–
(2)	Alabama	1908[a]	87.7	1.8	–
(3)	Georgia	1904[b]	66.6	28.3	–
(4)	Georgia	1910	73.9	4.3	–
(5)	Louisiana	1898[a,b]	46.6	9.5	–
(6)	Louisiana	1904[a]	52.5	1.1	–
(7)	Mississippi	1892[a]	53.8	5.4	–
(8)	Mississippi	1896[a]	76.2	8.5	–
(9)	Mississippi	1904	–	7.1	–
(10)	Mississippi	1908	62.9	7.5	–
(11)	North Carolina	1902	–	4.6	–
(12)	North Carolina	1904	–	4.6	–
(13)	South Carolina	1896	41.9	3.8	–
(14)	South Carolina	1897	73.7	8.2	–
(15)	South Carolina	1900	79.8	9.1	–
(16)	South Carolina	1904	–	13.8	–
(17)	Virginia	1900[b]	–	–	95.9
(18)	Virginia	1904	–	15.2	–
(19)	Virginia	1905	83.6	13.7	–

SOURCES: Sources for actual and estimated registration figures are listed below by the numbers preceding the states. Percentages were computed from raw totals and census data. Newspapermen and knowledgeable contemporary observers made the estimates. (1) *Montgomery Daily Advertiser*, Sept. 6, 1902. (2) *Alabama Official and Statistical Register*, 1911 (Montgomery, Alabama, 1911), pp. 262–263. (3) Clarence A. Bacote, "The Negro in Georgia Politics," p. 421. (4) Dewey W. Grantham, Jr., *Hoke Smith and the Politics of the New South*, p. 162. (5, 6) Louisiana Secretary of State, *Report, 1905* (Baton Rouge, La., 1905), pp. xxx-xxxi. (7) Vernon Lane Wharton, *The Negro in Mississippi*, p. 215. (8) George H. Haynes, "Educational Qualifications for the Suffrage in the United States," p. 506; James W. Garner, "The Fourteenth Amendment and Southern Representation," p. 203. (9, 12, 16, 18) Edgar Gardner Murphy, *Problems of the Present South* (New York: The Macmillan Co., 1904), p. 198, n. 1. (10) Alfred Holt Stone, *Studies in the American Race Problem*, p. 357. (11) *Raleigh* (N. C.) *News and Observer*, Nov. 4, 1902. (13) *Yorkville* (S.C.) *Enquirer*, Oct. 7, 1896, cited in George B. Tindall, *South Carolina Negroes, 1877–1900*, p. 88. (14) *New Orleans Daily Picayune*, Dec. 14, 1897; *Raleigh News and Observer*, Feb. 4, 1899. (15) *Congressional Record*, 56th Cong., 1st sess, p. 1036. (17) H. L. Horn, "Democratic Party in Virginia," p. 107. (19) *Lynchburg* (Virginia) *News*, quoted in *Richmond Times-Dispatch*, April 1, 1905, cited in Ralph Clipman McDanel, *The Virginia Constitutional Convention of 1901–1902*, p. 50.

[a]Official registration figures. All others are unofficial estimates.

[b]Denotes registration figure predating constitutional suffrage limitations.

Ph.D. theses. In only two of the seven states where post-disfranchisement statistics are available were more than 10 percent of the Negroes
registered. In no case did black registration exceed 16 percent. On the
other hand, the escape clauses for whites do not seem to have been as
elastic as the disfranchisers promised. Their repeated pledges that "no
white men will be disfranchised" must be somewhat discounted in light
of the fact that white registration reached only 53 percent in Louisiana
in 1904 and 63 percent in Mississippi in 1908.

Table 2.3 also allows us to compare the effect of the constitutional
changes with other factors that decreased participation. We noted previously that an 1896 Louisiana law cut white registration by half and
black by more than 90 percent. The 1898 constitution did little more
than insure that these declines were permanent. The white registration
increased somewhat after 1898, while the black could not drop too much
further than it had before the convention. In Georgia, the cumulative
poll tax, the white primary, and the demise of the Populists had depressed the proportion of whites registered to two-thirds and Negroes to
less than one-third even before passage of the suffrage amendment in
1908. It must be noted, however, that Negro registration in Georgia in
1904 was considerably higher than that in any state after constitutional
suffrage restriction. In sum, the constitutional suffrage plans insured
that the Southern electorate for half a century would be almost all
white; yet the plans did not guarantee all whites the vote.

3

"We Need the Strength Which Comes from Believing Alike" —The Poll Tax and the White Democratic Primary

Taxing the Right to Vote

The poll tax, adopted by every ex-Confederate state by 1904, further discouraged poor people from registering and voting. A South Carolina congressman in 1901 noted that many of the literate Negroes in his state did not bother to register "because they would rather save the dollar which would be required as poll tax." In light of its modern use as a restrictive device, it is ironic that the levy of a capitation tax in the nation's early years expanded the electorate. In British America, the franchise had generally been limited to property owners. After the Revolution, several of the new states shifted to a taxpaying qualification, and four, including Georgia and North Carolina, required all propertyless adult males to pay a small tax. These requirements provided for almost universal white male suffrage.[1]

The poll tax limited rather than expanded the suffrage in the South after 1870 because those in power made every effort not to collect the tax from men they deemed undesirable voters. There is no record of prosecution of a poll tax delinquent. In some states, only property holders received reminders of their poll tax assessment while other states assessed no one at all. More important, the tax usually fell due several months before election day. In the early part of the twentieth century, four states required payment six months before the November election, and three states asked voters to pay nine months ahead. An Alabama delegate clearly stated the discriminatory purpose of these provisions: ". . . the Negro and the vicious element will not pay two months ahead of time [sic; Alabama required payment nine months in

1. Representative Wilson in *Congressional Record*, 56th Cong., 2nd sess., p. 657; Williamson, *American Suffrage*, pp. 135–136.

63

advance] a dollar and a half in order to exercise this privilege, but if the business man knows he is liable for [the] tax, although he will not give a dollar and a half to vote or exercise the franchise, he will put it on the list of liabilities like he does everything else and tell his clerk to pay it when it is due. . . ."[2]

Although the $1 to $2 levies did not seem high to the middle-class convention delegates and legislators, they represented a significant charge to many inhabitants of the nation's economic backwater region. The estimated per capita income (including noncash income) for the inhabitants of the eleven ex-Confederate states was $86 in 1880 and $100 in 1900, in terms of dollar values at the time. Since these amounts were not apportioned equally, the vast majority of the population received a good deal less. Table 3.1 presents some (admittedly imperfect) estimates of the average incomes received by the bottom three-quarters of the Southern population.[3] It shows, for instance, that the bottom

Table 3.1. Southern Poverty: Estimated Income Received by the Bottom Three-Quarters of the Southern Population in 1880 and 1900.

% of the Population	% of Total Income Received	Average Income in Dollars[a]	
		1880	1900
7.17	2.29	27.46	31.92
16.70	6.35	32.69	38.00
26.08	11.20	36.92	42.92
38.92	19.02	42.08	48.85
51.54	27.86	46.48	54.08
61.33	35.48	49.74	57.82
69.43	42.48	52.61	61.15
75.96	48.73	55.16	64.12

SOURCE: Columns 1 and 2 were taken directly from King, table XLIV, p. 228. Columns 3 and 4 were computed from these figures and the averages computed from Kuznets, 2:185.

[a]The average income figures are in contemporary (1880–1900) dollars. They do not reflect inflation since that time.

2. Frederic C. Ogden, *The Poll Tax in the South*, pp. 42, 45–46, 50, 51, 59, 61–65, 69, 71; Ala. Con. Con. *Proceedings* (1901), vol. 3, p. 3374. See similarly Va. Con. Con. *Proceedings* (1901–1902), p. 600; *El Paso* (Texas) *News*, quoted in *Dallas Morning News*, Jan. 23, 1901; *New Orleans Daily Picayune*, Feb. 16, 18, 1898.

3. See speech by Wofford of Bartow County in Samuel W. Small, *A Stenographic Report of the Proceedings of the Constitutional Convention Held in Atlanta, Georgia, 1877* (Atlanta: Constitution Pub. Co., 1877), pp. 63–64. Per capita income figures are from Simon Kuznets, et al., *Population Redistribution and Economic Growth, United States, 1870–1950* (Philadelphia:

7.17 percent of the population received 2.29 percent of the income, which amounted to $27.46 per person per year in 1880. For a family of four or five, this would amount to about $100 to $125 per year. Incomes for the bottom 76 percent of the population averaged only $55-$64 per person!

Moreover, the cash income of most Southerners was probably much smaller. Under the ubiquitous lien and sharecropping systems, merchants or plantation owners advanced tools, food, and other essentials, and received, in return, a portion of the crop or a legally guaranteed sum from its sale. Many agriculturalists—three-fourths of the Negro farmers were sharecroppers or tenants by 1900—saw very little cash at all during the year.[4] In such cases, a dollar or two amounted to a substantial proportion of a man's cash income.

The cumulative features of capitation taxes in a few states raised another barrier to voting. The voter who neglected to pay his tax in an off-year or in the year of an unexciting election had to make up these taxes before he could exercise the franchise. The taxes could accumulate for two years in Florida and Mississippi, three in Virginia, and indefinitely in Georgia after 1877 and in Alabama after 1901. One knowledgeable observer termed Georgia's cumulative poll tax "the most effective bar to Negro suffrage ever devised."[5]

The efficacy of the poll tax in limiting the suffrage has long been a subject of controversy. Those who campaigned from about 1930 on for state and federal laws or constitutional amendments to repeal it no doubt exaggerated its impact. Simplistically comparing turnout and party competition in "poll tax states" with election returns from other areas, these crusaders often blamed Southern apathy and devotion to

---

American Philosophical Society, 1960), vol. 2, table A 4. 1, p. 185. He gives estimates of the per capita income for each state in 1929 dollars. I averaged these for the Southern states, weighted by population, and deflated the resulting figures according to the price index used in the calculation, given in vol. 2, pp. 143–144. The only estimates of income distribution we have for this period are estimates for the U.S. as a whole in 1910, given in Wilford Isbell King, *The Wealth and Income of the People of the United States* (New York: Johnson Reprint Corp., 1969), table 44, p. 228. I do not claim that they are absolutely reliable, but only that they may give some impression of the real distribution. Since the distribution for the South was no doubt more skewed than for the U.S. as a whole, table 3.1 probably *overstates* the incomes of the poorest groups.

4. On sharecropping and the lien system, see Woodward, *Origins of the New South*, pp. 175–186, 206–209.

5. Alfred Holt Stone, *Studies in the American Race Problem*, p. 355.

the Democratic party solely on that voting prerequisite. Reacting against such naïveté, V. O. Key and Frederic Ogden tended to belittle the power of the poll tax.[6] Ogden concluded that "the poll tax helped in a minor way to achieve disfranchisement but it primarily reflected in law a trend already begun" (p. 122). According to Key, "the poll tax has had little or no bearing on Negro disfranchisement, the object for which it was supposedly designed" (p. 618). How important was the poll tax?

Contemporaries thought it very important. A member of the Mississippi constitutional convention's Franchise Committee stated in 1902 that the poll tax had proven "the most effective instrumentality of Negro disfranchisement." An 1896 Mississippi survey made in preparation for a contested election case in the national House of Representatives found the poll tax, coupled with the requirement that voters register four months before the election, "more effective in disqualifying colored persons for suffrage than all other constitutional provisions on the subject." A Mississippi congressman stated that 90 percent of the Negroes in his state were disfranchised by the poll tax. The president of the Mississippi constitutional convention and "leading citizens of North Carolina" were quoted as saying that the provision gave the Democrats more "relief" than any other.[7]

A. J. McKelway testified that the cumulative poll tax in Georgia "practically disfranchised the Negroes" after 1877. Although some would have felt McKelway exaggerated, many politicians, travelers, and contemporary Southerners noted the restrictive effect of the "Georgia plan." Drawing on experiences from other states, Alabama

6. See, for instance, Jennings Perry, *Democracy Begins at Home* (Philadelphia & New York: J. B. Lippincott Co., 1944). Cf. Key, *Southern Politics*, pp. 578–618; Ogden, *Poll Tax*. For even more extreme deprecations of the poll tax as a force in limiting the electorate, see Boyce Alexander Drummond, Jr., "Arkansas Politics: A Study of a One-Party System" (Ph.D. thesis, Univ. of Chicago, 1957), pp. 12, 229, and Frank B. Williams, "The Poll Tax as a Suffrage Requirement in the South" (Ph.D. diss., Vanderbilt Univ., 1950), p. 327. A recent corrective to these views is Don Nimmo and Clifton McCleskey, "Impact of the Poll Tax on Voter Participation: The Houston Metropolitan Area in 1966," *Journal of Politics* 31 (1969): 682–699. It must be noted that Key was primarily concerned with the effect of the poll tax later on in the century, after the white primary and other restrictions on Negro voting had been instituted. See p. 579.

7. McNeilly, "History of the Measures," p. 136; *Proceedings of a Reunion of the Surviving Members of the Constitutional Convention of 1890, Held November 1, 1927* (Jackson, Mississippi: Premier Printing Co., 1928), pp. 49–50; *Congressional Record*, 56th Cong., 2nd sess., p. 736; Ala. Con. Con. *Proceedings* (1901), vol. 3, p. 3386; *Atlanta Constitution*, Aug. 15, 1906.

convention delegates insisted on the poll tax as the provision "by which the [whites in] the Black Belt will live or die," "the only thing that will give permanent relief." According to a recent scholar, Harold C. Livesay, "the Negroes were virtually disfranchised" by passage of a poll tax in Delaware in 1872. A Mississippi disfranchiser, Judge Simrall, appearing before the Louisiana constitutional convention's Suffrage Committee as a consulting expert, pointed out that the literacy test would soon be outmoded by Negro progress in education, but the poll tax would last as long as black poverty.[8]

Election returns also evidence the impact of the poll tax. Table 3.2 compares the turnout rates in poll-taxed Georgia with the participation in the other ten Southern states during the 1880s. Sixteen to twenty-eight percent fewer Georgians participated in elections than other Southerners. Although other factors were partly responsible for the unusually low turnout in Georgia, the contrast between that state's voting patterns and those of the states without effective legal restrictive devices does suggest the centrality of the poll tax in Georgia's late nineteenth-century politics.[9] A comparison of the estimated Negro turnout

Table 3.2. Impact of the Poll Tax on Overall Turnout: Rates for Georgia and the Rest of the South in Presidential Elections, 1880s.

Election	Georgia	Rest of South
1880	48.8	65.4
1884	40.6	65.7
1888	37.3	65.7

8. A. J. McKelway, "The Suffrage in Georgia," *The Outlook* 87 (1907): 63–64. For observations on the "Georgia Plan," see Alexander H. Stephens in James G. Blaine *et al.*, "Ought the Negro to be Disfranchised?" p. 251; Representative William H. Howard (D., Georgia), quoted in *Atlanta Constitution*, Aug. 12, 1906; Representative William D. Brantley (D., Georgia), quoted in ibid., Aug. 15, 1906; "Studies in the South," *The Atlantic Monthly* 50 (1882): 196–197; Stephen B. Weeks, "History of Negro Suffrage," pp. 692–693; Ralph Wardlaw "Negro Suffrage in Georgia," pp. 44–45, 64. For the Alabama delegates' remarks, see Ala. Con. Con. *Proceedings* (1901), vol. 3, pp. 3333, 3357. Cf. Harold C. Livesay, "Delaware Negroes, 1865–1915," *Delaware History*, 13 (1968): 96. On the Delaware law, see also Senator Anthony Higgins (R., Delaware), in *Congressional Record*, 51st Cong., 2nd sess., pp. 769–770. Judge Simrall's observations quoted in Ford, "Louisiana Politics," pp. 158–159. Future U.S. Senator Duncan Fletcher of Florida averred that the tax effectively disfranchised Jacksonville's Negro majority, and the 1892 figures, which show that only about 5 percent of Jacksonville Negroes paid their poll taxes, tend to bear Fletcher out. See Wayne Flynt, *Duncan Upshaw Fletcher*, pp. 15, 27–28.

9. For a fuller discussion of Georgia politics and the effect of the poll tax, see chapter 7.

in Georgia and Florida, both Deep South states and both 47 percent Negro in 1880, corroborates this view of the tax's impact (see table 3.3). No study of either state has suggested any variable or combination of variables besides the poll tax weighty enough to account for the fact that more than twice as large a proportion of Negroes seems to have voted in Florida as in Georgia in this period.

Though few deny that the chief target of the poll tax was the blacks, there is no scholarly consensus on whether those who framed it meant it to include whites among its victims. While one scholar claims that "no one seems to have intended the poll tax as a means of disfranchising the lower income white voters," another declares that it was mainly "a method of discouraging from voting that class of whites which was beginning to challenge [the disfranchisers'] control of southern politics."[10]

Had the disfranchisers wished the electorate to include the lower strata of whites, they could have written a grandfather clause or some equally efficacious exemption into the poll tax. In virtually every convention and legislative session that considered the prerequisite, newspapers and members of the assemblies warned that a poll tax would disfranchise at least some, and perhaps a great many, whites. That the final documents contained no exemptions from the tax for the white masses adds considerable weight to the view that the delegates wished to exclude the poorer whites from the electorate.[11]

Much of the direct evidence of the intentions of those who passed

Table 3.3. Impact of the Poll Tax on Blacks: Estimated Negro Turnout in Presidential Elections in Florida and Georgia, 1880s.

Election	Georgia	Florida
1880	39	88
1884	38	86
1888	19	64

10. Williams, "Poll Tax as a Suffrage Requirement," p. 283; Ogden, *Poll Tax*, p. 31.

11. As Senator Jeter Pritchard (R., North Carolina) noted in *Congressional Record*, 56th Cong., 1st sess., p. 1033. For examples of the warnings about the poll tax, see *Birmingham Age-Herald*, Feb. 12, 1901, quoted in McMillan, *Constitutional Development*, p. 273; Messrs. Flood, Thom, and Brown in the Virginia convention, and Smith, Fitts, and Duke in the Alabama convention, cited in Ogden, *Poll Tax*, pp. 22–23; *Jacksonville Florida Times-Union*, July 12, 22, 1885, and Oct. 14, 1886; Delegates O'Connor and Wickliffe in the Louisiana convention, quoted in *New Orleans Daily Picayune*, March 17, 1898; Messrs. Flournoy, Weaver, Pickett, and Johnson, in Seth Shepherd McKay, ed., *Debates in the Texas Constitutional Convention of 1875*, pp. 167–168, 172, 177, 184.

poll taxes and other restrictions on the electorate is difficult to evaluate. The framers could not have openly avowed a desire to disfranchise whites without courting defeat in the referenda on calling conventions or ratifying amended documents. Their stress on the effect of the suffrage restrictions on black voters, therefore, may have concealed an intent to strike whites from the rolls. Since a defense of Negro rights was politically suicidal at the time, parties or factions which opposed the disfranchisers naturally charged that the hidden purpose of the poll tax and other disfranchising schemes was to eliminate white voters. Their comments, consequently, do not prove that the restrictionists meant to disqualify whites any more than the restrictionists' silence proves the opposite. Furthermore, after passage and ratification of the suffrage plans, Southern propagandists seeking to persuade Yankees not to invoke the Reconstruction Amendments often denied that they had meant to discriminate on the basis of race.[12]

Nor does circumstantial evidence relating to political conditions at the time provide a sure guide to the motives of the disfranchisers. One historian argued that the impotence of the Populists in 1901 proved that Republican-oriented Negroes, not poor white Populists, were the targets of the Alabama tax. Conversely, the drop-off in Negro voting by 1902 convinced two political scientists that the Texas poll tax was aimed not at the blacks but at the Populists. But the significance of such immediate threats to the Democrats cannot be properly assessed without considering previous efforts to pass such laws and the probability of future challenges to the party from groups relatively powerless at the time of enactment.[13]

Private affirmations of the desirability of limiting white suffrage and

---

12. H. Clarence Nixon, "Influences of the Past," in American Council on Public Affairs, *The Poll Tax*, p. 20; Francis G. Caffey, "Suffrage Limitations at the South," *Political Science Quarterly* 20 (1905): 56–57, 59; Rep. Eaton J. Bowers (D., Mississippi), quoted in I. A. Newby, *Jim Crow's Defense*, p. 151; Edgar Gardner Murphy, "Shall the Fourteenth Amendment be Enforced?" *North American Review* 180 (1905): 126. For contemporaries' remarks, see *Clinton* (North Carolina) *Caucasian*, March 2, 1899, quoted in Mabry, *Negro in North Carolina Politics*, p. 63, and similar Populist utterances quoted on pp. 67 and 69; *Charleston News and Courier*, Oct. 2, 4, 13, 16, 19, 29, Nov. 3, 5, 1894; *Atlanta Constitution*, Aug. 5, 15, 19, 1906.

13. Frank B. Williams, "Poll Tax as a Suffrage Requirement," p. 244; Donald S. Strong, "The Poll Tax: The Case of Texas," *American Political Science Review* 38 (1944): 694; Dick Smith, "Texas and the Poll Tax," *Southwestern Social Science Quarterly* 45 (1964): 167–173. On previous efforts in Texas, see *Dallas Morning News*, Feb. 21, 1891; Rice, *The Negro in Texas*, pp. 133–139.

public statements made before or during the conventions or referenda provide more convincing testimony as to the objectives of the supporters of the poll tax and other disfranchising measures. Although he mentioned only black disfranchisement in public, William A. Anderson, a leading Virginia restrictionist, avowed privately that he favored eliminating many white voters, too. The *New Orleans Daily Picayune* assailed universal manhood suffrage as "the most unwise, unreasonable, and illogical notion that was ever connected with any system of government," and later stated that it was as desirable "to shut out every unworthy white man" from the franchise as to exclude "every unworthy Negro." Ex-Governor William C. Oates offered the Alabama convention a suffrage plan consisting of a literacy test, an understanding clause, and a poll tax, a proposal designed, he said, to "eliminate from the electorate 'the ignorant, incompetent and vicious' white men" as well as most Negroes. Similarly, a North Carolina Democratic paper remarked that the struggle for suffrage restriction was an effort to rid that state of "the danger of the rule of Negroes and the lower classes of whites." In the same vein, a Virginia convention delegate said he favored the poll tax "because I believe it will disqualify some white men in Virginia who ought to be disqualified," and an Arkansas newspaper supported restriction because it would disfranchise "the ignorant white man who votes without paying taxes," as well as the Negro.[14]

Despite the Louisiana convention's unanimity on the issue of Negro suffrage, a battle over the poll tax split the body into poll tax and anti–poll tax caucuses. This struggle further indicates many delegates' desire to use the tax to purge poor whites from the rolls. "The main purpose of the poll tax prerequisite," announced a Louisiana disfranchiser, "was to exclude not only the illiterate Negro, but also the unworthy white elements, who had been the curse to large cities." Those whites whom the tax would bar, he went on, were "as great a menace to the country as is the ignorant Negro." Delegates who agreed with his judgment of the tax's effect, but not the desirability of white disfranchisement, fought the provision. The New Orleans Democratic

14. Anderson to John W. Daniel, Dec. 24, 1900, quoted in Raymond H. Pulley, *Old Virginia Restored*, pp. 76–77; *New Orleans Daily Picayune*, Feb. 6, March 23, 1898; Oates is quoted in Ala. Con. Con. *Proceedings* (1901), vol. 4, pp. 4956–4957; *Charlotte Daily Observer*, June 6, 1900, quoted in Joseph F. Steelman, "Progressive Era in North Carolina," p. 215; R. Lindsay Gordon, quoted in Pulley, *Old Virginia Restored*, p. 83; *Little Rock* (Arkansas) *Democrat* (n.d.), quoted in *Pine Bluff Weekly Commercial*, Nov. 9, 1890.

machine opposed the poll tax because it would disfranchise its poor supporters, most of whom were white. Though they could not finally prevent inclusion of a poll tax qualification in the constitution, opponents did manage to force the suffrage committee to compromise. The final document provided that the tax would not go into effect until after the 1900 election, and could be repealed by referendum as early as 1902.[15]

Since it was usually enacted as part of a comprehensive plan, the precise effect of the poll tax on white voting is somewhat difficult to gauge. In Texas, where it was the only major restrictive device adopted, only 53 percent of the adult males paid their poll taxes in 1910. Assuming that all the Negroes defaulted, only 64 percent of the whites paid to vote in that year, at a time when the Democratic gubernatorial primary was hotly contested. Sheldon Hackney has estimated that 23.6 percent of the adult white males in Alabama in 1904 were disfranchised solely because of the poll tax. Senator Furnifold Simmons, boss of the North Carolina Democratic party, admitted that 17,000 whites in that state were voteless because of the poll tax, and Republican guesses ran as high as 40,000. The Virginia poll tax in effect from 1876 to 1882, according to a Richmond newspaper, kept a quarter of the whites from the ballot box.[16] If my estimates are correct, between 24 percent and 34 percent fewer white Georgians voted in presidential contests during the 1880s than their Florida counterparts (table 3.4). At least part of this difference must be attributed to the cumulative poll tax.

In summary, then, the poll tax amounted to a panacea for the restrictionists. Pushed through as the buttress of "white supremacy," the tax also disfranchised many whites, or, rather, encouraged them to think that their inability to spare a couple of dollars for a poll tax proved them

15. Wise of Shreveport, quoted in *New Orleans Daily Picayune*, March 9, 1898. For similar sentiments, see statements by Burke, March 10, 1988; Ransdell, Bruns, and Stubbs, March 11, 1898; and quotes from *Homer* (Louisiana) *Guardian-Journal*, *Shreveport Times*, *Baton Rouge Bulletin*, and *West Baton Rouge Sugar Planter*, March 15, 1898. The anti-poll taxer, A. L. Ponder, is also quoted in *Picayune*, March 11, 1898; Kruttschnitt, March 9, 1898. The clash and compromise may be followed in the *Picayune*, March 2, 12, 15, 17, 1898, and Ford, "Louisiana Politics," pp. 169–170.

16. The Texas percentages were computed from figures in Lewis W. Newton and Herbert P. Gambrell, *A Social and Political History of Texas* (Dallas, Texas: Turner Co., 1935), p. 381. For the other figures, see Hackney, *Populism to Progressivism*, pp. 207–208; Steelman, "Progressive Era in North Carolina," pp. 442–443; *Richmond State*, Nov. 18, 1882, quoted in Charles E. Wynes, *Race Relations in Virginia, 1870–1902*, p. 24.

Table 3.4. Impact of the Poll Tax on Whites: Estimated White Turnout in
Presidential Elections in Florida and Georgia, 1880s.

Election	Georgia	Florida
1880	56	80
1884	40	74
1888	56	84

unworthy to vote. As the *Montgomery Advertiser* put it, "any white man in
Alabama who will disqualify himself by the failure to take the trouble to
register or will refuse to pay $1.50 a year for the privilege, is not worthy
to be classed among the voters." "If our institutions are to be preserved,'
warned the *Little Rock Arkansas Democrat*, "it must be done by the intelligent voter—the man who at least thinks enough of the privilege of
the ballot to pay a dollar or two for it."[17] By lopping off the lower
economic strata, the poll tax preserved Southern institutions by creating
a fairly homogeneous polity—white, middle-class, and Democratic.

THE WHITE PRIMARY: PRESERVING ONE-PARTY RULE

Democrats attempting to persuade white Populists and Republicans
to support disfranchisement, and opponents of the Democrats seeking to
persuade themselves that franchise restriction did not spell the end of
their careers, often argued that the elimination of Negro voters would
reanimate the two-party system in the South. Future Governor Charles
B. Aycock of North Carolina promised in 1899 that disfranchisement
would bring "a larger political freedom and a greater toleration of
opinion. . . . The Republican party will be freed from the stigma of
being called the 'Negro party,' and . . . will have somewhat more
of influence in making and shaping a wholesome public opinion. Discussion of policies and principles will take the place of heated declama-
tion and partisan abuse." In spite of Aycock's assurances—a trifle ironic
in light of his own racist demagoguery during the vicious 1898 campaign to overthrow the Fusion government—there was less party competition in the South after 1900 than before. Nor was the section particularly noted for its tolerance or the reasoned, principled tone of its
political debate. One of the chief reasons for the South's failure to develop a two-party system was the institution of the white primary. Dean
Burnham has noted that in states where one party is dominant, the

17. *Advertiser*, Dec. 10, 1902; *Democrat* (n.d.), quoted in *Pine Bluff Weekly Commercial*, Nov.
9, 1890. Similarly, see *Jacksonville Florida Times-Union*, June 30, 1885.

primary has often "sapped the minority party's monopoly of opposition."[18] As we shall see, this was not an unintended consequence.

Many scholars have presented the direct primary as a triumph of democracy. Others have noted, however, that in the South it limited participation to whites only. Thomas B. Clark and Albert D. Kirwin went so far as to say that "from the time of its adoption [it] became the great obstacle to Negro voting, more effective than all others combined."[19] To understand the functions and effect of the primary in the evolution of Southern politics, we must review its development.

Almost from the first, Democrats utilized the primary to substitute intra- for interparty competition. County conventions or mass meetings nominated most candidates in the antebellum South. Use of the primary did not become widespread until the middle and late 1870s, when it was touted as the best means of uniting white Democrats and preventing defections to the Republicans and Independents in the general elections. In 1878, for example, Walter L. Bragg, chairman of the Alabama Democratic state executive committee, proposed that delegates to the state convention be elected in primaries in order "to promote harmony, secure a more full and satisfactory expression of the wishes of the great, patriotic and intelligent masses of the party, and to prevent as far as possible the occurrence of combinations injurious to the party and subversive of the best interests of the people of this state." It was no coincidence that this proposal came at the height of Greenback-Independent party activity which challenged Democratic hegemony with the spectre of a poor white–Negro coalition. In those circumstances, declared a black belt newspaper, the primary was "the only thing that can unite and hold the [Democratic] party together."[20]

18. For discussions of the "reanimation" idea, see Woodward, *Origins*, p. 347; Senator Samuel D. McEnery (D., Louisiana), quoted in *New Orleans Daily Picayune*, Jan. 4, 1898; Gov. Daniel L. Russell (R., North Carolina), quoted in Daniel Charles Roller, "Republican Party of North Carolina," p. 25; Tom Watson, quoted in Woodward, *Tom Watson*, p. 371. Aycock is quoted in Steelman, "Progressive Era in North Carolina," p. 229. Walter Dean Burnham's observations are taken from "The Changing Shape of the American Political Universe," *American Political Science Review* 59 (1965): 19–20. See, similarly, Seymour Martin Lipset, "Party Systems and the Representation of Social Groups," in Macridis, ed., *Political Parties*, pp. 56–57.

19. The primary appears a democratic device to Arthur S. Link, "Progressive Movement in the South," p. 188; Grantham, *The Democratic South*, p. 48; and Merriam, *Primary Elections*, pp. 163–164. Cf. Clark and Kirwin, *The South since Appomattox*, p. 109; Key, *Southern Politics*, p. 555.

20. Allen Woodrow Jones, "A History of the Direct Primary in Alabama" (Ph.D. diss.,

According to its proponents, deciding party nominations in semi-public primaries rather than in backroom caucuses would legitimate the nominees, settle intraparty differences before the general election, and greatly reduce the power of opposition voters—most often, Negroes—by confronting them with a solid Democratic party. Thus, in 1878, Wade Hampton advised Democrats in Anderson County, South Carolina, that "we cannot afford to be divided on State matters. Your county is the first to adopt the system of primary elections—be governed by its results and allow no independents to run." A Georgia newspaper favored the primary in 1876 because other methods of nomination might have encouraged disgruntled politicians to run as independents, and "support of an independent by a party in defiance of Democratic nomination may destroy or so cripple it [the local Democratic party] as to throw the balance of power into the hands of ignorant, illiterate, and corrupt radicals."[21]

In Louisiana, the contest between pro- and anti-Lottery forces in 1892 became so bitter that Democratic gubernatorial candidates from each faction agreed to hold a preelection white primary to prevent the possibility of a Republican or Populist victory against the divided Democrats in the general election.[22] This was the first direct statewide primary in the country's history, so far as I know. The fact that its purpose was clearly to prevent party defeat rather than to allow popular control of nominations or wrench power from the bosses should give pause to those who describe the primary simply as a beneficial, progressive reform.

There was little controversy over black participation in Democratic

Univ. of Alabama, 1964), pp. 1–110; Lynwood Mathis Holland, "The Direct Primary in Georgia" (Ph.D. diss., Univ. of Illinois, 1945), pp. 1–34; James Harris Fain, "Negro in Arkansas," pp. 56–57; Cooper, *The Conservative Regime*, pp. 38–39, 107. Bragg quoted in Jones, "Primary in Alabama," pp. 104–105. On the poor white–Negro coalition, see Francis Roberts, "William Manning Lowe," pp. 100–121; and for the response, Roberts (p. 110), quotes *Tuskegee Weekly News*, Jan. 30, 1879.

21. Oscar W. Underwood, "The Negro Problem in the South," *The Forum* 30 (1900–01): 215–219; Shadgett, *Republican Party in Georgia*, pp. 154–155. Wade Hampton quoted in Jarrell, *Wade Hampton and the Negro*, p. 140. See also a quotation from the *Columbia* (South Carolina) *Daily Register*, n.d., on the same page. The Georgia newspaper is *Dawson Journal*, Dec. 28, 1876, quoted in Holland, "Primary in Georgia," pp. 28–29, and similar quotations, pp. 29, 33.

22. Lucia E. Daniel, "The Louisiana People's Party," *Louisiana Historical Quarterly* 26 (1943): 1081–1082; Allie Bayne Windham Webb, "History of Negro Voting in Louisiana," pp. 187–188.

primaries in these years, since the vast majority of Negroes were staunch supporters of the party of Lincoln. A few were allowed to vote in primaries in scattered areas of the South, probably on the theory that black Democrats threatened the dominant whites less than black Republicans did. In other areas blacks were specifically excluded from the primaries as early as 1878. Practices varied from county to county until the early twentieth century, when most Democratic state committees or conventions adopted statewide whites-only regulations.[23]

During the nineties, the Alabama and Louisiana Populists realized that the Democrats would use their control to count black votes for themselves, whether or not those votes were actually cast. They also understood the effectiveness of the Democratic charge that they endangered white supremacy by putting the blacks in the position of holding the balance of power between divided white groups. The People's Party men therefore proposed that they and the Democrats settle their battles in white primaries. (In other cases, the Populists invited Negroes to participate in their primaries.) Unwilling to give up their advantages, the Democrats refused. After the presidential fusion arrangement of 1896 had weakened the Populists, however, the Democrats invited their erstwhile opponents to submerge their party identity in a solid white front.[24]

But the debility of the Populists and the disfranchisement of most Negroes after 1900 did not end the Democrats' difficulties. A Richmond paper reported that many Virginia Democrats believed that "the elimination of the Negro as a voting factor means the disintegration of the Democrats who have been held together by antipathy to the black race."[25] For the most reliable means of guarding against disintegration, Democrats turned to the primary.

23. Jones, "Primary in Alabama," pp. 114–117, 137–139, 325; Holland, "Primary in Georgia," pp. 55–56, 79–89; Fain, "Negro in Arkansas," pp. 61–65; Cooper, *Conservative Regime*, pp. 92, 107–109; Rice, *Negro in Texas*, pp. 113–126; John Hope, "The Negro Vote in the States Whose Constitutions Have Not Been Specifically Revised," in American Negro Academy, *The Negro and the Elective Franchise* (Washington, D.C.: The Academy, 1905), p. 53; Charles D. Farris, "The Re-Enfranchisement of Negroes in Florida," *Journal of Negro History* 39 (1954): 262–263.

24. Jones, "Primary in Alabama," pp. 140–141, 229–237. Moore, *History of Alabama and Her People*, 1: 729–730; Rogers, *One-Gallused Rebellion*, pp. 212, 241–243, 247–248; Hair, *Bourbonism*, pp. 237–242.

25. *Richmond Times*, May 4, 1900, quoted in Robert E. Martin, "Negro Disfranchisement in Virginia," *Howard University Studies in the Social Sciences* 1 (1938): 123.

Talks with Democratic leaders in Mississippi, South Carolina, and Louisiana convinced Josephus Daniels, editor of the *Raleigh* (North Carolina) *News and Observer*, that the white primary was necessary "in order to keep the white men united" after the limitation of the suffrage. "Without the legal primary," he went on, "the fear was expressed by several that the divisions among white men might result in bringing about a return to the deplorable conditions when one faction of white men call upon the Negroes to help defeat another faction." The primary would "secure permanent good government by the party of the White Man," by which Daniels meant the Democrats. Ex-Governor Thomas J. Jarvis of North Carolina favored the primary because, he explained, "I know of no better way to insure the continued success of the Democratic party." Tarheel Republicans opposed a legal statewide Democratic primary for the same reason. As a GOP spokesman commented, enactment of a primary law would mark "the final burial of Republican or other opposition parties in North Carolina."[26]

In Alabama, too, political leaders pushed the primary as the best means of aborting a nascent two-party system. A few spokesmen had broached the idea of using the statewide direct pirmary to minimize defections and prevent party division among the whites as early as the eighties.[27] After the 1901 disfranchising convention, leaders of both "conservative" and "liberal" Democratic factions took it up.

In the struggle to defeat the 1901 Alabama constitution, the remaining Populists coalesced with the "liberal" forces of ex-Governor Joseph F. Johnston. Their defeat in the referendum did not prevent them from establishing their own factional newspaper and setting up a continuing organization to contest the 1902 governor's race against the former Gold Democrat, incumbent William D. Jelks. Believing that the Jelks-controlled Democratic state executive committee would fear Johnston's popular appeal and therefore rebuff the "reformers'" demands for a primary, the Johnstonites apparently plotted to avenge their losses by bolting the party and campaigning on the charge that the "bosses" had rigged the election machinery—the same issue Reuben Kolb had used to animate the "Jeffersonian Democrats" a decade earlier.

Seeing through this strategy, conservatives advised the party leaders

26. *Raleigh News and Observer*, Feb. 4 and 12, 1899. GOP comments appeared in *Charlotte Daily Observer*, Jan. 1, 1915, quoted in Steelman, "Progressive Era in North Carolina," p. 458. For a further discussion of the primary in North Carolina, see pp. 451–461.

27. *Mobile Register*, June 16, 1886, quoted in Jones, "Primary in Alabama," p. 151.

to accede to half of Johnston's request by ordering a white primary, but keeping Populists and Republicans out, at least for the present. "Give him [Johnston] the Democratic primary he don't [*sic*] really want," the *Montgomery Advertiser* counseled party leaders. "Take away the opportunity of organizing a bolt from a State Convention. Cut off an independent movement like that of Kolb and other leaders in other Southern States on similar pretexts." The primary was a modest change designed to buttress the "harmony and strength" of the Democratic party by maintaining "a sense of fair dealing within its ranks," the newspaper explained. "The *Advertiser* wants to see the Party maintain its easy and deserved domination in Alabama affairs, and this can be ensured only by holding within its organization all the adherents it has, and by attracting all the others it can." "We have had turmoil and strife enough in our ranks," warned the conservative organ, "and if it can be avoided by adopting a primary, why not try it?"

Other newspapers and leaders agreed. A primary, announced the *Birmingham Ledger,* would "settle the matter and hold the party together and leave practically nobody outside the party lines except those persistently in opposition. Let us have a harmonious primary and a unanimous election." The *Mobile Register* advocated a primary "because its adoption is the only way of preserving the Democratic organization and the control of political machinery in this State by the Party organization." Noting that allowing white Populists and Republicans to participate in the 1896 local primaries "practically broke up the Populist Party in this State," former Governor William C. Oates argued that a statewide primary in 1902 "would allay all fears of fraud and save the grand old Democratic Party under which so many victories have been won, from further bickering, strife, and division within its own ranks." Johnston's party leader George P. Harrison predicted that a primary would restore "peace and harmony" and "reconcile all elements of the party," "This is necessary," he went on, "for the future success of the Democratic Party in both State and Federal elections." The Alabama state Democratic executive committee agreed to hold a primary in 1902 but carefully defined the election rules to exclude those who had supported Populist candidates in 1898 or 1900, most of whose votes would have probably gone to Johnston.[28]

28. All quotations in this paragraph and the preceding one are taken from *Montgomery Daily Advertiser*, March 7, 25, 26, 28, 29, April 1, 6, 10, 16, June 15, July 10, 12, 1902. See also Hackney, *Populism to Progressivism*, pp. 232–234; Jones, "Primary in Alabama," pp.

After the hatreds of the 1890s had had time to dissipate, Georgia "liberals" insisted on opening their primaries to white Populists and Republicans. Excluding them, the Democrats thought, would tend to "divide the white people of the state into two parties, rather than to build up the [D]emocratic party by obliteration of the factional lines." In North Carolina, Governor Charles B. Aycock declared in 1904 that "the Democratic party is alone sufficient. We need a united people. We need the combined effort of every North Carolinian. *We need the strength which comes from believing alike"* (my italics). Substitution of the primary for the convention may have slightly annoyed those who always opposed any change, but the irritation was bearable if the reform conserved the Democratic monopoly of politics.[29]

But the primary could not have worked so well for this purpose had the electorate not already been restricted. Before disfranchisement, Democrats in most states had to guard against even small defections, for large numbers of Negroes and hill country whites could be counted on to vote for the opposition. Add to them a small percentage of disgruntled Democrats and a modicum of honesty in the ballot count, and one had the recipe for Democratic disaster. The disfranchisement of a large proportion of opposition stalwarts in most states, however, greatly increased the number of Democratic turncoats necessary for a Republican or Populist triumph. With this much leeway, the primary, which pledged defeated candidates not to run in the general election, was sufficient to preserve Democratic hegemony except in the most extreme circumstances. It was the final step in transforming the Southern polity, but it required that the electorate be reduced before it could become a workable solution.

There were, of course, other reasons for adopting the primary. Politicos who felt their chances would be increased if the focal point of campaigns were speeches outside the courthouse rather than deals inside it naturally preferred primaries to conventions. Those in power hesitated to change the rules by which they got there, while those out of office tended to attack any system under which they lost. For example, in its attempt to elect the war hero John B. Gordon to the Senate in 1886 over a candidate who had already corralled most of the local

238–243, 266–270, 274–275, 288, 296, 309–311; Moore, *History of Alabama*, 1: 909–910.

29. Democratic party platform, 1906, quoted in *Atlanta Constitution*, Sept. 5, 1906. Aycock quoted in Oliver H. Orr, Jr., *Charles Brantley Aycock*, p. 252.

politicians, Henry Grady's *Atlanta Constitution* crusaded for local primaries. Its shout, "Let the People Revolt against the Politicians," was somewhat misleading, for Gordon had previously held the posts of governor, senator, head of the Ku Klux Klan, and servant to the Collis P. Huntington railroad lobby.[30]

In South Carolina, Ben Tillman called for a primary in 1886 and 1888, but his enthusiasm cooled when it became apparent that he would control the 1890 nominating convention. At that point the Conservatives reversed themselves and demanded a statewide primary. Tillman did agree in 1892 to set up an indirect primary in which, on a single election day, voters in each county would select convention delegates pledged to him or his opponent. But this temporary concession probably represented less a devotion to democratic procedures than a desire to head off formation of a permanent opposition party with white as well as black support, organized around the Conservative forces which contested the 1890 general election. In any case, the Tillman-bossed Democratic party did not authorize direct statewide primaries until 1896, after the disfranchisement convention, at a time when Ben was safely ensconced in the second year of a six-year United States Senate term.[31]

Virginia Congressman William A. Jones, who wanted Tom Martin's Senate seat, organized the "May Movement" in 1899 around the issue of a senatorial primary. Martin was a shy railroad lawyer, virtually unknown to the public when he persuaded (some said bribed) a majority of the state legislators to send him, rather than the popular Fitzhugh Lee, to the Senate in 1893. A master organizer and lobbyist, Martin was less proficient on the stump than Jones or several other aspirants for his Senate seat. After the disfranchising convention, Martin, realizing that a tight organization might win primaries in the limited electorate as well as it had previously controlled party conventions, and also desiring to remove the single issue which really divided the "Independents" from the "Machine" men, endorsed a senatorial

---

30. *Montgomery Daily Advertiser*, April 9, 10, 1902; Albert D. Kirwin, *Revolt of the Rednecks*, p. 33; Francis Butler Simkins, *Pitchfork Ben Tillman*, p. 229. For the *Atlanta Constitution* campaign, see Holland, "Primary in Georgia," pp. 36–38; Woodward, *Tom Watson*, pp. 61–63.

31. David Duncan Wallace, *The History of South Carolina*, 3: 347, 356, 364; Cooper, *Conservative Regime*, pp. 195–200; Ernest M. Lander, Jr., *A History of South Carolina, 1865–1960*, pp. 34–42. For a similar episode involving Joseph F. Johnston in Alabama, see *Montgomery Daily Advertiser*, March 25, April 1, 1902.

primary. This endorsement further evidenced the fact that quarrels over the primary between "Progressives" and their opponents were merely tactical maneuvers in the larger struggle to get and hold offices. And they were tactical maneuvers whose final consequences were not always clear to those who initiated them, for much to the chagrin of those who had been advocating the primary for a decade, Martin won handily in both 1905 and 1911.[32]

If the switch from the convention to the primary did not damage those politicians with well-run organizations, it did encourage demagoguery. Whereas earlier aspirants chiefly had to convince convention delegates of their fitness for office or their willingness to pass out favors, primary candidates had to lambaste their opponents publicly. Moreover, in the period before disfranchisement and the primary killed party competition and eliminated from the electorate those in the lower socioeconomic strata, Democratic nominees often had to contest general elections seriously. In those elections, real issues often divided the voters, and party organizations allowed some continuity and rationality in political choices. When the statewide primary became the only important election, candidates had to fabricate issues. Since no deep cleavages divided the voting public in the primaries, campaigns usually revolved around questions of personality, petty scandal, or charges that one or more candidates represented an evil political machine or a despised, but politically impotent group such as the Communists or the blacks. To attract attention, competitors were virtually forced to make charges they could not prove, promises they could not keep. Political campaigns in Arkansas became "a sort of legalized knife fight and perpetual stomping contest." A Mississippi newspaper believed that in the primaries, "the men who can shake hands best, wear the broadest smile, know the most people, and tell the funniest stories, have the best chance to win."[33]

32. Harry Edward Poindexter, "Copy Desk to Congress," pp. 185–192; Wythe W. Holt, Jr., "Virginia Constitutional Convention," pp. 70–74; Richard B. Doss, "John Warwick Daniel: A Study in the Virginia Democracy" (Ph.D. diss., Univ. of Virginia, 1955), pp. 216–258, 355–357; Burton Ira Kaufman, "Henry De La Warr Flood," pp. 128–129; Herman L. Horn, "Democratic Party in Virginia Since 1890," pp. 428–429.

33. Non-partisan elections, which are similar to Southern primaries, generally encourage candidates to avoid issues. See Charles R. Adrian, "Some General Characteristics of Non-Partisan Elections," *American Political Science Review* 46 (1952): 766–776. While primaries are certainly sometimes fought over real issues, they were not, by most accounts, in the South throughout most of the twentieth century. The leading authority on such matters, of course,

Probably more important than his smile, however, was the candidate's bankroll. In a polity divided along party lines, nominees can count on loyal campaign workers and voters. The contest is for the independent voters, the switchers, the normally apathetic. In a system with no consistent party or factional groupings, a much larger proportion of the active electorate is usually uncommitted to any candidate. Campaign organizations also must be constructed anew for every election. These tasks require money as well as the proper connections. Whereas a convention can afford to nominate a somewhat penurious candidate, relying on traditional party sources for funds, publicity, workers, and votes, the same man, unless he has rich friends, can rarely get enough exposure to contest a primary seriously.[34]

While it increased the power of affluent whites, the primary shut out Negroes almost entirely. But the extent of its effect on black political power in the early years of the twentieth century has been greatly exaggerated. Few blacks considered themselves Democrats until the New Deal. What they wanted was a chance to cast their ballots in the general election for opposition party candidates who would pose alternatives to the white supremacy rhetoric of the Democrats and the "lily-white" position which many Republicans espoused, especially after most blacks were disfranchised. Moreover, even if the blacks had desired to enter the Democratic primaries, and whites had let them, it is difficult to believe that they would have found any appealing can-

---

was V. O. Key. For more specific observations on campaign tactics, see Drummond, "Arkansas Politics," pp. 134–135; Clark and Kirwin, *South since Appomattox*, pp. 120–122; James Aubrey Tinsley, "The Progressive Movement in Texas" (Ph.D. diss., Univ. of Wisconsin, 1953), pp. 311–314; *New Orleans Times-Democrat*, April 29, 1907, quoted in Ray Stannard Baker, *Following the Colour Line*, p. 256; Stuart Towns, "Joseph T. Robinson and Arkansas Politics: 1912–1913," *Arkansas Historical Quarterly* 24 (1965): 300; Paige E. Mulhollan, "The Issues of the Davis-Berry Senatorial Campaign in 1906," *Arkansas Historical Quarterly* 20 (1961): 124–125; Key, *Southern Politics*, pp. 303–304. Comments on Arkansas and Mississippi appear in Milton MacKay, "The Senate's New Investigator," *Saturday Evening Post*, Aug. 13, 1955, p. 30, quoted in Drummond, "Arkansas Politics," p. 134; *Jackson* (Mississippi) *Clarion-Ledger*, Nov. 17, 1910, quoted in Clark and Kirwin, *South since Appomattox*, pp. 110–111.

34. Factions in the South from 1900 to about 1960 were far less persistent and organized than political parties usually are. See Allan P. Sindler, "Bifactional Rivalry as an Alternative to Two-Party Competition in Louisiana," *American Political Science Review* 49 (1955): 641–642; Julius Turner, "Primary Elections as the Alternative to Party Competition in 'Safe' Districts," *Journal of Politics* 15 (1953): 197–210; Key, *Southern Politics*, pp. 15–276. On the particular importance of money in primaries, see Drummond, "Arkansas Politics," pp. 151–155; Robert C. Brooks, *Political Parties and Electoral Problems* (New York: Harper & Bros., 1923), pp. 262–263.

didates. The Democratic party had been held together since the Civil War chiefly by its members' devotion to the doctrine of white supremacy; only a masochist would have openly bid for black votes in a turn-of-the-century primary. Most important, there would have been only a minuscule number of Negro electors to bargain for. For before they instituted their first permanent, statewide direct primaries, every Southern state had passed at least one major piece of restrictive legislation. Indeed, no seceding state passed any important suffrage qualifications *after* the establishment of the statewide white primary except Georgia in 1908, and that state's cumulative poll tax had barred the majority of Negroes almost since the date of its passage in 1877. Despite its name, the white primary had virtually no effect on Negro voting in the period from 1880 to 1910.

4

Insuring "the Safety of the Black Belt"

Suffrage restriction both reflected and affected political conditions. Having traced the development of Southern politics from 1877 to the early disfranchising statutes, explored how those laws worked, and examined their efficacy in reducing the number of voters and channeling them into the Democratic party, we must now seek to discover the human agents of electoral change. Which groups of men favored and opposed restriction and why? Why were the statutes in each state adopted at one time rather than another? How much of a threat did opposition parties and factions pose to the dominant interests at the time of disfranchisement? And what was the impact of franchise limitation on political conflicts? Answering these questions requires a detailed look at the political contexts of suffrage restriction in each of the eleven ex-Confederate states. Besides analyzing the passage of the disfranchisement acts, I will attempt in this and the following three chapters to revise some of the received wisdom about late nineteenth-century Southern politics.

The standard narratives discussing the legal restriction of the suffrage concentrate on the five disfranchising conventions and on the elaborate constitutional amendments submitted to the North Carolina and Georgia electorates. Other instances of the passage of restrictive laws, some requiring only action by the legislatures and some, the acquiescence of the voters, have been neglected. For example, in the most complete study of disfranchisement, William A. Mabry omitted the four ex-Confederate states where the poll tax and various quasi-literacy tests sufficed to constrict the franchise, and excluded from his discussion most of the nonconstitutional disfranchising laws passed by legislatures in the seven states he did cover.[1] As a consequence of this neglect,

1. Mabry, "Disfranchisement of the Negro." Similarly, C. Vann Woodward devoted just three paragraphs, by my count, to voting restrictions passed by legislatures in *Origins of the New South*, pp. 55–56, 275, 335. His general treatment of suffrage restriction, in chapter 12, "The Mississippi Plan as the American Way," concentrated on the same events Mabry examined.

historians have often misunderstood the timing and dynamics of disfranchisement, the conditions necessary for a successful movement to limit voting, the comparative efficiency of different techniques, and the identities and motives of the disfranchisers. Excessive stress on constitutional disfranchisement has, particularly, led historians to overemphasize race and underemphasize partisanship as motives for restriction. The convention delegates talked much more of racist aims than their counterparts in the legislatures. Furthermore, there were many more Republicans and Populists in the legislatures to damn the restrictionists' party-oriented purposes than there were in the conventions. By analyzing the passage of laws affecting the suffrage in five states and placing the struggles over their enactment in the context of each state's politics, I will attempt in the next two chapters to reemphasize these slighted episodes in the history of suffrage restriction.

SOUTH CAROLINA: BOURBON DISFRANCHISEMENT

South Carolina in 1880 linked the Southern reactionary past with its antidemocratic future. Identifying itself with the aristocratic antebellum tradition, the influential *Columbia Daily Register* derided majority rule as "a mere count of noses" and maintained that "whenever it crosses the substantial power of the State, its intelligence, its wealth and its established social appointments, [majority rule] ever melts away as a political myth and the philosopher's fair dream." All too aware of their race's minority status in the state, fearing that violence, intimidation, and fraud might not permanently maintain them in political power, and worried about the lasting effects of such practices on their state's existence as a social entity, the more foresighted white South Carolinians searched for an ultimate solution.[2]

The Palmetto State's Polity was perhaps farther advanced in 1881—more like the Southern political system of the first half of the twentieth century—than that of any other state. To Democrats, political contests seemed to "involve the very existence of society itself." Since Republican leaders were "the vilest class . . . ever known in American politics"

2. *Columbia Daily Register*, Jan. 3, 1882; three pamphlets by Edward McCrady, Jr., *The Registration of Electors* (Charleston, South Carolina, 1879), *The Necessity of Education as the Basis of Our Political System* (Charleston, South Carolina, 1880), and *The Necessity of Raising the Standard of Citizenship and the Right of the General Assembly of the State of South Carolina to Impose Qualifications upon Electors* (Charleston, South Carolina, 1881).

and their followers "a sea of brute force, ignorance and besotted prejudice," that party was "a perpetual menace to civilization." Unlike the border states, therefore, South Carolina had already abjured the luxury of a strong statewide Republican party. Unlike even such states as Mississippi, South Carolina suffered no potent Independent or Greenback movement. Lacking a viable opposition party which could hinder the passage of discriminatory laws or capitalize on the voter reaction to such legislation, and rid of the necessity of appearing "liberal" in their treatment of their former slaves (as had seemed requisite before and for a short time after Hayes's withdrawal of the troops), legislative leaders of the state which cradled secession felt free to take whatever steps were necessary to protect the political status quo permanently from upheaval.[3]

Though all Democrats, no doubt, agreed upon the desirability of shackling the Republicans—since by this time nearly all South Carolina GOP voters were black, discrimination against race and party coincided—no such consensus existed on the means of doing so. Some Democrats favored extralegal efforts. Former Governor Benjamin F. Perry, for example, advised systematic statewide economic intimidation as the best way to "crush out the Radical party in South Carolina." Others endorsed legal restriction. At the beginning of the 1880–1882 session of the legislature, a *Charleston News and Courier* poll of white Democratic state legislators found 25 in favor of calling a constitutional convention, 18 proponents of a registration law, 9 desirous of passing constitutional amendments providing for property or educational qualifications, 7 satisfied with the "old methods," 39 offering no opinion, and a scattered few members in favor of concessions to the blacks. Consequently, the legislature set up a commission on election laws and one on constitutional amendments to meet between the two sessions of the legislature and draft definite proposals.[4]

Probably the most important member of the election law commission and the chief author of its proposal was Edward McCrady, Jr., de-

3. *Columbia Daily Register*, Nov. 3, 1880. Restriction of the suffrage in this instance was clearly a partisan move. As the *Columbia Daily Register*, May 24, 1881, noted, "Nobody charges that the colored man is deprived of his vote on account of his color but on account of his politics."

4. Ibid., Nov. 18, 1880; *Charleston News and Courier*, Dec. 2, 1880. Unfortunately, the poll did not list the proponents of the several schemes by name. Legislation is recorded in S. C. *House Journal* (1880), p. 434.

scendant of an old Charleston family, lieutenant colonel in the Confederate army, civil service reformer, lawyer, and historian of the
glories of colonial South Carolina. His plan, expounded in several
speeches which circulated throughout South Carolina as pamphlets,
required each voter to be able to sign his name in order to register to
vote. In this manner, the Democrats could disfranchise illiterates
without going to the trouble, expense, and possible danger of calling a
constitutional convention. In addition to this literacy test, which he
thought would exclude about 71,000 blacks and 12,000 whites, Mc-
Crady favored setting the price for renewal of a lost registration certificate so high as to disfranchise the careless.[5]

To those who objected to robbing even 12,000 whites of the vote,
the Charleston patrician responded with perhaps the first form of what
was in the 1890s to become the grandfather clause. The Massachusetts
constitution of 1857 required literacy of all voters after its enactment,
but not of those who could vote in 1857. With fine legal logic, McCrady
analogously proposed guaranteeing the suffrage after 1881 to those
South Carolinians who had voted in 1857 or some similar date, thus
excusing from the literacy test at least the older whites. In this way,
South Carolina could constitutionally guarantee white supremacy
and thumb its nose at the symbol of abolitionism and radicalism at the
same time. The very cleverness of the stratagem led one major newspaper to fear that the bill would inflame Northern opinion, arouse
Congress, and meet defeat in the courts.[6]

McCrady's ingenious scheme had a rough time in the election law
committee and a rougher one in the legislature. At first, a majority of
the committee opposed the measure. The plan that the committee
presented to the legislature modified the Charlestonian's proposal in
several respects. Literacy was no longer required for registration;

5. Cooper, *Conservative Regime*, p. 98; Wallace, *History of South Carolina* 3: 441. McCrady's
father was one of South Carolina's premier jurists and Episcopal laymen. Educated at Yale,
he read law with U.S. Supreme Court Justice William Johnson. A Unionist in 1832, he, like
many other low country conservatives, became a "cooperationist" in the fifties. A prominent
member of the Southern Rights Association, he worked hard to break up the Union and
signed the secession ordinance. See his front-page obituary in the *Atlanta Constitution*, Nov.
18, 1892. For details of McCrady Jr.'s disfranchising plan, see his *Registration of Electors*, p.
8, and *Necessity of Education*, p. 14.

6. McCrady, *Registration of Electors*, pp. 10–11. Previous historians have overlooked the
Yankee origin of the grandfather clause. Fear of Northern opinion appears in *Columbia Daily
Register*, May 3, 1881; Jan. 19, 22, 1882.

instead, the literacy test was shifted to a new, second section of the law providing for eight separate boxes. If two separate boxes for federal and state elections were constitutional, McCrady's legalistic mind must have reasoned, then a mere multiplication by four would outrage no principle of jurisprudence. Besides this change, the committee's proposal included a 50-cent charge for registration and a $5 deposit in case of an appeal from an official's decision. The new plan excluded the exemption clause for older whites and the prohibitive price tag for re-registration. The committee's bill, in sum, altered McCrady's proposal significantly and closed the loophole for the whites.[7]

Though the committee's proposal sailed through the Senate with just one important record vote, the opposition made up in noise what it lacked in numbers. After assaulting the measure because "under it the poor white man would be driven to the wall with the black man," Senator Fishburne, a white who had been elected by a fusion of both races in Colleton County, promised to bolt the Democrats and set up a statewide "People's Party." In the major speech against the bill, black leader Thomas E. Miller charged that McCrady's device was "framed for the purpose of keeping the middle classes and the poor whites, together with the Negroes, from having anything to do with elections."[8]

Only extensive revision saved the bill in the House. First the provisions requiring a 50-cent fee for registration and a $5 deposit for appeals were eliminated. Then the registration section survived two tests by margins of only 56–50 and 53–52, despite Democratic caucus endorsement of the bill. Opponents of the eight-box section lost more decisively on motions to reduce the number of boxes to two, require the election officials to number the eight boxes and not shift their order during the voting, and allow an illiterate voter to bring a friend to read the labels for him. Most of the bill's critics were white Democrats, for the House was composed of 114 whites, all members of the dominant party, 6 black Democrats, and but 4 black Republicans. Many of the whites feared that the bill would disfranchise those whites who were illiterate, or neglected to register, or lost their certificates, Indeed, three members of the election law commission, McCrady, Murray,

7. *Columbia Daily Register*, Aug. 7, Nov. 23, 1881; *Charleston News and Courier*, May 25, Aug. 6, Nov. 24, 1881.

8. *Charleston News and Courier*, Jan. 3, 4, 1882; *Columbia Daily Register*, Dec. 3, 1881. A move in the Senate to strike out the registration section of the bill failed, 20–10. See S.C. *House Journal* (1881–1882), pp. 108–109.

and Hutson, freely acknowledged that they intended to disfranchise white as well as black illiterates.[9]

The pattern of voting among white Democratic legislators in the House confirms these notions. As table 4.1 shows, the members from counties over 70 percent black, fifteen of whom resided in the "low country," supported the bill overwhelmingly. Those legislators from counties with fewer Negroes, who presumably worried about the disqualification of whites more than the representatives of coastal planters did, opposed the bill by a slight margin. With the whites split over the registration section, the bill lost a third reading vote, 51–56.[10]

Table 4.1. Section, Racial Composition of Counties, and Support for Voter Registration among White Democrats in South Carolina Legislature, 1882.

Section of State	For Registration Section	Against Registration Section
Low-country	17	7
Midlands	14	19
Up-country	21	17
% Negro		
20–29	2	1
30–39	7	2
40–49	1	7
50–59	3	11
60–69	23	19
70–79	16	3

SOURCE: Information on which counties fell in each section of the state was taken from William J. Cooper, Jr., *The Conservative Regime*, p. 12.

NOTE: Abstainers are omitted.

9. The *Charleston News and Courier*, Dec. 3, 1881, reported the Democratic endorsement. S.C. *House Journal* (1881–1882), pp. 180, 327, 337, 367, 368, records the motions. Also cf. *Columbia Daily Register*, Jan. 13, 1882. One may conclude from the debates reported in the *Register* that most of those who wanted to reduce the number of boxes did not act out of antipathy to disfranchisement. Rather, they feared that federal officials would be able to supervise state elections (and thereby reduce fraud) if all the voting boxes were in the same polling place, or that the Republicans would overcome the literacy test by concentrating on only one of the eight offices and teaching their partisans how to recognize the name of that office on the box. For the expressions of intent to disfranchise whites, see *Charleston News and Courier*, Jan. 13, 1882.

10. S.C. *House Journal* (1881–1882), p. 369; *Charleston News and Courier*, Jan. 18, 1882. 92 percent of the white Democrats who opposed the registration section and voted on the third reading of the bill cast "no" votes on the latter. 86 percent of the white Democrats who favored the registration section and voted on the third reading cast "ayes" for the measure.

The surprise defeat forced concessions from the disfranchisers. On the next day, the third reading vote was reconsidered, and the bill was referred to a special committee, consisting of five opponents and five proponents of the bill, who proceeded to amend it in two crucial respects. The first amendment provided that at the close of registration, the registrar

shall revise the list; and in case it be made to appear to his satisfaction that there is a qualified voter in his precinct who has failed to register, he may, upon such evidence as he may think necessary, in his discretion, permit the name of such voter to be placed on said list and issue a certificate therefor.[11]

In other words, the registrar could add to his list the names of any whites who had neglected to register. If so inclined, of course, the registrars could use this provision as an invitation to effortless fraud, for, as the *Aiken Recorder* put it, "How easy it is to manufacture names . . . ."[12]

The other change made by the committee authorized election officials to read the labels on the ballot box to any voter who so requested. Now guaranteeing suffrage to persons acceptable to the white Democratic registrars and to election officials, who were appointed directly by the governor, the bill was ordered for a third reading by 57–39. Three days thereafter, the House indefinitely postponed a constitutional convention bill, which had been kept in reserve in case the legislature adopted no simpler solution to the suffrage problem.[13]

Since neither the *News and Courier* nor the *Register* printed biographical sketches of the legislators at this session, characterization of the proponents and opponents of the bill will necessarily be sparse. The chief author of the law, Edward McCrady, was an erudite low-country patrician, in style as different as possible from the later leader of the

11. S.C. *Acts* (1881–1882), section 5, p. 1112. The import of this section, which seems to have escaped the notice of previous historians, was noted by the black Republican Robert Smalls in an article, "Election Methods in the South," *North American Review* 151 (1890): 595–596: "All persons desiring to vote the Democratic ticket are registered, without personal application, and certificates are furnished them either before or on the day of election without even the formality of an oath as to eligibility."

12. *Aiken Recorder*, quoted in *Columbia Daily Register*, Feb. 2, 1882.

13. *Charleston News and Courier*, Dec. 8, 1881, Jan. 23, 26, 1882; S.C. *House Journal* (1881–1882), pp. 417–418. As in other states, many in South Carolina believed that a constitutional convention was dangerous because no one could be sure who would control it or what it would do. See statement of John D. Wylie, in *Columbia Daily Register*, May 17, 1881.

South Carolina disfranchising convention, Ben Tillman—whom Mc-Crady opposed. As for the other members, we many classify them into four groups on the basis of the three crucial votes of January 17–21, 1882: the roll calls on which the bill was defeated, on reconsideration of that vote, and on subsequent passage after amendment. One group is composed of the stalwart opponents of the bill, who voted against it at every turn; another (denominated "converts" in table 4.2), those who opposed it on January 17, but voted for reconsideration the next day and did not oppose final passage on January 21; a third, the constant proponents of the bill; and finally, those whose voting fits into no discernible pattern or who failed to vote.

Membership in these groups is cross-tabulated in table 4.2 with data on the section from which each delegate came and the racial composition of his home county. The first part of the table shows that while the disfranchisers were distributed fairly evenly throughout the state, opposition to the election law varied directly with distance from the ocean. Twice as high a percentage of uplanders as of lowlanders opposed the law. The second part of the table indicates that, in general, as the proportion of Negroes in the delegates' counties rose, support for the law grew and opposition subsided. One-third of the members from

Table 4.2. Who Opposed the Eight-Box Law in the 1882 South Carolina Legislature?

	PROPONENTS	CONVERTS	OPPONENTS	OTHERS	TOTAL
Section of State					
Low-country	16 (51.6%)	5 (16.1%)	6 (19.4%)	4 (12.9%)	31 (100%)
Midlands	19 (46.3%)	7 (17.1%)	13 (31.7%)	2 (4.9%)	41 (100%)
Up-country	19 (45.2%)	3 (7.1%)	16 (38.0%)	4 (9.5%)	42 (100%)
Total	54 (47.4%)	15 (13.2%)	35 (30.7%)	10 (8.8%)	114 (100%)
% Negro					
20–29	1 (25%)	0	3 (75%)	0	4 (100%)
30–39	8 (80%)	0	2 (20%)	0	10 (100%)
40–49	1 (12.5%)	4 (50%)	3 (37.5%)	0	8 (100%)
50–59	3 (17.6%)	3 (17.6%)	8 (47.1%)	3 (17.6%)	17 (100%)
60–69	27 (49.9%)	6 (11.3%)	16 (30.2%)	4 (7.5%)	53 (100%)
70–79	14 (63.7%)	2 (9.1%)	3 (13.6%)	3 (13.6%)	22 (100%)
Total	54 (47.4%)	15 (13.2%)	35 (30.7%)	10 (8.8%)	114 (100%)

NOTE: Opposition analyzed for white Democrats only. Abstainers are omitted.

counties below 60 percent Negro were classed as disfranchisers, and 41 percent as opponents. In the counties over 70 percent Negro, the respective figures were 64 percent and 14 percent.

Legend has it that the conservative followers of Wade Hampton, concentrated most heavily in the low country, favored Negro suffrage and practiced a benevolent paternalism toward the freedmen. The raw, uncultured upcountryman, led by the likes of Martin W. Gary and Ben Tillman, is usually pictured as the black man's real enemy. The Hamptonite intellectual Edward McCrady's central role in popularizing, drafting, and passing the registration and eight-box law tends to discredit these stereotypes. Moreover, table 4.2 demonstrates that opposition to the law was most prevalent among House members from the upcountry and those whose counties contained relatively small percentages of blacks. Their opposition apparently grew out of fear of white disfranchisement rather than any desire to protect the black man's vote. Since support for the law cut across sectional lines, blacks must have found little difference between the various groupings of whites. Perhaps most whites in South Carolina at the time would have agreed with a contemporary editorial in the organ of the conservative low country, the *Charleston News and Courier*. In an article entitled "Lynch Law—the Higher Law," this Hamptonite newspaper commended the recent lynching of two blacks. It worried, however, that quick hanging might not be a sufficient deterrent to crime. Instead, it advised burning at the stake or "chopping the offender into mince-meat."[14]

McCrady's law had an instantaneous effect on the politics of South Carolina, and it was exactly what he desired. As tables 4.3 and 4.4 show, the eight-box law cut the Republican vote by two-thirds, and it cut the Negro vote and overall turnout by half. The 1895 disfranchising convention merely finished the job by blotting out the tiny Negro and Republican percentages. Widely recognized as a potent disfranchising device, McCrady's 1882 scheme inspired a similar law later in the decade in Florida.

FLORIDA: THE ESTABLISHMENT OF "ARISTOCRACY AND DESPOTISM"

Markedly democratic during the 1880s, Florida became solidly

14. Jarrell, *Wade Hampton and The Negro*, expounds the Hampton myth. The Negro population and the geographical location were of course closely correlated. Twenty-five of the 39

Table 4.3. Republican Threat Dissolved Legally: Effect of Election Law
Changes in South Carolina on Turnout and Party Voting in Presidential
Elections, 1876–1896.

Year	Republican	Democrat	Not Voting
1876	45	44	11
1880	28	55	17
Eight Box Law			
1884	10	32	58
1888	6	29	65
1892	6	23	71
Disfranchising Convention			
1896	3	22	75

Table 4.4. Voting Participation Sliced by Half: Effect of Election Law Changes
in South Carolina on Estimated Turnout by Race in Presidential Elections,
1876–1896.

Year	White	Negro
1876	73	96
1880	96	70
1884	55	35
1888	45	26
1892	39	22
1896	46	11

Democratic by the 1890s. The registration, poll tax, eight-box, and
secret ballot laws simply exterminated the opposition. Though usually
ignored in studies of disfranchisement, Florida's election law changes
produced as dramatic effects as the property and literacy qualifications
instituted elsewhere. Three of every four adult males voted in 1888,
before the major amendments in the Sunshine State's electoral statutes;
in the next statewide contest four years later, only one-third voted. In
the 1888 presidential race the Democratic ticket prevailed by a 3–2
margin; in 1892, by better than 5–1.

Unlike the anemic South Carolina Republicans, Florida's opposition
party showed a good deal of vitality in the eighties, despite the usual
Democratic violence, harassment, fraud, and petty disfranchisement
devices. Perhaps partly because William E. Chandler, President

delegates from counties under 60 percent Negro lived in the state's westernmost section. For
the article, see *Charleston News and Courier*, Jan. 20, 1881, p. 2.

Arthur's Minister for Southern Affairs, had exceptionally close ties with Florida Republicans, the state spawned the most successful Independent movement in the South in the 1880s save Mahone's in Virginia. Alienated by planter Governor William D. Bloxham's sale of four million Florida acres to a Philadelphia promoter and other discriminations against the poor and the farmers, many whites threatened to bolt the Democratic party in 1884. Even though the Democrats patched over the feud between former governors Drew and Bloxham by awarding the gubernatorial nomination to the state's chief war hero, General Edward A. Perry, and in spite of the fact that the Independents ran a colorless local official, Frank W. Pope, the Democrats carried the 1884 gubernatorial contest by a mere 4,200 votes.[15]

After the failure of the Republican attempt to gain power through this front group and the general collapse of Southern Independentism when Cleveland's victory in 1884 left the Republicans bereft of federal patronage, the Florida GOP still polled a respectable 40 percent of the total votes for the state and national tickets in 1888. Furthermore, they continued to control local offices in such counties as Duval (Jacksonville), where they elected their whole slate in 1888. Consequently, although the GOP threat had been contained, especially in the legislature, where Democratic majorities fattened on the gerrymander, the opposition constituted a clear danger to Democratic control in the immediate as well as the far distant future. Both contemporary newspaper reports and election statistics belie the statement made by a recent student of the subject that Negroes "had largely surrendered the right to vote" in Florida by 1884.[16]

15. The Florida GOP's catalogue of Democratic abuses included most of those used in other states as well—disfranchisement of Republicans for petty larceny, gerrymandering, the employment of tissue ballots and ballot-box stuffing, refusal to allow Republican election inspectors and poll watchers to oversee the voting and the counting, appointment of ignorant or otherwise unqualified GOP representatives as inspectors over the protests of the county Republican committees, armed intimidation of Republican voters, and violence. See the *Report of the State Executive Committee of Florida to the Republicans of the State Upon the Election Held Nov. 2, 1880* (Washington, D.C.: National Republican Pub. Co., 1881). Edward C. Williamson, "Era of the Democratic County Leader," quotes many letters from Florida GOP leaders to Chandler. For example, see p. 97. The 1884 election is treated in Edward C. Williamson, "Independentism," pp. 131–156.

16. Regression analysis of party cross-overs from the 1880 governor's race to that of 1884 indicates that three-fourths of the 1880 Republican voters supported Pope in 1884, while only 10 percent of the 1880 Democrats left their party in the second election. GOP control of Duval reported in *Jacksonville Florida Times-Union*, Nov. 7, 1888. The student cited is Charlton

The need for restriction of the suffrage became particularly acute when white county Democrats threatened to substitute direct election for the provision of the 1868 constitution under which the governor appointed local officials. Unless supplied with other safeguards, black belt Democrats would then face the prospect of dealing with Negro county commissioners, judges, sheriffs, etc. A proposal to call a constitutional convention, fought out primarily on the issue of the election of local officials, failed in an 1880 referendum chiefly because white county Democrats had given their black belt compatriots no guarantee of protection against local Negro domination. Proponents of home rule hastened to provide the proper assurances, and an 1884 referendum on the same subject carried easily. Though both the Democratic and Independent gubernatorial candidates endorsed the convention call, statistical analysis of the vote on the referendum shows that virtually all the support for calling the convention came from white Democrats, while most Negroes and other Independent-Republicans either opposed the convention or abstained (table 4.5).[17]

Table 4.5. White Democrats Called the Convention: Estimates of Voting, by Race and Party, in Referendum on Calling 1885 Florida Constitutional Convention.

Race	% For Calling Convention	% Against Calling Convention	% Not Voting
White	70	0	30
Negro	11	21	68
Party[a]			
Democrat	100	0	0
Independent	0	21	78
Not Voting	0	0	100

[a]Party named in 1884 gubernatorial election.

W. Tebeau, *A History of Florida*, p. 289. Tebeau does recognize that the election laws finished off the Negro voters in particular and the Republicans in general, pp. 289–293.

17. This appointment provision had been adopted by the "moderate" Republicans who controlled the Reconstruction constitutional convention, in order to preserve white rule in the black belt. Jerrell H. Shofer, "The Constitution of 1868," *Florida Historical Quarterly* 41 (1963): 356–374. For the 1884 referendum, see J. E. Dovell, *Florida*, 2 : 593, 651. "Leon," in a letter to the *Florida Times-Union*, Feb. 5, 1885, stated that black belt Democrats had agreed to work for the convention only after promises of protection had been made to them at the Democratic state convention in June, 1884. Speaking for the black belt (Leon County had

If the white counties had provided the bulk of votes for the convention, the single most important agitator for it was Samuel Pasco of Jefferson County (77.4 percent black in 1890).[18] Born in London, England, raised in Massachusetts, a graduate of Harvard, Pasco moved to Florida in 1859 and fought in the rebel army. He was chairman of the state Democratic executive committee from 1876 to 1887, the liberal candidate for the Democratic nomination for governor in 1884, and the compromise winner of a U.S. Senate seat in 1887, a place he held for two terms. The ease with which he was elected president of the 1885 constitutional convention indicates the degree of control exercised by the Democratic leadership and the partisan nature of the convention from the beginning.

On the question of voting restriction, the convention's most important figure was the chairman of the suffrage committee, Austen S. Mann of Hernando County (36 percent black in 1890). Born, reared, and educated in Ohio, Mann had been a lawyer and manufacturer in the North before his removal to Florida in 1873—a strange career for someone later to become the most powerful Populist leader in Florida. As a Democratic state senator in the early 1880s, Mann had been chairman of the Senate committee on calling the constitutional convention. In the convention itself, he was a chief spokesman for the young, liberal Democrats and the leading opponent of the poll tax. Mann's chief adversary in the suffrage committee and on the convention floor, Samuel J. Turnbull of Jefferson County, had never before held political office. Born into a prominent Florida family, owner of a large plantation, Turnbull led the black belt proponents of disfranchisement in the convention.[19]

---

the highest proportion of Negroes in Florida), "Leon" threatened to torpedo ratification of the constitution, as he claimed he and his fellows had defeated the 1880 referendum, if black county Democrats were not sufficiently safeguarded in the convention. See also *Florida Times-Union* editorial, Aug. 4, 1885, corroborating "Leon's" account of events. Analysis of the November 1886 referendum on ratifying the constitution revealed a party and racial alignment similar to that of 1884 except that most Independents and Negroes opposed the constitution instead of abstaining.

18. *Florida Times-Union*, Nov. 12, 1886.

19. Observers have often wondered why the Farmers' Alliance chose to hold perhaps its most important national convention in a small Florida town, and why the railroads granted low rates or free passes to the agrarian delegates. According to the chief Alliance newspaper in Tennessee, it was A. S. Mann's "eloquence and magnetism" which convinced Alliance leaders to come to Florida and railroad owners to grant special rates. *Tennessee Weekly Toiler*,

In the five constitutional conventions from 1890 to 1902 in Mississippi, South Carolina, Louisiana, Alabama, and Virginia, the chief argument was over the *means* of limiting the suffrage. In the 1885 Florida convention, where the principal issue was not disfranchisement in the black counties but home rule in the white areas, there was strong opposition to any restriction at all. The issue was forced on the convention when the delegates voted to make all county officers elective except the most important ones, the members of the county commission. Thereafter, the chief problem of the convention, according to the *Florida Times-Union*, was how best to insure "the safety of the black belt."[20]

The suffrage committee, consisting of two black belt and four white county Democrats, three Independents, and two Republicans (one, T. V. Gibbs, an outstanding young Afro-American leader), split on the question of instituting a poll tax. The majority report favored submitting to the voters a poll tax article separately from the rest of the constitution. A minority report, signed by Turnbull and Odom, a white county Democrat, favored submission of the poll tax as part of the constitution. The Democratic caucus overwhelmingly endorsed the minority's views. After the convention adopted the minority report, the major issues became the amount of the capitation tax, the time for payment, and whether to make the tax mandatory or require the legislature to take positive action to put it into effect. The antirestrictionists won on the first two issues, defeating a proposal to require payment three years before the election as a prerequisite for voting and one setting the tax at $2 annually. On the third issue the convention followed a twisting course,

---

Dec. 18, 1889, quoted in *Florida Times-Union*, Oct. 21, 1890. The Florida Knights of Labor awarded Mann a medal, which he thereafter wore during election campaigns, for his defense of voting "without price." *Florida Times-Union*, Sept. 30, 1890. Biographical information on the convention leaders is from J. B. Whitfield, compiler, *Florida State Government, 1885* (Tallahassee, Fla.: Steam Book and Job Office, 1885); Samuel Pasco, Jr., "Samuel Pasco (1834–1917)," *Florida Historical Quarterly* 7 (1928): 135–138; Dovell, *Florida*, 2: 647–648, 688; Williamson, "Era of the Democratic County Leader," pp. 307–309.

20. An attempt to make county commissioners elective was beaten down, 57–38, and a motion to require the governor to appoint no more than three members of one political party to the five commissioners' posts failed 48–42. Fla. Con. Con. *Journal* (1885), pp. 409–412. See also *Florida Times-Union*, July 25, 1885. The Republicans and "young liberal Democrats" did succeed in making all judges elective, July 17, 1885. Mann voted with the Republicans on each of these issues. The chief purpose of the convention was exposed in the Aug 5, 1885 edition.

first voting for a mandatory poll tax, then sending the whole question back to the committee, which failed to resolve it, and finally investing the legislature with the power to make the tax a prerequisite or not. This final outcome was a compromise, more a victory for the opponents than the proponents of disfranchisement. The black belt's security, however, was insured through the gubernatorial appointment of county commissioners and the requirement that other county officeholders be heavily bonded by sureties acceptable to the county commissioners. The latter requirement was invoked in 1888, for example, to replace a Republican sheriff in Jacksonville with the future "Progressive" governor, Napoleon Bonaparte Broward.[21]

The lineup on suffrage restriction in the Florida convention was strongly related to party affiliation and the racial composition of the delegate's county. On the issue of requiring poll tax payments for the preceding year as well as the election year (a compromise between the proponents of paying it for three years and those who wanted it paid for only the election year), the Democrats voted 51–17 for, while the Republicans and Independents cast 26 of their 28 ballots against (table 4.6). Black belt Democrats voted 21–1 for the stiffest poll tax they could get. On the other hand, 16 of the 17 Democrats who opposed requiring poll tax payments for two years before the election came from predominantly white counties. Evidently, these deviant Democrats fought the tax because they feared that it would disfranchise many whites in their counties. In attacking the capitation tax the 16 delegates arrayed themselves with a "convention of the working people of

Table 4.6. Democratic Disfranchisers: Party Affiliation and Votes on the Poll Tax in the Florida Constitutional Convention of 1885.

Party	For	Against	Abstain
Democrat	51 (64%)	17 (21%)	12 (15%)
Independent	1 (17%)	5 (83%)	0
Republican	1 (4%)	21 (96%)	0

NOTE: Voting on the motion to require payment of the poll tax for election year and the preceding year.

21. The reports appear in Fla. Con. Con. *Journal* (1885), pp. 361–362; Democratic endorsement in *Florida Times-Union*, July 9, 21, 1885; the roll calls in Fla. Con. Con. *Journal* (1885), pp. 472–473, 510–513, 557–566, and in the debates in *Florida Times-Union*, July 30, August 2, 1885. Use of the appointment provision appears in Flynt, *Fletcher*, pp. 18–19; *Florida Times-Union*, March 24, 1889.

Jacksonville" (a white group), who protested against the tax in a memorial to the constitutional convention. The memorial claimed that the measure would hurt the "working classes," and tend to set up "aristocracy and despotism." Pointing to the shrunken political participation in Georgia, they attributed it to the operation of the poll tax, which limited voters to the "privileged class."[22]

The new constitution required poll tax prepayment for voting only when the legislature authorized it. In the 1887 session, a coalition of Republicans, Independents, and such white-county liberals as Stephen R. Mallory and Austen S. Mann defeated attempts in both houses to pass capitation tax bills introduced by Democrats from black-majority counties (table 4.7).[23]

The Democrats did, however, succeed in ramming through a registration bill over Republican protest on the last day of the session. Like the South Carolina law, the Florida annual registration act required the voter to present his registration certificate at the polls in order to vote.

Table 4.7. The Black Belt and the Poll Tax: Party, Proportion Negro, and the Poll Tax in the Florida Legislature of 1887.

Party and	Senate		House	
Racial Composition of County	For	Against	For	Against
Republican and Independent	1	8	1	19
Democrat, under 50% Negro	9	8	10	13
Democrat, black belt	4	0	12	4
Total	14	16	23	36

NOTE: Abstainers are omitted.

22. There were four significant roll calls on the poll tax. One was a motion to allow the legislature to impose any penalty (implicitly including disfranchisement) for nonpayment of taxes, which was so vague that it was withdrawn by its author the day after it passed. Another would have required payment of the poll tax two years in advance of the election. The other two suspended the tax as a suffrage prerequisite unless the legislature took positive action. See Fla. Con. Con. *Journal*, pp. 267–268, 509–510, 566. The motivation of deviant Democrats is exposed in Joseph B. Christie to *Florida Times-Union*, October 14, 1886; A. H. Curtin to ibid., July 12, 1885; editorial in ibid., July 22, 1885. Memorial appears in Fla Con. Con. *Journal* (1885), pp. 402–404; Williamson, "Era of the Democratic County Leader," p. 230.

23. Fla. *House Journal* (1887), pp. 72, 110–111, 133, 252–253, 459; *Senate Journal* (1887), pp. 88, 173, 676–680; *Florida Times-Union*, April 16, 18, May 8, 25, 27, 1887. Since Mallory held the conventional white supremacist opinions of a Southern Democrat, his staunch opposition to restrictive laws apparently stemmed from hostility to disfranchising any whites. See ibid., Sept. 13, 1890.

The Democrats also gerrymandered the legislature, transferring seats in both white and black areas where Republicans were strong to safely Democratic counties. These two actions and an apparent increase in frauds prepared the way for the disfranchisers' success in the next session. Before the 1888 election Democratic registrars, in what seems to have been a fairly concerted effort, refused to hold office hours on the designated days, unlawfully required blacks to produce white witnesses to prove their places of residence, refused outright to register Negroes, and registered Democrats fraudulently. On election day, ballots were rejected on the grounds, for instance, that an asterisk or a dash was printed on the ticket, that names were written in red ink, and that the ballot had "specks" on it. The chief federal election supervisor in Florida, Philip Walter, reported to the U.S. attorney-general that at least ten persons were denied registration in each of over 700 precincts and that "over 10,000 Republican votes were thrown out after they were cast." Such practices enabled the Democrats to gain control of the black belt, at least for one election. Grover Cleveland had carried only three of the ten Florida counties with Negro majorities in 1884; he took eight of them in 1888.[24]

These legal and extralegal actions reduced the opposition sufficiently to allow the Democrats to use their temporary top-heavy majorities to pass election laws, which, in effect, declared them rulers in perpetuity. Republicans and Independents had made up 31 percent of the 1887 legislature, but only 14 percent in 1889. In addition, several liberal Democrats and Independents, including Mann and Mallory, either lost their campaigns or chose not to stand for reelection. One indication of the power of the black belt in this legislature was the election of future Populist A. P. Baskin of Marion County (55 percent

24. On the registration act, see Fla. *Senate Journal* (1887), pp. 800, 901, 910–911, 923; Fla. *House Journal* (1887), pp. 919–922. The registration bill's provisions are given in Fla. *Acts* (1887), pp. 52–66. One white county Republican's amendment, disposed of without a record vote, would have added a little humor to the statute books: "Provided that when any person shall apply to the supervisor of election to be registered, it shall be the duty of the said supervisor to register him and also to brand him on the north part of his person with the initial letter of the party to which he belongs; if a Democrat, with the letter 'D'; if Republican, letter 'R'; if Mugwump, letter 'M', and if Knight of Labor, 'Let Her Up,'. . . ." Fla. *House Journal* (1887), pp. 910–911. On the gerrymandering, see Fla. *Senate Journal* (1887), p. 943. Walter's figures appear in *Goodrich* vs. *Bullock* (1889), summarized in Chester H. Rowell, compiler, *Digest of Contested Election Cases, 1789–1901*, pp. 464–466; *Memphis Daily Appeal*, February 13, 1890.

black) as head of the Democratic caucus. Another was the fact that Randall of Madison (61 percent black) and Turnbull of Jefferson (77 percent black) chaired the privileges and elections committees in the 1889 state Senate and the House, respectively, and black belt Democrats composed majorities of both committees. The state's leading newspaper, the *Florida Times-Union*, located in the Negro-majority county of Duval, spewed racist, antidemocratic editorials in a successful month-long campaign to replace Jacksonville's duly elected Republican government with one chosen by the governor and controlled by the Democrats.[25]

In this climate, the bills—all introduced by black belt Democrats—which provided for a more stringent registration procedure, payment of a poll tax as a prerequisite for voting, and an eight-box law met with little resistance. The poll tax law, which represented "the thoughtful deliberations of many weeks by the leading Democrats of the State," passed the House by 43–10 and the Senate by 15–7. Only five white-county Democrats in the House and four in the Senate, apparently fearing that the tax would discourage many white Democrats from voting, joined the Republicans in opposing the measure. The registration and eight-box law, written by William Milton, Jr., of Jackson (64 percent black), son of the antebellum Whig planter whom Andrew Johnson had appointed governor during Presidential Reconstruction, faced a slightly graver challenge. Despite Democratic caucus endorsement of the Milton bill, a move to strike the eight-box section in the House failed by only eight votes. The bill then passed the House by 43–15 and the Senate by 16–8. Every Democratic opponent of the bill on these votes represented a white county (table 4.8).[26]

Despite the fact that the "political war was being waged to the knife

25. For committee appointments, see *Florida Times-Union*, April 2, 1889; Fla. *Senate Journal* (1889), p. 45; Fla. *House Journal* (1889), p. 58. See editorials *Florida Times-Union*, April 3 to May 10, 1889, especially the issues of April 30 and May 10.

26. Poll tax bills were introduced by Theodore Randall and Hugh Patterson of Madison (61 percent black), Samuel Turnbull of Jefferson (77 percent), B. F. Walker of Leon (82 percent), W. C. Rives of Alachua (57 percent), and A. P. Baskin of Marion (55 percent). See Fla. *Senate Journal* (1889), p. 100; *House Journal* (1889), pp. 51, 61, 68, 419. Reports on the law occur in *Florida Times-Union*, April 30, 1889; Fla. *House Journal* (1889), pp. 589–590; *Senate Journal* (1889), p. 469. *Florida Times-Union*, May 19, 1889, indicates that fear of white disfranchisement determined the vote of the most important Democratic opponent of the poll tax in this legislature, Senate President J. P. Wall. On the registration and eight-box bills, see Fla. *House Journal* (1889), pp. 832–835, 995–996; *Senate Journal* (1889), p. 766.

Table 4.8. The Black Belt and the Eight-Box Section: Party, Proportion Negro, and the Eight-Box Section in the Florida House, 1889.

Party and Racial Composition of County	Position on Eight-Box Section		Total
	For	Against	
Republican or Independent White County	0	9	9
Democrat	18	14	32
Black Belt Democrat	13	0	13
Total	31	23	54

NOTE: Abstainers are omitted.

a whole year before the official campaign was opened," turnout in Florida in 1890 plunged below 50 percent for the first time in twenty years. Although the Republicans organized registration drives, disbursed money to pay poll taxes, and drilled their partisans on the new voting methods, the Democrats buried the GOP. The swollen Democratic majority, the *Times-Union* commented, was "due almost wholly to the operation of the new election law." While proclaiming that "the poll-tax pre-requisite was undoubtedly the greatest factor in the [R]epublican defeat in Florida," the *Times-Union* did not ignore the effect of the eight-box provision. In the black belt, "a large number of the Negroes could not read and placed their ballots in the first box they came to." Republicans charged that the election judges placed fresh Democratic ballots on the top of each election box (thereby eliminating the educational qualification for voters of the dominant party), but enforced the literacy test rigidly against Republicans. "The new election law," the *Times-Union* concluded, "is a God-send to the state, as it prevents ignorance from ruling and controling the destinies of the Land of Flowers."[27]

If the 1890 contest entombed the Republicans, the election of 1892 aborted the Populists. The captains of Florida Populism, former Democratic and Independent leaders Austen S. Mann, A. P. Baskin,

27. *Florida Times-Union*, Sept. 8, 9, 14, 20, October 6, 9, 11–12, 16, 18–19, 23, 28, 30–31, November 5, 6, 23, 1890; *Congressional Record*, 53rd Cong., 2 sess. (1894), pp. 1865–1866. Quotations are from the *Times-Union* issues of October 28 and November 5, 6, and 23.

and D. L. McKinnon, appear to have been as competent as any in the South. The Democrats canvassed actively in every county, delivered 1,600 speeches, and sent out 145,000 pieces of campaign literature. All this activity notwithstanding, overall turnout declined from 75 percent in 1888 to only 39 percent in 1892, and the Populist gubernatorial hopeful attracted less than a third as many voters as the Republican candidate had in the preceding governor's race (table 4.9). Negro turnout dipped to an estimated 11 percent, and despite Republican endorsement of the Populists—which had come in return for a Populist commitment to repeal "the infamous election law"—all Negro votes seem to have been cast, or at least counted, for the Democrats (table 4.10).[28] Substitution of the less openly revolutionary secret ballot for the notorious eight-box law in 1895 merely continued the practice of

Table 4.9. Populism Aborted: Effect of Election Laws in Florida on Turnout and Party Voting in Elections, 1880–1896.

Year	Republican and Independent	Populist	Democrat	Not Voting
1880	38	0	46	16
1884	37	0	42	21
1888	30	0	45	25
		Eight Box and Poll Tax		
1892	0	8	31	61
		Secret Ballot		
1896	7	4	22	67

Table 4.10. Black Suffrage Terminated: Effect of Election Laws in Florida on Estimated Turnout by Race in Gubernatorial Elections, 1880–1896.

Year	White	Negro
1880	96	71
1884	74	87
1888	86	62
1892	59[a]	11[a]
1896	57[a]	5[a]

[a]One deviant county deleted in making 1892 estimates, and three deviant counties deleted in making 1896 estimates. Ballot boxes were apparently stuffed in these black belt counties to inflate Democratic totals.

28. *Florida Times-Union*, October 2, 4–6, November 13, 1892.

eliminating illiterates under a new guise. The security of the black belt and the Democratic party had been purchased at the cost of abandoning popular government.

5

"The Magical Effects of The Dortch Law"

TENNESSEE: "GIVE US THE DORTCH BILL OR WE PERISH"

Tennessee's was the most consistently competitive political system in the South during the 1880s. Overall turnout levels in governors' races ranged from 63 percent to 78 percent. Estimated participation exceeded two out of three white voters in each election, while estimated Negro voting approached the same high levels in presidential years, but fell in the off-years. The Republicans polled more than 40 percent of the votes in each of the five gubernatorial contests from 1880 through 1888, winning the office when the Democrats split on the state debt issue in 1880 (see table 5.1A). Whereas the dominant party encountered little opposition for many congressional seats elsewhere in the South, Tennessee Democrats never garnered more than 54.3 percent of the total congressional votes during the decade. The Volunteer State's Republicans always took two or three of the ten districts, and managed to hold the official Democratic candidates to less than 60 percent of the votes in 34 of the 50 congressional races over the ten-year period (see table 5.1B).

Republicans drew their support from Negroes, from poor whites, especially in East Tennessee, and from those whites who stood to gain by the protective tariff and other positive governmental policies. In Middle and West Tennessee, where over 85 percent of the blacks lived, an estimated 48 percent of the Negro male adults voted Republican in the 1884 gubernatorial contest, while but 21 percent were counted for the Democrats. While it is difficult to determine directly the relation between wealth and voting behavior among whites for the 1880s, one can correlate economic and political variables after the vast majority of Negroes stopped voting in Tennessee. Republican support in the 1908 governor's race appears to represent the core of white GOP strength for the 1880s.[1] Assuming Negro wealth per male adult averaged $100,

1. This statement is based on an analysis of numerous graphs, several regression estimates

Table 5.1. Party Competition in Tennessee, 1880s.

A. GUBERNATORIAL ELECTIONS

	% of all Adult Males				Estimated % Turnout by Race[a]	
Election	Democrats	Republicans	Other	Not Voting	White	Negro
1880	23.9[b]/17.4[c]	31.5	1.1	26.1	68	92
1882	35.0	27.0	4.2	33.8	Not estimated	Not estimated
1884	36.8	34.9	0	28.3	72	67
1886	33.9	29.3	0	36.7	73	37
1888	40.4	35.8	1.8	22.0	84	62

B. CONGRESSIONAL ELECTIONS

	% of Congressional Vote for Democrats	Number of Congressional Districts in Which Democratic Percentage of Vote Was:		
Election		Less than 50%	50–60%	60%
1880	50.0	3	4	3
1882	51.3	2	4	4
1884	52.5	3	6	1
1886	54.3	2	5	3
1888	50.6	3	2	5

[a]All the estimates of voting behavior by race for the whole state are combinations, weighted by population, of separate linear regression estimates for East Tennessee, and for Middle and West Tennessee. For a fuller explanation of the procedures, see my "Ecological Regression" article.

[b]"State Credit Democrats."

[c]"Readjuster Democrats."

the differences in support for the major parties among whites is quite striking (see table 5.2A).[2] Whites in a typical poor county in which

---

of the way the 1884 white voters behaved in 1908, and reports in contemporary newspapers. I do not mean to claim here that lower-income whites voted for the GOP *because* they were poor, but only that poorer whites did, for whatever reason, end up disproportionately in the Republican camp.

2. One gets almost identical results for any value of Negro wealth between $50 and $200. Although Tennessee did not separate real and personal property assessments by race, several other Southern states in this period did. Analyses of data from the other states show that Negro wealth per male adult was remarkably stable from county to county, and that the average Negro adult male held between $100 and $150 worth of property in 1908. The formula for estimating white wealth is simply:

$$\frac{\text{total wealth} - (\$100) \times (\text{number of adult male Negroes})}{\text{number of adult male whites}}$$

For further details, see appendix A.

Table 5.2. Class, Section, and Race: Estimated Class, Sectional, and
Racial Composition of Political Parties in Tennessee, 1880–1884.

A. CLASS (WHITES ONLY)[a]

Party or Race	Pearsonian Correlation Coefficient	% Rise Per $1,000 Increase in Per Capita White Wealth
% Democratic	+.313	+11.4
% Republican	−.569	−23.2
% Negro	+.718	+24.8

B. SECTION[b]

	% of White Adult Males in Middle and West Tennessee				% of White Adult Males in East Tennessee			
Election	De-mocrat	Re-publican	Other	Not Voting	De-mocrat	Re-publican	Other	Not Voting
1880	49	11	3	37	30	49	0	21
1884	49	20	0	32	27	54	0	19

C. RACE

Election	% of Negro Adult Males			
1880	38	51	1	8
1884	25	42	0	33

[a]Correlation and regression statistics here are based on the percent of white adult males
voting for each party in the 1908 gubernatorial contest. The white wealth statistics are based
on the assumption that Negro wealth averaged $100 per adult male. For further discussion,
see appendix A.

[b]Estimates of voting from gubernatorial elections of 1880 and 1884.

wealth per white male adult averaged $400 gave the Republicans about
62 percent of their votes, leaving the Democrats only 38 percent. In an
affluent county with a per capita white wealth figure of $1400, the
whites could be expected to reverse those figures and provide the Democrats with a 65–35 margin. There were similar relationships between
white wealth and voting behavior within each section of the state. And
as table 5.2B shows, the GOP was much less attractive to Middle and
West Tennessee whites than to East Tennessee ex-Unionists who never
forgave the Democrats for leading Tennessee into the Confederacy.

In return for their support, black leaders during this period received
a good deal of recognition within the Republican party. In the legislative sessions from 1880 through 1886, black Republicans at various
times won seats from every Negro-majority county and from two

counties where the blacks made up less than 40 percent of the population. Though the number of offices they held was rarely if ever in proportion to Negro voting strength, blacks also often filled positions on county Republican tickets. Recognizing the political importance of their black constituency, white Republican leaders submerged the racism which they, as white Southerners, must have felt. In 1885, for instance, all 32 Republican state legislators voted for a black, Samuel Allen McElwee, for Speaker of the Tennessee House of Representatives. To nominate McElwee to such an important post not only directly challenged the shibboleth of Negro inferiority; it also presented the Democratic party with concrete evidence for their habitual cry that Republican rule meant Negro domination. Moreover, all three Tennessee Republican congressmen voted for the Lodge Elections Bill; the leading Republican newspaper openly favored integrated transportation facilities; and Republican legislators bitterly fought the convict leasing system and other racially discriminatory laws.[3]

If Republican strength forced Tennessee Democrats after 1880 to close ranks more tightly during election campaigns than elsewhere in the South and to rely more on caucus decisions during sessions of the legislature, the nature of the GOP constituency invited Democrats to restrict the suffrage when they got the chance. That chance came in 1889 when the Republicans, who had been able to filibuster a registration bill to death in the 1887 session, won only 35 seats in the 132-man state legislature.

The opportunity was hardly fortuitous. In 1886 and 1888 black belt Democrats employed some force and a great deal of fraud to overthrow their formerly potent Republican adversaries. When early returns from the November 1886 state elections showed a Democratic majority in Fayette County, more than two-thirds of whose residents were Negroes,

3. Robert Ewing Corlew, "The Negro in Tennessee, 1870–1900" (Ph.D. diss., Univ. of Alabama, 1954), pp. 165–178; *Memphis Daily Avalanche*, July 5, 1886, August 3, 1888. On McElwee, see Tenn. *House Journal* (1885), p. 7; and for biographical information, see William J. Simmons, *Men of Mark*, pp. 498–505. Editorials and news coverage in the *Knoxville Daily Journal*, March 13, April 12, 1889, November 14, 23, 24, 1896, indicate that newspaper's relative liberalism on racial questions; typifying the Democratic attitude in Tennessee was a speech by Congressman Josiah Patterson, reported in the *Memphis Daily Appeal*, November 5, 1890. See *Memphis Daily Avalanche*, March 21, 22, 30, 1889 for Republican efforts to destroy convict leasing. It must be noted that there were reasons other than antiracism for Republican opposition to leasing. Free miners, who seem to have had a large effect on public opinion, violently objected to having to compete with unpaid convicts for jobs in the mines.

a leading Democratic newspaper expressed "the greatest surprise." Republicans had carried that county in the August local elections by their "usual majority" of 1,500 out of a total voting population of about 5,700. The chief explanation for this startling upheaval, however, was not difficult to discover. Even Democratic newspapers noted that election officials from that party had refused to open the polls in one heavily Republican district and rejected the votes at another because of "irregularities," and these shenanigans no doubt represented only the most overt Democratic tricks. In another black belt county, Shelby, the Republicans charged that during the August local elections, Democrats forced blacks to leave the polls and neglected to count 3,000 votes which Negroes had managed to cast.[4]

The 1886 contests were mere rehearsals for 1888. As the *Memphis Daily Appeal* noted, GOP activity in the Tenth Congressional District, where almost half of the potential voters were black, typically declined in off-years but increased enough in presidential years to allow the Republicans to elect their candidate to Congress. Yet despite what the *Appeal* termed "an extraordinary effort" by the Republicans in 1888, the Democrats carried the district by nearly two to one.[5]

Republicans immediately charged the Democrats with massive frauds. "For the first time in the history of the state," intoned the *Knoxville Journal,* "fraud carried Tennessee for the [D]emocratic party." The contest in the Tenth was a "notorious highway robbery . . . one of the most flagrant outrages ever perpetuated [*sic*] upon the ballot-box in a free republic . . . a wholesale steal . . . an infamous election conspiracy . . . ." Federal election supervisors reported unmistakable frauds in at least three wards in Shelby county, two districts in Fayette County, and one in Haywood County. Republican allegations that Democratic majorities in some Memphis wards exceeded the total number of possible voters several times over elicited no specific denials from spokesmen for the victorious party. Democrats also kept down the Republican vote by issuing wholesale, dilatory challenges to Republican voters, by changing polling sites at the last minute, and, in Haywood, by calling out a local white militia, the Mason Guards, to "maintain order." What the Republicans lost at the polls they could not regain in

4. *Memphis Daily Appeal,* November 4, August 8, 1886; *Memphis Daily Avalanche,* August 6, November 5, 1886.

5. *Appeal,* October 24, 1888. The GOP carried the Tenth in 1880 and 1884.

the courts: federal judges dismissed a Shelby case on a technicality; the Republican congressional candidate finally abandoned his contest after more than a year of gathering evidence to overcome his opponent's reported 8,000-vote majority; and Negro witnesses failed to convince four all-white juries of the guilt of Fayette County election officers.[6]

Having vanquished their local opponents at least temporarily, the black belt Democratic leaders adjourned to Nashville to push legislation to insure their newly won positions against potential counterattacks at home and against the efforts of national Republicans to mandate fair election procedures throughout the nation. Democrats from Negro-majority counties controlled all but one of the legislative posts key to the passage of election legislation in 1889. House Speaker W. Lucas Clapp, a native of Mississippi and a graduate of Ole Miss, represented Shelby county. Senate Speaker Benjamin J. Lea, a farmer and Wake Forest graduate who had sat in the Tennessee secession legislature, resided in Haywood County. J. H. Dortch was chairman of the Senate privileges and elections committee. This 31-year old son of an antebellum planter-politician, a graduate of both Southwestern Presbyterian College in Clarksville and Vanderbilt Law School in Nashville, edited the local newspaper in Fayette County. As chairman of the Democratic county executive committee, he managed the political overthrow of the blacks in 1888. C. A. Stainback, son of another antebellum Fayette County planter, chaired the committee which considered the election bills in the House. The only important post which escaped the black belt, the chairmanship of the Democratic caucus, was held by Thomas O. Morris of Nashville. Negroes, who comprised 38 percent of that city's population, provided the bulk of

6. *Knoxville Journal*, November 21, 23, 1888. The *Journal's* November 21 statement indicates that the paper did not make charges of fraud lightly; this was by no means the first close statewide election of the decade. Democratic behavior is reported in *Memphis Daily Avalanche*, August 3, 4, 5, November 7, 18, 1888; *Memphis Daily Appeal*, December 8, 1888, July 20, 1890. When Haywood went Democratic in the 1888 local elections, it was, according to the *Avalanche*, the first time since the Civil War. In the 1886 state election, Haywood had been 2–1 Republican; in 1888, the count went 2–1 Democratic. For GOP attempts to recover their losses, see *Knoxville Journal*, December 8, 1888; *Memphis Daily Appeal*, December 21, 1888, March 27, 1889, February 9, 15, 1890; *Memphis Daily Avalanche*, February 15, 1890. Significantly, three prominent local Democrats volunteered to defend the accused Fayette officials: General J. J. Dupuy, Tenth District Congressman Josiah Patterson, and State House Speaker W. Lucas Clapp.

Republican votes in the tight party competition for control of the capital city.[7]

The election measures pushed by the Democrats fell into four categories. The first, the "Myers law," required voters in districts or towns which cast 500 or more votes in 1888 to register at least 20 days before every election. Written in Dortch's Senate committee, the bill passed both houses on strictly party votes; only two East Tennessee Democrats in the House crossed party lines to oppose the act. Likewise, party loyalty determined almost every vote on the "Lea law," which provided for two separate ballot boxes for federal and state elections in order to prevent federal supervisors from overseeing state elections in the event that the pending Lodge Elections Bill passed the U.S. Congress. Only five East Tennessee Democrats deserted their party on this issue.[8]

The secret ballot act, drafted and managed by Senator J. H. Dortch, was the third major proposal. The principal purposes of the Dortch law were to disfranchise Republicans, especially Negro Republicans, and, by eliminating the necessity for stuffing so many ballot boxes, to rob the GOP of a telling campaign issue. When a Republican newspaper charged that "Democrats do not hesitate to say that the Dortch bill is framed especially for the protection and preservation of the Democratic party," the Democratic *Memphis Daily Avalanche* responded by confirming the allegation: "The Democratic party represents nine-tenths of the intelligence and property of the state and a measure for its protection is therefore for the preservation of the best interests of the state. Certainly the Dortch bill is for the benefit of the Democratic party."[9] The *Avalanche* also touted the legislation as an answer to the "Negro Question":

7. A black belt newspaper discussed and endorsed the secret ballot in the month following the 1888 contest. See *Memphis Daily Appeal*, December 13, 1888. The *Memphis Daily Avalanche*, February 28, 1890, called on the state legislators to pass a law restricting the suffrage in order to counteract the threatened Lodge Elections Bill. Biographical details for the legislators are from *Nashville Daily American*, January 5, 7, 1889, and *Nashville Banner*, March 15, 1890. Nashville had twice sent black Republicans to the state legislature. See Corlew, "Negro in Tennessee," pp. 122, 165.

8. The vast majority of Tennessee's Negroes, who were more likely to reside in cities and towns than the whites, lived in the area covered by the Myers Act. See *Nashville Daily American*, March 9, 1889. The text of and roll calls on the Myers Act are in Tenn. *Acts* (1889), pp. 414–420; Tenn. *Senate Journal* (1889), p. 652; *House Journal* (1889), pp. 741–745. On the "Lea law," see Tenn. *Acts* (1889), pp. 437–438; Tenn. *Senate Journal* (1889), pp. 678–679; *House Journal* (1889), pp. 804–805.

9. Cf. Corlew, "Negro in Tennessee," p. 139. The standard history of the state views the

The first thing to be done is to cut off the great mass of innate ignorance from its baleful influence in our elections, and then we will be able to see further what can be done upon a more permanent basis. It is certain that many years will elapse before the bulk of the Negroes will reawaken to an interest in elections, if relegated to their proper sphere, the corn and cotton fields, by some election law which will adopt the principle of the Australian ballot . . . .[10]

The provisions of the bill as initially drafted confirm the *Avalanche's* view of the objects of the legislation. The secret ballot first applied to the 78 civil districts in 37 counties which contained nearly all the state's blacks, and any person who could have voted in 1857 (before Negro enfranchisement) was allowed assistance in marking his ticket. The majority party leadership thought, in addition, that the bill "will also stop the *cry* of fraud," as the chairman of the Shelby County Democratic executive committee put it. In other words, the Dortch law allowed Democrats to appear honest, but still retain the possibility of artificially inflating their totals if the need arose.[11]

Myers, Lea, Dortch, and poll tax laws as measures, "designed to preserve the purity of the ballot box, facilitate honest elections, and raise revenue for schools." See Stanley J. Folmsbee, Robert E. Corlew, and Enoch L. Mitchell, *History of Tennessee*, 2: 158; and similarly, Frank B. Williams, "Poll Tax As a Suffrage Requirement," pp. 130–133. Drafted by the chief defilers of the ballot box, the first three laws lacked effective enforcement mechanisms. Since poll tax payment, far from mandatory, was discouraged, that tax can hardly be considered a school revenue measure. Quotations are from *National Review*, n.d., quoted in *Memphis Daily Avalanche*, March 31, 1889, and *Avalanche* editorial following the quotation. The *Memphis Daily Appeal* headlined its April 3, 1889 edition "Safe at Last—Goodbye Republicanism, Good-bye—The Myers Registration and Dortch Election Bills Passed. . . ." Another Democratic newspaper, the *Nashville American*, stated on March 27, 1889, that "the Democratic party would be the chief beneficiary of this law." The politically independent *Nashville Banner*, April 3, 1889, decried the Dortch law as "a party and race discrimination." Similarly, see editorials in *Knoxville Journal*, April 9, 10, 1889.

10. *Avalanche*, March 27, 1889. Republican newspapers agreed that one of the Dortch bill's chief objects was to disfranchise blacks. See *Knoxville Negro World*, quoted in *Knoxville Daily Journal*, July 18, 1892, and *Knoxville Daily Journal*, July 24, 25, 1892.

11. *Nashville Daily American*, March 9, 13, 1889. Since the 1857 Massachusetts Constitution had proclaimed that henceforth new voters had to be literate, its 1888 secret ballot law contained a provision prohibiting election inspectors from aiding illiterates who had not been qualified to vote in 1857. Dortch lifted the section of the 1888 Massachusetts act whole into the Tennessee law to assist Southern defense of that statute in congress. The Dortch law as finally passed allowed no help at all to illiterates. Democratic chairman, quoted in *Memphis Daily Avalanche*, April 1, 1889, emphasis added. For a similar statement, see editorial, March 24, 1889. According to the *Knoxville Daily Journal*, July 27, 1892, the Dortch law "was passed for the simple reason that ballot-box stealing, fraudulent voting and corrupt counting had become dangerous" to the Democratic party.

Despite its partisan and racial purposes, the Dortch bill aroused a good deal of opposition among Democrats from overwhelmingly white counties. When Speaker Clapp first attempted to obtain Democratic caucus endorsement of the bill, the uproar was so great that the caucus had to be adjourned. Though opponents of the bill tried a filibuster at the next caucus, its proponents obtained a 22–11 endorsement. Even then, the bill's Senate backers, realizing that they could not produce the necessary 17 votes (24 of the 33 senators were Democrats), had to postpone consideration of the bill for five days. One newspaper correspondent remarked that the bill's course at this point "looked squally"; another characterized its condition as "precarious," its fate "very uncertain." The day before the third reading roll call in the Senate, the opposition counted at least 16 votes, and a visitor thought Dortch seemed "like a man who was getting ready to die game."[12]

Why did some white county Democrats oppose the bill? First, even though tailored to assist Democratic fortunes in the state as a whole, the bill, many believed, would disfranchise poorer, less literate whites of both parties, particularly in the predominantly white hill country. As we have already seen, Democrats usually polled over a third of the white votes even in the poorest counties, and they gained majorities in slightly wealthier ones. While its greatest strength among whites lay in the richest counties, the Democrats did compete with the GOP in less affluent regions. In these places, universal manhood suffrage, at least for whites, commanded strong support, and the threat of restriction gave the Republicans a potent campaign issue.[13] Consequently, some white-county Democratic legislators were less than enthusiastic about helping the party in the state, and especially about supporting their black belt compatriots, for they feared that supporting the Dortch law might cost them their own seats. The second reason for Democratic deviations was that no one could predict precisely what the impact of

12. The progress of the Dortch bill in the legislature may be followed in the March 13 to April 5 issues of the *Memphis Daily Appeal, Memphis Daily Avalanche, Nashville Daily American,* and *Nashville Banner.* Votes are taken from Tenn. *Senate Journal* (1889), pp. 707–708, and Tenn. *House Journal* (1889), p. 743. Caucus action and visitor's observations are reported in *Memphis Daily Appeal,* March 19, 1889; *Memphis Daily Avalanche* March 28, 29, April 4, 1889.

13. Recognizing the unpopularity of the new laws among many whites, the Republicans screamed denunciation of them in their 1890 platform. The Democrats apparently shared the opposition's appraisal of the election law issue, for they did not mention the measures in their own platform. See Charles A. Miller, *The Official and Political Manual of the State of Tennessee,* pp. 343–345. The Democrats, of course, made no move to repeal the obnoxious statutes.

the Dortch law would be on every group in the electorate. Men elected under the old laws hesitated to change the rules of the game. Thirdly, the spectre of Republican control in the black belt did not seem so horrible to upland Democrats as it did to those who would be more directly affected. If the parochial needs of black belt Democrats were to be fulfilled, the party's leaders would have to quiet the parochial apprehensions of white county Democrats.

Democratic leaders salvaged the bill by offering concessions to senators from their party who feared the disfranchisement of some of their white constituents, and, more important, by appealing to their partisanship. Afraid that without the Dortch law the state would "witness a sweeping Republican victory next year," the *Avalanche* issued "one final appeal to the Democrats of the Legislature. For the first time since the war we [i.e., legislators potentially favoring disfranchisement] have a majority of the General Assembly. Shall we utilize this, or fritter away a golden opportunity? . . . Ask anybody who is familiar with the politics of this county, and he will say give us the Dortch bill or we perish." To defeat it would "turn Shelby county bound hand and foot to the venality and corruption of Negro rule." Three Shelby Democratic leaders who rushed to Nashville at the last moment to lobby for the bill undoubtedly used the same argument to change the mind of a senator whose "nay" would have killed it. After Dortch, in a gesture to quiet the fears of rural white county Democrats, agreed to reduce the coverage of the bill to the state's four largest cities, he closed the debate fittingly by "urg[ing] especially that [his bill] was to the interest of the Democratic party." All five of the Democratic Senate opponents of the law represented counties containing few Negroes, four of which lay in East Tennessee. Every Republican, of course, also voted against the bill.[14]

Although less difficult, House passage of the Dortch law further emphasized the bill's partisan purposes. The secret ballot was railroaded through the House on the same day as the Myers law and an act gerrymandering the Third Congressional district in order to oust the Re-

14. *Memphis Daily Avalanche*, March 26, 30, April 1, 3, 4, 1889. Actually, the 1889 law applied to Chattanooga, Knoxville, and the entire counties of Davidson (Nashville) and Shelby (Memphis). In 1891, the secret ballot and registration laws were put into operation throughout all four counties. For the provisions of these laws, see Tenn. *Acts* (1889), pp. 364–371, 414–420; Tenn. *Acts* (1890), pp. 438–440. About one-third of the state's blacks, and nearly 20 percent of the total state population resided in these four counties.

publican incumbent. Democratic high-handedness provoked what one veteran correspondent called "the wildest scenes that were probably ever enacted in any Tennessee legislature."[15] Speaker Clapp refused to allow a recorded vote on amendments to the Dortch law, refused to record votes on the third reading passage of the Myers law, refused to read the Dortch act the third time (as the legislative rules required), and even refused to allow the Republicans to enter a protest against the passage of these laws in the *House Journal*. In response, the Republicans tried to prevent a roll call on the Dortch act by shouting, stamping, and beating on their desks. They also at first abstained from voting, hoping that the Democrats would be unable to maintain a quorum. Their efforts failed, despite the fact that 12 white county Democrats joined the 23 Republicans in recording their votes against Dortch's literacy test.

The fourth law, the poll or capitation tax, attracted much less attention in 1889–90 than the Dortch Act. In the 1889 session, Democrats were not so united on the capitation tax, for many critics thought it would disfranchise more white Democrats than Negro Republicans, even though it was aimed principally at the blacks. The chief poll tax bill considered during the 1889 session appears to have been a hybrid of measures introduced in the House by Pearson of Madison (48 percent Negro in 1890) and Callicott of Obion (only 16 percent black, but in the most heavily Negro, western section of the state). After the House judiciary committee reported the bill unfavorably, it failed to pass on third reading, 32–39. The *Memphis Daily Appeal* deeply regretted this defeat, for it believed the tax on voting would have eliminated from the electorate "criminals . . . the bummer class . . . strikers . . . heelers . . . [and] machine men." The Senate tabled a similar bill without a record vote. Except for one dissident member, every Republican recorded on the House vote opposed the bill. Democratic resistance generally varied with the proportion of Negroes in each county (table 5.3), but party sentiment had not yet coalesced. The Democratic caucus took no position on the measure at the time, and one of the party's most important leaders, Joel Fort of Robertson County, opposed the bill. The opposition cry that the bill oppressed the poor, white as well as black, infected even such conservatives as Stainback of Fayette.[16]

15. *Memphis Daily Appeal*, April 3, 1889.
16. Although the Tennessee Redeemer Convention of 1870 authorized the use of the poll

Table 5.3. The Party Whip Cracks: Increasing Democratic Cohesion on
Three Roll Calls on the Poll Tax in the 1889–1890 Tennessee House.

	March 11, 1889		*February 26, 1890*		*March 11, 1890*	
% *Negro*	*For*	*Against*	*For*	*Against*	*For*	*Against*
0–9	1	9	1	7	5	6
10–19	5	4	7	5	9	1
20–29	11	2	13	3	17	0
30–39	7	1	8	1	8	1
40–49	4	5	9	2	10	2
50–59	1	2	5	0	7	0
60–69	1	0	1	0	1	0
70–79	1	0	1	0	1	0
Total	31	23	45	18	58	10

NOTE: Abstainers are omitted.

In the extra session a year later, the Democrats, for reasons not clear from the available sources, solidified their position on the poll tax. H. l, a poll tax measure written by T. Bun Carson of Lauderdale (42 percent black), fell a single vote short of the number constitutionally necessary for passage in the House. A similar bill carried the Senate, where only three white county Democrats bucked the party whip. Despite virulent opposition from several hill-country Democrats opposed to denying poor men the franchise, the Democratic caucus endorsed the Senate poll tax bill five days after the defeat of the Carson measure.[17] As table 5.3 shows, rebellion among the Democrats was correlated with the percentage of Negroes in each delegate's county. As party pressure to support the poll tax increased, the number of dissenters dropped off, roughly in proportion to the "whiteness" of their counties.

The scene on the day of the final vote in the House was rather dramatic, since the Tennessee Republicans, reversing their national party's

tax to limit the electorate, a coalition of Republicans and followers of ex-President Andrew Johnson struck down the only serious effort to pass enabling legislation before 1889. See Tenn. Con. Con. *Journal* (1870), pp. 159–161, 174–181, 210–211, 397–398; Williams, "Poll Tax as a Suffrage Requirement," pp. 57–95; Philip M. Hamer, *Tennessee, A History, 1673–1932,* 2: 679–681. For 1889 session, see *Nashville Banner,* February 28, 1890; *Knoxville Daily Journal,* March 13, 1889. Quotation from *Memphis Daily Appeal,* March 12, 1889; roll calls in Tenn. *House Journal* (1889), pp. 363, 377, 472–474; Tenn. *Senate Journal* (1889), p. 485; opposition remarks in *Nashville Daily American,* February 28, March 12, 1889.

17. Tenn. *House Journal* (extra sess., 1890), pp. 26–27, 99–100; *Senate Journal* (1890), p. 66; *Nashville Banner,* March 4, 1890; *Memphis Daily Avalanche,* March 4, 1890.

tactic under the Reed rules in Congress, tried to subvert the business of the legislature by refusing to answer roll calls. Two of the House Democrats whose votes were necessary for a quorum on the poll tax bill had to answer from sickbeds in an adjacent committee room.[18] But the partisan effort finally succeeded.

And the new laws had the predicted effect, as newspaper reports of the returns from the first elections after the 1889–90 legislative session stressed. In a Shelby County district, one of several the Democrats carried for the first time since the Civil War, "the magical effects of the Dortch law was [sic] nowhere more strikingly manifested than in this precinct, once a Republican stronghold of formidable dimensions." In Hamilton County, the Democrats won the local elections "thanks to the righteous Dortch and registration laws." In Tipton County, "The poll tax requirement cut off nearly one-half of the Republican vote and consequently the Republican or People's ticket was beaten by more than two to one." "Owing to the new registration law a very light vote was cast [in Union City]. The greater portion of the Negroes refrained from voting on account of the poll tax law." From Jackson came the report, "The registration in the city and the poll tax law caused a light vote"; in Dyersburg, "The poll tax and registration laws have played havoc with the colored vote." "From all over Middle and West Tennessee," the *Avalanche* announced, "reports show that the Negro was practically disfranchised by the law compelling every voter to show his poll tax receipt before voting." "From a Democratic standpoint," the *Appeal* found the Dortch law's effect "most admirable. The vote has been cut down wofully [sic] and wonderfully to be sure, but the ratio of Democratic majorities has been raised at least four-fold. . . . The enemy is completely annihilated." Furthermore, the Tennessee Populists charged that the poll tax disfranchised 50,000 voters, while the Republicans estimated that the new statutes cost them between thirty and forty thousand votes. "But for the Dortch law and the poll-tax law," asserted the *Knoxville Journal,* "Tennessee would be a [R]epublican state."[19]

A careful analysis of the election statistics confirms the impressions of contemporary observers (see figure 5.1). In 1888, before the passage

18. *Nashville Banner*, March 10, 11, 1890.

19. *Memphis Daily Appeal*, August 8, November 5, 6, 1890; *Memphis Daily Avalanche*, August 8, November 4–8, 1890; Robert Saunders, "Southern Populists and the Negro, 1893–1895," pp. 242–243; *Knoxville Daily Journal*, Nov. 6, 9, 1892, Oct. 31, 1896.

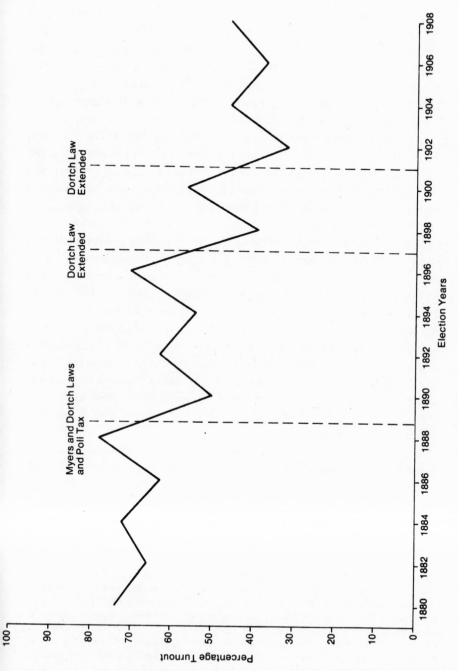

Figure 5.1. Effect of Election Law Changes on Turnout in Tennessee Gubernatorial Contests, 1880–1908.

of the registration, poll tax, and secret ballot laws, 78 percent of the adult males in Tennessee went to the polls. In the 1890 election, overall turnout crashed to a mere 50 percent. Apparently dispirited by the prospect of contending with the Democrats under the new, one-sided electoral laws, the Republican machines collapsed in 1890. The capture of the Democratic party by the Farmers' Alliance as well as the evaporation of the strength of the GOP seem to have disjointed the majority party's organization. Although presidential contests revivified both parties in 1892 and 1896, although the 1895 legislature eliminated the requirement that voters present their registration receipts at the polls, and although the Republicans benefited from the nationwide revulsion against the depression-ridden Cleveland administration, turnout in Tennessee never quite returned to its 1888 peak. Meticulous campaigning and huge contributions to funds for paying poor voters' poll taxes throughout the state, as well as alleged relaxation of the capitation tax requirement in several East Tennessee counties raised participation to only 70 percent in the furiously contested election of 1896. Before 1897, four counties containing 19 percent of the Tennessee population used the secret ballot. For the 1898 election, that literacy test was extended to towns and civil districts in 34 more counties. The disorganization and confusion which must have attended the concurrent use of the secret ballot in towns and the old party ballot in rural areas of the same counties probably further decreased turnout in 1898 and 1900. After 1901, the secret ballot applied in areas containing over 80 percent of Tennessee's populace.[20]

To demonstrate the tremendous impact of the secret ballot law, one need only compare voting patterns in the four urban counties with those in the state as a whole from 1880 to 1896 (figure 5.2). In presi-

20. *Knoxville Daily Journal,* August 4, November 8, 9, 1894, November 2, 1896. Republicans gained added strength by fusing with the Populists for many offices in 1894. Good coverage of the 1896 campaign appears in ibid., November 4, 6, 9, 16, 22, 24, 27, 1896. Newspaper reports of candidates and parties who paid poll taxes for their followers probably represent only the tip of a large iceberg. The *Journal* noted the following expenditures for poll taxes (which amounted to $2 per person): $4,000 by one candidate in Nashville, 1894; $4,000–$6,000 in Knoxville, 1894; $1,000 on election day alone in Knoxville, 1896; $10,000 by the Republicans in the Ninth (West Tennessee) Congressional District, 1896; and $5,600 by Republicans in Fayette County, 1896. The spread of the secret ballot is treated by Arthur C. Ludington, in "American Ballot Laws, 1888–1910," in University of the State of New York, *Education Department Bulletin* (Albany, New York: State Education Dept., 1910), pp. 67–68. The proportional coverage figures were computed from statistics given in the *Thirteenth Census of the U.S., 1910* (Washington, D.C.: G.P.O., 1913), *Population,* vol. 3, pp. 724–735.

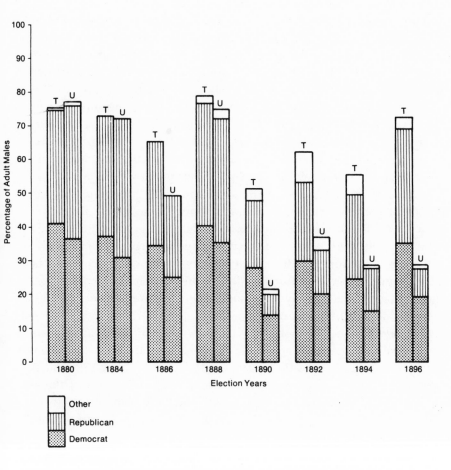

Figure 5.2. Impact of the Secret Ballot: Overall Voting Patterns in Tennessee Contrasted to Urban Counties Where Dortch Law Applied after 1888.

dential years during the 1880s, turnouts in the cities and the state as a whole were approximately equal. The Republican party carried the combined urban areas, but lost the state, in each of these three elections.[21] In 1890, when voting participation slid by about a third in the state as a whole, it plummeted by two-thirds in the counties covered by the secret ballot. City voting participation lagged 25–30 percent behind the statewide percentages in the elections from 1892 through 1896. Moreover, the GOP dropped far behind the Democrats in 1890 and 1892 in the cities, and only temporarily regained its strength in 1894 and 1896 as a result of the reaction against the party in power during the economic depression and of deals with Gold Democrats in 1896. Clearly, the secret ballot cut turnout substantially and hurt the Republicans disproportionately, especially in Nashville and Memphis, where the party of Lincoln had depended heavily on Negro votes.

A comparison of turnout in the 1900 and 1904 gubernatorial elections further strengthens this conclusion about the disfranchising power of the secret ballot. In the counties completely covered by the secret ballot in 1900, there was a 1 percent decline in turnout from 1900 to 1904. In the counties free from that literacy test in both elections, the decline was 2.6 percent. But the decline in participation in counties where the secret ballot's coverage was extended between 1900 and 1904 amounted to a full 13.3 percent.[22]

As figure 5.3 shows, moreover, the new election laws largely accomplished their racist aim. While participation among whites continued at high levels until the secret ballot's extension after 1896, black turnout declined dramatically in 1890 and remained very low thereafter. Those Negro votes recorded in 1892 and 1896 seem to have been counted almost entirely for the Democrats. Estimates of Negro turnout after 1896 are approximately zero.

21. Votes from both Democratic factions were combined for this figure to give a realistic idea of the party's strength in 1880.

22. Many of the counties in this third group were partially covered by the secret ballot in 1900. If we could separate the returns from the newly covered *precincts* from those where the secret ballot had been used before, the apparent effect of the secret ballot would probably seem even greater.

There does not appear to be any other ready explanation for the differences in turnout patterns in these three groups of counties. The only common characteristic of the counties in the third group is that they were more rural than those in the first, and less rural than those in the second group. Counties in all three groups were roughly evenly matched in the percentage of Negroes they contained, the section of the state they were in, and the average wealth of whites.

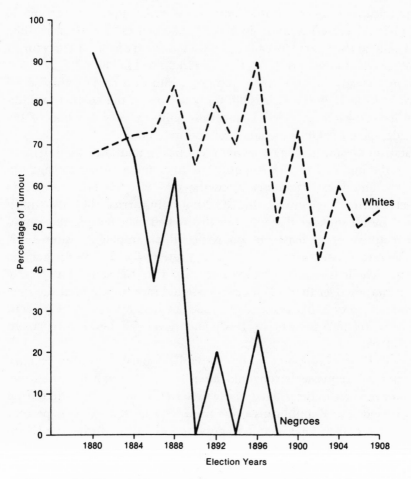

Figure 5.3. Differential Impact of Election Laws on Whites and Negroes in Tennessee: Estimated Turnout, by Race, in Gubernatorial Contests, 1880–1908.

The statutes also had a great impact, especially in the middle and western portions of the state, on the battle between the two chief political parties. Among those voting, the Democratic margin over the Republicans in gubernatorial contests was less than 15 percent in Middle and West Tennessee in 1884. It climbed to 21 percent in 1886 and 1888 at least partly because increases in fraud distorted the returns. After nearly doubling in 1890, the margin dipped in 1894 and 1896, for reasons already explained, but jumped again to a comfortable 30–46 percent from 1898 through 1906. Only the rise of the volatile prohibition issue, which exploded Democratic unity toward the end of the decade, gave the GOP a chance for the state house.

Statistics from the congressional races before and after 1888 demonstrate the inability of the Republicans to maintain their strength in Middle and West Tennessee once the new election laws went into effect. During the eighties, the GOP not only carried their two traditional East Tennessee districts, but threatened seats outside the mountain country or at least put on respectable campaigns. After 1888, Democratic congressional candidates rarely faced serious general election challenges except in the eastern part of the state. The Democratic margin over the GOP in congressional races throughout the state amounted to only 2.3 percent in 1888, but it jumped to 18.4 percent in 1890, to 26.2 percent in 1892, and never fell below 10 percent thereafter.

Other figures also point up the Republican party's growing reliance on its East Tennessee stronghold after 1888. Although less than one Tennessee voter in three lived in the eastern division of the state during this period, the Republicans drew from 39.5 percent to 43.4 percent of their votes from that section in gubernatorial races during the 1880s. From 1890 through 1908, a majority of GOP votes came from East Tennessee in most elections, and the figure never dropped below 47 percent. The election laws, then, fulfilled their chief proponents' purposes by largely demolishing the Republican organization in Middle and West Tennessee.[23] Only in the east, where the GOP had much

23. This is not to deny entirely the continued influence of violence and fraud in the process of subordinating the opposition after 1890 in Tennessee. An independent candidate for sheriff in Fayette County in 1896 was killed by a friend of the Democratic incumbent; Democratic militias continued to prevent Negro voting in close black belt elections; and election officials continued to concoct imaginary totals. See *Knoxville Daily Journal*, August 3, November 22, 27, 1896. But such methods were necessary after 1890 only when the Republicans made

greater influence over the election machinery, did active party opposition to the Democrats persist.

ARKANSAS: DISFRANCHISEMENT "IN THE INTERESTS OF THE DEMOCRATIC PARTY"

Arkansas Democrats in 1891 had withstood two successive assaults on their power. The Republican party there was stronger than in some Southern states in the 1880s, regularly polling a third of the votes in governors' races and about 40 percent in presidential contests. Militant farmers' organizations added to the Democratic party's difficulties. In 1885 the "Brothers of Freedom" and the "Agricultural Wheel" fused and the next year, after political pressure forced a prominent Democrat to decline the Wheel nomination, gathered 11 percent of the votes in the state race despite their ticket of unknowns. In 1888 the Wheelers, now organized as the Union Labor party, accepted Republican proffers of support and ran a fusion ticket which polled 46 percent of the officially totaled votes in a fraud-filled contest. The coalition elected two congressmen, one of whom was assassinated while gathering evidence for a congressional committee investigation of the contest for his seat. The fusionists fared worse in the gerrymandered legislature, winning only 26 of 95 seats in the House and 2 of 32 in the Senate. These minorities could be decisive, however, whenever the House Democrats divided on an issue. In 1890, the Union Labor-Republican ticket polled only 44 percent of the votes, their state legislative delegation dropped to 20, and all their congressional candidates lost. Nevertheless, the Democrats could not rest easy, for the news of the state treasurer's extensive defalcation followed closely the announcement of the 1890 results. This blight on the Democrats' vaunted honor handed the opposition a dangerous issue for the 1892 campaign. Moreover, by 1891 the stirrings of the Populist party shook Southern Democrats everywhere. Leaders of the dominant party in Arkansas must have been tempted to silence the opposition while the temporary lull lasted.[24]

---

frenetic efforts to overcome the voting barriers.

24. On the Wheel, Union Laborites, and the 1886–1890 campaigns, see Clifton Paisley, "The Political Wheelers and Arkansas's Election of 1888," pp. 3–21; and Francis Clay Elkins, "The Agricultural Wheel in Arkansas, 1882–1890." See the two contested congressional election cases in Rowell, *Digest of Contested Election Cases*, pp. 441–447, 468–470. The election results for the 1888 race appear in *Chicago Daily News Almanac for 1890* (Chicago: Chicago Daily News, 1890), p. 93; *The American Almanac for 1889* (New York and Washington,

They did not have to look far for the means to avert the threat to their party's supremacy. The overwhelmingly Democratic State Senate had passed both poll tax and secret ballot measures in 1889, the latter authored by James P. Clarke, the 1891 Senate Speaker. In the 1889 House, where the Republicans and Union Laborites were more numerous, neither these bills nor more moderate substitutes for them could be brought to a vote.[25]

But the 1891 legislators did not simply dig up the old bills and forward them for the governor's signature. At first, the House elections committee drew up a more moderate secret ballot law. From the floor, White of Nevada County (29 percent Negro), the elections committee chairman, offered amendments to the bill, one vesting in local party committees the power to nominate election judges, and the other permitting the listing of the party designation after each candidate's name. The first amendment would have gone far toward ensuring the selection of qualified election judges and a fair count, and the second would have made it easier for illiterates to vote, since they could easily be taught to recognize the name "Republican" or "Populist." This bill and the amendments, however, were dropped when eleven days later Ambrose H. Sevier, Jr., introduced a tougher bill, similar to the 1889 Clarke secret ballot act. Sevier's bill, which had been rushed through the Democratic caucus in one hour, left out the guarantee of fairness in choosing election judges and prohibited all party designations, though it did allow judges to help illiterates mark their ballots. The Democrats openly avowed the partisan purposes of the bill. A Democratic newspaper termed it "a partisan measure" which would prove "beneficial to the Democratic party," and Sevier recommended it as "conceived in the interests of the Democratic party." All efforts to amend the bill were brushed aside. Three white-county Democrats in the Senate and 10 in the House joined the Republicans, the Union Laborites, and the single black Democrat in opposing the measure.[26]

Clarke and Sevier, the authors of the 1889 and 1891 secret ballot acts, closely resembled the disfranchisers in other states. Clarke of

D.C.: The American News Co., 1889), p. 201; and those of the 1890 race in *Little Rock Arkansas Gazette*, Nov. 4, 1890.

25. Ark. *Senate Journal* (1889), pp. 365, 461, 501–502; Ark. *House Journal* (1889), pp. 806–807, 850–854, 922.

26. Ark. *House Journal* (1891), pp. 262–263, 407, 419–423; Ark. *Senate Journal* (1891), p. 334; *Arkansas Gazette*, Feb. 26–28, 1891; *Interstate News*, n.d., quoted in ibid., Jan. 18, 1891.

Phillips County (78 percent Negro in 1890) had been born in Mississippi in 1854. A graduate of the University of Virginia law school, he followed the prototypical career of a successful politician: law practice, member of the state house of representatives and the state senate, state attorney general, governor, and finally, U.S. senator, where he served as President Pro-Tempore. Described by the Pine Bluff newspaper as "the old [D]emocratic wheelhorse," he was "a firm believer that the Anglo-Saxon was the only race on earth fit to govern" and was given to urging his Democratic audience "to stand united and fight their old enemies [the Republicans] *to the death*" (my italics). Sevier of Lafayette County (58 percent Negro) was a member of a distinguished Arkansas family. His father was a plantation owner who served as the first congressman and one of the first two U.S. senators from Arkansas, and Sevier Jr. married the daughter of the other senator. After attending Georgetown University and attaining the rank of major in the C.S.A., A. H. Sevier, Jr., returned to Arkansas, entered business and the law, and became owner and publisher of the state's largest newspaper. Although often mentioned for higher office, he retired after his one legislative term, reemerging into politics only as the conservative Gold Democratic candidate for governor in 1896.[27]

After the partisan battle over the secret ballot, the poll tax bill came as something of an anticlimax. Passage of the bill authorizing a referendum on a poll tax amendment was interrelated with the issue of calling a constitutional convention. In 1888 the voters soundly defeated a referendum proposal to convene such a convention. At issue then was not disfranchisement, but a new usury law, a road law, and other innocuous propositions. Regression analysis shows that virtually all the Democrats and about 65 percent of the Republicans and Union Laborites who participated in the referendum opposed calling a convention in 1888. By 1891, however, with the example of the Mississippi disfranchising convention so close at hand, many Democrats changed their position on the issue. Accordingly, a bill authorizing a

27. John L. Ferguson, *Arkansas Governors and United States Senators*, pamphlet, p. 12; Myrill Cheney Murdock, *National Statuary in the Nation's Capitol* (Washington, D.C.: Monumental Press, Inc., 1955), pp. 16–17; Dallas T. Herndon, *Annals of Arkansas, 1947* (Little Rock, Ark.: The Historical Record Assn., 1947), pp. 225–226; *Pine Bluff* (Ark.) *Weekly Commercial*, Aug. 26, 1894. Details on Sevier are from Ferguson, *Arkansas Governors*, pp. 6, 17; *Little Rock Arkansas Democrat*, March 31, 1894; *Arkansas Gazette*, Feb. 27, 1908. I want to thank State Historian Ferguson for providing me with biographical details on Clarke and Sevier.

convention without calling a referendum on the issue passed the Senate, 14–12. Responding to criticism of the Senate bill, the House later passed a substitute which required a referendum. Only after the Senate refused to accede to the House bill did the legislature's attention turn from the convention issue to the poll tax. The poll tax was pushed through both houses in the session's last three days; the Senate did not even bother to record a vote on it. Eight white county Democrats and six Republicans and Union Laborites opposed the law in the House.[28]

Analysis of the poll tax referendum sharply challenges those who regard the Populists as chief culprits in the movements to limit the suffrage. The Democratic *Pine Bluff Commercial* neatly summed up the partisan and racist purposes of the poll tax by "most prayerfully" asking party members to vote for it on the grounds that "the most dangerous foe to [D]emocracy [the party] is the Negro." Conversely, both the Republicans and the Populists strongly condemned the secret ballot act and opposed the poll tax during the 1892 campaign. The Republican candidate denounced the secret ballot as "unjust" and the poll tax as a relic of "the middle ages." The Populists, whose gubernatorial candidate was the most outspoken opponent of the amendment, denounced the poll tax in their platform as a "partisan effort to strengthen a corrupt party in their hold on power by limiting the right of suffrage." Regression analysis of the referendum and the 1892 governor's race shows that Populist voters adhered to the platform (table 5.4).

Table 5.4. Who Voted for the Poll Tax in Arkansas, 1892?

	Position on Poll Tax		
	For	*Against*	*Not Voting*
Party[a]			
Populist	0	92	8
Republican	20	55	25
Democrat	62	21	19
Not Voting	4	0	96
Race			
White	27	31	43
Negro	32	0	68

[a]Party in 1892 governor's race.

28. *Arkansas Gazette*, March 15, 1889, Feb. 17, March 11, 1891. For evidence of Arkansas' awareness of the Mississippi disfranchising convention and the calls for Arkansas to follow her southern neighbor's example, see *Pine Bluff Weekly Commercial*, Aug. 24, 1890, Aug. 28,

The Republicans, by nearly a three-to-one margin, joined the men of the People's Party in opposing the tax on voting. As in the legislature, the great bulk of support for the measure came from the Democrats.[29]

Even more important, the results of this referendum underscore the importance of antecedent disfranchisement in the referenda on suffrage restriction, a theme which will receive more attention in the next chapter. In the off-year governor's race in 1890, an estimated 75 percent of the whites and 71 percent of the Negroes had turned out to vote. With the secret ballot in effect in 1892, however, only 58 percent of the whites and just a third of the Negroes were recorded in the poll tax referendum. As the *Arkansas Gazette* reported after the announcement of the results, "Many Negroes from pride failed to vote at all, and others scratched their tickets so badly that the judges had great trouble deciding for whom they intended to vote. . . . The [secret ballot] law demoralized the Negro." And in black belt Pine Bluff, the *Commercial*, exulting in the fact that the Democrats in 1892 overcame the normal three-to-one Republican majority to carry Jefferson county for the first time in 31 years, trumpeted that Sevier's was "A GREAT ELECTION LAW—It Works Like a Charm in the Cause of Intelligent Government." The Democrats had won "thanks to the Australian system."[30]

Figure 5.4 portrays the effect of the secret ballot graphically by comparing nonvoting in the governors' races of 1890 and 1892. In 1890, turnout in the predominantly white counties barely topped that in the black belt. Other graphs, not presented here, show that Republicans dominated all the heavily Negro counties except one. There was little variance in voting rates between counties, most achieving rates of 65 percent to 85 percent. In 1892, however, nonvoting rose throughout the

1892. After the passage of the secret ballot act but before defeat of the constitutional convention bill, the *Gazette* listed 13 important bills yet to be acted on by the legislature. The poll tax was not among them. *Arkansas Gazette*, March 8, 1891. Passage of the poll tax is detailed in the *Gazette*, April 4, 1891; Ark. *House Journal* (1891), p. 916.

29. *Pine Bluff Weekly Commercial*, July 17, 1892. It is clear from the context and from the *Commercial's* habit of referring to the Democratic party with a small "d" that this reference is, indeed, to the party. Similarly, see *Little Rock Arkansas Democrat* (n.d.). quoted in *ibid.*, Nov. 9, 1890. The Populists' and Republicans' response appears in *Pine Bluff Weekly Commercial*, Aug. 7, 1892; Ogden, *Poll Tax in the South*, pp. 16–17; James Harris Fain, "Political Disfranchisement of the Negro in Arkansas," p. 42.

30. *Arkansas Gazette*, Sept. 7, 1892, quoted in Graves, "Arkansas Negro and Segregation," p. 95; *Pine Bluff Weekly Commercial*, Sept. 11, Nov. 13, 1892. Republicans charged that the law's purpose was to give the Democratic party the power "to perpetuate itself forever in power. . ." (Oct. 9, 1892).

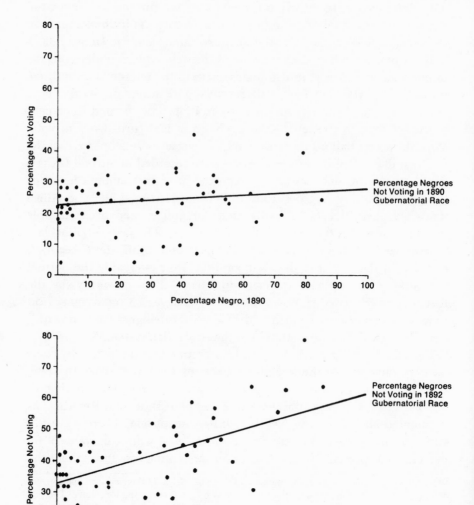

Figure 5.4. Secret Ballot and Disfranchisement of Negroes in Arkansas.

state, but especially in the black belt. The regression line shifts upward and tilts much more sharply from left to right (compare the 1892 regression line with that on the lower 1890 graph). Turnout in most white majority counties in 1892 ranged from 50 percent to 70 percent, a drop-off of about 15 points. Fewer than half of the electors cast ballots in most Negro majority counties. Most of the Negroes who did vote seem to have been recorded for the Democrats and for the poll tax, an indication of ballot box stuffing unless we can believe that the Negroes stupidly plotted to disfranchise themselves.

Thus, the process of suffrage restriction in Arkansas developed in three stages: the Democrats repulsed the opposition party challenge, rammed through a secret ballot law disfranchising many illiterates, and enacted a poll tax act as an extra shield against lower-class political activity. "The ignorant, uneducated whites and blacks cannot vote the ticket," announced the *Pine Bluff Commercial*. This "ought to be, and is a blessing to the state, for ignorance should never rule a great commonwealth like Arkansas."[31]

As tables 5.5 and 5.6 show, the secret ballot contracted voting by about 17 percent (21 percent among Negroes and 7 percent among whites). Then, the poll tax curtailed voter participation by an additional 10 percent (15 percent among Negroes, 9 percent to 12 percent among whites). Together, these two laws shrank opposition strength enough to ensure permanent Democratic hegemony. Little wonder that both the Populists and the Republicans attributed their losses in 1892 and 1894 to the secret ballot and poll tax laws.[32]

Table 5.5. Populism Avoided: Effect of Election Law Changes in Arkansas on Turnout and Party Voting in Gubernatorial Elections, 1888–1896.

Year	Republican	Democrat	Other	Not Voting
1888	0	41	35[a]	24
1890	0	41	34[a]	25
		Secret Ballot		
1892	13	33	12	42
		Poll Tax		
1894	9	27	9	55
1896	12	31	7	51

[a]Union Labor–Republican Fusion

31. *Pine Bluff Weekly Commercial*, Sept. 9, 1894.
32. Thomas, *Arkansas and Its People*, 1: 241–242, 248–252.

Table 5.6. Blacks Disfranchised: Effect of Election Law Changes in Arkansas
on Estimated Turnout, by Race, in Gubernatorial Elections, 1888–1896.

Year	White	Negro
1888	78	72
1890	75	71
1892	68	39
1894	56	24
1896	59	24

ALABAMA: DISFRANCHISEMENT TO "RESTORE THE DEMOCRATIC PARTY"

On the surface, the Alabama political scene in 1890 seemed calm. Grover Cleveland carried Alabama in 1884 by 5 to 3 and in 1888 by 2 to 1. The state's Republican party, seriously split throughout the decade into "lily white" and "black and tan" factions, lost the 1886 and 1888 gubernatorial races by 4 to 1 margins. No Negro had sat in the legislature since 1876. Such Negro leaders as William H. Councill and H. C. Binford advised the blacks to conciliate the Democrats or avoid politics altogether. The "Independent" movement among whites in northern Alabama had petered out after the death of its leader, William Manning Lowe.[33]

Those who looked closer, however, knew that Democratic supremacy was more fragile than it seemed. It depended on the inertia of three groups: disgruntled Democratic politicians, hill-country whites, and Negroes.

Though one word—"nigger"—sufficed to sum up the Alabama Democrats' strategy for neutralizing white opposition, the party's formula for controlling the blacks was more complex, blending widespread intimidation with minor favors and a great deal of fraud. Openly admitting—even boasting—that Negro votes were cast for the opposition but counted for the Democrats, leaders of the dominant party had ample reason to fear Republican and Populist pledges of "a free vote and a fair count."[34]

33. Joseph H. Taylor, "Populism and Disfranchisement in Alabama," *Journal of Negro History* 34 (1949): 413; Joseph Matt Brittain, "Negro Suffrage and Politics in Alabama," pp. 48–65, 120–124, 76–77; William H. Councill, speech at Tuscumbia, Alabama, 1881, quoted in Stone, *American Race Problem*, p. 279; Going, *Bourbon Democracy*, pp. 51–59.

34. Bond, *Negro Education in Alabama*, pp. 138–141; Moore, *History of Alabama and Her*

The organization of the "Jeffersonian Democratic" and Populist parties, who united on the gubernatorial candidacy of Reuben Kolb in 1892, posed a real threat to the Democrats.[35] Kolb, a watermelon farmer and former head of the state agriculture department, had used his Alliance contacts to become the leading candidate for governor in the 1890 Democratic convention. Defeated at that gathering by backroom bargaining engineered by the Louisville and Nashville railroad, Kolb tried for the nomination again in 1892. When it became clear he would fail once more in the convention, he dropped out of the race and accepted the nominations of the Populists and the "Jeffersonian Democrats," a front group set up to propitiate those hesitant to desert the Democratic banner. Kolb attracted Republicans, trade unionists, former Greenbackers, and the poorer whites in general. Pledging "protection of the colored race in their political rights" in their platform, the Jeffersonians also made a strong bid for black votes. Their alliance with the predominantly white Moseley faction of the Republicans, however, cost them the support of the state's leading black Republican, Bill Stevens, and the Democrats used all the traditional weapons to ensure that the Negro vote would end up in their column. According to William Rogers' close analysis of the election, "It seems certain, on the basis of available evidence, that Kolb was the legitimately elected governor but was counted out in the black belt" (p. 226). Even so, the Populists polled 48 percent of the votes.

What the Democratic *Birmingham Age-Herald* termed the "razzle dazzle" of the 1892 election count also gave the Kolbites a powerful issue for 1894. "Prior to this time," the chief Democratic organ of the state noted, "the practice of piling up fictitious majorities, of stuffing

---

*People,*1: 736; Rowell, *Contested Election Cases*, pp. 363–368, 394–395, 411, 424–426, 454–457; Going, *Bourbon Democracy in Alabama*, pp. 33–39; McMillan, *Constitutional Development*, pp. 220, 226, 284–285. For boasts of intimidation and fraud, see the statements of William C. Oates, quoted in Going, *Bourbon Democracy*, p. 39; Going, "Critical Months in Alabama Politics, 1895–1896," p. 279, and *Congressional Record*, 51st Cong., 1st sess., p. 6724; and the revelations during the constitutional convention, in Ala. Con. Con. *Proceedings* (1901), vol. 3, pp. 2771, 2780, 2786–2789, 2820, 2867, 2982, 3009, and especially a statement by Rogers of Lowndes County, p. 3062.

35. On the 1890 and 1892 elections, see Hackney, *Populism to Progressivism*, pp. 3–27; Charles Grayson Summersell, "The Alabama Governor's Race in 1892," pp. 5–35; Moore, *History of Alabama*, 1: 722 ff.; Brittain, "Negro Suffrage and Politics in Alabama" pp. 102–108; Rogers, *One-Gallused Rebellion*, pp. 165–235. Similarly see David Ashley Bagwell, "The 'Magical Process': The Sayre Election Law of 1893," *Alabama Review* 25 (April, 1972): 86–88.

ballot boxes, has made little or no impression on the public mind because it was exercised against the Negroes of a few counties and against
an opposition that was too weak to arrest attention." But in 1892 the
same methods had defeated a popular party, most of whose members
were native whites. Unless something was done, the Democrats could
not "escape destruction at the hands of the same opposition more ably
and wisely led, with a moral issue [fraud] to give them standing and
respect."[36]

As usual in such circumstances, the Democrats turned to suffrage
restriction to escape their difficulties. In 1889, several party chiefs met
at the black belt home of Judge Thomas Coleman to consider whether
to follow Mississippi's example by holding a disfranchising convention.
Many of the leaders feared that the problem of setting outwardly nonracial qualifications for the vote might split the Democrats. Despite
Governor Thomas Seay's public endorsement of the idea, a House-
passed bill providing for a convention died in the 1889 Senate. Instead
of adopting the Mississippi plan, the Alabama Democrats followed the
example of Tennessee.[37] Future "Progressive" Governor Joseph Forney
Johnston was the author of a plank in the 1892 state Democratic
platform which stated:

We favor the passage of such election laws as will better secure the government of the State in the hands of the intelligent and the virtuous [presum-
ably, all Democrats], and will enable every elector to cast his ballot secretly
and without fear of restraint.[38]

Democratic representatives from counties with heavy concentrations
of Negroes dominated the 1892–93 legislature. The President of the
Senate and the Speaker of the House both came from Dallas County
(84 percent black in 1890). The House Democratic caucus chairman

36. *Birmingham Age-Herald*, Dec. 11, 1892, Jan. 23, 1893.

37. Thomas H. Watts, quoted in *Memphis* (Tennessee) *Daily Appeal*, Dec. 11, 1888; Coleman
in Ala. Con. Con. *Proceedings* (1901), vol. 3, p. 3865; McMillan, *Constitutional Development*, pp.
249–250; Rogers, *One-Gallused Rebellion*, p. 237; Ala. *House Journal* (1888–89), p. 511; Ala.
Senate Journal (1888–89), pp. 659, 720; Ala. *Senate Journal* (1890–91), pp. 12, 31–34, 203; Ala.
House Journal (1890–91), pp. 51, 1035. The Lawson secret ballot act, which would have disfranchised all illiterates, failed in Alabama in 1889 despite endorsement from at least two of
the leading newspapers of the state. For its provisions, see *Memphis Daily Appeal*, Feb. 8, 1889.

38. The Democratic plank is quoted in Rogers, "Agrarianism in Alabama, 1865–1896"
(Ph.D. dissertation, Univ. of North Carolina, 1959), p. 366. The quotation does not appear
in the published version of this work. On Johnston's authorship of this plank, see Moore,
History of Alabama, 1: 744.

represented Lowndes County (86 percent Negro); his Senate counter-
part, Madison County (49 percent Negro). Districts with black majorities sent to the legislature 3 of the 5 members of the privileges and
elections committee in the Senate and 9 of the 13 members of that
committee in the House. The chief author and floor manager for the
secret ballot law was the chairman of the House privileges and elections committee, Anthony Dickinson Sayre, a prominent lawyer from
Montgomery County (74 percent Negro). Sober and grave, Sayre
was "a brilliant idealist," "a model of respectability and conservatism."
He had all the proper family connections for a conservative politician.
He was the son of a black belt newspaper editor, the nephew of U.S.
Senator John Tyler Morgan (D., Alabama), and the son-in-law of
U.S. Senator Simon Bolivar Bruckner (D., Kentucky), the rebel general
and vice-presidential candidate on the Gold Democratic ticket in
1896.[39]

Regardless of the Democrats' platform commitment to the secret
ballot, some prominent legislators and newspapers still favored writing
new suffrage requirements into the fundamental law.[40] House Speaker
Frank L. Pettus of Dallas County, grandson of an antebellum planter,
son of "the grandest of all [Alabama's] old war time and reconstruction
leaders," and close relative of two governors, proposed holding a constitutional convention specifically to consider an amendment that
limited the vote to those who were literate or owned $250 worth of
property or had served in the Civil War. His bill answered one common
criticism by apportioning convention seats so as to make a Populist
majority in the body virtually impossible. According to the *Mobile
Daily Register*, the chief argument its proponents made in private discussions of the bill was that it was necessary to settle the suffrage ques-

39. Malapportionment of the legislature limited the Populists and Republicans to 29 of the
101 House seats and perhaps 4 or 5 in the Senate. Committee appointments are recorded in
Ala. *Senate Journal* (1892–93), p. 76; Ala. *House Journal* (1892–93), p. 84; *Mobile Daily Register*,
Nov. 16, 1892. Biographical information is from Thomas M. Owen, *History of Alabama and
Dictionary of Alabama Biography*, 4 vols, (Chicago: S. J. Clarke Pub. Co., 1921), 4: 1507–1508;
Nancy Milford, *Zelda, A Biography*, pp. 17, 211. The quoted phrases are those of F. Scott
Fitzgerald, who was Sayre's son-in-law, and Nancy Milford.

40. Newspapers which favored a Mississippi-type disfranchising convention in Alabama
included the *Shelby Chronicle*, the *Evergreen Star*, the *Mobile Register*, the *Tuskaloosa Gazette*, the
Huntsville Argus, the *Anniston Hot Blast*, the *Eutaw Whig*, the *Selma Times*, the *Birmingham Age-
Herald*, and many others. See the *Age-Herald*, Dec. 24, 1892–Jan. 18, 1893 for their endorse-
ments.

tion then, while the Democrats were still in control of the government. "We doubt," the *Register* announced, "whether there is one more governor and one more legislature in the stuffed ballot box." The *Birmingham Age-Herald* added that, unless robbed of their chief argument—that fraud in the black belt had defeated Kolb—the Populists might well carry the state in 1894. "Every day but lends recuperative power to the now beaten or dissolved opposition. The Democratic party stands before the people as resting for its power on Negro votes, fair or false, and a constitutional convention presents an escape from the inevitable results of that" (i.e. defeat). Nonetheless, most delegates turned to the secret ballot, which, the *Register* noted, "might obviate the necessity for calling a convention," and the convention bill was decisively shelved.[41] The chief reasons for the convention's defeat appear to have been opposition from the Jeffersonians, an unwillingness on the part of some black belt Democrats to give up the practice of stuffing ballot boxes, and the South Alabama fear that the capitol might be moved from Montgomery.

The Sayre secret ballot act had the same partisan and racist purposes as the constitutional convention. "We do not think this is an issue of 'reform,' " intoned the *Age-Herald*. "It is, to be exact, a necessity to find some legal and honest way of preventing Negro control in the black counties, the present 'system' having produced evils that threaten the existence of the [Democratic] party and the safety of the State." Agreeing with the newspaper's interpretation, Sayre claimed (in a reporter's summary) that his bill "would restore the [D]emocratic party in Alabama. . . . It el[i]minates the Negro from politics, and in a perfectly legal way." Emerging from Sayre's committee, the bill met a hostile reception in the House committee of the whole, where it was amended to let most voters register up to the day of election, thus minimizing its disfranchising effect. Sayre's motion on February 13, 1893, to table the amendments made in the committee of the whole failed. And despite Sayre's stress on the argument that the bill would largely remove Negroes from politics, the measure went down to defeat on third reading, 40–46.[42]

41. *Mobile Daily Register*, Nov. 16, 17, 1892; Jan. 20–27, Feb. 4, 7, 1893; *Age-Herald*, Dec. 19, 1892, Jan. 21, 1893; Rogers, *One-Gallused Rebellion*, pp. 237–239. Pettus' father was reportedly the first to call for a disfranchising convention in Alabama. This fact and the description of him appeared in ibid., Jan. 29. 1893.

42. *Birmingham Age-Herald*, Dec. 25, 1892, Feb. 14, 1893. For a different interpretation of

The compromise which made House passage possible involved help to illiterates in order "to satisfy the white counties." After the House resurrected the bill by a 49–44 vote on February 15, Sayre failed to prevail upon the body to table an amendment allowing the voter to bring in a friend to help him mark the ballot. He succeeded, however, in limiting such "friends" to justices of the peace and assistants appointed by the election officials. The bill, described by a leading newspaper correspondent as "a party measure," then passed the House, 50–46.[43]

In the Senate, the opposition, led by Populist Albert Taylor Goodwyn, tried to filibuster the bill to death. Goodwyn charged that the bill would disfranchise 60,000 Alabamians, including about 30,000 whites. In an action paralleling that of the national Republicans during the Lodge Elections Bill debate in the U.S. Senate, the Democrats introduced a cloture rule that allowed a simple majority to stop debate by calling the "previous question." After pushing through the rule while Goodwyn, according to the *Mobile Register*, was "off his guard," the Sayre bill's proponents quickly passed it by a 17–13 margin on the bill's only record vote in the Senate. The Senate President, Compton of Dallas County, facilitated the bill's progress by ruling Populist motions and amendments out of order.[44]

Since the Senate had amended the bill, the lower house had to concur before the measure could become law. The only important amendment added by the Senate prohibited justices of the peace from assisting voters unless they were designated "assistants" by the election officers. This kept Populist or Republican justices of the peace from aiding their parties' illiterates without the approval of the election officials, all of whom were Democrats. The Senate amendments were hammered through the House on the last day of the session.[45]

As finally passed, the Sayre law provided for biennial registration during May, over a month before the state, and five months before the

---

the bill's purposes, see Bagwell, "Sayre Election Law," pp. 95–104. The progress of the Sayre bill is covered in *Mobile Daily Register*, Jan. 22, Feb. 5, 14, 1893; *Birmingham Age-Herald*, Feb. 8, 9, 1893; Ala. *House Journal* (1892–93), pp. 911, 917–920.

43. Ala. *House Journal* (1892–93), pp. 928–930, 948–949; *Birmingham Age-Herald*, Feb. 16, 17, 1893.

44. *Mobile Daily Register, Birmingham Age-Herald*, Feb. 19, 1893; Ala. *Senate Journal* (1892–93), pp. 790–793.

45. Ala. *House Journal* (1892–93), pp. 1084–1088; *Mobile Daily Register*, Feb. 22, 1893.

national election. The voter had to bring his registration certificate
with him to the polling place. The governor directly appointed all
registrars. There was no guarantee of representation for Populists or
Republicans on registration or election boards. The publicly printed
office-block ballot contained no party names or initials. Candidates were
listed in alphabetical order, and the local printers could list the offices
themselves in any order they desired.[46]

The legislative lineup on the Sayre Act followed a pattern familiar to
the reader by now. Populists, Republicans, and those Democrats who
cooperated with the opposition during the legislative session (labeled
"Independent Democrats" in table 5.7), opposed the law, and Democrats from the black belt were somewhat more likely to favor it than
their white county compatriots.[47] Table 5.7 cross-classifies the February
15 roll call on the bill's third reading with each House member's party
affiliation and his constituency's racial makeup. Though the table is
not given here, division in the Senate followed similar lines. When the

Table 5.7. A Party Measure: Relation of Party and Racial Composition
to Voting on the Sayre Law in the Alabama House, 1893.

	For Sayre Law	*Against Sayre Law*	*Total*
Party			
Populist and			
Republican	0	28	28
Independent Democrat	0	10	10
Democrat	50	8	58
Total	50	46	96
% *Negro in*			
Representatives' County[a]			
Less than 50% Negro	26	5 (16%)	
More than 50% Negro	24	3 (11%)	

NOTE: Abstainers are omitted.

[a]Populists and Independent Democrats omitted.

46. Ala. *Acts* (1892–93), pp. 837–851.

47. "Independent Democrats" are those, classed as Democrats at the beginning of the
session, who voted for seating the Kolbite candidate in the contested election case from Con-
ecuh county. See *Birmingham Age-Herald* and *Mobile Daily Register*, Feb. 2, 1893, and *Age
Herald*, Feb. 28, 1893. The cleavage on the bill was unusually stable. For example, only three
House members who opposed the bill on third reading (Feb. 13) before the amendments
which liberalized voting arrangements for illiterates voted for the measure in its final form;
and none who favored the bill on Feb. 13 later switched sides.

two houses forwarded the bill to the conservative governor, Thomas G. Jones, he allegedly "pushed aside everything else and said: 'Let me sign that bill quickly, lest my hand or arm become paralyzed, because it forever wipes out the Kolbites, all the third partyites, and all the niggers.' "[48]

Election returns and estimates of voting by race show that the Democrats essentially fulfilled their goals. Tables 5.8 and 5.9 illustrate the rise and decline of the Populists in Alabama, and indicate the role that the

Table 5.8. Populist Threat Diminished: Effect of Sayre Law on Turnout and Party Voting in Alabama Gubernatorial Races, 1890–1896.

	Percentage of Adult Males				*% of Those Voting Republican or Populist*
Year	*Democrat*	*Republican*	*Populist*	*Not Voting*	
1890	43	13	0	43	24
1892	37	0	34	29	48
			Secret Ballot		
1894	31	0	23	46	43
1896	34	0	23	43	41

Table 5.9. Participation Declines: Effect of Sayre Law on Voting Patterns, by Race, in Alabama, 1890–1896.

Year	*Democrat*	*Republican*	*Populist*	*Not Voting*
	WHITES			
1890	34	13	0	51
1892	27	0	53	20
1894	22	0	45	33
1896	27	0	41	32
	NEGROES			
1890	59	12	0	30
1892	49	0	4	36
1894	44	0	−2[a]	58
1896	45	0	4	51

[a]For an explanation of estimates outside the 0–100% logical limits, see my "Ecological Regression" article.

48. *Birmingham Age-Herald*, July 20, 29, 1893. Since this story came from a Populist, it is somewhat suspect, but the fact that the *Age-Herald*, the leading Democratic newspaper, reported it and that neither Jones nor the *Age-Herald* denied it lends the story a good deal of credibility.

Sayre law, combined with the black belt frauds, played in ensuring Democratic victory. The Republicans attracted only about 13 percent of the potential electors in 1890. With the organization of the People's party, turnout jumped from 57 percent to 71 percent, and Kolb received nearly half of the recorded votes. From 1892 to 1894, the percentage of the total electorate supporting the Populists dropped by more than a third. The two-party balance shifted from a tight 52–48 to a fairly comfortable (for the Democrats) 57–43 margin. According to the statewide estimates, the Populists in 1894 lost 15 percent of their 1892 white supporters and virtually all their black ones.[49] The fact that the estimated black voting percentage dropped by 22 points from 1892 to 1894, and remained below 50 percent thereafter, shows that the Sayre law was administered to disfranchise Negroes—especially those hostile to the Democratic party—and not merely to facilitate fraud.

Apart from the change in election laws, there was no reason to expect the Populists to weaken in 1894. The governor's contest of that year rematched the 1892 contestants, and Kolb should have benefited from a reaction against the obvious 1892 frauds. The deepening depression should have hurt the party in power. Given this situation, it is logical to conclude that the Sayre law—which Kolb spent much of his 1894 campaign attacking—was largely responsible for the decline of the Populists and the decrease in Negro turnout after 1892.[50]

49. The estimates of black and white voting here are obviously tarnished by the notorious black belt fraud, which unreasonably lowers the estimates of white Democrats and Negro Populists. Estimates of black voting calculated by dividing the counties at 30 percent, 50 percent, and 70 percent Negro, respectively, show the Populists in 1892 garnering from four to six times the estimated Negro percentages in table 5.9. In 1894, the Populists seem to have won a third of the Negro votes in the white counties, but counters allowed them none in the areas over 50 percent black. For a corroborating contemporary analysis of black voting, see *Birmingham Age-Herald*, Aug. 9, 10, 1894.

50. On fraud in the 1894 election, see *Birmingham Age-Herald*, Aug. 8–10, 1894, and Bagwell, "Sayre Election Law," p. 101.

6

The Disfranchising Conventions: "Family Meetings of the Democratic Party"

In contrast with the legislative activities described in chapters 4 and 5, the disfranchising conventions held between 1890 and 1902 in Mississippi, South Carolina, Louisiana, Alabama, and Virginia are familiar to students of late nineteenth-century America. But the notoriety of these spectacles, the comparative wealth of easily available information on them, and the colorful personages who dominated some of the convocations have tended to obscure the fact that these assemblies were largely anticlimactic. By focusing on the conventions themselves, scholars have tended to slight the political battles that prepared the way for disfranchisement in each state and exaggerate the disagreements within the safely Democratic gatherings. The fact is that the suppression of dissenting groups and parties by legal and illegal means *preceded* the conventions. The contention over various disfranchisement plans has sometimes concealed the wide extent of the underlying consensus that existed among the delegates. On the other hand, the eclipse of the opposition was neither complete nor necessarily permanent at the time any of the conventions met, and both the collapse of the enemies of restriction and the consensus among its friends often predated the conventions by only a few months. To see the conventions and their accomplishments in proper perspective, therefore, we must shift the emphasis to the events which led up to them.

Mississippi: "Proper Patriotism"

The Mississippi Democrats faced threats from within and without in 1889–90.[1] Not only did the national Republicans push a federal

1. On the reasons for calling the convention and the Mississippi political situation at the time, see Kirwin, *Revolt of the Rednecks*, pp. 58–64; Wharton, *Negro in Mississippi*, pp. 207–211; James Sharbrough Ferguson, "Agrarianism in Mississippi, 1871–1900: A Study in Nonconformity" (Ph.D. diss., Univ. of North Carolina, 1952), pp. 443–482; Mabry, "Disfranchise-

fair elections bill, the state GOP in 1889 nominated a complete state ticket for the first time since 1875. Although extensive Democratic violence led to the Republican candidates' quick withdrawal, their nomination proved that the opposition was only dormant, not moribund.

The agitation for a constitutional convention originated in the counties where there were comparatively few Negroes. Led by Farmers' Alliance activist and future Populist gubernatorial candidate Frank Burkitt, many small farmers wanted a convention to repeal convict-leasing, reapportion the state legislature and the school funds, enact prohibition, provide for an elective judiciary, and regulate corporations. Burkitt's resolution for a convention passed the 1886 House, but died in the Senate.[2] A similar resolution in 1888 passed both houses, but was vetoed by Governor Robert Lowry. His veto message indicated that he feared that Alliance men might be able to write some of their reforms into the state constitution. Mississippi politics were peaceful, he went on:

Why disturb society under such circumstances and surroundings? Why agitate and convulse the country when quiet is so desirable and important for the public welfare? . . . It is important to the people that there should not be disturbance of elections and the disquieting issue of race questions and other exciting issues, for they know that their success and prosperity depends, not so much on constitutional laws, as on their own efforts and the blessings of Heaven.[3]

Apparently the Deity Himself sanctioned electoral chicanery.

But Lowry's passive conservatism gave way the next year to the activist conservatism of U.S. Senator James Z. George. Frightened by the Lodge Elections Bill, George realized that radical changes in the electorate were necessary to maintain the established party in power. In 1889, therefore, he campaigned throughout the state for a constitutional convention. His call for suffrage restriction converted many political leaders from the overwhelmingly black counties who had

---

ment of the Negro," pp. 104–123; McNeilly, "History of Measures," pp. 131–132; Frank Johnston, "The Public Services of Senator James Z. George," pp. 209–216.

2. Kirwin, *Revolt*, p. 60; Wharton, *Negro in Mississippi*, pp. 207–208. Burkitt's actions and comments during and after the convention, detailed below, make it exceedingly unlikely that his motive in calling for a convention was "to eliminate blacks from politics," as Jack Temple Kirby claimed in *Darkness at the Dawning*, p. 10.

3. Miss. *Senate Journal* (1888), pp. 146–149.

opposed a convention aimed at socioeconomic reforms or hesitated to replace the familiar methods of election control with legal ones. The ballot-box stuffers felt they could trust Senator George, chief organizer of the bloody 1875 overthrow of the Radicals, to discover a way of maintaining white Democratic supremacy without openly violating the U.S. Constitution. Although legislators from the counties with fewer Negroes had little immediate interest in disfranchising the blacks and balked at any action which would deny the vote to whites, many of them continued to favor a convention as the only means of instituting other changes. By refusing to discuss plans for suffrage qualification, George retained enough support for the convention from legislators from the hills and piney woods to pass a convention bill through the 1890 legislature.[4]

Table 6.1. Who Called the Constitutional Convention in Mississippi? Changes in Support for the Convention in Mississippi Legislature, 1888–1890.

% Negro in Member's District	For	Against	Total	For	Against	Total
	1888 HOUSE			1888 SENATE		
Less than 50%	34	4	38	7	1	8
	(89%)	(11%)	(100%)	(88%)	(12%)	(100%)
More than 50%	33	24	57	12	15	27
	(58%)	(42%)	(100%)	(44%)	(56%)	(100%)
Totals	67	28	95	19	16	35
	(70%)	(30%)	(100%)	(54%)	(46%)	(100%)
	1890 HOUSE			1890 SENATE		
Less than 50%	27	14	41	8	5	13
	(66%)	(34%)	(100%)	(62%)	(38%)	(100%)
More than 50%	39	26	65	16	9	25
	(60%)	(40%)	(100%)	(64%)	(36%)	(100%)
Totals	66	40	106	24	14	38
	(62%)	(38%)	(100%)	(63%)	(37%)	(100%)

NOTE: All the votes given in table 6.1 are on third readings of the constitutional convention bills, except the 1888 Senate vote, which was the attempt to override Governor Lowry's veto. This required a two-thirds majority, and the bill therefore failed to pass. Only Democrats are included. Abstainers omitted. Percentages in parentheses add up to 100% across rows.

4. Kirwin, *Revolt*, pp. 60–64; George, quoted in Mabry, "Disfranchisement of the Negro," p. 109; McNeilly, "History of the Measures," p. 132; Johnston, "Public Services of Senator George," pp. 213–216; and "Suffrage and Reconstruction in Mississippi," p. 209.

Table 6.1 demonstrates the changes from 1888 to 1890 in support for calling the constitutional convention. Nearly 90 percent of the delegates from predominantly white counties favored a convention in 1888, but only about 65 percent in 1890. A majority of black belt senators actually opposed the attempt to override Governor Lowry's veto in 1888, whereas by 1890 over 60 percent of the black belt senators and representatives favored the convention. Moreover, the vote on the bill shows how little support existed—or was necessary—for disfranchisement in Mississippi. Since the Mississippi constitution required a referendum neither on calling a convention nor on ratifying its results, all the proponents of disfranchisement needed to attain their ends were bare majorities in the legislature and the convention. They got only 62 percent of the Democratic legislators. And a mere 15 percent of the eligible voters bothered to turn out in the elections for delegates to the convention. No grass roots upsurge was responsible for disfranchisement in Mississippi. It was strictly a movement by the elite.[5]

The convention itself was composed of 130 Democrats and four men from other parties. Senator George's candidate, Solomon Salidin Calhoun, a wealthy lawyer and planter, won the presidency, and all accounts agree that George was the dominating figure in the convention.[6]

In the consideration of the suffrage article, the delegates split along white county–black belt lines. The Farmers' Alliance opposed any educational or property qualifications. Frank Burkitt, who eventually refused to sign the constitution, and John E. Gore, the convention's only Greenbacker, opposed disfranchising anyone, white or black. James L. Alcorn, a Republican governor of the state during Reconstruction, earnestly but unsuccessfully appealed to the convention to allow Negroes to control the lower house of the legislature and gradually reenter

5. For consideration of the bills, see Miss. *House Journal* (1888), pp. 109–113; Miss. *Senate Journal* (1888), pp. 91, 159–162; Miss. *House Journal* (1890), pp. 165, 211–218; Miss. *Senate Journal* (1890), pp. 165, 168, 172–175. The Senate was solidly Democratic in both sessions. Two of the nine lower house members classed as Republicans or Independents in 1888 favored the convention, six opposed, and one cast no vote. Five of the six Republicans in the 1890 House voted against the bill, and the other did not vote. The turnout for the election of convention delegates was computed from figures in Kirwin, *Revolt*, p. 65. For a similar analysis of the change in motives for calling the convention, see Ferguson, "Agrarianism in Mississippi," pp. 443–454, 461, which I encountered only after reaching the conclusions in this paragraph.
6. E.g., Kirwin, *Revolt*, pp. 65–70; Johnston, "Suffrage and Reconstruction," p. 222.

the entire political system. In Mississippi, as elsewhere in the South, political and racial unorthodoxy often went hand in hand.[7]

The contradiction between white county opposition to limitations on the electorate and black belt insistence that the qualifications be high enough to destroy Negro voting majorities in every county forced an elaborate series of compromises. The delegates apportioned the legislature so that the white counties had a majority in the House and the black belt in the Senate. They also set up an electoral college scheme that gave the gubernatorial candidate "electoral" votes for carrying each county proportional to the number of lower house seats assigned to the county. To win, a candidate had to have a majority in both the electoral college and in the popular vote, which would prevent the election of a governor supported chiefly by Negroes if the federal courts ruled the new constitution invalid. In the most important compromise, the delegates allowed illiterates to register if they could prove to the registrar's satisfaction that they understood the constitution. Although most delegates apparently expected that discriminatory administration would allow all white and few black illiterates to vote, the early history of the operation of the clause belied the predictions. As pointed out in chapter 2, only about 2,000 adult males, nearly half of them black, qualified under this clause in 1892. Other provisions of the suffrage article required residency for a year in the precinct and payment of a $2 poll tax annually for two years before the election, and allowed municipalities to set additional suffrage qualifications. The suffrage article as a whole passed by an 82–37 margin. Twenty-two of the thirty-four dissenters whose home counties were given (the others were at-large delegates) resided in areas under 50 percent Negro.[8]

7. Memorial to the convention by the Farmer's Alliance, printed in Miss. Con. Con. *Journal of the Proceedings* (1890), pp. 50–51. For Burkitt's exceedingly liberal views on the suffrage, see *New Orleans Daily Picayune*, Dec. 6, 1897, and Norman Pollack, *The Populist Mind*, p. 397. For Gore's opinion, see Kirwin, *Revolt*, p. 68; for Alcorn's, *Jacksonville Florida Times-Union*, Sept. 20, 1890, but cf. Alcorn's more orthodox racist views cited in Lillian A. Pereyra, *James Lusk Alcorn*, pp. 196–197. Burkitt also strongly opposed a move to segregate school taxes by race and appropriate only Negro taxes for Negro schools. See Miss. Con. Con. *Journal* (1890), p. 349.

8. On the compromises, see a statement of G. T. McGehee, a black belt member of the Franchise Committee, quoted in *Congressional Record*, 51st Cong., 2nd sess., pp. 734–735; Mc-Neilly, "History of the Measures," pp. 133–137; Alfred Holt Stone, "Address to the Jackson Lions Club, May 30, 1947," quoted in Frank B. Williams, "Poll Tax as a Suffrage Requirement," p. 175; Kirwin, *Revolt*, pp. 66–73; *Proceedings of a Reunion of the Surviving Members of the*

The new constitution not only prevented a resurgence of Negro opposition, it also aborted the Populist party (tables 6.2 and 6.3). Rural, poverty-stricken Mississippi should have welcomed a new party that sought to remedy many farmers' grievances. And with the Republican party clearly dead in Mississippi by 1892, the Populists had no competition for the votes of those disenchanted with the Democrats. Moreover, the knowledge that almost no Negroes were left in the electorate should have freed whites to split without fear of "Negro domination." Nonetheless, the Populists garnered but 4 percent of the adult males in 1892 and 6 percent in 1895. According to my estimates, less than a fifth of all adult white males, which equaled only a third of those who turned out to vote, backed the well-known and widely respected Populist Frank Burkitt for governor in 1895.[9] The constitution cut Negro turnout from about 30 percent in the 1888 presidential race to virtually nothing thereafter.

Such figures lend credence to a statement made in 1904 by Mississippi Congressman Eaton J. Bowers. According to the congressman, Mississippi had "disfranchised not only the ignorant and vicious black, but the ignorant and vicious white as well, and the electorate in Mississippi is now confined to those, and to those alone, who are qualified by intelligence and character for the proper and patriotic exercise of this great franchise."[10] Bowers no doubt believed only Democrats properly patriotic.

Table 6.2. An Innoculation against Populism: Effect of Election Law Changes on Turnout and Party Voting in Mississippi, 1888–1895.

Election	Percentage of Adult Males			
	Democrat	Republican	Populist	Not Voting
1888 Presidential	32.3	11.0	0.0	56.7
	1890 Constitution			
1892 Presidential	14.3	0.5	3.9	81.3
1895 Gubernatorial	15.1	0.0	5.6	79.3

Constitutional Convention of 1890, Held November 1, 1927 (Jackson, Mississippi: Premier Printing Co., 1928), pp. 55–56; Wharton, *Negro in Mississippi*, pp. 209–213. On the operation of the understanding clause, see Johnston, "Suffrage and Reconstruction," pp. 229–230; Kirwin, *Revolt*, p. 74. For the roll calls, see Miss. Con. Con. *Journal* (1890), pp. 229–239, 245–247.

9. On Mississippi Populism, see Kirwin, *Revolt*, pp. 93–102.

10. Quoted in Newby, *Jim Crow's Defense*, p. 151.

Table 6.3. Blacks Disfranchised: Effect of Election Law Changes on
Voting, by Race, in Mississippi, 1888–1895.

Election	Percentage of Adult Males			
Whites	Democrat	Republican	Populist	Not Voting
1888 Presidential	55	6	0	38
1892 Presidential	28	0	11	59
1895 Gubernatorial	35	0	19	45
Blacks				
1888 Presidential	14	15	0	71
1892 Presidential	2	0a	0	98
1895 Gubernatorial	0a	0a	0a	100a

aEstimates within 3% of the 0–100% logical limits have been set at 0% and 100%. For an explanation of the procedures involved, see my "Ecological Regression" article.

SOUTH CAROLINA: "PERPETUATING THE RULE OF THE DEMOCRATIC PARTY"

Although fraud, violence, and the 1882 election law had severely damaged the Republican party in South Carolina, by the end of the eighties the Democrats there could not rest too easily. As Governor John P. Richardson remarked in 1888, "We now have the rule of a minority of four hundred thousand [whites] over a majority of six hundred thousand [Negroes]. . . . The only thing which stands to-day between us and their rule is a flimsy statute—the Eight-Box Law—which depends for its effectiveness upon the unity of the white people."[11] That unity broke in the early nineties with the rise of Benjamin Ryan Tillman.

The split between Tillman and the Conservatives involved no fundamental matters of political principle. The "Conservative" and "Reform" platforms of 1892 could have been interchanged with few corrections or deletions. Tillman and Senator Matthew C. Butler endorsed the same parts of the Alliance's Ocala platform in their 1894 contest for the Senate, and Tillman was perhaps more vigorous than the aristocratic Butler in denouncing the Populist schemes for railroad nationalization and the subtreasury. As governor, Tillman authored no startling economic programs to raise up the lower or tear down the

11. *Charleston News and Courier*, July 31, 1888, as quoted in Thomas B. Reed, "The Federal Control of Elections," *North American Review* 150 (1890): 677. See similarly Ben Tillman's speech at the disfranchising convention, in S.C. Con. Con. *Journal* (1895), pp. 443–472.

upper strata. When he pushed through a bill strengthening the railroad commission, for example, he appointed to it conservative men who did the corporations no harm. A large farmer himself, Tillman brought into the government not roughhewn tenants or small landowners, but such men as his successor as governor, John Gary Evans, a well-dressed, Northern-educated son of a Confederate general. While his manner no doubt seemed radical and "populistic" to cultivated businessmen in Charleston or New York, Tillman's actions were solidly in the mainstream of contemporary Southern Democrats. He endorsed Grover Cleveland in 1892 and Alton Parker in 1904, assailed the more substantive economic changes proposed by the Populists as "socialistic," and denounced any attempt to set up a party opposed to his own in South Carolina as a conspiracy to turn the state over to the blacks. Genteel Carolinians were put off not so much by his programs as by his manners and his willingness to discard the older, honored political leaders. He retired war heroes Wade Hampton and Matt Butler from the Senate, irresponsibly charged honest state legislators with taking bribes, and uttered curse words on public platforms to please rowdy audiences.[12]

Nonetheless, he rekindled opposition to the Democrats. Conservatives revolted against his rhetoric, less wealthy whites against the timidity and irrelevance of his economic programs, unsuccessful politicians against his failure to back them for office, and Negroes against his virulent racism. The Republican state committee joined a few conservatives behind the independent candidacy of Alexander C. Haskell for governor in 1890. Notorious among the blacks for his racist activities as state Democratic chairman during the 1876 Red Shirt campaign, Haskell offered Negroes neither patronage nor specific policy commitments. Nor did he tender economic proposals to attract lower strata whites. In addition, the *Charleston News and Courier*, Wade Hampton, and most other Democratic officeholders loyally backed Tillman as the party nominee. Haskell, the first man to contest a South Carolina governor's race since 1882, was lucky to get a sixth of the votes. Two years later, Tillman scotched a proposed coalition between the conservatives and the Farmers' Alliance by investing in the state Alliance

12. Wallace, *History of South Carolina*, 3: 351–353, 363–364; Cooper, *Conservative Regime*, pp. 17–20, 156–157, 203, 208–213; Simkins, *Tillman*, pp. 161, 166–167, 189, 198, 204–206, 209–214, 218–220, 265–267, 274.

newspaper and having the state Democratic convention endorse the subtreasury plan, a plan which he opposed before and after the convention. In 1894, Tillmanite John Gary Evans faced a surprisingly strong challenge in the governor's race from a former follower of Tillman who ran as an independent. Lacking either newspaper support or any semblance of a campaign organization, Samson Pope did strongly appeal to Negroes by defending, in court, their right to register and vote freely. He gained about 30 percent of the ballots in that contest. After his defeat, Pope called for a conference of white and Negro Republicans and anti-Tillmanites to meet in early 1896 to prepare for that year's race for governor.[13]

To end the possibility of Democratic defeat by a coalition of Negroes and some disaffected white group, Tillman promoted a constitutional convention. Enabling legislation for a referendum on calling a convention failed to get the necessary two-thirds in the Conservative-dominated 1892 House, but passed in 1894. Along with the referendum bill, the Tillmanites passed a new registration law designed to prevent Negroes from surging back into the electorate to defeat the convention. The new system allowed those already registered—most of whom were whites—to vote, but set up virtually incomprehensible regulations for those previously unregistered. In addition, Tillman and Evans instructed local officials to refuse registration blanks to Negroes, and they removed uncompliant functionaries. Local officials did their duty in the classic Southern manner, failing to appear on designated registration days, intimidating those who tried to register, conducting their business in such a dilatory way as to leave hundreds waiting in line at the day's end. Only ten thousand Negroes managed to register, and, said a Republican complaint, "one hundred thousand, after unparalleled suffering and sacrifice, remain unregistered." Although a federal district judge ruled the registration law unconstitutional, the circuit court overturned the decision on the grounds that the courts lacked jurisdiction over such "political questions."[14] Nevertheless, the renewal of political interest among blacks and the extent to which Democrats went to discourage the Negroes' activity proved the necessity of sub-

13. Simkins, *Tillman*, pp. 162–168, 204–206, 280–281; Wallace, *History of South Carolina*, 3: 367; *Jacksonville Florida Times-Union*, Nov. 5, 1890; *Birmingham Age-Herald*, Nov. 7, 1894.

14. Rowell, *Contested Election Cases*, pp. 530–534, 541–546; Simkins, *Tillman*, pp. 175, 282, 289–291; Tindall, *South Carolina Negroes*, pp. 75–80.

stantial changes if the Democrats were to insure against future black uprisings.

The campaign on the referendum itself indicated the difficulty the Tillmanites might have in the future without suffrage restriction. The Democratic state executive committee appealed for a "yes" vote in the referendum on the grounds that only disfranchisement would prevent the blacks from holding the balance of power in the expected campaign between Democrats and independents in 1896. Many spokesmen for the poorer whites, especially Larry Gantt, an upcountry editor, theretofore a staunch Tillmanite, feared that any suffrage plan would eliminate large numbers of whites as well as blacks. Tillman himself confirmed these fears when he remarked that "a Constitutional Convention can deal with the suffrage question in a way to save the suffrage to *every white man who is worthy of a vote*, while at the same time reducing the Negro voters at least one-half, possibly more" (my italics). He left vague what standards of fitness he would apply, but his statement made clear that mere membership in the Caucasian race was not enough. Many Conservatives also opposed calling the convention, charging that the idea of Negro domination was merely a "bugaboo" to hide the Tillmanites' desire to write the state liquor dispensary and other "reforms" into the constitution.[15]

Amid widespread charges of fraud, the convention call barely passed, 31, 402 to 29, 523—a recorded turnout of less than a quarter of the potential electors. The *Charleston News and Courier*, which had opposed the convention, headlined its story on the election outcome "A Machine Election—White Men Cheat White Men in South Carolina." In preparation for a contested election case in the Second Congressional District, Republican leaders took down the names of their followers who tried unsuccessfully to register and vote. If the GOP figures were accurate, over 4,500 people were denied the right to vote

15. The Democratic fear is enunciated in a pamphlet on the referendum, quoted in *Charleston News and Courier*, October 10, 1894. Gantt's and similar views appear in *Yorkville* (South Carolina) *Enquirer*, quoted in *Charleston News and Courier*, October 2, 1894; W. W. Sellers to *News and Courier*, October 4, 1894; *Piedmont* (South Carolina) *Headlight*, quoted in *News and Courier*, October 13, 16, 1894; and summaries of newspaper opinions opposing the convention because of the fear of white disfranchisement given in *News and Courier*, October 29, Nov. 5, 1894. Tillman's pledge quoted in *Charleston News and Courier*, October 30, 1894. The Conservative opposition appears in *Charleston Sun*, quoted in George Brown Tindall, "The Campaign for the Disfranchisement of Negroes in South Carolina," *Journal of Southern History* 15 (1949): 226–227.

in that district alone, a margin large enough to have defeated the convention by nearly 3,000 votes.[16]

Regression analysis of the official returns also indicates fraudulent practices as well as the pattern of white opposition to the convention (table 6.4). In view of the fervent activity against the convention in the black communities, it is likely that the estimated 8 percent of the Negroes recorded for the convention were products of election officials' imaginations. The four contested election cases make it clear that the 17 percent turnout figure for Negroes resulted not from apathy, but from discriminatory operation of the registration law. The fact that only 38 percent of the whites turned out indicates that in South Carolina as elsewhere, the impetus for disfranchisement derived not from the masses, but from a fairly small elite.

Part B of table 6.4 shows that support and opposition for the convention cut across factional lines. The Conservatives who supported Sheppard in the white primary in 1892 opposed the convention 18 to 14, but two-thirds of them failed to vote at all. Nearly a third of those who supported Tillman in 1892 and voted in the referendum split with their leader, presumably because of opposition to white disfran-

Table 6.4. Tillman's Convention? Estimated Relations between Race, Party, Faction, and Voting in the Referendum on Calling a Constitutional Convention in South Carolina, 1894.

	1894 Referendum		
	% For Convention	% Against Convention	% Not Voting
Race			
White	21	17	62
Negro	8	10	83
Faction in 1892ᵃ			
Tillman	35	15	49
Sheppard (Conservative)	14	18	68
Not Voting	6	11	83
Party in 1894ᵇ			
Evans (Democrat)	72	13	15
Pope (Independent)	0	90	10
Not Voting	3	5	92

ᵃFaction in 1892 refelects the vote in the 1892 Democratic primary for governor.
ᵇParty in 1894 reflects the vote in the 1894 general election for governor.

16. Tindall, "Disfranchisement of Negroes in South Carolina," pp. 230–231.

chisement. In the 1894 governor's race, the Conservative faction, hesitant to bolt the Democratic party in support of a former Tillmanite, gave Samson Pope little backing.[17] Most of Pope's votes probably came from disgruntled Tillmanites and Negroes. In any case, to vote for Pope against the Democratic nominee signified disloyalty to the old party, and his followers no doubt found it easier to reject the party position in the referendum. Democratic loyalists stood by Evans and the convention. In sum, table 6.4 tends to confirm the theory that the election was carried only by fraud and spreads the blame for calling the convention to the Conservative, as well as the "Reform" faction.

Once the referendum was over, the lines between the two factions blurred even more. After all, leaders of both sides agreed that blacks did not deserve the vote. In the same speech in which he appealed for Negro support in 1890, for instance, the Conservative, Alexander Cleves Haskell, rather undiplomatically announced that he hoped for their future disfranchisement. Although a compact to divide the seats to the convention equally between the factions broke down, the contests for delegates proceeded equably enough in a special Democratic primary. In the convention itself, Tillman worked closely with the actual author of the suffrage plan, J. P. K. Bryan, a Charleston lawyer aligned with the Conservative faction. In fact, the leader of the opponents of the suffrage plan in the convention was U.S. Senator J. L. M. Irby, erstwhile Tillman crony and self-proclaimed "poor man's friend." Irby believed that the plan would disfranchise many white illiterates.[18]

The suffrage committee proposed to limit the vote to those who paid a poll tax six months before the election and who were literate or owned $300 worth of taxable property. Illiterates who applied before January 1, 1898, would be permanently registered if they could convince an

17. Ibid., pp. 222–223. According to my estimates, only one-third of those who voted for Sheppard (Conservative) in the 1892 primaries and voted in the 1894 general election supported Pope in that contest. Two-thirds of the Sheppardites, apparently unwilling to vote against the Democratic nominee, backed John Gary Evans. The Tillmanites of 1892 who voted in 1894 split three-to-one for Evans over Pope. Factional alignments between South Carolina Conservatives and Tillmanites were considerably weaker than contemporary Democratic-Populist splits in other states.

18. Haskell is quoted in Tindall, *South Carolina Negroes*, p. 52. Convention events are detailed in Simkins, *Tillman*, pp. 286–289, 293–297; S.C. Con. Con. *Journal* (1895), p. 468; Tindall, *South Carolina Negroes*, p. 85.

election official that they understood a section of the Constitution when read to them.[19]

Opposition to the Bryan-Tillman scheme encompassed both extremes on the question of white suffrage. Irby proposed to require every voter to explain sections of the Constitution read to him, thus bypassing the literacy and property tests altogether. The Senator obviously expected virtually all whites to be registered and all Negroes tidily excluded by administrative discrimination. Some of the extreme Conservatives joined Irby's effort to torpedo the suffrage committee's report because they believed it left too many whites enfranchised. McMahan of the Conservative stronghold of Richland County, for instance, wanted only large property-holders to vote. Expressing a philosophy seldom heard in America since the 1820s, McMahan stated that the right to vote was "a privilege to be bestowed by the State" only upon citizens who had a "vested interest" in it. "Book-education," he went on, "is no indication of judgment, of character, or of patriotism." The only true test was "property in land." But most Tillmanites and Conservatives apparently trusted their leaders, for they passed the suffrage plan with no important amendments.[20]

Former students of suffrage restriction in South Carolina have distorted its nature in several respects. Some concentrate almost entirely on the 1895 convention. But tables 4.3 and 4.4 showed that the 1882 registration and eight-box law caused larger percentage declines in Negro and Republican voting. It would be wrong, however, to conclude with George Tindall that "disfranchisement already had been substantially accomplished" by the nineties, and the 1894 registration law and the convention had only a "psychological impact." For the sudden, vigorous reawakening of the blacks in 1894, the crack in Tillman's ranks which Pope's surprising 1894 showing exposed, and the widely publicized plans for an 1896 coalition of Republicans and disgruntled Democrats all would have spelled trouble for the Tillman-

---

19. S.C. Con. Con. *Journal* (1895), pp. 297–299. The property qualification was higher than it appeared to be, since property was never assessed at 100 percent of its value. Actually, one had to own $1,500 to $3,000 worth of real property to qualify under that provision of the constitution. See David Duncan Wallace, *The South Carolina Constitution of 1895*, p. 34.

20. For Irby's proposition, see William Alexander Mabry, "Ben Tillman Disfranchised the Negro," *South Atlantic Quarterly* 37 (1938): 181. For McMahan, see S.C. Con. Con. *Journal* (1895), pp. 151–153. For the passage of the suffrage plan see ibid., pp. 423–427, 430–434, 438–443, 482–484, 516–518.

ites if they had not limited the electorate when they did. As Georgia Populist Tom Watson commented at the time, "The whole scheme of the [D]emocrats of South Carolina [i.e., the disfranchising convention] is to perpetuate the rule of their party." Finally, the South Carolina example should offer little comfort to those historians who believe that "the democratization of politics robbed the Negro of his democratic rights," and that Conservatives merely "acquiesced" in the black man's disfranchisement. McCrady's role in 1882, the support for the convention by an estimated 43 percent of the 1892 Sheppard supporters who voted in the 1894 referendum, the extensive cooperation between Conservatives and Tillmanites in the selection of delegates and the drafting and passage of the suffrage plan—all these facts show that the "aristocrats" must share the responsibility for suffrage restriction in South Carolina.[21]

LOUISIANA: ELIMINATING "THE FORCE OF BRUTE NUMBERS"

Most delegates to the Louisiana constitutional convention of 1879 resisted moves to limit the vote because they feared federal intervention. They therefore rejected clauses containing education or literacy tests by votes of 81–14 and 107–4. Apparently reasoning that it was a more subtle qualification, one less likely to invite Northern Republican wrath, a few black belt Democrats, however, advocated a poll tax prerequisite. Although backed by such important figures as future Congressman, Senator, and Governor Newton C. Blanchard of Caddo Parish (74 percent Negro in 1880), the capitation tax failed by votes of 83–34 and 59–43. In the most important roll call, the 32 Republicans and a few Greenback and independent delegates opposed the tax by a 31–1 margin, while white parish Democrats voted 32–13 against it, and black belt Democrats split evenly, 20–20. On a later attempt to insert the prerequisite in the suffrage article, majorities of both white and black parish Democrats favored the measure. It was defeated only by the virtually solid opposition of the Republicans and other anti-Democrats, led by the erudite, race-conscious Theophile T. Allain, a wealthy Negro sugar planter.[22]

21. Mabry, "Ben Tillman Disfranchised the Negro," concentrates too much on the convention. The Tindall quotation is from his *South Carolina Negroes,* pp. 88–89; Watson's, from *People's Party Paper,* Nov. 8, 1895, quoted in Woodward, *Tom Watson,* p. 371. The "conservative acquiescence" thesis appears in Stark, *Damned Upcountryman,* p. 29.

22. For Louisiana's fear of federal intervention, see Governor Murphy J. Foster, quoted

Failing to secure legal suffrage restriction, the Democrats turned to perfecting fraud. The brazenness with which the Louisianians fabricated returns still shocks one accustomed to tales of election chicanery in this period. For instance, Robert H. Snyder of Tensas Parish (93 percent Negro in 1890), a key leader in the machine faction of the Democrats and future lieutenant governor, told the Louisiana legislature in 1890, "We all admit that when it comes to our elections 'we suspend the law until the danger is passed.' " In 1896, the official newspaper organ of the Democratic party charged its opponents with the awful crime of desiring to "fasten indefinitely upon the people the Negro vote and [compel] it to be counted as cast." Likewise, the Democratic *Shreveport Evening Judge* declared that the Populists "even go so far as to say that they are in favor of voting the Negro honestly. . . . Think of this, Louisianians! Are you willing to go this far with them?" No wonder that William Pitt Kellogg, a Republican governor of the state during Reconstruction, believed that in late nineteenth-century Louisiana, "after the polls are closed the election really begins."[23]

Selected returns from the 1888 governor's race substantiate these statements. After losing renomination in the Democratic convention, Governor Samuel D. McEnery threatened to use his powers to insure a fair count in the general election. Shocked by such an ungentlemanly threat, Francis T. Nicholls, the former Redeemer governor who had been the candidate of the "best people" in the 1888 convention, promised to name McEnery to the state supreme court. This bribe succeeded, and McEnery stumped the state for his opponent, telling audiences, "It is time we shall say that the law shall be silent and uphold

---

in *New Orleans Daily Picayune*, Jan. 4, 1898; Congressman Charles J. Boatner, quoted ibid., Jan. 6, 1898; Judge Lawrason, quoted ibid., Feb. 15, 1898. For the proceedings on education and literacy tests, see La. Con. Con. *Journal* (1879), pp. 256, 309. For poll tax prerequisite, see Edwin Aubera Ford, "Louisiana Politics and the Constitutional Convention of 1898," p. 114. Philip D. Uzee, "Republican Politics in Louisiana," p. 62, says there were 97 Democrats, 2 Greenbackers, 3 Independents, and 32 Republicans in this convention. I could identify only 36 of the non-Democrats from votes recorded in the La. Con. Con. *Journal* (1879). The votes on the poll tax are given on pp. 258–259, 309. On Allain, see Simmons, *Men of Mark*, pp. 208–230.

23. Snyder, quoted in *Congressional Record*, 51st Cong., 2nd sess., p. 558; *Baton Rouge Daily Advocate*, June 11, 1896; *The Evening Judge*, Aug. 9, 1895, and Kellogg quotes are taken from William Ivy Hair, "Agrarian Protest in Lousiana, 1877–1900" (Ph.D. diss., Louisiana State Univ., 1962), pp. 95–96, 357. The *Evening Judge* statement is also given in the published version of Hair's dissertation, *Bourbonism*, p. 249.

our liberty at all hazards." The Republican threat to Democratic "liberty" was Henry Clay Warmouth, who, like Kellogg, had occupied the governor's chair during Reconstruction. The GOP ticket, which included a black man, James F. Patty, as secretary of state, as well as the widely known Warmouth, should have drawn almost unanimous Negro support. But as table 6.5 shows, Nicholls rolled up remarkable majorities in several black belt parishes. In a commendable show of patriotic fervor and attention to civic duty, 104 percent of the eligible voters of Madison Parish trooped to the polls and cast their tickets unanimously for Nicholls. Election officials in Tensas and Concordia Parishes atoned for allowing a few Warmouth votes by putting in 112 percent and 115 percent, respectively, for Nicholls. The same Democrats, a decade later, led what they called a crusade for ballot reform and purity in elections.[24]

Such methods carried Louisiana Democrats safely through the eighties. In 1890, the convention in next-door Mississippi attracted a good

Table 6.5. Democracy, Louisiana Style: Election Returns from
Selected Parishes, 1888 Gubernatorial Race.

Parish	% Negro	% of Estimated Adult Males[a]	
		Democrats[b]	Republicans
Concordia	85	115	4
Tensas	90	112	3
Madison	90	104	0
Bossier	78	98	2
East Carroll	90	87	9
Red River	68	77	4
Caddo	70	68	5
West Feliciana	81	67	12
East Feliciana	66	66	0

[a]Estimates of adult males in each county made by straight-line interpolations between population data in the 1880 and 1890 censuses.
[b]Only two candidates ran in this election.

24. For McEnery's statement, see Hair, *Bourbonism*, p. 140; Uzee, "Republican Politics," p. 83. On the election returns, an anonymous but knowledgeable correspondent wrote the *New Orleans Daily Picayune*, June 11, 1894, that the 1882 election law, under the provisions of which the 1888 election operated, "is confessedly an act in the interest of fraud and for the purpose of thwarting popular will and juggling with figures in the distribution of popular offices." Obviously a Democrat, he opposed changing the law on the grounds that even if Negroes were disfranchised, Republicans or Populists would probably carry four of Louisiana's six congressional districts.

deal of interest in New Orleans and Baton Rouge. "Everybody," said the *Picayune*, "will wait to see what Mississippi will do." But the struggle between proponents and opponents of the fantastically profitable Louisiana Lottery Company, the emergence of the Farmers' Union and the Populist party as political forces, and the defection of many wealthy subsidy-hunting sugar planters from the Democrats to the high-tariff Republicans threw Louisiana's politics into chaos. To call a convention in such times, the *Picayune* pointed out, might disturb "the existing order of things." Consequently, Louisiana Democrats turned to a simpler vehicle. The 1892 legislature set up a constitutional commission, composed entirely of Democrats, to recommend separate amendments at the 1894 legislative session. The commission proposed to limit the electorate to those who paid poll taxes and could read or owned $200 worth of assessed property.[25]

The commission's was but one of several remedies before the legislature in 1894. The New Orleans Ballot Reform League, a typical middleclass "Progressive" organization, favored an Australian ballot law both to end frauds and disfranchise illiterates, thereby depriving the New Orleans machine of some of its followers. The Australian system, the League told the legislature, "will at once eliminate from politics the great mass of black ignorance and incompetence. If it works well in Tennessee, Florida, and Mississippi, why not in Louisiana?"[26]

Another plan that illustrated the cooperation of disfranchisers across the South was written by E. H. Farrar, who had presented a similar scheme to the Mississippi Convention of 1890. This patently unconstitutional bill required mere registration for voting in predominantly white parishes. In parishes with black majorities, however, the voter had to be literate and also own property assessed at $500.[27]

25. *New Orleans Daily Picayune*, quoted in *Natchez* (Mississippi) *Daily Democrat*, February 4, 1890, quoted in Mabry, "Disfranchisement of the Negro," p. 113. On the chaotic political climate, see Berthold C. Alwes, "The History of the Louisiana State Lottery Co.," *Louisiana Historical Quarterly* 27 (1944): 964–1118; Hair, *Bourbonism*, pp. 201–223; Henry C. Dethloff, "The Alliance and the Lottery: Farmers Try for the Sweepstakes," *Louisiana History* 6 (1965): 141–159. The statement from *New Orleans Daily Picayune* appeared June 4, 1894; similarly, see *New Orleans Times-Democrat*, May 27, 1894, quoted in Ford, "Louisiana Politics," pp. 69–71. The Constitutional Commission's propositions are from *New Orleans Daily Picayune*, May 2, 17, 1894; Ford, "Louisiana Politics," pp. 34–39.

26. *New Orleans Daily Picayune*, May 11, 22, 1894; La. *Senate Journal* (1894), pp. 319–320.

27. *New Orleans Daily Picayune*, June 6, 1894. The bill was actually introduced in the legislature by C. C. Cordill of Tensas Parish (93 percent Negro in 1890).

These bills and others including poll tax, property test, and under-standing clause provisions encountered opposition from several sides. Legislators identified with the Populists, the Farmers' Union, and the New Orleans machine were against disfranchisement through the secret ballot or property qualifications. Representatives of the state machine fought any law that might encourage a fair count, because, as one of the machine leaders put it, "the very social, financial, and political existence of Louisiana depends upon the continued triumph of the Democracy." Many middle-class reformers, on the other hand, de-nounced fraud, but, in the words of the *Picayune*, favored an electorate restricted to "the men who own the land, who conduct the industries, who pay the taxes." "The ignorant and brutal classes," they believed, should be disqualified.[28]

Unable to agree on any real changes in election statutes, the Demo-crats passed a bill which differed very little from the infamous 1882 law. The conflict and confusion in the legislature ended only when Governor Murphy J. Foster proposed a constitutional amendment to be submitted to a referendum on the same day as the April 1896 state and local elec-tions. The amendment allowed literate or propertied voters to retain the franchise, but contained no poll tax, secret ballot, or understanding clauses. The joker in the bill was a provision that allowed the 1896 legislature to alter the qualifications by a two-thirds vote without sub-mitting its changes to a referendum. The proposition breezed through the Democratic caucus, the Senate, 27–0, and the House, 74–9. Five

28. Ibid., June 3, 9, 16, 17, 19, 1894. The Populist state platform of 1897 stated, "We favor the adoption of an Australian ballot system which will disfranchise no one, but shall effectually preserve the secrecy of the ballot." This declaration, said the state Democratic newspaper, signified that the Populist party had "come out flat footed as the advocate of Negro suffrage." *Baton Rouge Daily Advocate*, November 23, 1897. Henry C. Dethloff confuses Populist support for a secret ballot which would not disfranchise illiterates with Ballot League and Democratic support for the ballot as a literacy test, a grave error typical of his failure to discriminate between the very different motives and behavior of the several groups of "reformers" in Louisiana. See his "Populism and Reform in Louisiana" (Ph. D. diss., Univ. of Missouri, 1964), p. 306. Robert H. Snyder is the machine spokesman quoted in *New Orleans Daily Picayune*, June 29, 1894, p. 1, and see a similar justification by another proponent, Gates, on the same page. See also ibid., June 28, 1894. When the Farmers' Union leader in the legislature savagely attacked the 1894 election bill as an invitation to fraud, Democratic leaders Snyder and Lott again admitted its partisan purposes. Ibid., June 29, 30, July 3, 4, 1894. For "reformers," see La. *Senate Journal* (1894), pp. 339–343, 346–369; *New Orleans Daily Picayune*, June 20, 21, 23, 1894.

Farmer's Union members and the four blacks opposed the bill in the House. The Senate's only Populist did not vote on the bill.[29]

The year 1896 was easily the most critical in Louisiana political history between the end of Reconstruction and the rise of Huey Long. First, sugar planters, Populists, and the Warmouth faction of the regular Republican organization gingerly drew together into a coalition. After some maneuvering among themselves, these groups settled on John N. Pharr, a millionaire Republican sugar planter, to head the "Fusion" state ticket, which included four Populists and two other sugar planters. The combination of adequate campaign money, a comprehensive organization, and adherents with high social status made the Fusion movement formidable and outweighed the incongruity of the temporary association. Despite the fact that it did not formally endorse Pharr, the organization of a "Citizens' League," successor to numerous businessman-reform organizations in New Orleans, further split the Democrats.[30]

Believing the Fusionists, in the words of the *Baton Rouge Advocate*, "a grave menace to our civilization," the Democrats buried their factional differences by putting out a state ticket carefully balanced between the McEnery and Foster wings of the party. They also buried several Populists and Republicans, and intimidated many others. In six heavily Negro cotton parishes among the nine listed in table 6.5, the Democrat, Murphy J. Foster, received 15,976 votes to Pharr's 139.[31]

The gravity of the Fusion challenge and the general unpopularity of the suffrage amendment, with its clause allowing the legislature to set any qualifications it liked, led Democrats across the state to abandon the amendment during the campaign. For instance, when the New

29. The text of the 1894 law is given in La. *Acts* (1894), pp. 223–236. On the confusion and partisan conflict in the legislature, see *New Orleans Daily Picayune*, May 30, 31, June 2, 15, 1894, and La. *House Journal* (1894), pp. 187–209. For the votes, see *New Orleans Daily Picayune*, June 22, 1894; La. *Senate Journal* (1894), p. 367; La. *House Journal* (1894), p. 836.

30. Hair, *Bourbonism*, pp. 247–261; *Baton Rouge Daily Advocate*, Jan. 3–April 28, 1896; Philip D. Uzee, "The Republican Party in the Louisiana Election of 1896," pp. 332–344; Lucia E. Daniel, "The Louisiana People's Party," pp. 1099–1109; Ford, "Louisiana Politics," pp. 55–64; Jackson, *New Orleans in the Gilded Age*, pp. 30–50, 313–318; Dethloff, "Populism and Reform," pp. 241–320.

31. *Baton Rouge Daily Advocate*, Jan. 9, Feb. 4, 6, 7, 9, March 16, 1896; Hair, *Bourbonism*, pp. 257–264; Uzee, "Republican Party in the Louisiana Election of 1896," p. 341.

Orleans machine, apparently fearing disfranchisement of its poorer white followers, came out against the amendment, the Citizens' League, too, had to oppose it or alienate the lower classes. The Fusionists, of course, denounced the amendment. Pharr declared that the legislature passed it "avowedly for the purpose of maintaining the government in the hands of the Democratic party, and for that sole purpose." Hardy Brian, a prominent Populist, castigated it as "infamous, damnable and hell born . . . a stepping stone to perpetually place this government in the hands of the rich, depriving the poor of any rights except to eke out their lives in hovels." Fervid enemies and tepid friends swamped the amendment, 34,761 to 3,534.[32]

In spite of Governor Foster's 56–44 margin in the official count, the Democrats' difficulties continued. In an attempt to heal Democratic wounds and present a solid front against the expected Populist-Republican threat in 1896, Foster two years earlier had appointed Congressman Newton C. Blanchard, a McEnery supporter and archenemy of the Anti-Lottery League, to a vacant seat in the United States Senate. Blanchard, however, had alienated south Louisiana sugar planters by voting to end their subsidy. Many of the sugar planters who remained Democratic preferred Congressman Andrew Price, who favored reestablishing the subsidy, for the Senate in 1896. The rift between the Blanchard and Price supporters also involved the monetary system. Price backed the gold standard, while Blanchard endorsed free silver.[33]

The irreconcilable split between the followers of Blanchard and those of Price and the fact that only 72 of the 134 legislators were officially Democrats invited an opposition coalition. Thirty-one of the legislators were Populists or Republicans, and 31 listed themselves as Independents, Independent Democrats, or Citizens' Leaguers.[34] After five days of deadlock, the Populist-Republican caucus threw its support to

32. According to the *New Orleans Daily Picayune*, July 9, 1896, Richard Henry Lea, the chief organizer of the Citizens' League, was not chosen president of the League because he was a strong advocate of the suffrage amendment and also a strong Democratic partisan. On the referendum, see *Baton Rouge Daily Advocate*, Jan. 19, June 5, 1896; Ford, "Louisiana Politics," pp. 49–52; Daniel, "Louisiana People's Party," pp. 1100–1104; Hair, *Bourbonism*, pp. 234–237. For the Populist party platform's bitter denunciation of the amendment and disfranchisement, see Dethloff, "Populism and Reform," pp. 244–246.

33. Ford, "Louisiana Politics," p. 26; *New Orleans Daily Picayune*, May 27, 1896; *Baton Rouge Daily Advocate*, May 21, 1896.

34. The Citizens' Leaguers refused to enter the Democratic caucus from the beginning of

the Citizens' League candidate, a young New Orleans reformer named Walter Denegre. The count then stood: Denegre, 60; Blanchard, 45; Price, 13; Samuel D. McEnery, 9; and others, 6. The *Picayune* Commented that "the proximity of Mr. Denegre to an election has driven the Democrats to desperation." On the first ballot the next day, May 27, Denegre picked up 6 more votes, only one short of a majority of those present, and all observers thought another vote-count that day would surely elect him senator. To stave off defeat, the Senate's presiding officer, Lieutenant Governor Robert H. Snyder, high-handedly refused to entertain a motion for another ballot and declared the session adjourned.

In the next 24 hours, Governor Foster, Lieutenant Governor Snyder, former New Orleans Mayor John Fitzpatrick, and Democratic State Chairman Ernest Kruttschnitt labored intensely to save the party. In a final move to reconcile the party's old factional difficulties, the leaders persuaded all the other Democratic candidates to withdraw in favor of former Governor McEnery. On May 28, McEnery was elected by a 71–63 margin over Denegre. "Never in the history of the State, since [1876]," said the *Picayune*, "has the Democratic party been so near its overthrow."[35]

Denegre's election to the Senate might have profoundly changed the history of this legislative session and, consequently, of Louisiana. While it is not clear what the Populists and Republicans asked from the Citizens' Leaguers in return for supporting Denegre, their quid pro quo was probably a promise of opposition to disfranchising laws and backing for an unlimited constitutional convention not focused on disfranchisement. A victory in the senatorial contest might have solidified the anti-Democratic coalition. With Denegre's defeat, however, the alliance collapsed, the Citizens' Leaguers joined the Democratic caucus, and the legislature passed two laws that severely restricted the suffrage and provided for calling a constitutional convention.

The defeat of the suffrage amendment in April 1896 convinced many Democratic sachems of the necessity for calling a disfranchising con-

---

the legislative session until the Senate race was decided. *Baton Rouge Daily Advocate*, June 2, 1896.

35. *New Orleans Daily Picayune*, May 27–29, 1896; *Baton Rouge Daily Advocate*, May 21, 28–30, 1896. Foster later musically chaired Blanchard into a state supreme court seat. Dethloff, "Populism and Reform," p. 295.

vention. In early May, the Democratic state central committee put out a pamphlet in support of such a convention. In his inaugural address, Governor Foster added his voice to the chorus.

The aggregation of the mass of ignorance, vice and venality, without any proprietary interest in the State, real or personal [said the Governor in reference to those who had had the bad taste to vote against him], is a standing menace to good government, when thrown as a body into the scales of popular elections. The elimination of this force of brute numbers is, and must be, the paramount question on the solution of which the success of a *truly representative government* must turn (my italics).[36]

Before calling a convention, the State Committee pamphlet stated, the legislature must enact "a proper election law." The Democrats' official organ, the *Baton Rouge Advocate*, explained shortly after the April election why such a law was desirable:

It would be the sheerest folly to go into a constitutional convention without adopting some sort of law the practical effect of which would be to restrict the right of suffrage. The defeat of the suffrage amendment renders such a law absolutely necessary, and the new legislature should proceed to enact it at its first session . . . . If an election for delegates to a constitutional convention were called under our present unrestricted suffrage laws, the experience of the late campaign would be re-enacted, practically the same majority that was rolled up against the suffrage amendment would be given in favor of men who would promise not to interfere with the elective franchise, the result would be that the advocates of Negro domination would be in absolute control of the convention.[37]

To protect the party's interest against Populists and Republicans who favored a convention because they hoped to write socioeconomic reforms into the constitution, the Democratic caucus in the legislature set up a joint committee of fifteen members to consider all election and convention bills. Two-thirds of the committee's members came from predominantly Negro parishes. Most important was Dr. P. J. Trezevent of Caddo Parish (68 percent Negro in 1900), a druggist, contractor, legislative clerk for two decades, and the chief Democratic leader in the House. With advice from Governor Foster, Senator McEnery,

36. *Baton Rouge Daily Advocate*, May 6, 19, 1896.
37. *Baton Rouge Daily Advocate*, May 1, 1896. Similarly, see ibid., May 5, June 19, 1896; *Amite* (Louisiana) *Florida Parishes*, quoted in *New Orleans Daily Picayune*, June 1, 1896; *Picayune*, May 29, June 13, 1896; Ford, "Louisiana Politics," pp. 86–90.

and other party chiefs, Trezevant drafted a constitutional convention bill which prohibited the body from discussing six important topics. After a few minor changes in caucus, the Democrats rushed Trezevant's bill through the House without even printing it, thereby catching the Populists and Republicans off guard. Every Populist and Republican recorded, six Citizens' Leaguers, and eleven white parish Democrats opposed the bill in the legislature.[38]

The joint committee coupled the convention bill with an Australian ballot law designed, in the *Advocate*'s words, to "secure the control of the convention to the Democratic party." Protected by such a law, the paper went on, the Democrats could enter the contest for convention delegates "fully assured of victory from the very outset." The law was also necessary to protect the Democrats against defeat in the November 1896 election. For unless the electorate was restricted, the *Picayune* and an anonymous "power in the Democratic party" predicted, McKinley would carry the state.[39]

Based on a draft offered by the Ballot Reform and Citizens' Leagues, the secret ballot bill absolutely prohibited election officials from assisting illiterates. The spectacle of city "progressives" and former Fusionist sugar planters working closely with the Democratic machine against the Republicans and Populists on the Australian ballot question demonstrated the extent to which Pharr's and Denegre's defeats had broken down the anti-Democratic coalition. The celerity with which the upper-class elements of that defunct coalition turned on their erstwhile allies and voted to disfranchise them also underlines the complete opportunism with which they solicited Populist and Republican votes. The bill's origin and its failure to make any provision whatever for a fair count, moreover, reveals the New Orleans businessmen-reformers' claim to favor "honest elections" to be pure cant. In the final vote on the secret ballot bill, eight white parish Democrats, every recorded Populist and Republican, only three Citizens' Leaguers, and

38. *New Orleans Daily Picayune*, June 11, 18, 25, 26, July 21, 1896; La. *House Journal* (1896), pp. 415–417; La. *Senate Journal* (1896), pp. 295–297. Two Democrats from the black belt county of Ouachita opposed the bill on the grounds that it would given the Populists too strong an issue for 1898, and therefore hurt the Democrats. See Sholars' comments in ibid., pp. 295–297.

39. *Baton Rouge Daily Advocate*, June 18, 1896; *New Orleans Daily Picayune*, June 13, 15, 1896. Cf. the account of the Australian ballot as a "reform" and Governor Foster as a reluctant reformer in Dethloff, "Populism and Reform," pp. 293–301.

one lone black belt Democrat stood in opposition. The *Advocate* at first believed the bill would disfranchise 60–75 percent of the state's Republicans, but later changed the estimate to 90 percent.[40]

As additional insurance against Populist or Republican efforts to elect delegates to the constitutional convention, the Democrats passed a law proposed by J. D. Wilkinson of Red River Parish (65 percent Negro in 1900), requiring voters to register anew after January 1, 1897. A friend or registrar could write down an illiterate's exact words in answer to the form's often obscure questions, but could not explain a question or suggest a reply. Moreover, any two representatives of a political party or the registrars themselves could purge the voting lists, for any reason whatever, of any names they desired. The names of those purged from the lists were supposed to be published in a newspaper. Unless the purged elector filed a challenge against the deletion of his name within five days after the publication, he could not vote. All registration and election officials, of course, were Democrats. As on the other roll calls, virtually every Democrat favored the bill. The opponents included all the recorded Republicans and Populists, one Independent, three Citizens' Leaguers, and six Democrats from predominantly white parishes.[41]

The passage of these two election laws allowed the Democrats to escape the threat of an opposition breakthrough. With the Australian ballot in effect, opposition totals in November 1896 fell off nearly 75 percent from the April state election. Overall nonvoting more than doubled (table 6.6). To express the figures another way, 56 percent of those voting favored Foster in April, while 76 percent backed William Jennings Bryan in November. The registration act, which went into

40. *New Orleans Daily Picayune*, June 19, 1896, reported that an important Negro Republican politician, T. B. Stamps, circulated around the Louisiana House the preceding day, cornering Citizens' Leaguers and accusing them of duplicity in soliciting Negro support and then breaking their promises by backing the limited convention and secret ballot laws. The Citizens' Leaguers apparently offered no defense. The narrative of the bill's progress may be followed in *New Orleans Daily Picayune*, June 2, 15, 16, 19, 27, 30, 1896; *Baton Rouge Daily Advocate*, June 19, 23, 1896; La. *House Journal* (1896), pp. 468–471; La. *Senate Journal* (1896), pp. 325–326; La. *Acts* (1896), section 76, pp. 214–215; Uzee, "Republican Politics in Louisiana," pp. 162–163. The estimates of disfranchised Republicans appear in *Baton Rouge Daily Advocate*, July 1, 1896.

41. On the Wilkinson proposal, see *New Orleans Daily Picayune*, June 9, 12, 23, 24, 30, 1896. The voting is recorded in ibid., June 23, 1896; *Baton Rouge Daily Advocate*, June 26, 1896; La. *Senate Journal* (1896), p. 343; La. *House Journal* (1896), pp. 495–496.

Table 6.6. Pre-Convention Suffrage Restriction: Effect of Election Law
Changes on Registration and Voting in Louisiana, 1892–1900.

A. Registration

Year	% White Adult Males Registered	% Negro Adult Males Registered
January 1, 1896	96.3	93.0
January 1, 1897	103.2	95.6
New Registration Law		
January 1, 1898	46.6	9.5
Constitution		
January 1, 1902	58.9	2.9
January 1, 1904	52.5	1.1

B. Voting

| Election | Percentage of Adult Males | | | |
	Democratic	Republican	Populist	Not Voting
1892 Gubernatorial	47.5	15.1	3.2	34.2
1896 Gubernatorial	39.4	30.5 (*Fusion*)		30.1
Secret Ballot Law				
1896 Presidential	26.1	6.2	1.9	65.6
Registration Law and Constitution				
1900 Gubernatorial	18.5	3.6	1.5	76.4
1900 Presidential	16.5	4.4	0.0	79.1

effect after January 1, 1897, cut the white registration by more than
half and the Negro by 90 percent. The percentage of whites registered
actually climbed after the enactment of the new constitution. The
disfranchisement of almost all Negroes and many whites was, therefore, a fait accompli by the time of the constitutional convention, but
it was a fact accomplished by the passage of election laws intended to
restrict the vote.

The new laws also made short work of potential opponents of a
constitutional convention. In 1896, Louisianans turned down a suffrage amendment by 34,671 to 3,534. In the January 1898 referendum
on the question of calling a convention, the chief aim of which would be
to restrict the electorate, the voters proved themselves remarkably
fickle. Despite a joint regular Republican-Populist effort against the
convention, the question carried, 36,178 to 7,578. The effect of the

secret ballot on illiterates in this contest may be gleaned from the fact
that the four-foot long official ballot contained more than 100 names,
including 92, listed alphabetically, for the 36 delegate-at-large posts.
Each voter had three minutes to fill out his ballot. One justice of the
state supreme court failed to finish in the allotted time.[42]

Every faction of the Democratic party cooperated in the referendum
campaign. In New Orleans, the Citizens' League and the Choctaw
Club, as the reorganized machine was known, joined in the effort to
disfranchise (in the words of the League chairman) "the ignorant, the
vicious and the degraded classes." Old enemies Murphy J. Foster and
Samuel D. McEnery spoke from the same platform at proconvention
rallies. All but one of the delegates elected to the convention was a
Democrat. Ernest Kruttschnitt, president of the convention and
chairman of the Democratic state executive committee, did not exaggerate when he said in his opening address: "We have here none of the
clash of faction. We have here no political antagonism, and I am called
upon to preside over what is little more than a family meeting of the
Democratic party of the State of Louisiana."[43]

In a passage packed with the tender solicitude characteristic of the
Southern paternalistic tradition, Kruttschnitt, nephew of Confederate
Secretary of State Judah P. Benjamin, went on:

My fellow-delegates, let us not be misunderstood! Let us say to the large
class of the people of Louisiana who will be disfranchised under any of the
proposed limitations of the suffrage, that what we seek to do is undertaken
in a spirit, not of hostility to any particular men or set of men, but in the
belief that the State should see to the protection of the weaker classes;
should guard them against the machinations of those who would use them
only to further their own base ends; should see to it that they are not allowed
to harm themselves. We owe it to the ignorant, we owe it to the weak, to
protect them just as we would protect a little child and prevent it from
injuring itself with sharp-edged tools placed in its hands.

42. *New Orleans Daily Picayune*, December 5, 9, 11, 1897; Uzee, "Republican Politics in
Louisiana," p. 176; Ford, "Louisiana Politics," pp. 95–97; Hair, *Bourbonism*, p. 275. According to the machine Democratic *Opelousas Courier*, Jan. 15, 1898 cited in Dethloff, "Populism
and Reform," p. 329, the Populists in this election tried, but "were unable to rally opposition
to Negro disfranchisement."

43. *New Orleans Daily Picayune*, December 16, 18, 19, 1897, January 4, 1898; La. Con.
Con. *Journal* (1898), pp. 8, 9, 68, 374. The only Populist in the convention refused to sign
the new constitution. See Hair, *Bourbonism*, p. 275.

With equal gravity, he predicted that the convention would "establish the relations between the races upon an everlasting foundation of right and justice."[44]

The divisions in the convention itself were not very important. Quarrels over whether to adopt an obviously unconstitutional grandfather clause or a patently fraudulent understanding clause did not hide the fact that the vast majority of delegates wanted some kind of temporary escape mechanism for whites. Under the watchful eye of Governor Foster, who established a special office in New Orleans so that he could superintend the convention, the conventioneers also compromised on the poll tax issue. The actual qualifications finally agreed upon—literacy in the voter's tongue or ownership of $300 property, with a grandfather clause exemption for those whites who registered within the next four months, and payment of a poll tax after 1900—were less significant than the fact that the restrictions were permanent. Within the Democratic consensus, the chief critics of the new document were those who believed it enfranchised too many whites. Until the rise of Huey Long, at least, their fears proved unjustified.[45]

ALABAMA: "A SMALL VOTE AND A LARGE COUNT"

The question of calling a constitutional convention plagued Alabama throughout the nineties, for despite the fact that most Democrats desired to replace the Sayre law with a more permanent restriction of the suffrage, every faction and interest group feared that a convention might damage the group's present power. Efforts to qualify the electorate through amendments submitted to voters in referenda also aroused opposition. After persuading the 1899 legislature to repeal its call for a convention, Governor Joseph Forney Johnston tried to push a property-or-literacy qualification through the legislature. But his amendment fell short of the constitutionally required two-thirds in the legislature, as poll tax amendments had earlier in the decade. Although enabling acts for a convention passed the House in the 1896–97 session, and both houses in the 1898–99 session, it was not until the conservative faction

44. La. Con. Con. *Journal* (1898), p. 10.

45. Those who wish to untangle the minor squabbles in the convention should consult the La. Con. Con. *Journal* (1898); *New Orleans Daily Picayune*, February 8 to March 27, 1898; Ford, "Louisiana Politics"; George E. Cunningham, "The Italian, A Hindrance to White Solidarity in Louisiana, 1890–1898," *Journal of Negro History* 50 (1965): 22–36; and Mabry, "Disfranchisement of the Negro," pp. 218–257.

of the Democrats took firm control in 1900–01 that the convention was finally called.[46]

Unlike other states, Alabama instituted no law to restrict the suffrage immediately before calling its convention, and submitted the new constitution to the voters, instead of merely proclaiming it. The voting patterns in the two referenda on calling the convocation and ratifying the changes it proposed deserve close analysis.

As in other states, only a small minority of the population voted for disfranchisement. Turnout in the referenda amounted to 27.3 percent and 44.9 percent, respectively. Only 16.6 percent of the adult males voted in favor of calling the convention, and but 25.6 percent for ratifying the constitution.

Suffrage restriction attracted widespread support only in Alabama's black belt. As table 6.7 shows, only 52.4 percent of those from counties

Table 6.7. Black Belt Disfranchisers: Election Returns in the Constitutional Referenda in Alabama Counties, by Percentage Negro.

A. Groupings of Counties

County Group	% for Calling Convention	% for Ratification
All 66 Alabama counties	60.7	57.1
11 counties over 70% Negro	93.5	88.3
55 counties under 70% Negro	52.4	49.7
21 counties over 50% Negro	87.3	78.9
45 counties under 50% Negro	47.7	45.2

B. Selected Individual Counties

County	% Negro 1900	For Convention	Against Convention	For Ratification	Against Ratification
Dallas	80	5668	200	8125	235
Hale	80	2318	66	4698	95
Greene	84	1479	19	1077	101
Marengo	74	2197	241	1958	341
Perry	76	2295	43	3209	88
Sumter	79	1440	69	2930	168
Wilcox	78	1689	25	4652	178

46. For the uneasiness about what a convention might do, see McMillan, *Constitutional Development*, pp. 232–257; Hackney, *Populism to Progressivism*, pp. 147–174. On efforts to call a constitutional convention, see Ala. *Senate Journal* (1896–97), pp. 42–43, 73–74, 288–289, 1042–1044, 1195; Ala. *House Journal* (1896–97), pp. 1044–1045; Ala. *Senate Journal* (1898–99),

less than 70 percent Negro in 1900 backed the call for a convention, and a majority from these 55 counties actually opposed ratification. If all 21 counties with Negro majorities had been excluded, both the convention and ratification referenda would have lost. On the other hand, nearly nine of every ten votes in the predominantly Negro counties were recorded for the convention, and nearly 80 percent for the finished constitution.

In a Democratic state executive committee meeting shortly before the first referendum, one black belt politico is reported to have remarked, "All we want is a small vote and a large count." The spectacular vote totals from the seven counties in table 6.7B indicate that this was no idle comment. The disfranchisers carried every county over 50 percent Negro in the first referendum, and lost only four of the twenty-one, three by small margins, in the second. In seven of the eleven counties over 70 percent Negro, the number of votes recorded for the convention and/or ratification substantially exceeded the number of white adult males. These figures demonstrate that the promise of one prominent black belt delegate, Thomas W. Coleman—"We will ratify your constitution"—was more than braggadocio. In several counties, at least, the Negro vote was not merely suppressed; it was counted for suffrage restriction.[47]

Estimates of the relation between voting patterns in the referenda and those in the decade's gubernatorial contests should disprove any notion that most Populists approved of disfranchisement (table 6.8). Those voters who backed Kolb in 1892, at the time he still attracted some conservative farmers, split better than four-to-one against calling the convention. Virtually all of those who still managed to vote after the Sayre law's passage and stayed loyal to the declining Populists voted negatively in both referenda. The tiny number of Democratic defectors to the antirestriction forces does not alter the overall picture:

pp. 47, 296–297, 326, 433–434, 495; Ala. *House Journal* (1898–99), pp. 452–453, 459; Ala. *Senate Journal* (extra session 1899), pp. 17, 34, 36–37, 51, 56; Ala. *House Journal* (1900), pp. 351–352; Ala. *Senate Journal* (1900), p. 320; Joseph F. Johnston, "Negro Suffrage in Alabama," *The Independent* 51 (1899): 1535–1537; Joseph H. Taylor, "Populism and Disfranchisement in Alabama," p. 420; Joseph Matt Brittain, "Negro Suffrage and Politics in Alabama Since 1870," p. 83.

47. The anonymous black belt politico quoted in McMillan, *Constitutional Development*, pp. 261–262, n. 93. Some Democrats publicly admitted the fraud in the black belt. See, e.g., *Montgomery Daily Advertiser*, June 11, 1902. Coleman of Greene (80 percent Negro), quoted in Ala. Con. Con. *Proceedings* (1901), vol. 4, p. 4853.

Table 6.8. Populists against Suffrage Restriction: Estimated Relationships between Party and Voting in the 1900 Constitutional Referenda in Alabama.

A. The 1892 Governor's Race and the First Referendum

| Vote in 1892 | Vote in 1901 Referendum on Calling Convention | | |
Governor's Race	% For	% Against	% Not Voting
Democrat	29	0	81
Populist	8	34	52
Not Voting	17	3	78

B. The 1898 Governor's Race and the First Referendum

| Vote in 1898 | Vote in 1901 Referendum on Calling Convention | | |
Governor's Race	% For	% Against	% Not Voting
Democrat	42	11	39
Populist	0	53	65
Not Voting	9	3	91

C. The 1896 Governor's Race and the Second Referendum

| Vote in 1896 | Vote in 1901 Referendum on Ratifying Constitution | | |
Governor's Race	% For	% Against	% Not Voting
Democrat	70	0	31
Populist	0	69	36
Not Voting	6	11	79

[a]Since some of the original estimates came out to be less than 0% (logically but not statistically impossible results), I set several of the estimates at zero and recalculated the other estimates accordingly. As a consequence, some totals do not add to 100% across rows. For procedures see my "Ecological Regression" article.

suffrage restriction in Alabama was a partisan issue. As the *Montgomery Advertiser* crowed, "The Democratic Party, through its most patriotic spirits, called the convention, framed the new instrument, [and] adopted it at the polls."[48]

The convention itself reflected the aims of its conservative, Democratic, black belt sponsors. Of its 155 delegates, 141, including each of the 25 Suffrage Committee members, were Democrats. Judge Thomas W. Coleman, ex-slaveholder, Princeton graduate, Confederate officer, justice of the Alabama Supreme Court, and small town banker, led the

48. Similar matrices relating each of the 1892–1900 gubernatorial contests to the two referenda show exactly the same relationship between partisanship and suffrage restriction. The quotation is from *Montgomery Daily Advertiser*, April 8, 1902.

black belt majority on the Suffrage Committee. The convention elected John B. Knox, perhaps Alabama's richest railroad lawyer, to its presidency, and brushed aside all efforts at social reform. The body refused to strengthen the railroad commission or impose limitations on other corporate activity, refused to abolish child labor or the convict leasing system, and it straitjacketed the government's ability to provide social services by cutting the constitutionally set maximum state tax rate.[49]

Despite the Democrats' pledge not to disfranchise a single white man, the suffrage article was obviously calculated to discourage from voting "the ignorant and vicious" whites (a much-repeated formula in the convention). In the words of Malcolm McMillan, representatives of the black belt and the businessmen "wished to disfranchise most of the Negroes and the uneducated and propertyless whites in order to legally create a conservative electorate." The new qualifications included lengthy residency requirements, a $1.50 cumulative poll tax, and a literacy or property test with temporary exemptions for ex-soldiers, the descendants of ex-soldiers, and men of "good character." Any registrant after 1902 had to be able to read and write, as well as be employed regularly for a year preceding the election, or own 40 acres of land or $300 worth of real or personal property. Judge Coleman thought the employment clause alone would exclude 10,000 "tramps." Although ultraconservative delegates fought the broad white suffrage guaranteed by the fighting grandfather clause, the majority realized that without the clause the constitution would lose in the contest for ratification. Moreover, if the courts declared the temporary plan unconstitutional, "the chief effect of such a decision," as a writer in a contemporary magazine recognized, "would be to aid in purging the registration lists" of whites. One white county delegate charged that the black belt representatives, believing the courts would throw out the grandfather clause, plotted in the Suffrage Committee to exclude white illiterates by writing that flagrantly discriminatory provision into the constitution.[50]

49. Taylor, "Populism and Disfranchisement," pp. 422–423; McMillan, *Constitutional Development*, pp. 264–269, 315–317, 339; Hackney, *Populism to Progressivism*, pp. 191, 209–227.

50. McMillan, *Constitutional Development*, pp. 268–269. The suffrage provisions are detailed in Taylor, "Populism and Disfranchisement," p. 421; Ala. Con. Con. *Proceedings* (1901), vol. 3, p. 3160; *ibid.*, vol. 1, pp. 1257–1264; *ibid.*, vol. 3, pp. 3163, 3172–3175. The contemporary observer was Francis G. Caffey, "Suffrage Limitations at the South," pp. 56–57, 59. The references in the *Proceedings* to the issue of white disfranchisement and the fighting grand-

The only delegates to defend universal suffrage for both whites and blacks were the Populists and Republicans. Most of the Democrats believed that suffrage "is not a right that belongs to any citizen or any man. It is a pure privilege which the State extends to certain men in the interest not of the man, but of the State itself." The preamble to the 1875 constitution had designated suffrage a "right"; the draft of 1901 changed that to a "privilege." One black belt delegate, future U.S. Senator Tom Heflin, even propounded the theory that suffrage was "an inherent right with the white man and a privilege with the Negro." The Populists, on the other hand, kept to the older belief in universal manhood suffrage. Pointing out that Negroes had to pay taxes and obey the laws of the state, N. B. Spears stated, "I do not believe it is right to disfranchise any man simply because he is a Negro." The Populist-Republican John H. Porter opposed disfranchising "any citizen of Alabama except for crime." The Negro was law-abiding and patriotic, Porter continued. "All he asks is the right to choose between two or more the one he prefers to rule over him. This right, in my judgment, he should have."[51]

Toward the end of the convention, N. H. Freeman, a Republican from the old Unionist stronghold of Winston County, offered what at first seemed a racist amendment to the suffrage article. Since everyone knew that the Alabama Constitution contravened the Fifteenth Amendment indirectly, he reasoned, it would be more bold and manly to limit the vote on ratification to whites only. Predicting that only extensive fraud in the Negro-majority counties could carry the constitution, Freeman went on, "I respectfully submit that it is enough to

father clause are too numerous to note. For a sample, see vol. 1, pp. 1264–1266; vol. 2, pp. 2715–2739; vol. 3, pp. 2789–2797, 2809–2811, 2849, 2856, 2866, 2869, 2952–2953, 3101–3107, 3115. The white county delegate's statement is in ibid., vol. 3, p. 3086. One piece of evidence to substantiate this charge is that when the suffrage article was first drafted, it contained a provision allowing the legislature, by a two-thirds vote, to rewrite any section of the qualifications voided in the courts. This provision was later replaced with one stating that if any section were declared unconstitutional, the rest of the constitution would stand as written. See Mabry, "Disfranchisement of the Negro," pp. 350–363.

51. On the "privilege" of voting, see Cobb of Macon (81.6 percent Negro in 1900), in Ala. Con. Con. *Proceedings* (1901), vol. 4, pp. 4870–4871; ibid., vol. 2, p. 1759 for changing of the preamble. Heflin's theory appears in ibid., vol. 3, p. 2842. During this speech Heflin noted his upperclass descent. His father had been the largest slaveholder in Randolph County. See ibid., vol. 3, p. 2846. For the Populist-Republican response, see Spears, in ibid., vol. 3, pp. 2971–2981; Porter in ibid., vol. 3, pp. 3018–3019; Reynolds in ibid., vol. 3, p. 3285.

disfranchise the Negro, without making him an involuntary party to his own disfranchisement. We should not call upon him in the Black Belt to be the victim of a ballot he never cast."[52] But the convention quickly tabled the amendment, the promised fraud occurred, and Alabama settled down to decades of a shapeless, partyless politics dominated, not accidentally, by the black belt–"Big Mule" coalition which controlled the convention.

VIRGINIA: "THE DEMOCRATIC SALVATION"

Since Negroes made up more than 40 percent of Virginia's populace in the 1870s and since a goodly number of white mountain folk translated their Unionist sympathies into membership in the Republican party after the War, the Virginia Conservative-Democratic Party was fortunate that it did not lose a statewide contest during the decade. In 1869, the Conservatives backed a moderate Republican for governor, and four years later, in a contest that involved extensive vote-buying, intimidation, and race-baiting, the Conservatives elected a Confederate general. By enacting a poll tax in 1876, they hoped to avoid the rule of an elected Radical government entirely.[53]

But in the latter part of the decade, the Conservatives made two crucial mistakes: they passed over their ambitious wire-puller General Billy Mahone for governor in 1877, and they committed themselves to complete repayment ("funding") of the state debt, most of which had been accumulated by state financing of antebellum railroads and most of which was owned by Northern and foreign bondholders. Mahone bolted the Conservatives and organized the Readjuster party which promised to scale down the debt, increase school expenditures (the Funder candidate for governor in 1881, John W. Daniel, declared

---

52. Ibid., vol. 4, pp. 4782–4784. On the ratification campaign, see McMillan, *Constitutional Development*, pp. 341–352; and Hackney, *Populism to Progressivism*, pp. 227–229, 343–344.

53. For the 1869 and 1873 elections, see Richard L. Morton, *The Negro in Virginia Politics, 1865–1902*, pp. 77, 87; Wynes, *Race Relations in Virginia, 1870–1902*, p. 11. On virtually all issues relating to the Virginia Democrats in this period, the authoritative work is Jack P. Maddex, Jr.'s *The Virginia Conservatives, 1867–1879*. On the poll tax, see Maddex, *Virginia Conservatives*, pp. 197–198. The poll tax was less effective in restricting the suffrage in Virginia than elsewhere because the political parties, in this highly competitive period, regularly paid their poor followers' taxes. For evidence on this point, see Morton, *Negro in Virginia Politics*, pp. 93, 112; Wynes, *Race Relations*, p. 24; DeSantis, *Republicans Face*, p. 153; Robert E. Martin, "Negro Disfranchisement in Virginia," p. 86; Rowell, *Contested Elections*, pp. 402–404, 410–411.

he would rather burn the schools than default on the debt), repeal the poll tax, and carry out a generally liberal program. Gradually fusing with the GOP, the Readjusters took over the legislature in 1879 and the governorship in 1881, kept their promises, including poll tax repeal, and barely lost the 1883 contest for the legislature.[54]

After gaining control of the legislature, the Democrats passed the Anderson-McCormick election law, a law which, according to Democratic chieftain Hal Flood, permitted the election judges, all Democrats,

when the polls were closed to turn everyone out of the election room until they had an opportunity to make the number of ballots in the ballot box tally with the number of names on the poll book. In the black counties this enabled them to change the ballots to suit themselves. This was done in many instances to save those counties from Negro domination.[55]

Though the Democrats, employing the usual fraud, carried the three governor's races from 1885 to 1893, the tenure of the dominant party was not as secure as it appeared on the surface. For one thing, the Populist party won the support of several prominent Virginia aristocrats, and the new party's label had the potential to attract normally Democratic voters who had hesitated to back the party of Lincoln. Furthermore, the 1893 election to the U.S. Senate of the hitherto unknown railroad lobbyist Thomas S. Martin over the popular war hero Fitzhugh Lee lent credibility to the Populist claim that a political machine, financed by out-of-state corporations, ruled Virginia by means of fraud and bribery. The fact that allegations about Martin's underhanded dealings later fueled the "Independent" faction of the Democratic party for more than a decade indicates what the Populists and Republicans, had they operated in an unrestricted electorate, might have done with these issues.[56]

54. On the Readjusters, see Pearson, *Readjuster Movement*; Blake, *William Mahone of Virginia*; Wynes, *Race Relations*, pp. 18–26; Pulley, *Old Virginia Restored*, pp. 34–40.

55. Flood to R. D. Haislip, July 28, 1911, quoted in Harry Edward Poindexter, "Carter Glass," p. 87. On the partisan purposes of the law and the fraud it encouraged, Pulley, *Old Virginia Restored*, pp. 46–47; Wynes, *Race Relations*, pp. 40–46; and William C. Pendleton, *Political History of Appalachian Virginia*, p. 359.

56. On the 1885–1893 elections, see Pendleton, *Appalachian Virginia*, p. 365; Herman L. Horn, "The Growth and Development of the Democratic Party in Virginia Since 1890," pp. 28–29; and Blake, *Mahone*, pp. 219–223. For evidence of widespread fraud, see Joseph B. Cheadle to Benjamin Harrison, November 16, 1889, quoted in Daniel W. Crofts, "The

The Democrats took advantage of the widespread demand for election reform, fostered chiefly by the Republicans and Populists, to pass a secret ballot law. Although known as the "Walton Act," the statute was probably written by the head of the Democratic organization, Senator Thomas S. Martin. The law, which another Democratic leader, Richard E. Byrd, called "the [D]emocratic salvation," provided for a publicly printed ballot containing neither party names nor symbols. Voters had two and a half minutes to draw lines three-fourths of the way through the names of all candidates for whom they did *not* want to vote. Special constables (all Democrats, of course) could assist illiterates.[57]

Election statistics, as well as contested congressional elections, testify to the effectiveness of the secret ballot law (table 6.9).[58] The shift of labels for the opposition between 1889 and 1893 apparently attracted fewer Democrats than it lost Republican loyalists. The 1893 race also failed to inspire as large a turnout as the epic contest of 1889, in which the best-loved and best-hated character in postbellum Virginia politics, Mahone, had been a candidate. Still, the Populists garnered 41 percent of the votes in 1893.

The GOP must have expected to lose in 1897. Mahone had died two years earlier. Some Populists backed the Democratic "farmer" J. Hoge

---

Blair Bill and the Elections Bill," pp. 238–239. Cheadle, an Indiana Congressman who observed the 1889 election in Virginia for the president, concluded that the only way to guarantee fair elections in such cases was to pass a federal regulatory bill. See also Rowell, *Contested Elections*, pp. 451–454, 457–460. The Populists gathered strength when Mahone indirectly endorsed the new party in 1893, declaring that he favored "any ism that will bust the Democracy." Quoted in Horn, "Democratic Party in Virginia," p. 39. Regression analysis shows that virtually every Populist vote in 1893 came from those who had backed Mahone four years earlier. On the Populist party in Virginia, see Sheldon, *Populism in the Old Dominion*. The Populist charges about the Martin organization were true. See Allen W. Moger, *Virginia, Bourbonism to Byrd, 1870–1925*, pp. 98–100, 102–105, 111–121. On the 1893 Senate election, see, in addition to Moger, Pulley, *Old Virginia Restored*, p. 165; Burton Ira Kaufman, "Henry De La Warr Flood," pp. 31, 67; Poindexter, "Carter Glass," pp. 185–192; Holt, "Virginia Constitutional Convention," p. 70. For Populist charges of election fraud, see Sheldon, *Populism in the Old Dominion*, pp. 94–95, 111–112.

57. On the authorship and operation of the "Walton Act," see the evidence offered in Poindexter, "Carter Glass," p. 196, and Byrd to Hal Flood, April 1, 1894, quoted in ibid., p. 197. For the law, see Va. *Acts* (1894), pp. 862–867.

58. For more detailed information on the Walton Act's abuses, see Rowell, *Contested Elections*, pp. 534–540, 547–552, 565–574, 578–580, 606, 611–613. Anger at these abuses forced a few token changes in the law in 1897, on which see Poindexter, "Carter Glass," pp. 211–212, 215, 220–221.

Table 6.9. Two-Step Disfranchisement: Effect of Election Law Changes
on Voting by Party and Race in Gubernatorial Elections in Virginia,
1885–1905.

A. *Party*

	Percentage of Adult Males			
Year	*Democrat*	*Republican*	*Other*	*Not Voting*
1885	43	38	0	19
1889	44	32	0	24
1893	32	0	22[a]	46
		Secret Ballot		
1897	26	13	1[b]	60
1901	26	18	0	56
		Constitution		
1905	17	10	0	73

B. *Race*

	Percentage of Negro Adult Males			
Year	*Democrat*	*Republican*	*Other*	*Not Voting*
1885[c]	27	71	0	3
1889[c]	30	56	0	15
1893[c]	19	0	46	35
1897	20	2	0	78
1901	24	0	0	76
1905	10	−13	0	103

[a]Populist and Prohibitionist.
[b]Prohibitionist.
[c]These estimates were calculated by splitting the state into groups—those counties under 30 percent Negro, and those over that figure. The estimates for each group were then weighted according to population and summed. In the other elections, a simple straight-line linear equation fit the data better than separate lines for each group.

Tyler for governor. The switch from Republican to Populist to Republican must have disjointed some voters' party loyalties. Nonetheless, the Walton Law undoubtedly accounted for much of the decline in GOP strength and in overall turnout from 1893 to 1897. Whereas in 1889 the GOP had the sympathies of nearly a third of the potential electors, it attracted but one in eight in 1897. The opposition percentage of those voting dropped from 42 percent in 1889 and 41 percent in 1893 to 31 percent in 1897. More important, table 6.9B shows that the estimated percentage of Negroes who cast their ballots for the opposition fell from 46 percent in 1893 to 2 percent in 1897. The estimated 20 percent of the black vote counted for the Democrats in 1897 probably existed only in the minds of election officials. The Walton Law ended most actual black voting in Virginia.[59]

Nevertheless, many Democrats in Virginia wished to replace the election law with more permanent, constitutional restrictions. Accordingly, in 1894, State Senator Eugene Withers of Danville (54 percent Negro in 1890) introduced a bill calling for a constitutional convention. But the usual fearful attitude of interest groups toward constitutional conventions, the threat of "populist ideas," and splits within the Democratic party over monetary policy and "machine control" prevented Withers' bill from passing and doomed the convention in an 1897 referendum.[60] As table 6.10 shows, the chief support for the convention in the referendum came from the black belt. What appear to be black votes in the estimates undoubtedly represent either stuffed ballot boxes or considerable white support for the convention in the predominantly Negro areas.

Rejection in the 1897 referendum did not end the movement to call a convention. If the Republicans in Virginia were still too weak and divided to win elections on the issue of Democratic fraud, the Re-

Table 6.10. Only the Black Belt Wanted a Convention in Virginia in 1897: Estimates of Voting, by Race, in the Referendum on Calling a Constitutional Convention in Virginia.

Race	Vote on Referendum		
	For	Against	Not Voting
White	8	35	57
Negro	12	0	89

59. The Walton Act seems to have had little effect on white voting, which indicates that it was not enforced very strictly in the mountain counties. For other evidence of the Walton Law's effect, see Va. Con. Con. *Proceedings* (1901–02), pp. 3029, 3070; Martin, "Negro Disfranchisement in Virginia," p. 114; Morton, *Negro in Virginia Politics*, pp. 133–134; McDanel, *Virginia Constitutional Convention*, pp. 29–32; Wynes, *Race Relations*, pp. 53–54.

60. Pulley, *Old Virginia Restored*, pp. 68–69; Martin, "Negro Disfranchisement in Virginia," p. 119; Poindexter, "Carter Glass," pp. 198–199, 216–217, 231, 265, 269–274; Holt, "Virginia Constitutional Convention," p. 72; Richard Burke Doss, "John Warwick Daniel," pp. 216–230, 238–248, 264–269; Morton, *Negro in Virginia Politics*, pp. 147–148; *Richmond Times*, February 6, 1900, quoted in McDanel, *Virginia Constitutional Convention*, p. 10; J. A. C. Chandler, "History of Suffrage in Virginia," in *Johns Hopkins University Studies in Historical and Political Science* (Baltimore, Maryland: Johns Hopkins Univ. Press, 1901), pp. 72–73; Allen W. Moger, "The Rift in Virginia Democracy in 1896," *Journal of Southern History* (1938) 4: 295–317.

publicans in Congress could unseat candidates elected by egregious chicanery. From 1894 to 1900, the Republicans and Populists initiated ten contested election cases in Virginia and won four of them. Pointing out that the Virginia constitution guaranteed adult males the right to vote, the Republican minority in one case declared that the secret ballot was a literacy test and therefore unconstitutional according to Virginia's fundamental law.[61] If the GOP ever applied this doctrine consistently, they could contest and throw out every Virginia congressman.

It was also safer to call a convention by 1899, for the split between Gold and Silver Democrats which caused defections to McKinley by several leading Democrats in 1896 had healed. The threat of "Kansas ideas" had faded with the Populists. The state's Republicans wrangled amongst themselves. Despite the growing strength of antiorganization Democrats, Tom Martin easily won reelection to the Senate in 1899. With Martin safe for another six years, such organization members as Hal Flood and State Democratic Chairman J. Taylor Ellyson felt free to work for a convention.[62]

Flood, chief spokesman for the corporations and the Martin machine in the legislature, introduced the enabling act for the constitutional convention in 1899. A descendant of some of the most distinguished planters and politicians among the Virginia gentry, Flood had risen quickly in Virginia politics. Winning a seat in the House of Delegates in 1887 at the age of 21, he attached himself to Tom Martin, whose 1893 and 1899 Senate campaigns he managed, and played a large role in blocking attempts in the state legislature to regulate railroads and provide for fair elections. His patrician heritage never deterred him from race-baiting in close elections. His typical Southside prejudices against Negro voting led him to support a convention, which his mentor Martin opposed, when it became safe to do so without endangering Democratic hegemony. Practically all the "Independents" also favored a disfranchising convention.[63]

61. Rowell, *Contested Elections*, pp. 534–537. For discussions of the relation between contested elections and the decision to call the convention, see *Richmond Times*, March 14, 1900, quoted in Mabry, "Disfranchisement of the Negro," p. 400; Wynes, *Race Relations*, p. 55.

62. Horn, "Democratic Party in Virginia," pp. 49–50.

63. On Flood's support of the constitutional convention, see Kaufman, "Flood," pp. 80–88. For the "Independents'" sympathies, see Holt, "Virginia Constitutional Convention," pp. 72–77; Poindexter, "Carter Glass," pp. 301–302; Doss, "Daniel," pp. 250–251; Moger,

This consensus on the desirability of a convention among important leaders of both Democratic factions enabled the proponents to push their bill through the legislature over the opposition of the small Republican minority. To guarantee its passage by the electorate, the legislators scheduled the referendum to coincide not with the state or national elections, when GOP turnout might be large, but with the contests for local office. They also biased the ballots, printing on them only the words, "For the Convention." To vote as the Democrats wished, one had merely to place the ticket in the ballot box. To oppose the convention, one had to mark through all three words and place no other mark on the paper, a provision which made it easy for officials to discard ballots against the convention.[64]

The Democrats' stratagems were successful. In the November 1900 presidential election, 60 percent of Virginia's adult males turned out, and the Republicans received the backing of 44 percent of those who voted. In the May 1900 referendum, the same percentage, 44 percent, stood with the GOP platform against the convention, but overall turnout amounted to only 31 percent of the electorate. Fewer than 18 percent of the eligible voters cast their ballots for the convention. As table 6.11A shows, voting in the referendum split sharply along party lines. Part B of table 6.11 indicates the similarity of patterns of support for and opposition to a constitutional convention in the 1897 and 1900 referenda. Most of those who voted in both elections chose the same side each time. The convention picked up support in 1900 from some of the 71 percent of the adult males who had not voted three years earlier. Sixty percent of those who had opposed the convention in 1897 do not appear to have voted in 1900. The Democratic party's endorsement of the convention in 1900 obviously activated some voters previously apathetic toward calling one and quieted the apprehensions of others who had heretofore feared what a convention might do.

The estimates of voting in the referendum by race given in part C of table 6.11 indicate that the convention was most popular among whites in the heavily Negro counties. Southside Democrats turned out in large numbers, compared to the rest of the state, and either voted

---

Bourbonism to Byrd, p. 186; McDanel, *Virginia Constitutional Convention*, pp. 12–15; Horn, "Democratic Party in Virginia," p. 60.

64. Poindexter, "Carter Glass," pp. 358–362; McDanel, *Virginia Constitutional Convention*, pp. 59–60.

Table 6.11. Black Belt Democrats Called the Virginia Convention:
Estimates of Relationships between Voting Patterns in 1900 Referendum
and Party, Race, and Voting in the 1897 Referendum.

	% For Convention	% Against Convention	% Not Voting
Democratic[a]	35	0	65
Republican[a]	0	56	44
Not voting[a]	14	0	86
White	13	16	71
Negro	24	16	59
1897 referendum, compared			
For convention	57	14	28
Against convention	2	37	60
Not voting	17	10	74

[a]Party preferences estimated by votes in 1900 presidential election.

overwhelmingly for the convention or stuffed the ballot boxes for it.[65]
These estimates and the graphs (not presented here) which relate referendum voting to the Negro percentage in each county also demonstrate that there was a fairly sizable black vote against the convention.
The opponents of the convention carried 18 of the 35 counties with
Negro majorities. In no Virginia county did the returns in this referendum approach the blatant falsification in the comparable Alabama
and Louisiana elections.

Once in session, the convention lasted off and on for over a year,
principally because of inability to agree on a suffrage article. The chief
reasons for the delay were factional divisions among the Democrats in
this period, the presence in the convention of too many moderately
important politicians—several ex-congressmen and ex-governors, a
senator, and some intelligent and stubborn local leaders—and the
absence of a single dominant figure. Senator George in Mississippi,
Senator Tillman in South Carolina, Governor Foster and Convention
Chairman Kruttschnitt in Louisiana, and Judge Coleman in Alabama
had pushed suffrage plans through their conventions. Senator John W.

65. For analyses of the campaign and returns, see *Richmond Times*, May 30, 1900, quoted
in McDanel, *Constitutional Convention*, p. 18; *Petersburg* (Virginia) *Daily Index-Appeal*, May 25,
1900, quoted in Horn, "Democratic Party in Virginia," p. 60; Poindexter, "Carter Glass,"
pp. 390–397, 406.

Daniel, chairman of the Elective Franchise Committee in the Virginia convention might have played an analogous role, but was apparently incompetent at anything but stump speaking. It was only when Daniel retired from the convention after suffering a nervous breakdown that Southside newspaper editor Carter Glass emerged to patch up a compromise which could win a majority of the committee and the Democratic "conference."[66]

Four factions vied to write the suffrage article. At the extreme right, a group of men primarily representing counties with large proportions of Negroes urged setting the qualifications so high that no Negro could be elected to any office in Virginia. They also wished to eliminate a substantial number of poor whites. The black belt group first proposed a property test as the sole qualification for registering, a plan which, according to contemporary tax statistics, would have allowed less than 5 percent of the Negro and one-third of the white adult males to vote. To meet objections that this plan would affect too many whites, Alfred P. Thom, a wealthy railroad lawyer, proposed dividing the electorate into categories based on employment, and disfranchising all unskilled laborers. When this, too, proved unacceptable to white county Democrats, the black belt men demanded a free hand to discriminate administratively by requiring all potential registrants to prove they understood the duties of all officers for whom they might vote. A man who could not explain the duties of justices of the peace well enough to please a registrar could, under this provision, be denied the right to vote entirely. This group also desired a cumulative poll tax.[67]

These reactionaries made up for their relatively small numerical strength by their strategic placement. They held a majority on the Elective Franchise Committee. Most of the others on the committee, only slightly less conservative, wanted to eliminate as many Negroes as they could while still allowing virtually all white Democrats to regis-

66. Poindexter, "Carter Glass," pp. 463–465, 477, 487–499; Doss, "Daniel," pp. 279–280; Holt, "Constitutional Convention," pp. 93–99.

67. Alfred P. Thom, in Va. Con. Con. *Proceedings* (1901–02), pp. 2961, 2968, 2972, 2986–2988. "There is no reason," Thom said, "for enfranchising the whites." See also McIlwaine, in ibid., pp. 2988–3004; Walter A. Watson, "Diary," April 4, 1902, quoted in McDanel, *Constitutional Convention*, p. 43. The effect of the property tax proposal can be seen by noting tax statistics quoted in Morton, *Negro in Virginia Politics*, p. 158. For the other proposals of the reactionaries, see Thom, in Va. Con. Con. *Proceedings* (1901–02), pp. 2970–2971, 2982–2985, 2989–2990; Daniel, in ibid., p. 2943.

ter. The poorer whites, they realized, would "disfranchise themselves" by failing to pay the poll tax six months in advance.[68]

The conservative grouping shaded off towards a band of moderates, mostly Democrats from overwhelmingly white counties in the western region. This third group acquiesced in suffrage restriction because of party loyalty and an implicit bargain which swapped eastern votes for a strong corporation commission for western support of a limited electorate.[69]

Most of the one hundred-man convention's twelve Republicans fell into a fourth category of delegates who opposed any restriction whatever on the suffrage. A. L. Pedigo of Henry County (44 percent Negro in 1900) spoke for them when he remarked, "I cannot tolerate the thought of depriving even one of the humblest of our citizens of his right to vote, and to have his vote counted, and honestly weighed in making the returns. No matter how humble, or poor, or ignorant, or black he may be . . . yet I would keep a ballot in his hand."[70]

The final suffrage plan was a compromise between the conservatives and the reactionaries. Every voter had to satisfy lengthy residency requirements and, six months in advance, pay a poll tax which could accumulate for three years. Three classes of persons could register before 1904: soldiers and their sons, those who held $333 worth of assessed property, and men who could give a reasonable explanation of some part of the constitution. After 1904, new registrants had to prove their literacy by filling out, with no aid whatsoever, a very complex blank registration form.[71]

Aware of the difficulty the Alabama Democrats had in ratifying their constitution in 1901, the Virginia delegates broke a Democratic party pledge to submit their finished document to a referendum. After

68. Daniel, in ibid., p. 2955; Thom, in ibid., pp. 2961, 2989; Glass, in ibid., p. 3076; Goode, in ibid., pp. 20–21; Doss, "Daniel," p. 276; Pulley, *Old Virginia Restored*, pp. 76–77, 83; Poindexter, "Carter Glass," pp. 269–270, 473–474, 492–493.

69. Holt, "Constitutional Convention," pp. 84, 87; Wysor, in Va. Con. Con. *Proceedings* (1901–02), p. 2996; Kendall and Gordon, in ibid., pp. 3027–3028.

70. Va. Con. Con. *Proceedings*, p. 3047. See similar comments of Gillespie, p. 3001; Davis, p. 3058.

71. Ibid., pp. 2937–2940. Known as the "Glass Amendment," the final proposal was more restrictive than the earlier "Daniel plan," against which the Southside delegates had waged a long battle. See John W. Daniel, "The Work of the Constitutional Convention," in *Report of the Fourteenth Annual Meeting of the Virginia State Bar Association* (Richmond, Virginia, 1902), pp. 264–272; Poindexter, "Carter Glass," p. 498.

proclaiming the constitution, the party used its control of the electoral process to discriminate against white and black Republicans, register Democrats, and guarantee that loyal followers' poll taxes were paid. The restriction of the electorate and partisan domination of the electoral bureaucracy paved the way for the Byrd machine. The active electorate was so small that from 1905 to 1948 state employees and officeholders cast approximately one-third of the votes in state elections.[72]

72. For the Democratic failure to submit the constitution to a vote, see Va. Con. Con. *Proceedings* (1901–02), pp. 3032, 3037, 3259–3260; Pulley, *Old Virginia Restored*, p. 88, gives evidence of the direct effect of Alabama's experience; McDanel, *Constitutional Convention*, pp. 114–129 shows that delegates thought the constitution would lose in a referendum. For the party's discriminatory tactics, see Pendleton, *Appalachian Virginia*, p. 457; Ernest H. Mc-Clintic to Hal Flood, September 20, 1902, and C. W. Manger to Flood, September 29, 1902, both quoted in Buni, *The Negro in Virginia Politics*, p. 21; Horn, "Democratic Party," pp. 89–91; Pulley, *Old Virginia Restored*, pp. 75–77. On the reduced electorate and the Byrd machine, see Horn, "Democratic Party," pp. iii-iv, 111–113, 119, 223–228, 329–331.

"A Good, Square, Honest Law That Will Always Give a Good Democratic Majority"

By amending the suffrage clauses of their constitutions in referenda from 1900 to 1908, Democrats in North Carolina, Texas, and Georgia excluded dangerous voters permanently, without the risks and expense of calling conventions. The final episodes in the disfranchisement campaigns in these three states closely resembled corresponding events elsewhere: the character and motives of the restrictionists and their opponents and the timing and development of the successful movements for limitation fell, for the most part, into familiar patterns. Even the texts of the amendments were patterned after those in other states.

Nevertheless, the experiences of North Carolina, Texas, and Georgia differed in important respects from those of the rest of the South in the post-Reconstruction period. North Carolina was the only state where the Democrats lost control during the nineties. The reasons for Democratic defeat, the programs of the Populist-Republican administration, and the difficulties which helped to break up that bipartisan, biracial coalition indicate how opposition parties throughout the South might have operated had the election machinery not been so geared to their defeat. Since farmer parties were stronger and black belt Democratic politicians weaker in Texas than elsewhere, neither coalition-building by the opposition nor disfranchisement by the Democrats followed exactly the same lines as in other states. It took a quarter of a century of repeated efforts to enact a major restrictive device in Texas. Georgia was the first Southern state to enact a cumulative poll tax and the last to adopt a comprehensive suffrage clause in its constitution. The only state which had an effective restrictive law from Reconstruction on, it also had one of the two weakest Republican parties in the South before disfranchisement. Because these peculiarities deserve thorough examination, North Carolina, Texas, and Georgia will receive more attention here than the more typical Southern states.

NORTH CAROLINA: DISFRANCHISING "LOW-BORN SCUM AND
QUONDAM SLAVES"

The North Carolina political system was perhaps the most democratic in the late nineteenth-century South (table 7.1). Turnout at gubernatorial elections in the last two decades of the century never fell below three-quarters of the adult males. From 1880 through 1896, the Democrats never won more than 54 percent of the vote in the races for governor. Since there were relatively few restrictions on the suffrage before 1900, black men voted in large numbers.[1] Ballot box stuffing seems to have occurred on a less extensive scale than in most other Southern states.

Essentially a coalition of upland, ex-Unionist whites and lowland blacks, the Republicans gradually added to their ranks Piedmont

Table 7.1. Strong Party Competition and Heavy Negro Participation in
Gubernatorial Races in North Carolina, 1880–1896.

Year	Democratic	Republican	Other	Not Voting	% Voting Favoring Democrats
		% OF ADULT MALES			
1880	41.3	39.2	0	19.4	51.3
1884	45.6	39.2	0	15.2	53.8
1888	44.6	40.2	0.9	14.3	52.0
1892	37.9	26.5	14.1	21.6	48.3
1896	37.5	39.7	8.3	14.6	43.9
		ESTIMATED % OF NEGRO ADULT MALES			
1880	17	69	0	14	—[b]
1884	20	74	0	2	–
1888	19	49	1	32	–
1892	34	27	2	36	–
1896	20	59	8	13	–

[a]These estimates computed by splitting state into 2 groups of counties—those with more than 30% Negro, and those with less—and weighting and summing the estimates for the separate groups.

[b]Not estimated.

1. The Democrats did extensively gerrymander congressional, legislative, and city districts, and the election officials from time to time used their broad powers to deny Negroes and other Republicans and Populists the right to vote. See Logan, *Negro in North Carolina*, pp. 49–63; Mabry, *Negro in North Carolina Politics*, pp. 16–22.

manufacturers who favored protective tariffs for their products. When a Democratic-sponsored amendment to prohibit the sale and manufacture of liquor failed by 100,000 votes in an 1881 referendum, the Republicans took advantage of the Democratic split. Allying themselves with some of the "wet" Democrats, the GOP came within 400 votes of winning the statewide race for congressman-at-large in 1882. Many drinking Democrats thereafter preferred the party of emancipation to that of prohibition. The Republicans capitalized, too, on the fact that to prevent Republicans from winning local offices in the black belt and the mountains, the Democratic legislature appointed all officers of the county governments, instead of allowing the people to vote for them. Democratic favoritism towards a small number of business interests, particularly the largely Northern-owned railroads, also probably drove some voters into the Republican or Populist parties.[2]

Alienated by the national Democratic party's nomination of the conservative Cleveland for president in 1892, and angry at the nominally pro-farmer state legislature's inaction on their demands, leaders of the Farmers' Alliance put up a Populist state ticket in 1892. After the election, the Democratic legislature punished the agrarian apostasy by circumscribing the Alliance charter so as to prohibit its business activities. At the same time, the Democratic governor, former state Alliance president Elias Carr, leased the state-owned railroad to a private corporation for ninety-nine years. These actions led the Populists to fuse with the Republicans on a joint legislative ticket in 1894, a tactic which, in the midst of the economic depression, produced opposition majorities in both houses of the legislature.[3]

Because North Carolina produced two of the most prominent Populists, Leonidas L. Polk, editor of the *National Economist,* and Marion Butler, Populist national chairman in 1896, historians have put a great deal of emphasis on the Populists' role in this period.[4] Actually, the Populists garnered a smaller proportion of the votes in

2. Steelman, "Progressive Era in North Carolina," pp. 11–15, 66, 86–96; Mabry, *Negro in North Carolina Politics,* pp. 29–30; David Charles Roller, "Republican Party in North Carolina," pp. 3–6, 48–49; Edmonds, *Negro and Fusion Politics,* pp. 10–11; J. G. de Roulhac Hamilton, *North Carolina since 1860* (Chicago and New York; The Lewis Pub. Co., 1919), pp. 197–199, 207–212; DeSantis, *Republicans Face,* pp. 162–163.

3. Steelman, "Progressive Era in North Carolina," pp. 14–56, 98–100; Mabry, "The Disfranchisement of the Negro," pp. 262–263.

4. Mabry, "Disfranchisement of the Negro," p. 260.

North Carolina governors' races than in seven other Southern states. The bulk of those who wished to oppose the Democrats voted Republican during the nineties, just as they had in the seventies and eighties.

In a state as closely divided as North Carolina, however, the Populists' role, though small, was crucial. As table 7.2 shows, the People's Party drew virtually all its strength in the 1892 governor's race from formerly Democratic areas. Running best in counties about one-third Negro, the Populists perfectly complemented GOP strength in the overwhelmingly white and the predominantly black districts. Whites in counties above 30 percent Negro seem to have been hesitant to vote for the "Black Republicans," but many felt free to go into the People's Party in 1892, and, having voted against the Democrats once, were willing to vote against them again after the death of the Populists (table 7.3). In 1896, when the Populist total dropped from its 1892 figure of 13 percent of the adult males to only 8 percent, two-thirds of the Populist defectors appear to have voted Republican. When four years later the Populists fielded no gubernatorial candidate, the 1892 Populists who turned out in 1900 split about three-to-two for the GOP.

In addition to providing votes for the Republicans and denying them to the Democrats in statewide contests, the Populists cooperated with the GOP in congressional and legislative races and in the legislature itself. From 1894 through 1898, Populists and Republicans usually agreed to fuse behind a single candidate in each legislative and senatorial district and, after the election, formulated a common legislative program. Winning control of the legislature in 1894, the Fusionists added the statehouse two years later with Republican Daniel Russell's victory. The furious "white supremacy campaign" swept Populists and Republicans out of the legislature in 1898 (table 7.4).

While they controlled the legislature, however, the Fusionists put

Table 7.2. Populists in North Carolina Were Former Democrats: Estimates of the Relation between Voting in 1888 and 1892 Governors' Contests.

% of Adult Males in 1888 Governor's Race	% of Adult Males in 1892 Governor's Race			
	% Democrat	% Republican	% Populist	% Not Voting
Democrat	63	0	27	12
Republican	18	64	0	18
Not Voting	22	20	0	58

Table 7.3. Most North Carolina Populists Voted Republican in 1896 and
1900 Gubernatorial Races: Estimates of Relationships between Voting
Patterns, 1892–1900.

% of Adult Males in 1892 Governor's Race	% of Adult Males in 1896 Governor's Race			
	Democrat	Republican	Populist	Not Voting
Democrat	76	14	0	10
Republican	19	87	−9[b]	2
Populist	11	21	51	18
Not Voting	10	38	17	34

% of Adult Males in 1892 Governor's Race	% of Adult Males in 1900 Governor's Race[a]		
	Democrat	Republican	Not Voting
Democrat	84	18	−2
Republican	6	83	11
Populist	33	48	19
Not Voting	29	−17[b]	88

[a]The Populists did not run a candidate in 1900.
[b]For an explanation of estimates below zero, see my "Ecological Regression" article.

Table 7.4. Rise and Fall of Fusionism in North Carolina: Party
Composition of Legislature, 1892–1898.[a]

Year Elected	Representatives			Senators		
	Democrats	Republicans	Populists	Democrats	Republicans	Populists
1892	93	16	11	47	0	3
1894	46	38	36	8	18	24
1896	26	54	40	7	18	25
1898	94	23	3	40	7	3

[a]Adapted from J. G. de Roulhac Hamilton, *North Carolina since 1860*, pp. 241, 246, 262, 299.

through an impressive reform program, indicative of what opponents
of the Democrats might have accomplished had they come to power
elsewhere in the South. After restoring and liberalizing the Alliance
charter and seeking to lower bank interest rates, the legislature repealed the old county government law, thereby enabling localities to
elect their own officials. Whereas the conservative Democratic regimes
had starved public services, the Fusionists—in the midst of a severe
depression—substantially increased state appropriations for public
schools from the elementary to college level, set up teacher training
institutes for local schools, and provided incentives for local school
districts to raise their tax rates. The legislature also augmented the

expenditures for charitable and correctional institutions and intensified taxation of railroads and businesses. Governor Russell attacked the lease of the state-owned rail line to J. P. Morgan's Southern Railway Company and called for public ownership of all railroads. As a result of these reforms and threats, railroads, bankers, and manufacturers heavily subsidized the Democrats in the 1898 campaign. Leaders of the denominational colleges, who wished to keep the state university weak, also backed the Democrats in exchange for a promise not to increase funds for the public college.[5]

In addition to attacking upper-class privilege and democratizing local government, the Fusionists reformed election procedures. Stigmatizing the 1889 Democratic registration law as a "force bill," the Fusionists replaced it with what was probably the fairest and most democratic election law in the post-Reconstruction South. To insure a fair count, the county clerk was required to appoint one election judge from each party and allow all of the judges to be present during the counting of ballots. To prevent the clerk from appointing incompetents from parties other than his own, each local party chairman actually nominated his own party's representative. To end disfranchisement by deliberate delays in large precincts, the clerk had to set up a voting place for every 350 voters. To debar registrars from illegally and capriciously disqualifying voters, the Fusionists strictly limited the registrars' powers. To eliminate repeated partisan challenges against voters, the legislature put the burden of proof on the challenger, rather than the voter. Finally, to make voting easier for illiterates, the 1895 law allowed colored ballots and party emblems on the ballots.[6] Partly as a consequence of the new law, turnout in 1896 rose by seven points to 85.4 percent; the Republicans elected a governor in North Carolina for the first time since Reconstruction; and the Fusionists increased their majorities in both houses of the legislature.

5. Steelman, "Progressive Era in North Carolina," pp. 119–123, 150–152, 162–164; Edmonds, *Negro and Fusion Politics*, pp. 139–140, 151–154; Roller, "Republican Party in North Carolina," pp. 14–15.

6. On the 1889 law and fraud in North Carolina during the nineties, see Logan, *Negro in North Carolina*, pp. 58–60; Edmonds, *Negro and Fusion Politics*, pp. 67–70; Hamilton, *North Carolina since 1860*, p. 217; Steelman, "Progressive Era in North Carolina," pp. 36–37; and Josephus Daniels, *Tar Heel Editor*, p. 504. On the 1895 law, see Simeon A. Delap, "The Populist Party in North Carolina," in Trinity College Historical Society, *Historical Papers*, series XIV (Durham, North Carolina: The Seeman Printery, 1922), pp. 54–56. Edmonds,

Liberal and fair election laws, however, did not save the Fusionists from the tremendous onslaught of violence and fraud, financed from corporate coffers, which the Democrats unleashed in 1898. Weakened by personal feuds and jealousies among their leaders and by the continual difficulty of operating a coalition between two parties which differed on such national issues as monetary policy and the protective tariff, the white Republicans and Populists were also ambivalent in their attitudes towards the black voters who provided the bulk of their support. While most white Republicans and Populists probably remained loyal to their parties in 1898, a significant number capitulated to the Democratic argument that racial identity should override disagreement on all other questions. Still, the Democrats got only 52.8 percent of the votes in the only statewide race (for chief justice of the state supreme court) in 1898, a contest in which 84.2 percent of the adult males, the highest turnout in a non-presidential year in North Carolina's postbellum history, were recorded as voting. And the Democratic totals, a prominent North Carolina clergyman admitted in a national magazine shortly after the election, were considerably padded through frauds.[7]

To the Fusionists' personal bickering and uncertainty over racial policies, the Democrats presented a solid, violently racist front. Led by Furnifold Simmons, Charles B. Aycock, and Josephus Daniels, the North Carolina Democrats borrowed the idea of Red Shirt Clubs from South Carolina. These clubs, composed, according to J. G. de R. Hamilton, primarily of "respectable and well-to-do farmers, bankers, schoolteachers, and merchants," paraded around in bright costume intimidating opposition voters, breaking up Republican and Populist meetings, and cheering when outside agitators like Ben Tillman congratulated them for their valiant defense of white supremacy. Although the fact of gentry domination of the Red Shirts may surprise

---

Negro and Fusion Politics, pp. 70–74; Mabry, "Disfranchisement of the Negro," pp. 269–276; Steelman, "Progressive Era in North Carolina," pp. 67, 120–122.

7. On the weakening of the Fusionists in 1898, see Steelman, "Progressive Era in North Carolina," pp. 47–53, 123–155, 167–177, 186, 196; Edmonds, *Negro and Fusion Politics*, pp. 40–56, 133–137, 144–145; Mabry, "Disfranchisement of the Negro," pp. 262–263, 280–282; Hamilton, *North Carolina since 1860*, pp. 199, 257–258; Logan, *Negro in North Carolina*, pp. 13–18; Durden, *Climax of Populism*, pp. 11, 167; Daniels, *Editor in Politics*, pp. 123–131; Orr, *Charles Brantley Aycock*, pp. 85, 105, 122; Joseph L. Morrison, *Josephus Daniels Says . . .*, pp. 94–95. On the fraud, see A. J. McKelway, "The Cause of the Trouble in North Carolina," pp. 1488–1492. Later a nationally known "Progressive," McKelway approved the frauds, disfranchisement, and the postelection slaughter of Negroes at Wilmington.

those who believe that lower-class whites were solely responsible for Southern violence, it did not seem strange to contemporaries. As a scribbler for the *Raleigh News and Observer* summarized the Democratic view of the campaign,

> Shall low-born scum and quondam slaves
> Give laws to those who own the soil?
> No! by our gransires' bloody graves,
> No! by our homesteads bought with toil.[8]

The Democratic triumvirate's talents meshed perfectly. Simmons, chief protégé of the former Democratic boss and U.S. Senator Matt Ransom, was adept at quietly cajoling campaign contributions and building up an efficient organization. Future Wilson cabinet member Daniels, editor in 1898 of the newspaper with the largest circulation in North Carolina, turned out a widely circulated barrage of editorials and "news" stories portraying the state in the clutches of corrupt, pro-Negro radicals. Another of Matt Ransom's brood, Aycock, supplied the flamboyant, race-baiting oratory. Gesturing wildly, this prototypical Southern Progressive (and railroad lawyer) would wrap himself rhetorically in the Stars and Bars and assure his crowds that the choice in the election was between the "Anglo-Saxon heritage" and "white womanhood" on one side, and "Negro rule" and a return to Reconstruction on the other.[9]

When the Populists and Republicans during the 1898 campaign charged that the Democrats would restrict the suffrage if they won, Furnifold Simmons denied the charges unequivocally. After the election, however, the party of Southern honor and upper-class rectitude promptly reneged. Fearing to call a constitutional convention because the Fusionists might overturn the slim 18,000 vote majority of 1898, the Democrats decided to propose a constitutional amendment. Accordingly, Simmons sent Josephus Daniels junketing around to seek advice from disfranchisers in other Southern states and write propaganda pieces expatiating on the benevolent consequences of restriction elsewhere in Dixie.[10]

8. Hamilton, *North Carolina since 1860*, p. 287. *Raleigh News and Observer*, November 6, 1898, quoted in Mabry, "Disfranchisement of the Negro," p. 292.

9. Steelman, "Progressive Era in North Carolina," pp. 168, 178–179; Daniels, *Editor in Politics*, pp. 283–312; Orr, *Aycock*, pp. 118–124.

10. Edmonds, *Negro and Fusion Politics*, p. 144; Mabry, "Disfranchisement of the Negro," p. 291; Daniels, *Editor in Politics*, pp. 312, 374–380; Steelman, "Progressive Era in North Carolina," p. 198.

But before they could be sure of passing an amendment, the Democrats had to change the election law. Daniels may have picked up this tactic in his conversations with the important Louisiana disfranchisers. In any case, the *News and Observer* announced that before the vote on the amendment, the legislature should "make it impossible for any element of white voters to appeal to the Negro voters upon any public question." Similarly, a black belt correspondent, in a letter to the newspaper, asked the legislature to "give us an election law by which the amendment can be adopted." A Democratic state senator declared himself in favor of "a good square, honest law that will always give a good Democratic majority." Drafted by a three-man Democratic committee with the help of State Chairman Simmons, the law passed the legislature with every recorded Democrat but two in favor, and every recorded Populist and Republican in opposition. In the thirty minutes that the majority party allowed for the House Republicans to state their case against the bill, the GOP spokesmen declared the election law a subterfuge to get the constitutional amendment past the electorate.[11]

The new law snatched appointment of election officers from local officials chosen by the voters and placed it in the hands of a state election board selected by the Democratic General Assembly. To prevent possible federal interference, the law changed the date of the state election from November to August. To negate the lingering effect of the liberal Fusionist law, the Democratic statute required all voters to register anew and gave the registrars enough discretion to exclude anyone. Finally, the law provided that any ballot placed in the wrong box—there were six—whether by election officers or the voter himself, would be void. As Representative Richmond Pearson (R., North Carolina) charged in Congress, this multiple box provision amounted to an educational qualification, at least for the oppositionists, who could not trust Democratic election officers.[12]

The purpose of the constitutional amendment, according to the Speaker of the 1899 North Carolina House, was "to settle this question

11. *Raleigh News and Observer*, January 12, 21, 28, February 5, March 1, 1899. N. C. *House Journal* (1899), pp. 984–988; N.C. *Senate Journal* (1899), pp. 778–782.

12. N.C. *Public Acts* (1899), pp. 658–687; Roller, "Republican Party in North Carolina," p. 20; Edmonds, *Negro and Fusion Politics*, pp. 184–185; Mabry, *Negro in North Carolina Politics*, pp. 62–63; Rep. Pearson, in *Congressional Record*, 56th Cong., 2nd sess.. pp. 667–669.

once and forever." Expanding on this reasoning, the *News and Observer* declared:

The victory won last November will be short-lived and almost barren unless it is garnered. To leave on the registration books every ignorant Negro in the State, who is merely a tool of selfish and designing men, would be to invite a repetition of the disgraceful rule of 1895–1899 whenever there is any considerable division among the white voters.[13]

Populist newspapers, however, charged that the amendment aimed to disfranchise whites as well, and a Democratic sheet lent credence to these charges when it remarked, "The struggle of the white people of North Carolina to rid themselves of the danger of the rule of Negroes *and the lower classes of whites* is being watched with interest outside the state" (my italics).[14]

As in other states, the disfranchisement managers were black belt aristocrats. The "chief engineer" of the amendment, according to the *News and Observer*, was Francis D. Winston of Bertie County (58 percent Negro in 1900). Born in 1857 of F.F.V. lineage, Winston attended Cornell and graduated from the University of North Carolina. A member of the proper gentry church (Episcopal), Winston followed his father's path into law and the state legislature, and he surpassed his parent by attaining the lieutenant-governorship in 1904. The only other man who spoke for the amendment in the House was the chairman of the Constitutional Amendments Committee, George Rountree of New Hanover County (51 percent Negro in 1900). Though Rountree's ancestors settled in Virginia too late to be among the first families, they did predate the Revolution, and his father was a rich North Carolina businessman. Graduating from Harvard in 1877, George Rountree became a lawyer, politician, and pillar of the Episcopal church. A leader in the 1898 Wilmington uprising which overturned the legally elected government and killed twenty black men, Rountree displayed small concern for either Negroes or lower-class whites. As he noted in a private manuscript written later in his life, he and the Constitutional Amendments Committee wished to exclude from the electorate all

13. *Raleigh News and Observer*, January 29, February 3, 1899.
14. *Charlotte Daily Observer*, June 6, 1900, quoted in Steelman, "Progressive Era in North Carolina," p. 215. See Populist, Republican, and Democratic papers quoted and cited in Steelman, p. 215. The text of the amendment is given in N. C. *Public Acts* (1899), pp. 341–343.

illiterates as soon as possible. Apprehensive about the passage of the amendment without some concession to poor whites, they agreed to the most temporary grandfather clause they could obtain.[15]

The votes on the amendment in the House and Senate split sharply along party lines. Five House Democrats who had pledged during the 1898 campaign not to vote for a restricted suffrage chose to honor their promises, but every other Democrat recorded on the House and Senate roll calls abided by the party's new position. The Populists split three in favor to three opposed. The three in the lower house stated that they agreed to the bill in order to submit it to the voters. Every recorded Republican opposed the measure.[16]

After the bill's passage, Republican lame-duck Governor Daniel L. Russell and his close adviser J. C. L. Harris traveled to Washington in an apparent attempt to induce national GOP leaders to assist them in fighting the amendment in the courts and in Congress. If this was their mission, they failed to obtain the McKinley administration's backing, and North Carolina Republican Senator Jeter Pritchard's effort to persuade the United States Senate to condemn the amendment's grandfather clause likewise proved unsuccessful.[17]

The campaign for the amendment continued the brutal partisanship of 1898. Throughout the state, registrars used their newly regained powers to deny the vote to nearly every black man. The chief speaker for the amendment, Charles B. Aycock, branded his opponents "public enemies" who deserved the "contempt of all mankind." Taking him at his word, Red Shirt Clubs, which enrolled as many as a quarter of the whites in some counties, openly intimidated opposition voters of both races and prevented such antiamendment orators as Populist U.S.

15. For Winston's role, see *Raleigh News and Observer*, March 5, 1899. For biographical details, see Charles B. Aycock, "Francis D. Winston," in Samuel A. Ashe, ed., *Biographical History of North Carolina* 2:475–480; J. O. Carr, "George H. Rountree," in ibid., 3:365–371. For Rountree's view, see George H. Rountree, "My Personal Recollections of the Campaign of 1898," manuscript quoted in Mabry, *Negro in North Carolina Politics*, p. 59. The Progressive Charles B. Aycock threatened to oppose the amendment if the temporary grandfather clause were extended. See Orr, *Aycock*, p. 170.

16. N. C. *House Journal* (1899), p. 656; N. C. *Senate Journal* (1899), p. 495; *Raleigh News and Observer*, February 18, 19, 1899; Daniels, *Editor in Politics*, p. 326.

17. Daniels, *Editor in Politics*, pp. 332–334; Edmonds, *Negro and Fusion Politics*, p. 198. United States Senator John T. Morgan (D., Alabama) thought Pritchard's resolution so grave a challenge to disfranchisement that he stayed in Washington during part of the time when he could have been campaigning at home in his tough 1900 reelection contest. See Ala. Con. Con. *Proceedings* (1901), vol. 3, p. 2917.

Senator Marion Butler from speaking. Perhaps the Red Shirts' real spokesman, however, was not Aycock, but an upper-class ex-congressman from black belt Wilmington, Alfred Moore Waddell, who told an election eve crowd to "go to the polls tomorrow and if you find the Negro out voting, tell him to leave the polls and if he refuses, kill him, shoot him down in his tracks." Against such powerful and determined forces, the official opposition of the Republicans and the Populists, who charged the amendment would "end popular government in this state," could not prevail. With a recorded turnout of 74.6 percent for the referendum, the amendment carried by a 59–41 margin.[18]

Table 7.5 indicates that the 1898 election law and a very large, one-sided turnout in 1900 in heavily Negro counties rolled up the majority for the amendment. Under the Fusion election laws, the Negroes voted overwhelmingly for the Populists and Republicans in 1896. The statewide GOP percentage did not change from 1896 to 1898, but the Fusionist percentage in the predominantly white counties probably rose because of the Populist-Republican agreement on a single statewide candidate in 1898, while intimidation and fraud probably depressed their totals in the black areas. From 1898 to 1900, the Fusionist percentage statewide dropped by about a quarter, and their support in the regions of Negro concentration completely disappeared. Since there was a large amount of intimidation in both of these elections, most of the Fusionist decline from 1898 to 1900 must be attributed to the workings of the new election law. The strong correlation between votes for Aycock and the amendment on the one hand, and the percentage of Negroes in each county on the other, no doubt represents a combination of a disproportionately large turnout for disfranchisement among black belt whites as well as simple fraud. As a North Carolina Re-

18. On the actions of the registrars, see editorials, *The Independent*, 52 (1900): 1874–1876, 1885; Marion Butler, "Elections in North Carolina," in ibid.: 1953–1955; A. J. McKelway, in ibid.: 1955–1957; editorial, *The Outlook* 65 (1900): 841–843. Both of these national magazines favored suffrage restriction, and neither usually showed much sympathy for either black people or Southern Republicans. Aycock is quoted in Orr, *Aycock*, p. 157; Waddell, quoted in Daniels, *Editor in Politics*, p. 368. Statement of the Populist State Executive Committee is quoted in Mabry, *Negro in North Carolina Politics*, p. 67. The Populists and ex-Populists split over the amendment. Senator Butler's faction fought it strenuously, while other former Populist leaders campaigned for it. See ibid., pp. 63–69; Hamilton, *North Carolina since 1860*, pp. 306–308; Steelman, "Progressive Era in North Carolina," pp. 209–217; Orr, *Aycock*, pp. 163–170. One prominent Republican campaigned for the amendment, according to Roller, "Republican Party in North Carolina," p. 52.

Table 7.5. Election Law, Intimidation, and Fraud Carried the Suffrage
Amendment: Election Returns and Estimated Negro Voting in North
Carolina, 1896–1904.

Election	*% Democratic*	*% Republican*	*% Populist*	*% Not Voting*
PARTY BALANCE, 1896–1900				
1896 Governor	37.5	39.7	8.3	14.6
1898 Supreme Court	44.4	39.7		15.8
1900 Governor	44.8	30.3		24.7
1900 Referendum	43.8*a*	30.8*b*		25.4
ESTIMATES OF NEGRO VOTING, 1896–1904*c*				
1896 Governor	20	59	8	13
Election Law and Intimidation				
1900 Governor	67	0		33
1900 Referendum	73*a*	0*b*		27
Constitution				
1904 Governor	0	0		100

*a*For Constitutional Amendment.
*b*Against Constitutional Amendment.
*c*No estimates were made for Negro voting in the 1898 state supreme court contest.

publican congressman pointed out at the time, the Negroes "according
to the election returns, actually voted to disfranchise themselves."
In the first statewide election after the amendment went into effect,
the estimated number of Negroes voting dropped drastically. The crisis
having passed, whites in regions of high Negro concentration did not
need to turn out again in such large proportions or artificially inflate
the returns.[19]

Table 7.6 demonstrates the split over suffrage restriction in North
Carolina. Virtually every Republican and Democrat who voted in 1900
followed his party's line on the amendment. It is more difficult to
discern what course former Populists took, for their party never ran
a strong statewide candidate. Since the People's Party made by far its
best statewide showing in 1892, returns from the governor's race of
that year provide the least unsatisfactory indication of who the Populists

19. I have not been able to obtain county-by-county figures on the race for the Supreme
Court in 1898. Republican Congressman Linney is quoted in *Congressional Record*, 56th Cong.,
2nd sess., pp. 611–616. For other evidence of fraud in the 1900 referendum, see Steelman,
"Progressive Era in North Carolina," pp. 222–226; Orr, *Aycock*, pp. 181–182.

Table 7.6. Party and Suffrage Restriction in North Carolina: Estimates
of Relations between Voting in Gubernatorial Races and Referendum on
Suffrage Amendment.

% of Adult Males in 1900 Governor's Race[a]	% of Adult Males in 1900 Suffrage Referendum		
	For	Against	Not Voting
Democrat	96	0	4
Republican	0	100	0
Not Voting	14	0	87
% of Adult Males in 1892 Governor's Race			
Democrat	74	23	2
Republican	6	80	15
Populist	37	42	22
Not Voting	40	−16[b]	75

[a]There was no Populist candidate in 1900.
[b]For an explanation of estimates below zero, see my "Ecological Regression" article.

were. The 1892 Populists split in the 1900 referendum, and a slight majority of those who voted opposed the amendment.

With the suffrage restricted, both the Republican and Democratic parties shifted to the right, and turnout declined from 75 percent in the 1900 governor's race to less than 50 percent in 1904. No longer did either party have to concern itself with the illiterate or those too poor to pay the poll tax. Democratic legislatures kept taxes low, cut appropriations in some cases and failed to increase them in others, continued to pass partisan election laws and gerrymander voting districts, enacted few of the usual "Progressive" reforms, and none which protected workers or trade unions. The party convention almost endorsed the gold standard in 1902, elected the Southern Railroad's candidate to the United States Senate in 1903, a corporation lawyer to the governorship in 1904, and felt quite comfortable with the conservative Alton B. Parker as presidential candidate in that year. Abandoning the disfranchised Negroes as a lost and damaging cause, the state GOP adopted a lily-white line, and spent the first decade of the century trying to paint the Democrats as pro-Negro and antibusiness. Settled party loyalties and a political structure devised to ensure Democratic victory aborted the new Republican appeals.[20]

20. On the Democrats, see Steelman, "Progressive Era in North Carolina," pp. 237–248,

TEXAS: ELECTIONS—"THE MOST TERRIBLE ENEMY"

Texas was in many respects the least "Southern" of the ex-Confederate states. Settled by Americans late in the antebellum period, it entered the Union only in 1845. Slavery lasted for 200 years in Virginia and the Carolinas; for twenty in Texas. The aristocratic planter class, the fixed racial attitudes, and the stable, elitist power structure which characterized a slave society had little time to mature in the Lone Star State. In Alabama and Virginia the antebellum black belt slave-holders began a tradition of political expertise which their descendants cherished and developed. In North Carolina and Tennessee, mountain whites, by banding together against the lowland slaveholders' schemes of secession and war, willed their progeny an inclination to oppose the established politics even if opposition meant alliances with Yankees and Negroes. Postbellum Texans inherited neither of these traditions.

Nor did a post-War Texan's birthright include the profound sense of grievance, the corresponding regional and state pride, and the desire for unity against a common enemy which were shared by inhabitants of states more battered by the Civil War. Cut off from the main theater of the conflict in 1863, Texas never saw its coasts infested with opponents, its towns and crops burned, large numbers of its sons sacrificed. Consequently, Confederate generals received a little less automatic reverence, orators slipped a bit less easily into paeans to the lost cause, the North inspired somewhat less fear and hatred in Texas after the War than in other ex-Confederate states. Texas society after 1865 also differed from the rest of the South in another respect: it included fewer Negroes. In 1880, 36 percent of the population in the 16 states and the District of Columbia which comprised the Census Bureau's South were black, but only 24.7 percent in Texas. By 1910, Texas had the smallest proportion of Negroes, 17.7 percent, among the 11 ex-Confederate states.[21]

Since the percentage of Negroes was too small to pose a plausible

---

264–268, 272–279, 542–580, 694–721; Roller, "Republican Party in North Carolina," pp. 29–31; Orr, *Aycock*, pp. 213–214. According to Steelman, pp. 386–394, North Carolina in 1916 had the lowest taxes per capita of any state in the United States. On the Republicans, see Steelman, "Progressive Era in North Carolina," pp. 228, 339–409, 423–431; and, generally Roller, "Republican Party of North Carolina."

21. U.S. Department of Commerce, Bureau of the Census, *Negro Population, 1790–1915* (Washington, D.C.: G.P.O., 1918), pp. 46, 49.

threat of "Negro domination," opposition political parties could be tolerated more easily than in the rest of Dixie. If an opposition party did triumph in Texas, its victory would not automatically spell a large increase in the number of Negro officials who were given an office as a reward for black support, because Negro votes would constitute a smaller percentage of the dissenters' totals. Conversely, Democrats would have less reason to demand disfranchisement of the Negroes. Moreover, the black belt was smaller and less potent in Texas politics than in other Southern states. Only 14 of Texas' 144 counties had black majorities in 1880; and by 1910, only 8 of 217. In contrast, 66 of Georgia's 146 counties were predominantly black in 1910. These figures translated into legislative impotence for the Texas black belt. For instance, only 7 of 107 members of the 1891–92 Texas House came from counties with Negro majorities.

All this is not to imply that Texas was utterly different from the rest of the South, but only that the forces which shaped late nineteenth-century Southern politics were muted in Texas. The Democrats, predominantly white and drawing their support from all classes, although dominated by businessmen and rich landowners, struggled against the repeated efforts of a poor white–Negro coalition to gain power and office. Since there was no mountain whites' Unionist tradition, few whites adhered to the Texas GOP. Men with economic grievances and those unsuccessful in achieving their ambitions within the Democratic party therefore gravitated to the third-party movements, which consistently attracted a larger proportion of the adult males in Texas than in any other Southern state (table 7.7). Since Negroes regularly voted for the Republicans and third parties, and poor whites often did also,

Table 7.7. Texas Was Hospitable to Third Parties: Percentage of Adult Males Voting for Third Parties in Presidential Elections, 1880–1896.

Party	Year	% in Texas	% in Ten Other Southern States
Greenback	1880	7.2	2.2
Union Labor	1888	6.6	0.6
Populist	1892	19.0	8.0
Mid-Road Populist[a]	1896	13.5	1.1

[a]The "Middle of the Road" faction refused to cooperate with either the Democratic or Republican parties, keeping instead its independent identity.

Democrats made repeated efforts to enact laws restricting the suffrage. But since Democrats from counties with large numbers of Negroes had less power in Texas than elsewhere, it took 27 years to enact poll tax legislation.[22]

Though it reflected these differences from the rest of the South, the course of Texas politics from the Civil War to the turn of the century was quite similar to that in other areas below the Mason-Dixon line. The Republican party elected only one governor during Reconstruction in Texas, and his margin over an "independent" opponent was less than 800 votes. Thereafter, Texas Republicans provided a constant, though small opposition to the Democrats. It should be noted that Republican support did not erode very much during the eighties. The GOP candidate for governor got 24.4 percent of the votes in 1880 and 22.6 percent in 1890, while turnout remained fairly constant.

The Republicans, about three-fourths of whom were black, posed more of a threat to the Democrats when they supported third-party candidates.[23] In 1880, for example, the Democratic gubernatorial candidate enjoyed a margin of 26.8 percent of the adult males over the Republican nominee; whereas, in 1882, a Greenback-Republican hopeful cut the majority party's margin to 11.6 percent of the potential electorate (table 7.8). Under the skilled generalship of Norris Wright Cuney, a Negro, the Republicans also gave substantial backing to a Farmers' Alliance candidate in 1888, a conservative Democrat in 1892, and a Populist in 1896. In fact, a considerable portion of the votes for unorthodox parties, left or right, came from the blacks, and those parties could not hope to contend with the Democrats without widespread black support.

22. For evidence of blatant favoritism toward privileged economic groups under Democratic rule, see Frank W. Johnson, *A History of Texas and Texans*, 1: 586–593; James Aubrey Tinsley, "The Progressive Movement in Texas," pp. 15–22, 91–106, 177–187. Roscoe C. Martin, *The People's Party in Texas*, presents proof from correlations of subcounty election returns and economic statistics that the Populists represented poor whites, while the large landowners on good land were Democrats. In the four presidential elections cited in table 7.7, the third party received a larger percentage of the votes than in any other state with one exception. The Populists in Alabama got 24.8 percent of the vote in the 1892 presidential race.

23. Rice, *The Negro in Texas*, pp. 34–112, is the best treatment of Republicanism and Texas elections in this period. Robert Saunders, "Southern Populists and the Negro, 1893–1895," p. 257, treats the 1894 contest. For the attitudes of white Republicans and Populists toward the blacks, see, in addition, Pollack, *The Populist Mind*, pp. 284–285; Martin, *People's Party Party in Texas*, pp. 82, 93–99, 137, 236–237; Casdorph, *History of the Republican Party in Texas*, pp. 44–45, 49–50, 58, 68–71.

Table 7.8. Stiff Party Competition in Texas Gubernatorial Contests, 1880–1896: Actual Votes and Estimates of Voting by Race.

Election	Democratic	Republican	Third Party	Other	Not Voting
		% OF ALL ADULT MALES			
1880	43.7	16.9	8.9[a]	0	30.5
1882	36.7	0	24.9[a]	0	38.4
1888	49.6	0	19.5[b]	0	30.9
1890	49.0	14.5	0	0	35.9
1892	33.6	0	19.2[c]	23.6[d]	23.7
1894	40.5	9.3	26.7[c]	1.4[e]	26.6
1896	47.6	0	36.1[c]	0	14.3
		ESTIMATED % OF WHITE ADULT MALES			
1880	53.6	4.9	8.7[a]	0	36.9
1882	44.1	0	18.0[a]	0	37.8
1888	55.6	0	10.1[b]	0	34.3
1890	63.3	6.6	0	0	29.4
1892	36.2	0	23.1[c]	23.2[d]	17.0
1894	41.7	5.3	29.5[c]	0	22.0
1896	47.6	0	34.1[c]	0	18.0
		ESTIMATED % OF NEGRO ADULT MALES			
1880	26.5	62.2	4.0[a]	0	11.2
1882	9.9	0	61.8[a]	0	28.3
1888	27.9	0	58.3[b]	0	13.3
1890	11.5	56.1	0	0	32.7
1892	24.1	0	8.3[c]	29.4[d]	38.2
1894	21.4	34.5	22.4[c]	0	22.9
1896	47.0	0	49.9[c]	0	3.2

[a]Greenback
[b]Alliance
[c]Populist
[d]Conservative Democrat
[e]Prohibitionist

Politicians of every party no doubt recognized these facts and sought to bargain for the endorsement of black leaders when possible, and undercut those leaders by appealing over their heads to the black masses when necessary. The Democrats and Populists concentrated on the latter tactic particularly in 1892, with a fair amount of success. The Democrats continued to seek black support outside regular Republican channels throughout the nineties, but the Populists, after their substantial defeat in 1894, chose to deal with Cuney directly. Unfortunately for the People's Party, one of Cuney's young lieutenants who was feuding with his captain revolted against the older man's choice and openly backed the Democratic candidate. The Democrats also swelled their totals in the 1896 contest through extraordinary efforts, legal and illegal, in black belt counties in which they had gained control by violence and intimidation.[24]

The attempt to restrict the suffrage began long before 1896. Delegates to the 1875 constitutional convention beat down three efforts to enact a poll tax by votes of 52–28, 44–28, and 56–22. Led by former Confederate postmaster-general and future United States Congressman and Senator John H. Reagan of Anderson County (44.7 percent Negro in 1880) and by W. L. Crawford of Marion County (65.6 percent Negro), proponents of the poll tax argued that the restriction would eliminate "irresponsible" voters. Voting, according to these conservatives, was not a natural right, but a privilege which the state should deny to those unwilling to pay the tax.[25] As the *Houston Telegraph* summed up the poll taxers' stand,

Must the low, groveling, equal-before-the-law, lazy, purchasable Negro, who pays no taxes, have the privilege of neutralizing the vote of a good citizen and taxpayer? Ought the miserable apologies for men with white skins, who exercise the right to vote only because it furnishes them with whiskey, be allowed to vote, if they dont [*sic*] pay the state a pittance for its protection and the privileges afforded them?[26]

Almost every Democrat who joined the fourteen Republicans in opposition to the tax was a member of the Grange, a farmers' organization. Most of those who spoke against the voting restriction came from counties with very few Negroes. Defending the traditional belief that suffrage was a natural right, these men charged that the capitation tax would disfranchise many whites, encourage fraud, invite the federal government to overthrow Texas' constitution, and "oppress the poor."

24. Rice, *Negro in Texas*, pp. 68–85; Casdorph, *Republican Party in Texas*, pp. 53–54. Graphs of the series of gubernatorial election returns by county make clear which counties deviated from the general pattern and when those deviations occurred.

25. In analyzing the conventions, I have relied upon the Tex. Con. Con. *Journal* (1875); McKay, ed., *Texas Constitutional Convention*, and McKay, *Making the Texas Constitution*. The roll calls are given in the *Journal*, pp. 306, 309, 310. For the conservatives' arguments, see *Texas Constitutional Convention*, pp. 167–190. An opponent of the poll tax identified Reagan and Crawford as its chief backers in ibid., p. 185.

26. *Houston Telegraph*, October 10, 1875, quoted in McKay, *Making the Texas Constitution*, p. 98.

"Is this a covert design, cunningly devised," asked B. D. Martin of Hunt County (7 percent Negro), "to plant the germ of aristocracy in this land? . . . It cannot affect the *rich*; they can always pay their taxes. It afflicts the *poor* man and the poor man alone." J. W. Barnett of Parker County (3.9 percent Negro) more bluntly castigated the tax as "a stepping stone toward aristocracy and imperialism."[27]

The convention defeat of the "aristocratic design" proved temporary. Four years later, Alexander Watkins Terrell pushed a poll tax amendment through the state senate. Terrell, who served in the state senate from 1876 to 1884 and in the lower house from 1890 to 1892 and 1902 to 1906, was the most prominent and constant advocate of the poll tax in Texas. Born in Virginia in 1827 of a slaveholding family, Terrell migrated to Missouri, where he attended the state university, read law, and married the daughter of a wealthy tobacco farmer and politician. Moving on to Texas, Terrell became a lawyer, Democratic politician, and Confederate general in the Civil War.

After the War and his first wife's death, Terrell married a Texas plantation owner's daughter. Averse to appearing in courts where Negroes served on juries, he retired from the law temporarily and devoted himself entirely to running the plantation from 1867 to 1871, but he entered politics again in 1872. Throughout the rest of his life, he divided his time between law, politics, and the plantation. One of the first bills he introduced in the state senate was aimed at eliminating blacks from Texas juries. Strongly challenged by a Greenback candidate in 1878, Terrell introduced his poll tax bill in 1879 because, in his biographer's words, he "thought that the only way to prevent the people of Texas from voting to confiscate property for educational and eleemosynary purposes was to reform the ballot box by requiring a poll tax for the privilege of voting." In fact, Terrell wished to destroy public elementary education in Texas, though he eagerly supported allocations for the University of Texas, which primarily served those wealthy enough to prepare at private secondary schools. He also fought valiantly to reward, with three million acres of public land, the builders of an opulent new capital building.[28]

---

27. On the opposition Democrats, see ibid., pp. 97–98, 101–102. Spokesmen include Weaver, in *Texas Constitutional Convention*, pp. 170–172; Martin, in ibid., pp. 173–175; Flournoy, in ibid., pp. 167–168; J. F. Johnson, in ibid., p. 184; Pickett, in ibid., p. 177; John Johnson, in ibid., p. 177; Barnett, in ibid., p. 176.

28. Charles K. Chamberlain, "Alexander Watkins Terrell, Citizen, Statesman," pp. 140–

Although his 1879 bill died in the House, Terrell introduced poll tax bills in the 1881 and 1883 legislatures, again meeting defeat. His minority report on the bill to a state senate committee in 1883 may be coupled with a speech he gave to the "Progressive" National Civic Federation in New York City in 1906 to indicate Terrell's views on the necessity of a restricted suffrage and on the purposes of the poll tax.[29] Characterizing the Fifteenth Amendment as "the political blunder of the century," Terrell proposed the poll tax to eliminate "the thriftless, idle and semi-vagrant element of *both races*" (my italics). "Though liberty requires elections," this adherent of the "Democratic" party remarked in 1883, "yet when they are not controlled by intelligence and patriotism they become the most terrible enemy." And in 1906 he added this non-sequitur: "Whether universal manhood suffrage is good for the country depends entirely on the sort of men who vote."

Stressing his desire to regulate, but not disturb the railroads, Terrell ran unsuccessfully for the United States Senate in 1886. After this defeat, he attached himself to the "reform" governor Jim Hogg and returned to the state legislature, where he quickly became one of the most important leaders. In the 1891 session, Terrell was the principal sponsor, according to the *Dallas Morning News*, of a poll tax amendment (February 20, 1891). After a debate in which Terrell declared, in the *News*'s summary (February 21, 1891), "that the chief object in view was to collect the tax on the wooly scalp" (i.e., to disfranchise Negroes), the bill passed the House. Opposition was apparently so substantial in the Senate, however, that the bill was never brought to a vote.[30]

141, 191–192, 230, quote at p. 140. Biographical details on Terrell are taken from this thesis. The Greenback Party platforms from 1878 through 1882 endorsed "universal manhood suffrage" and strongly denounced any attempts to set up "property suffrage" through a poll tax. See Winkler, *Political Parties in Texas*, pp. 181, 200, 208. Terrell may well have had a financial interest in the "Capital Syndicate's" operations.

29. Recognizing Terrell's central role in the adoption of the poll tax, despite the fact that he did not serve in the legislature which finally passed the amendment, the *Austin* (Texas) *Daily Statesman* reprinted his 1883 minority report during the 1902 campaign for ratification. See the issue of October 19, 1902. Terrell's 1906 speech to the National Civic Federation in New York is reported in Chamberlain, "Terrell," pp. 493–494, and Tinsley, "Progressive Movement in Texas," pp. 195–196.

30. Chamberlain, "Terrell," pp. 268–329; *Dallas Morning News*, February 20, 21, 26, 1891. Terrell was apparently chief author of the railroad commission law which so angered the Farmers' Alliance leaders that they broke with the Texas Democrats and launched the Populist Party. See Harry Tracy (Alliance lobbyist) to the *News*, March 23, 1892. For the progress of Terrell's bill in the Senate, see *Austin* (Texas) *Daily Statesman*, February 21, 1891; Tex. *House Journal* (1891), pp. 84, 162, 565–566, 572–573. During the debate, Ed Patton, the only

The 1891 legislature also considered a bill to call a constitutional convention. Terrell, the leading opponent of the proposal, objected to calling a convention at this time because (again in the *News*'s summary),

The people are confused over new theories, projects, crankiness about subtreasury schemes, state ownership of railroads, and [Henry] Georgeism, and . . . a large element is in favor of confiscation and a general divide. It is, therefore, a dangerous time to elect men for the essentially conservative work of constitution making.[31]

The legislature did pass a bill providing for voter registration and a secret ballot in cities of ten thousand or more people. The registration bill was a direct response to the outcome of the "nonpartisan" Dallas city election of April 1891, in which incumbent Mayor Connor beat a candidate endorsed by the local Democratic party. Much of Connor's majority came from Negro and lower-class white precincts. Furious at their defeat, the local Democratic leaders rushed to Austin and persuaded the legislators to jam through a registration law during the last three days of the session.[32]

The secret ballot law, introduced in the special session of 1892 by W. H. Pope of Harrison County (68 percent Negro in 1890), at first applied to every county in the state. Before final passage, however, it was grafted onto another bill that limited its effect to the ten largest cities, which together contained fewer than one of every ten Texans. The bill also allowed election judges to assist illiterate voters, despite one representative's protest that "the object of the bill could hardly be accomplished" if illiterates were allowed to vote.[33] These provisions severely limited the bill's restrictive impact.

---

black member of the House, charged that while the bill was aimed chiefly at Negroes, it would affect many whites as well. The *News*, March 5, 1891, endorsed disfranchisement of Negroes and the "agrarian agitators of the large cities" (by definition, presumably, a rather miniscule group). After one day of hot debate in the Senate, the bill languished. See *News* March 20, 1891; *Statesman*, March 20, 1891; Tex. *Senate Journal* (1891), pp. 436–437. Neither newspaper explained precisely why the sponsors allowed the bill to die. Robert C. Cotner asserts in *James Stephen Hogg*, p. 226, that Governor Hogg opposed a poll tax, but offers no evidence for his assertion, and does not specify whether or not Hogg ever threw his considerable political weight into active opposition to the tax.

31. *Dallas Morning News*, February 6, 7, 1891. Terrell's proposal to kill the convention bill passed the House by 67–13.

32. Ibid., April 8–14, 1891. The election took place on April 7; the bill was introduced April 10. The legislature adjourned April 13.

33. Tex. *House Journal* (extra session, 1892), pp. 180–191, 242, 260; Tex. *Senate Journal* (extra session, 1892), pp. 69, 73, 78–80, 83, 84, 88, 153, 227–229; *Austin Daily Statesman*, April

Throughout the rest of the decade, various legislators proposed certain changes in election laws, but none of their bills passed either house. In 1893, for example, Rowell of Marion (64 percent Negro in 1890) proposed to extend registration and the secret ballot throughout the state, but a majority of the House refused to take up his bill. A majority, but not the two-thirds of the House members necessary to pass a constitutional amendment, did favor a poll tax in the same session. Other poll tax bills met with even less success. Since there were so few votes on the actual bills, and since historians have written so little on Texas politics during these years, it is difficult to tell which groups pushed and which fought the measures.[34]

At the beginning of the twentieth century, Texas was unnaturally quiet politically. After Norris Wright Cuney's death, two black leaders, Henry Ferguson and William McDonald, fought for control of the state's Republican organization. Although Ferguson had clearly won by 1900, he had to struggle continuously for the next decade against a lily-white faction of the party. By 1900, too, most Populists had found the middle of the road overgrown with weeds. In the gubernatorial election of 1900, the Populist candidate attracted only about 6 percent of the white adult males and almost none of the Negroes.[35]

12, 1892; Tex. *General Laws* (extra session, 1892), pp. 13–19.

34. Tex. *House Journal* (1893), pp. 100, 218, 780, 862–863, 1248, 1286; Tex. *House Journal* (1895), pp. 382, 1026, 1063; Tex. *Senate Journal* (1895), p. 748; Texas *House Journal* (1897), pp. 318, 1420, 1447–1448; Tex. *Senate Journal* (1895), pp. 375, 903; Tex. *House Journal* (1899), pp. 1169, 1531–1532; Tex. *Senate Journal* (1899), pp. 619, 792, 1150. Grover Cleveland appointed Terrell ambassador to Turkey in 1893, and Terrell did not return to the legislature during the decade. Though members of dissenting parties unanimously opposed all disfranchising measures brought to a vote in the 1891, 1893, and 1899 legislatures, there were too few Populists or Republicans in the legislature at any time to stop any bill which the vast majority of the Democrats wanted passed. Nor were there enough Democrats from heavily Negro counties to push through bills without the aid of a great many white-county Democrats. I therefore tried a variety of dividing lines between "whiter" and "blacker" counties. Although Democrats from counties over 30 percent or 40 percent Negro did support the poll tax more strongly than those from overwhelmingly white counties in these sessions, the differences in the two groups' voting patterns during the nineties were slight. Nor do correlations of roll calls with the strength of Populist or Republican candidates in each legislator's home county unveil any pattern. These facts, in addition to the secret deaths of many of these measures in committees or on the calendar of one house, lead me to place particular stress on the few legislative leaders about whom we have some information.

35. The Ferguson-McDonald struggle may be followed in Rice, *Negro in Texas*, pp. 49–52; Winkler, *Political Parties in Texas*, pp. 405–409, 433–441, 454–461, 474–478, 487–491, 514–519. The tiny Populist vote in this election and in the 1902 contest, when the Populists received the

The Democrats were no less drowsy. Each of the three governors who held office from 1894 to 1906 put himself under the tutelage of Col. Edward M. House and repeatedly reassured the conservative wire-puller that he felt inactivity the best course for government. A leading student of the period describes the two terms of Governor Joseph D. Sayers (1898–1902) as "placid." Headlining an article on the 1901 legislature "Demand for 'Reform' Is No Longer Heard," the *Dallas Morning News* reported that "not one [legislator] in fifty wants to discuss with another member the importance of disturbing the present apparent placid and satisfactory conditions."[36] The adoption of the poll tax in Texas, then, was neither part of a general "reform" program nor the result of a frantic racist upsurge. It was the quiet climax of a long drive by a few men, a drive which succeeded when the opposition became dormant.

In the 1899 legislature, Representative Pat Neff of McLennan (24 percent Negro in 1900), and Senator A. B. Davidson of DeWitt (23 percent Negro) had introduced poll tax bills. The former failed, 50 ayes, to 50 nays; the latter, 18 to 11, neither of which received the necessary two-thirds vote. In 1901 Neff and Davidson re-introduced their bills, and Davidson's eventually became the constitutional amendment. Both legislators were aspiring, legislatively talented politicians. Neff, 28 years old in 1901, became House Speaker in the 1903 session and governor from 1920 to 1924. Davidson rose to be President Pro-Tem of the Senate in 1903. His bill passed both houses fairly easily in 1901, 87–15 in the House and 23–6 in the Senate, with the voting patterns showing no significant difference between legislators from counties over and counties under 40 percent Negro.[37]

---

franchises of 1.6 percent of the adult males, destroys the contention of Strong and Smith that the poll taxers aimed to quell an immediate Populist threat, although they may have wished to guard against the renascence of a Populist-type party. See Donald S. Strong, "The Poll Tax: The Case of Texas," pp. 693–709; Dick Smith, "Texas and the Poll Tax," pp. 167–173.

36. Tinsley, "Progressive Movement in Texas," pp. 32–43; *Dallas Morning News,* January 13, 1901.

37. For the 1899 vote on the poll tax bill, see Tex. *House Journal* (1901), p. 1368; Tex. *Senate Journal* (1901), p. 29. For the 1901 passage of the bill, see Tex. *House Journal* (1901), pp. 481–482; Tex. *Senate Journal* (1901), pp. 55–56, 63–64, 80. When the vote on final passage in the House was announced, the bill lacked a two-thirds margin by three votes. Several members, including a freshman representative named John Nance Garner, switched sides so the bill could pass. *Dallas Morning News,* February 22, 1901. On an earlier vote in the House to make the 1901 amendment self-enacting without further legislative action—thus precluding

The 1902 referendum took the character of a party, race, and class battle. The Democrats endorsed the amendment. The Populists blasted it, charging that it was a plot to rob "the laboring people . . . of their liberties at the ballot box. Every laboring man who loves liberty, who believes in freedom of suffrage, who prizes his rights of citizenship should vote against the poll tax amendment." Citing the Declaration of Independence, the State Federation of Labor denounced the tax as a "cunning effort of the wealthier classes to defeat the will of the people by disfranchising the poorer classes . . . a step in the direction of disfranchising a larger part of the people whenever the ruling class sees fit to increase the tax." Likewise, Negroes and white Republicans organized to defeat the tax, and the precinct returns for at least one large county, Travis, show a close correlation between votes for the GOP candidate for governor and votes against the poll tax.[38]

Only 41 percent of the adult males cast ballots in the November 1902 referendum, which was 7 percent less than the percentage cast in the governor's race held at the same time. Sixty-five percent of those who voted, or just over a quarter of the potential electors, favored the poll tax. The estimates of voting by race indicate that there was a great deal of fraud and/or intimidation in the counties of high Negro concentration. Whereas the Republican candidate for governor in 1902 got better than three-fourths of the estimated Negro votes (table 7.9B), more than four-fifths of the same voters appear to have backed the poll tax (table 7.9A). Since it is ludicrous to assume either that Negroes

---

possible legislative delay or de facto nullification later—there was something of a white county –black belt split. Eighty-five percent of those from counties over 40 percent Negro voted for the automatic provision, while only 62.5 percent from the counties under 40 percent Negro favored it. See Tex. *House Journal* (1901), pp. 388–391.

Printed sources for Texas biography in this period are abominable. This sparse information was gleaned from Seth S. McKay and Odie B. Faulk, *Texas After Spindletop*, pp. 77–87; C. W. Raines, ed., *Year Book For Texas*, vols. 1 and 2 (Austin, Texas: Gammel Book Co., 1902, 1903).

38. *Dallas Morning News*, October 14, 1902. Editorials and letters to the editor make it clear that the Democrats represented the tax as a white supremacy measure. See *El Paso* (Texas) *News*, quoted January 23, 1901; editorial, February 15, 1901; George T. Todd to ibid., October 14, 1902; editorial, October 26, 1902. The Democrats also tried to confuse the issue by arguing that the tax would protect the poor from the "outrages" of "corrupt office-holders." See ibid., November 2, 1902; *Austin Daily Statesman*, October 28, 1902. For the Populists' and state Federation of Labor's response, see Ogden, *Poll Tax in the South*, pp. 18–19; *Dallas Morning News*, October 26, 1902. Republican efforts are detailed in *Dallas Morning News*, October 19, 1902. The Travis County results are from *Austin Daily Statesman*, October 30, November 7, 1902.

Table 7.9. Violence, Disorganization, and Fraud: Estimates of
Negro Voting in Texas, 1902.

Race	*For Poll Tax*	*Against Poll Tax*	*Not Voting*
		A. Referendum, 1902	
White	34	18	48
Negro	23	4	73

Race	*Democratic*	*Republican*	*Populist*	*Not Voting*
		B. Governors' Contest, 1902		
White	50	9	2	38
Negro	6	21	0	77

voted for the tax or that black belt whites voted Republican, one can
only conclude that election officers, realizing that the Democrats were
safe in the gubernatorial election but fearing that the referendum might
be close, changed the figures on the poll tax. The very low turnout in
counties with large percentages of blacks probably reflects the disorganization of Negro voters after the Ferguson-McDonald struggle and
the decline of the Populists, as well as a consolidation of power by whites
in those counties, a consolidation which had often been delayed because of the fervid competition for votes in the nineties. Estimates of
votes in the referendum according to party alignments in 1900 (table
7.10) reflect the evident tampering with returns—surely the Republicans did not vote three-to-one for the tax—as well as the opposition
of the few remaining Populists to suffrage restriction.[39]

In 1903 A. W. Terrell returned to the legislature to author what

Table 7.10. Texas Populists Opposed the Poll Tax: Estimates of
Relationships between Party and Voting in 1902 Referendum.

Party in 1900 *Governors' Race*	*1902 Poll Tax Referendum*		
	For Tax	*Against Tax*	*Not Voting*
Democratic	39	12	48
Republican	66	18	16
Populist	0	81	19
Not Voting	2	5	94

39. These conclusions are based on a series of graphs of votes in gubernatorial elections and
the percentage Negro in each county. The graphs are too numerous and complex to include
in the text. Since the Populists did not control the election machinery even in the counties
where they remained strong, one must assume that that group's partisans really voted against
the tax.

became known as the "Terrell Election Law." That law, together with a more comprehensive statute passed two years later also written by Terrell, provided for a noncumulative poll tax to be paid six months before the election and an office-block secret ballot in every county for general elections and primaries. Only election judges could assist illiterates in voting. Minority parties were not guaranteed roles in the election machinery. Chiefly to allow counties to conduct white primaries, the county committees of each party were authorized to prescribe additional qualifications for voting in their primaries.[40]

Texas election returns from the first decade of the century tend to undermine some contentions crucial to V. O. Key's fait accompli hypothesis, a hypothesis which rested largely on the example of Texas. Key asserted that by the time the poll tax was passed, the "Negroes [had] been disfranchised . . . and the electoral abdication of a substantial part of the white population signed and sealed . . . " (p. 535). To be sure, most blacks in Texas had been pushed out of the electorate by 1902 through violence and intimidation, or had at least temporarily ceased voting because of the disarray of the Populist and Republican parties.[41] Yet an estimated 36 percent managed to vote in the 1900 governor's race, and 21 percent in 1902. And much larger proportions of whites continued to participate in the pre–poll tax elections—80 percent in 1900 and 62 percent in 1902. If their abdication was already "signed and sealed," delivery awaited the institution of the poll tax. In the first general election for governor in which tax payment was required (1904), estimated white turnout dropped to 46 percent, and the figures in successive elections were 27 percent, 39 percent, and 29 percent. The analogous turnout percentages for blacks were 15 percent, 11 percent, 16 percent, and 2 percent. Moreover, the voters did not turn out for post–poll tax Democratic primaries, either. Only about a third of the Texas adult males—about 40 percent among the whites—voted in the hard-fought Democratic gubernatorial primaries of 1908 and 1910.

The Terrell election laws also sealed the doom of opposition parties in Texas until the late 1950s. In the 1900 presidential contest, 23 per-

---

40. Tex. *General Laws* (1903), pp. 133–158; Tex. *General Laws* (1905), pp. 532–565.

41. On the disarray of the opposition, see Chester Alwyn Barr. Jr., *Reconstruction to Reform*, pp. 176–208; Lawrence C. Goodwyn, "Populist Dreams and Negro Rights: East Texas as a Case Study," *American Historical Review* 76 (1971): 1435–1456.

cent of the adult males in Texas voted for the Republican or Populist candidates, compared to 39 percent for the Democrats. In 1904, after the poll tax went into effect, the combined GOP-Populist percentage dropped to 8 percent, and the opposition did not attract as many as one eligible voter in ten in any of the decade's remaining presidential or gubernatorial elections. Each decade since the Civil War had witnessed a major challenge to Texas Democrats—Radicalism in the sixties and seventies, the Greenback-Independent movement in the eighties, and the Populists in the nineties. Depressions, which seemed to strike about every ten years, had nurtured the Greenback and Populist parties. The recessions of 1907–08, 1914–15, or 1920–21 might have bred similar protests. Moreover, the Socialist party, which attracted many voters west of the Mississippi after 1900, might have provided the vehicle for Texans' economic protests.[42] Or perhaps—had their Northern stronghold begun to crumble in the face of Democratic victories—the Republicans would have turned South again in an effort to regain national predominance. The point is that if the electorate had not been restricted and the remaining voters channeled into the Democratic fold by the primary, some party might well have arisen to challenge the status quo. At the very least, the Democrats who framed the poll tax and similar restrictions elsewhere must have feared that possibility.

GEORGIA: THE "TOOMBS PLAN"

"Give us a convention," Bob Toombs is reported to have said in 1876, "and I will fix it so that the people shall rule and the Negro shall never be heard from." A planter, congressman, and U.S. senator before the War, Toombs was considered too rash and bibulous for the Confederate presidency. Although he was an antebellum Whig, Toombs did not become a "New South" paternalist after the conflict. Indeed, he was the prototypical unreconstructed rebel, carrying to his grave a passionate hatred of a Yankee-dominated Union and an unshakable

---

42. On Socialist party activities in the South and West, see James Weinstein, *The Decline of Socialism in America, 1912–1925* (New York: Vintage Books, 1967), pp. 16–19. The party was especially strong among ex-Populists in Texas and Oklahoma. See also Don Nimmo and Clifton McCleskey, "Impact of the Poll Tax on Voter Participation," pp. 682–699, who found that repeal of the poll tax alone increased turnout by about 15 percent in Harris County. They showed that the increases were highest among white collar workers, Mexican Americans, and the young. They predicted larger changes in the character of county politics as politicians realized the necessity of catering to the new voters.

belief that Negroes were subhuman beasts fit only for slavery. He got his constitutional convention, ruled it autocratically as head of its chief committee, and came close to keeping his promise to eliminate black men from Georgia politics. His method, later referred to as the "Georgia plan," was the cumulative poll tax.[43]

The 1868 Georgia constitution had required each male adult to pay a $1 poll tax each year or lose the right to vote. Realizing the damage this requirement would do their cause, the Republicans suspended the requirement from 1868 to 1871. The Democrats, however, resorted to widespread terrorism and fraud, and many self-appointed election officials disfranchised nontaxpayers regardless of the actions of the Republican governor and legislature. When the Democrats took over in 1871, one of their first acts was to reinstitute the poll tax prerequisite. Nevertheless, the 1868 provision did not guarantee Democratic success, for under it taxes cumulated only in the election year. Even if poor citizens could not pay their tax, politicians in tight contests might be able to pay the $1 taxes for large numbers of their partisans.[44]

The cumulative poll tax, adopted at Toombs' 1877 constitutional convention, insured that the Georgia GOP would never rise again. Several knowledgeable contemporary observers believed that it was the most effective device for restricting the suffrage.[45] An analysis of

43. Toombs's quotation from *Atlanta Constitution*, January 26, 1876, quoted in Allie M. Allen Jackson, "The Georgia Constitutional Convention of 1877" (M.A. thesis, Atlanta University, 1936), p. 15. The most recent biography of Toombs is William Y. Thompson's *Robert Toombs of Georgia* (Baton Rouge, Louisiana: Louisiana State University Press, 1966). Rarely if ever has one man so dominated a constitutional convention in America as Robert Toombs dominated the Georgia convention of 1877. Every convention bill had to be submitted to the Committee on Final Revision, which Toombs chaired. When the legislative appropriation for the convention ran out, Toombs personally advanced the money to pay for the rest of the session. Jackson, "Georgia Constitutional Convention," pp. 21, 26. There was no record vote and little discussion on the poll tax provision. See Samuel W. Small, *A Stenographic Report of the Proceedings of the Constitutional Convention Held in Atlanta, Georgia, 1877* (Atlanta, Georgia: The Constitution Co., 1877), pp. 36, 63–65, 480–481, 489. Congressman William H. Howard (D., Georgia) said in 1906 that "our poll-tax qualification was put in the constitution by [Confederate] General Toombs as his idea of disfranchisement," *Atlanta Constitution*, August 12, 1906.

44. On events from 1868 through 1871, see Elisabeth Studley Nathans, *Losing the Peace*, pp. 141, 202; Alan Conway, *The Reconstruction of Georgia*, p. 175; Shadgett, *The Republican Party*, p. 44. Governor Colquitt's followers were able to pay the taxes of their poor followers in Macon in 1880, but the cost of doing so became increasingly high. The Georgia comptroller-general stated in 1904 that most Negroes were 10–25 years in default on their poll taxes. Clarence A. Bacote, "The Negro in Georgia Politics, 1880–1908," pp. 46, 421.

45. See above, chapter 3, footnote 8.

election returns bears out their estimate (see also chapter 3, tables 3.2, 3.3).

Figure 7.1 portrays actual turnout figures for presidential elections from 1876 to 1908 in Georgia and in the ten other ex-Confederate states, and estimates of black turnout in Georgia. Political participation in Georgia was markedly lower than in the rest of the South except in 1892 and from 1904 on. The emergence in 1892 of the Populists, the first significant opposition party since Reconstruction in statewide Georgia politics, and the passage of restrictive laws between 1888 and 1892 in four other states account for the narrowing of the gap in 1892. The turn-of-the-century disfranchising efforts in other states explain the convergence of the two lines after 1900. Black participation always trailed white in Georgia, reaching a post-1880 peak of only an estimated 41.7 percent in the 1892 election. After 1900, fewer than one in ten Georgia Negroes seems to have voted.

Ignoring the 1892 election for a moment, note the gradual steady decline in voting in Georgia—just the cumulative impact one would expect from a tax which placed increasing burdens on defaulters. In other Deep and Border Southern states, turnout was relatively stable until they passed restrictive laws. This comparison implies that Georgia's pattern cannot be brushed off as the result of a general falling-off in political interest or a regional rise in Negro apathy.

The poll tax also influenced the course of party politics during the period. The Republican party was weaker in Georgia during the 1880s than in any other Southern state except South Carolina after the eight-box law took effect. Only in Mississippi and Georgia did the GOP fail to run a single statewide party campaign after 1876. As table 7.11 shows, the Republicans almost always garnered a smaller percentage of the adult male population in Georgia than in any other "Deep South" state. (The GOP usually did much better, of course, along the Dixie periphery.)

Why were the Georgia Republicans so weak? A recent student of Reconstruction in that state chastizes the GOP leaders for refusing to adopt a more moderate stance in order to attract the wealthy antebellum Whigs. Relying too much on the protection of the Congressional Radicals and on a yeoman white–black coalition, the Republicans, according to this view, collapsed in the face of the "natural Democratic majority" in Georgia. Another student blames violence, intimidation,

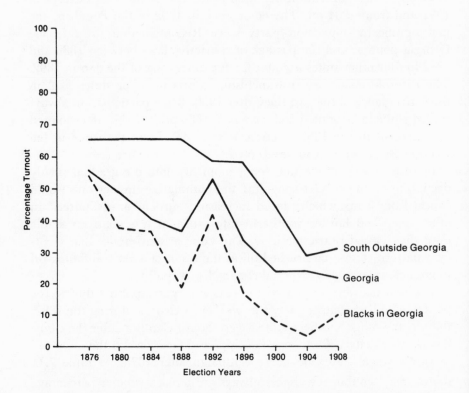

Figure 7.1. Effect of Cumulative Poll Tax: Overall Turnout and Estimated Black Turnout in Georgia Compared with Turnout in Ten Other Southern States in Presidential Elections, 1876–1908.

Table 7.11. The Poll Tax Weakened the Georgia GOP: Votes in
Presidential and Congressional Races in Six Deep South States, 1880s.

A. % *of Adult Males Voting Republican in Presidential Elections*

State	1880	1884	1888
Mississippi	14.4	17.3	11.0
South Carolina	28.2	10.0	6.0
Georgia	16.8	13.6	10.6
Alabama	21.7	20.7	18.3
Florida	38.4	37.1	29.7
Louisiana	17.7	20.1	12.6

B. % *of Adult Males Voting Republican in Congressional Elections*

State	1880	1882	1884	1886	1888	1890
Mississippi	10.3	8.4	15.1	4.3	10.5	5.0
South Carolina	29.5	13.0	9.2	2.7	4.4	5.5
Georgia	7.8	4.3	7.8	0.5	5.1	4.2
Alabama	12.2	0.8[a]	16.2	7.3	17.5	7.5
Florida	37.3	29.4	36.7	19.1	29.7	15.8
Louisiana	16.6	12.1	15.4	8.8	11.0	5.1

[a]In 1882 the Alabama Republicans obviously backed candidates running under the "opposition" label, who received the franchises of 17.3 percent of the adult males.

and the ineptitude of the white GOP chiefs Rufus Bullock and Foster Blodgett.[46]

Such contentions demonstrate again the need for comparative state history. Were Bullock and Blodgett any less capable than their Republican counterparts in Florida, Alabama, or Tennessee, or some of their Democratic successors in Georgia? Was there more violence and intimidation in Georgia than in Louisiana or Mississippi? How could there have been a "natural Democratic majority" in a state 47 percent Negro in 1880, a state in which the defection of a minuscule number of whites would have ensured the victory of a solidly voting black party? Why did the poor white–black coalition do so much worse in Georgia than in other Southern states? These questions have no simple answers, but we do know that generous amounts of violence and ineptitude, as well as tactical errors, were not peculiar to Georgia, and that poll tax laws in other states severely damaged lower-class opposition parties. These considerations suggest that the unusual frailty of the Republican

46. Nathans, *Losing the Peace*; Conway, *Reconstruction of Georgia*, pp. 198–199, 225.

party in Georgia was directly related to the fact that Georgia was the only Southern state with a poll tax prerequisite throughout the 1880s.

The impotence of the Republicans led opponents of the Democratic party to run as independents, and later, as Populists. That Georgia was the scene of the first sustained independent movement in the South is but another evidence of the premature demise of the Republican party there. As early as 1874 William Felton captured the predominantly white seventh district in north Georgia, a poor, hill-country district with large portions of small farmers and pre-War Unionists. He held the district until 1878, and Emory Speer, also an independent, won another northern congressional seat in 1878 and 1880. In 1880 the state Democratic convention split and both Alfred Colquitt and Thomas M. Norwood claimed to be at once independent and Democratic. Colquitt appealed to whites as a former Confederate hero, while Norwood, a dull speaker with no war record, could not rid himself of the stigma of having represented Northern railroad bondholders during Reconstruction. Norwood's bitterly racist views were also well known. Consequently, Colquitt, who pictured himself as an "anti-Bourbon" racial moderate before black audiences, and whose friends controlled most of the election machinery, received almost 80 percent of the votes of the Negroes who turned out. This was the last statewide election for eighty years in which a majority of the blacks voted.[47]

Unlike several other Southern Republican parties, the Georgians did not court the independents in order to build a formidable statewide fusionist movement in the early eighties or cajole those who had bolted the Democratic party into becoming full-fledged Republicans. Perhaps the obvious hopelessness of the GOP prospects repelled the followers of Felton. Not until 1892 did the Democrats face serious statewide opposition.

The Populists ran serious statewide campaigns for governor in 1892, 1894, and 1896. Even though these were the most exciting and hotly contested statewide races since Reconstruction, only a minority of male

47. Arnett, *Populist Movement in Georgia*, pp. 33–36, 41–43; Shadgett, *Republican Party in Georgia*, pp. 62–65; Felton, *Memoirs of Georgia Politics*, pp. 273–274, 307; Raymond B. Nixon, *Henry W. Grady, Spokesman of the New South*, pp. 170–177; C. Vann Woodward, "Tom Watson and the Negro in Agrarian Politics," p. 15; Ralph Wardlaw, "Negro Suffrage in Georgia, 1867–1930," pp. 42–50. Several of these authors indicate possible fraud in the vote count. My estimate, which rests on the published totals, is that 44.5 percent of the Negro adult males voted for Colquitt, 11.9 percent for Norwood, and 43.7 percent did not vote.

adults turned out to vote. Even these figures reflected extensive fraud and, in all probability, relaxation of the cumulative poll tax requirement.[48]

The Negro vote probably never held the balance of power in Georgia during the nineties because the poll tax crippled black turnout and because the majority of the whites who voted stayed loyal to the Democrats. Democratic majorities among whites probably exceeded the estimates given in table 7.12. The estimates of Negro voting cast considerable doubt on Woodward's early view that "never before or since have the two races in the South come so close together politically" as in the Populist movement.[49]

Table 7.12. Race and Populism in Georgia: Actual Votes and Estimates of Votes, by Race, 1892–1896.

Election	Democratic	Populist	Republican	Not Voting
% OF ALL ADULT MALES				
1892	33.6	14.1	0	52.3
1894	27.6	22.1	0	50.3
1896	26.3	18.7	0	55.0
1892 Presidential	30.9	10.3	11.6	47.2
ESTIMATED % ADULT WHITE MALES				
1892	42.6	29.0	0	28.3
1894	34.7	33.8	0	31.4
1896	39.9	31.7	0	28.4
1892 Presidential	36.3	16.4	12.5	34.8
ESTIMATED % OF NEGRO MALES				
1892	28.4	7.5	0	64.1
1894	23.4	15.0	0	61.7
1896	15.6	8.2	0	76.4
1892 Presidential	22.6	6.4	12.2	58.3

48. For evidence of fraud, see Arnett, *Populist Movement in Georgia*, pp. 154–155, 183–184, 209; Bacote, "Negro in Georgia Politics," pp. 181, 193–194. It is difficult to believe that many poor Georgians could have paid their poll taxes, already $10–15 in arrears in many cases, or that politicians could have assumed the burden for them. Consequently, many registrars must have winked at the law.

49. Woodward, "Tom Watson and the Negro," p. 21. Similarly, Jack Abramowitz referred to Georgia Populism as "the most unique [*sic*] experiment in race relations in the history of the South." See his "The Negro in the Populist Movement," in Sheldon Hackney, ed., *Populism: The Critical Issues* (Boston: Little Brown and Co., 1971), p. 39. Woodward seems recently to have moderated his enthusiasm for the Populist-Negro coalition. See his article,

Twice as high a percentage of blacks appear to have voted for Harrison as for Weaver in the 1892 presidential contest, and Cleveland and the Democratic gubernatorial candidate attracted even more Negroes. To be sure, ballot-box stuffing and overwhelming support for the Democrats among black belt whites probably distort the estimates. And both newspaper reports and the election returns imply that black support for the Populists was stronger in the Third and Tenth (Watson's) Congressional Districts than in other areas. Perhaps a majority of the Negroes who participated in 1894 cast Populist ballots.[50] Still, the relative size of the estimated statewide Negro support for the Populists from election to election correlates closely with the Populist and Democratic vote-getting strategies and with contemporary impressions of the way most blacks voted.

In 1892, the Populists, stressing the economic similarities between black and white farmers, attempted to appeal to Negro voters through the Colored Alliance, instead of through the Republican party and the established Negro leaders. Apparently realizing their error, the Populists in 1894 addressed themselves openly and directly to the issue of Negro civil rights, gave more prominence to black campaign workers, and seem to have cooperated more closely with the traditional black leadership. Two years later, the Populists seem to have courted Negro support less eagerly, and refused for the first time to place a Republican on their state ticket. The Democrats throughout the decade sought black votes through conventional channels, and especially in 1896, according to the Negro *Savannah Tribune*, "wined, dined, and slept with colored men in order to get their votes." Moreover, the Democratic legislature passed a registration law in 1895 that tightened the procedures requiring proof of poll tax payment before voting. This new law may have dampened Negro turnout in 1896.[51]

Party competition and turnout quickly declined after 1896 (table

"The Negro in American Life, 1865–1918," in John A. Garraty, ed., *Interpreting American History: Conversations with Historians*, 2 vols. (New York: The Macmillan Co., 1970), 2: 58. The most bitter—and unfair—attack on Woodward's view of the Populist-Negro coalition in Georgia, is Lawrence J. Friedman's *The White Savage, Racial Fantasies in the Postbellum South*, pp. 77–98.

50. *Atlanta Journal*, Nov. 9, 1892; *Atlanta Constitution*, October 4, 5, 1894, quoted in Abramowitz, "Negro in the Populist Movement," p. 47; Georgia state Democratic executive committee chairman A. S. Clay, quoted in Bacote, "Negro in Georgia Politics," p. 206.

51. On the 1892 election, see *Bulletin of Atlanta University*, November 1892, p. 4, quoted in Bacote, "Negro in Georgia Politics," p. 183, which reported that most Negroes had voted for the Democratic candidate for governor in 1892. On Populist, Democratic, and Republican

7.13). Populist failure bred apathy among both Populists and Democrats. Furthermore, enforcement of the taxpaying requirement for voting undoubtedly stiffened after 1895, and election officers had less reason to inflate returns.

This decline in competition, the desire to prevent a recurrence of partisan battling, the news of suffrage restriction in other states, as well as some politicians' extreme racism led Georgia Democrats to propose two major changes in 1898. The state committee introduced coordinated white primaries in each county for statewide elections, and State Representative Thomas W. Hardwick proposed a literacy test for voters.

Before 1898, delegates to state Democratic conventions could be chosen by county primaries, conventions, mass meetings, or other methods. After 1898, the party made primaries mandatory and provided for a uniform primary day, although the election was for delegates instead of directly for candidates and each candidate's strength was apportioned by county units rather than total votes. The purpose of the primary, according to the *Atlanta Constitution*, was to "permit the *conservative people* of the state to control affairs without depriving any person of the vote" (my italics). That substituting intra- for inter-party competition was another purpose was implied in Governor Terrell's statement in 1905 that "the primary elections have become, *as they deserve to be*, the all important elections in our State" (my italics).[52]

tactics during the campaign, see pp. 166–183; Arnett, *Populist Movement in Georgia*, pp. 153–155; Shadgett, *Republican Party in Georgia*, pp. 109–114; John Hope, "The Negro Vote in the States Whose Constitutions Have Not Been Specifically Revised," in American Negro Academy, *The Negro and the Elective Franchise*, p. 53; Woodward, "Tom Watson and the Negro," pp. 21–24. On the 1894 election, see Arnett, *Populist Movement in Georgia*, pp. 183–184; Bacote, "Negro in Georgia Politics," pp. 198–209; Saunders, "Southern Populists and the Negro," pp. 241–255; Shadgett, *Republican Party in Georgia*, pp. 116–117. On the 1896 election, see Bacote, "Negro in Georgia Politics," pp. 212–223, 518–519; *Savannah Tribune*, October 30, 1897, quoted in Bacote, "Negro Officeholders in Georgia Under President McKinley," *Journal of Negro History* 44 (1959): 232; Durden, *The Climax of Populism*, pp. 105–106. For the registration act, see Ga. *Acts and Resolutions* (1894–95), pp. 116–119; Ga. *House Journal* (1894–95), pp. 181, 510–512, 595–596; Ga. *Senate Journal* (1894–95), pp. 121, 533. Since there were no important struggles after the relatively innocuous bill emerged from committees, I will not treat the bill at greater length. And for the effect of this law on Negro voting, see Bacote, "Negro in Georgia Politics," pp. 218–219, who noted that Negro registration in Fulton County (Atlanta) dropped from about one-third of the total in the period before 1895 to one-seventh of the total in 1896. Unfortunately, we do not have similar figures for other counties.

52. Lynwood Mathis Holland, "The Direct Primary in Georgia;" *Atlanta Constitution*, May 15, 1900, quoted in Shadgett, *Republican Party in Georgia*, p. 154. Terrell is quoted in Holland, "Direct Primary in Georgia," p. 99.

Table 7.13. Declines in Party Competition and Estimated White and Negro
Turnout in Georgia after 1896.

Election	Democrat	Populist	Republican	Not Voting
	% OF ALL ADULT MALES			
1898 Gov.	24.7	10.7	0	64.6
1900 Gov.	18.1	4.6	0	77.3
1902 Gov.	15.6	1.1	0	83.3
1900 Pres.	16.2	1.2	6.8	75.8
1904 Pres.	15.3	4.1	4.4	76.2
	% OF WHITE ADULT MALES[a]			
1898 Gov.	42	20	0	38
1900 Gov.	33	8	0	59
1902 Gov.	28	2	0	70
1900 Pres.	26	2	12	60
1904 Pres.	24	7	8	61
	% OF NEGRO ADULT MALES[a]			
1898 Gov.	11	4	0	85
1900 Gov.	0	0	0	100
1902 Gov.	0	0	0	100
1900 Pres.	8	0	0	92
1904 Pres.	4	0	0	96

[a]Logically impossible estimates of Negro voting have been set at the 0% or 100% limits, and estimates of white voting have been accordingly recalculated. For the procedures involved see my "Ecological Regression" article.

The Hardwick Disfranchisement Bill, a literacy test with a grand-father clause loophole, easily emerged from committee, but failed in the House by overwhelming margins in 1899 and 1901. Although conservative Governor Allen D. Candler strongly endorsed literacy and property tests to prevent the possibility of Negro influence in future elections, many conservatives seem to have felt the poll tax and white primary had removed the need for further racial agitation and voting restrictions. Moreover, the bill aroused intense opposition from such Negro leaders as W. E. B. DuBois and John Hope of Atlanta University, Booker T. Washington, and John H. Deveaux, the leading Negro politician in southern Georgia. A New York magazine thought Negro protests responsible for the bill's defeat. Hardwick himself believed the bill failed in 1898 because Democratic legislators feared the

Populists would use the issue in 1900 to secure the votes of Negroes and poor whites concerned about being cast out of the electorate.[53]

With almost no Negroes voting and no opposition party operating in the first decade of the new century, most Georgians saw no need for more limitations on voting.[54] In 1905–06, however, the issue of further restrictions was thrust into a Democratic primary campaign for governor. Once again, it was Thomas W. Hardwick, by then a congressman, who focused attention on the issue and manipulated events.

Congressman Hardwick first endorsed Pope Brown, a proponent of disfranchisement and Negro repatriation to Africa. When Brown's early canvass proved him a sure loser against *Atlanta Constitution* editor Clark Howell, Hardwick persuaded Brown to withdraw in favor of Hoke Smith, editor of the *Atlanta Journal* and former Cleveland cabinet member. The congressman then induced his friend Tom Watson, old racial egalitarian, new ultra-racist, to endorse Smith, Watson's archenemy during the nineties.[55]

Clark Howell and Hoke Smith vied before the white-primaried, poll-taxed electorate for the title of most rabid racist. Smith, a former moderate who had opposed the Hardwick bill in 1898, now assailed "Negro domination" from every rostrum, approving the use of "any

53. Candler's 1898 and 1900 addresses to the legislature are quoted in Bacote, "Negro in Georgia Politics," p. 276; and Alton DuMar Jones, "Progressivism in Georgia, 1898–1918" (Ph.D. diss., Emory Univ., 1963), p. 137. Like James K. Vardaman, Candler believed educating Negroes only resulted in a higher crime rate. Candler wanted to disfranchise the propertyless and illiterate, regardless of race, and cut appropriations for Negro education. The magazine noted was *The Independent* 51 (1899): 3306–3307; Bacote, "Negro in Georgia Politics," pp. 282–288. It should be noted that the predominately white trade unions also opposed the bill. See ibid., pp. 289–290. Hardwick is quoted in *Atlanta Journal*, October 23, 1900, cited in Bacote, "Negro in Georgia Politics," p. 290.

54. From 1878 to 1908, Negroes representing only three counties sat in the Georgia legislature. From 1902 to 1908, only W. H. Rogers of McIntosh managed to win a seat. This fact indicates that a few Negroes were still voting. See Monroe N. Work, "Some Negro Members of Reconstruction Conventions and Legislatures and of Congress," *Journal of Negro History* 5 (1920): 63–119.

55. For Hardwick's and Brown's views on Negro suffrage and Hardwick's central role in the shenanigans, see Bacote, "Negro in Georgia Politics," pp. 276–278, 335; Dewey W. Grantham, "Some Letters from Thomas W. Hardwick to Tom Watson Concerning the Georgia Gubernatorial Campaign of 1906," *Georgia Historical Quarterly* 34 (1950): 328–340; Grantham, *Hoke Smith*, pp. 134, 138–148; Woodward, *Tom Watson*, pp. 372–374. Watson supported Smith because of his stand on disfranchisement and railroad regulation, despite Smith's record as a Gold Democrat and staunch opponent of Populism, and Smith's tepid support for the liberal Democratic candidate for president, William Jennings Bryan.

means" to expel Negro elected officials from any community in the state. Backing Hardwick's new plan, Smith charged that Howell's willingness to rely on the present safeguards might lead to an eventual Negro takeover in Georgia.[56] Howell, on the other hand, blasted Smith for the grievous sin of appointing Negroes to office while he was secretary of the interior. Charging that a literacy test would lead Negroes to flock to school and thereby rise above their traditional field-hand positions, Howell also declared that the Hardwick-Smith plan would disfranchise many poor whites. When his campaign faltered Howell applied the tattered whip of party loyalty, accusing Smith of plotting with Tom Watson to break up the Democratic party.[57]

Watson claimed he had swung "90,000" Populists to Smith, a claim which lends credence to charges that the Populists were largely responsible for passage of the literacy test. Watson, however, puffed up his power over his followers in an attempt to increase his influence with politicians. As the forlorn Populist presidential candidate in 1904, he had drawn only 22,310 votes in Georgia, and the Populist candidate for governor in 1900 had tallied only 23,235. Regression estimates of the way those who participated in the 1892 and 1894 gubernatorial campaigns voted in the 1906 primary indicate that between 22,000 and 27,000 Populists voted for Hoke Smith. Smith would have had a comfortable plurality if all the Populists who turned out in 1906 had voted for his closest competitor. Far from dominating the Democrats in 1906, Watson could not even win a seat from his home county in

56. For the Howell-Smith campaign, see Grantham, *Hoke Smith*, pp. 147–149, 151; *Atlanta Constitution*, August 1, 2, 1906. Conservative opposition to the Hardwick-Smith proposal during the 1905–06 campaign did not imply that they opposed disfranchisement in general. Governor Allen Candler, an earlier proponent of literacy and property tests, denounced Smith and his plan, as did Senator A. O. Bacon, author of a bill to repeal the 15th Amendment. See *Atlanta Constitution*, August 12, 1906; Dewey W. Grantham, Jr., "Georgia Politics and the Disfranchisement of the Negro," *Georgia Historical Quarterly* 32 (1948): 9. Headlines from Howell's newspaper show how far the "conservatives" were willing to engage in racial demagoguery and how much of the burden they bear for the racist climate which made the 1906 Atlanta riot possible: "In Presence of Outraged Girl Black Fiend is Shot to Death by Enraged Atlanta Citizens" (a lynching, *Constitution*, August 1, 1906); "Assaults Girl with Meat Knife—Negro makes diabolical assault on young woman" (ibid., August 15, 1906); "Girl's Father Favors Torture for Assailant . . ." (ibid., August 17, 1906). Examples of such grisly headlines could easily be multiplied.

57. Ibid., August 5, 15, 19, 1906. Interestingly enough, the old Independent Dr. William H. Felton echoed Howell's charges that the plan would disfranchise poor whites. For the party loyalty issue, see ibid., August 1, 21, 1906. Howell's charges may well have led historians to exaggerate Watson's power and his role in the campaign.

the state convention. It was, rather, staunch Democrat Thomas Hardwick, who had coached Smith on disfranchisement and drafted the plan, who gave the chief speech in favor of the proposal at the state convention. Moreover, the legislature which overwhelmingly passed the amendment in 1907 contained no avowed Populists and only a handful of former Populists.[58]

The object of the suffrage amendment was not to cut down a serious immediate threat, for few Negroes were still voting, but to ensure "that the Negro shall not be left around the corner, awaiting the awakening hand of the corruptionist whenever division shall again break the white ranks and discord lift its threatening hand."[59] The actual bill, based on the Alabama amendment, provided for a literacy test easy to administer in a discriminatory manner, along with a property qualification and a number of escape clauses. It passed both houses easily, the chief dissent arising from those who thought the bill might eliminate too many whites.[60]

The campaign for the referendum in 1908 resembled those in other states. Blacks tried hard to organize against passage, calling several conferences, urging Negroes to register in large numbers, denouncing federal neglect and state destruction of the civil rights of black men.[61] Democrats responded typically, making registration difficult, threatening, burning churches, lynching, stuffing ballot boxes. Even the sustained efforts of the highly competent Negro leadership of Atlanta and Savannah resulted in the registration in Fulton and Chatham Counties

58. Watson quoted in Woodward, *Tom Watson*, p. 378. William A. Mabry in effect makes the charge against the Populists in "The Disfranchisement of the Negro," pp. 439–440. For Hardwick's speech, see *Atlanta Constitution*, September 5, 1906.

59. Ibid., Hardwick's speech. It is instructive to note that the chief disfranchiser, far from desiring to remove the Negro so that the whites could safely split into parties, perceived division as "threatening."

60. During the campaign, the Smith followers had asked for and received advice on what plan to adopt and how each worked from leading Democrats in states which had already passed restrictive amendments. See Bacote, "Negro in Georgia Politics," pp. 412–413; Grantham, *Hoke Smith*, p. 150; Mabry, "Disfranchisement of the Negro," pp. 453, 457. The text of the amendment is given in Ga. *Acts* (1907), pp. 47–50. For the passage, see Ga. *Senate Journal* (1907), pp. 294–299; Ga. *House Journal* (1907), pp. 922–929; Grantham, *Hoke Smith*, pp. 159–160; Mabry, "Disfranchisement of the Negro," pp. 464–466; Bacote, "Negro in Georgia Politics," pp. 452–467. Eleven of the fifteen white House members who opposed final passage of the bill came from white-majority counties.

61. Bacote, "Negro in Georgia Politics," pp. 434–512, details this story, proving conclusively that the Negro leadership was far from accepting Booker T. Washington's public counsel to drop out of politics.

of only 2,500 Negroes, or less than one-tenth of the Negro adult males. The election returns themselves demonstrated how little the amendment represented a popular upsurge of feeling, how effective previous restraints on the suffrage were, and how anticlimactic the campaign had been (table 7.14). Only one Georgian in five—about one in four among whites—turned out. Both supporters and opponents of Hoke Smith among the whites who voted seem to have favored the amendment overwhelmingly.

The model of voting most in accord with contemporary judgments and statistical criteria indicates that antiamendment strength varied directly with the proportion of Negroes in each county.[62] As the figures in the table indicate, about 16 percent of the white adult males in a county that contained no Negroes could have been expected to vote against the amendment, compared to 24 percent for it. As the Negro proportion rose from county to county, white opposition to the amendment dropped off markedly. In typical counties that were 10 percent, 20 percent, and 30 percent Negro, respectively, the proportion of white males voting against the amendment amounted to 13 percent, 10 percent, and 6 percent, in that order. According to this interpretation of the data, virtually no black belt whites opposed the amendment. The rationale for the white voting pattern which this model expresses is simple: some whites in almost entirely white counties opposed the amendment because of a hostility to white disfranchisement, but whites in counties with more Negroes increasingly feared Negro domination more than the restriction of the white vote.

The pattern of Negro voting appears to have been just the reverse of the whites'. The black leaders apparently concentrated their limited resources in the counties with the most Negroes. Thus, in a county where Negroes made up 10 percent of the population, only an estimated 2.5 percent of them turned out against the amendment, while in a 50 percent Negro county, 12.5 percent of the blacks registered votes against

62. The model employed here is based on the assumptions that no Negroes supported the amendment, and that opposition can be represented by the following equation:

$$Y = a + b_1x + b_2x^2$$

where Y is the proportion against the amendment, x is the proportion Negro, and a, b_1 and b_2 are the multiple regression coefficients. This equation explains 16.7 percent of the variance of Y, whereas, an equation containing no x^2 term explains only 2.1 percent. Of the several possible soluble models which could underlie this multiple regression equation, the one given in the text best satisfies contemporary impressions of voting behavior.

Table 7.14. Votes and Estimated Voting, by Race, in 1908 Georgia
Disfranchisement Referendum.

	Percentage of Adult Males		
	For Amendment	*Against Amendment*	*Not Voting*
All Males	13.4	6.8	79.8
Whites	23.6	3.8 $(15.7-31.4X)^a$	73.6
Blacks	0	12.5 $(24.9X)^a$	87.5

[a]These estimates are based on a curvilinear model, $Y = a + b_1X + b_2X^2$, where $Y = \%$ against the amendment, $X = \%$ Negro, and a, b_1, and b_2 are regression coefficients. Estimates of Negro and white turnout were changed from the straight-line estimates slightly to accord with the estimates of anti-amendment voting.

disfranchisement. In the state as a whole an estimated 3.8 percent of the whites and 12.5 percent of the blacks opposed the amendment. That the amendment had some effect in reducing whatever slight possibility of black participation remained is indicated by the fact that Negro registration dropped from 28.3 percent in 1904 to 4.3 percent in 1910.[63]

63. Bacote, "Negro in Georgia Politics," pp. 421, 499–500; Grantham, *Hoke Smith*, p. 162.

8

The Post-Disfranchisement Political System

FROM DEMOCRACY TO OLIGARCHY

By 1910 the Southern political system which was to last through mid-century had been formed. The new system posed a striking contrast to that of the eighties and nineties. Figure 8.1 presents the percentages of adult males voting for the Democrats and opposition party candidates, and not voting in selected elections in each decade from 1880 to 1910. During the 1880s, 64 percent of the Southern adult males, on the average, turned out to vote in the elections selected. This figure increased to 73 percent in the 1890s in those states which passed no major piece of restrictive legislation before 1894 (group A), but dropped to 42 percent in those states which did enact such legislation (group B). In the next decade Southern turnout fell to an average of 30 percent. The political system had changed from a democracy to what Dean Burnham has termed a "broadly-based oligarchy."[1]

Likewise, one of every four adult males voted for Republican or Independent candidates during the 1880s; whereas, by the first decade of the twentieth century, the percentage had dropped to one in ten. Post-Reconstruction Southern politics had a moderately active electorate and fairly vigorous, if somewhat sporadic, competition between parties. In the early twentieth century the electorate was tiny and party competition almost nonexistent. Between the eighties and the first decade of the twentieth century, there was a decrease of 47 percent in the average percentage of adult males for the Democrats, but a 62 percent drop in the already lower opposition totals.

There was some variance in the amount of competition and turnout from state to state (table 8.1). But only in Tennessee and North Carolina, where mountain Republicanism persisted, was there much party competition or voter participation, and even in those two states turnout

1. W. Dean Burnham, "Party Systems and the Political Process," in William N. Chambers and Burnham, eds., *The American Party Systems*, p. 301.

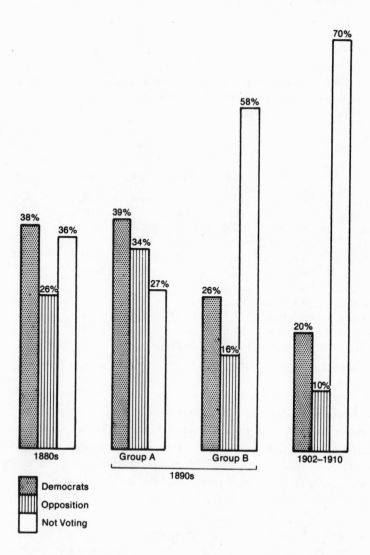

Figure 8.1. Southern Politics from Active Competition to Mandatory Tranquility: Percentage of Adult Males Voting for Democrats and Their Opponents and Not Voting in Selected Elections in the South, 1880–1910.

SOURCE: For the 1880s and 1890s, the elections selected were the gubernatorial races in which opposition candidates ran up their highest percentages (the same elections presented in tables 1.3 through 1.6). For the final period I selected the gubernatorial or presidential election where the turnout was highest in each state after the final disfranchising law was passed. Had the selection for this latter period included only gubernatorial elections, which often went uncontested, the turnout and opposition party percentages would have been even lower. Because each state's polity was somewhat autonomous, and because the elections occurred at different times during the decade, I did not weight the percentages by the population of each state.

NOTE: Group A in this table corresponds to Group II in tables 1.5 and 1.6, Group B corresponds to Group I.

Table 8.1. Apathy Settles In: Voting and Turnout Patterns in Eleven
Southern States in the General Election with the Highest Turnout after
Disfranchisement and between 1902 and 1910.

| State | Election | Percentage of Adult Males | | | | % White Turn-out, Assuming No Negroes Voted |
		Demo.	Repub.	Other	Not Voting	
Alabama	1904 Pres.	17.6	5.0	1.4	76.0	42.0
Arkansas	1904 Gov.	26.6	15.6	1.1	56.8	60.0
Florida	1908 Pres.	15.6	5.4	3.8	75.2	42.9
Georgia	1908 Pres.	12.1	6.9	3.0	77.9	38.9
Louisiana	1908 Pres.	16.1	2.3	0.7	81.0	33.2
Mississippi	1908 Pres.	14.7	1.1	0.5	83.8	36.2
No. Carolina	1908 Gov.	29.8	22.1	0.1	48.0	73.6
So. Carolina	1908 Pres.	19.2	1.2	0	78.6	41.8
Tennessee	1908 Pres.	25.1	21.9	0.7	52.3	61.0
Texas	1906 Gov.	27.8	4.8	3.5	63.9	43.8
Virginia	1904 Pres.	17.0	10.1	0.4	72.5	40.4
Unweighted average		20.1	8.7	1.4	69.6	46.7

never surpassed 52 percent in any election from 1902 to 1910. In most of the Southern states, the Democrats won by landslides, and only about one potential elector in four bothered to cast a ballot. The decline in participation was not confined to Negroes. Assuming that no Negroes voted after disfranchisement, which is certainly an exaggeration, turnout averaged only 46.7 percent of the adult white males.[2] Under this assumption, a majority of whites could have voted in the elections of only three of the eleven states.

The substitution of intra- for inter-party competition after institution of the Democratic primary amounted to much more than a mere change in name. Table 8.2 demonstrates that participation in the primary with the highest turnout in each state, 1902–1910, averaged only 29.9 percent, or slightly less than the average turnout in general elections in the same period. Assuming that no Negroes voted in these primaries, the maximum possible white turnout averaged a mere 48.8 percent, surpassing 50 percent in but four states. Moreover, the primary did not everywhere immediately replace the general election as the chief arena of combat. In the five border states of Arkansas, North Carolina,

2. Regression estimates indicate that Negro turnout was very close to zero in several states after disfranchisement, and rarely above 10 percent.

Table 8.2. The Primary Did Not Immediately Replace Party
Competition: Voting and Turnout Patterns in the Primary with
the Highest Turnout in Each State, 1902–1910.

State	Election	Percentage of Adult Males				Percentage of White Males, Assuming No Negroes Voted	
		Leading Candidate	Second Candidate	Other	Not Voting	Highest Candidate	Turnout
Alabama	1906 Sen.	10.2	7.6	18.2	64.0	17.8	52.6
Arkansas	1906 Sen.[b]	18.7	15.2	0	66.1	26.0	47.1
Florida	1908 Gov.	16.3	11.7	0	72.0	28.2	48.5
Georgia	1908 Gov.	18.4	16.6	0	65.0	29.2	61.7
Louisiana	1904 Gov.[a]	11.7	8.3	0	80.0	20.8	35.5
Mississippi	1907 Gov.[a]	7.3	7.0	16.1	69.7	16.2	67.7
No. Carolina	none						
So. Carolina	1908 Sen.[b]	21.7	12.2	0	66.1	44.3	69.3
Tennessee	1908 Gov.	15.8	13.6	0	70.6	20.7	37.6
Texas	1910 Gov.	14.6	8.0	13.1	64.3	17.5	42.8
Virginia	1905 Gov.	8.8	4.2	4.2	82.8	12.9	25.2
Unweighted average (ten states)		14.3	10.4	5.1	70.1	23.4	48.8

[a]First primary.
[b]Run-off primary.

Tennessee, Texas, and Virginia, voter participation in the general
elections surpassed turnout in the primaries (compare tables 8.1 and
8.2).

The reduction in turnout also meant that politicians could forego
trying to reach voters they had had to capture before disfranchisement.
During the 1880s, and in the 1890s in those states which did not en-
cumber the franchise before the rise of Populism, the average Democratic candidate won the allegiance of four voters in ten. In the
primaries after 1902, the highest candidate attracted one potential
voter in seven, on the average. Assuming that no Negroes voted, the
average primary winner gained the support of less than one potential
voter in four even among the whites. This decrease in the proportion
of the populace that a candidate needed to appeal to in order to win,
along with the disorganization that always characterizes primaries,
increased the power of such interest groups as the Anti-Saloon League
and such political machines as those of Simmons in North Carolina and

Martin in Virginia. At the same time, the new order reduced the possibility that the lower socioeconomic strata might be able to use political means to promote their economic well-being.

Between Reconstruction and disfranchisement, Negroes had held governmental posts throughout the South. Negroes sat in every Congress except one from 1869 to 1901. Hundreds of blacks were elected to the state legislatures. Thousands served as sheriffs, judges, magistrates, customs collectors, census officials, and clerks. White Southerners might have preferred to see these posts filled by whites, but they tacitly recognized the right of the blacks to serve. As long as Negroes voted, the Democrats realized, even members of the "party of white supremacy" would have to recommend some Negroes for patronage posts.[3]

After disfranchisement, however, the prospect of a Negro in or even near office, particularly in an integrated situation, became an anathema to the Southern Democrats. Since no Negro could any longer be elected to a Southern post, the race had to depend entirely on federal patronage for any official recognition. But help from this quarter also diminished under growing Southern pressure and an ever-decreasing Northern Republican commitment to Negro rights. Theodore Roosevelt's famous meal with Booker T. Washington, his nomination of a Negro as collector of the port of Charleston, and his refusal to dismiss a Negro postmistress in Indianola, Mississippi, immediately became causes célèbres. Earlier, such events would have been dismissed as normal patronage politics, as similar acts by President Cleveland had been. And when an avowedly racist national administration took over in 1912, the remaining blacks in federal employ were placed in humiliating segregation and relegated to minor duties.[4]

The loss of offices was both a very real blow to members of the black intelligentsia and a symbolic statement that Negroes were no longer worthy of recognition by their government. At the same time the Southern state and local governments increased the discrimination

3. Logan, *Negro in North Carolina*, pp. 43–44.
4. On Roosevelt's activities, see William F. Holmes, *The White Chief*, pp. 104–105; Willard B. Gatewood, "Theodore Roosevelt and Southern Republicans: The Case of South Carolina, 1901–1904," *South Carolina Historical Magazine* 70 (1969): 251–266; William A. Sinclair, *The Aftermath of Slavery*, reprint ed. (New York: Arno Press, 1969), pp. 186–197. On Wilson, see Nancy J. Weiss, "The Negro and the New Freedom: Fighting Wilsonian Segregation," *Political Science Quarterly* 84 (1968): 61–79.

against blacks in the only important service those governments provided
—education. By allocating state funds to local school districts on the
basis of the total school-age population, but allowing the localities to
spend the money in any manner they chose, the Democratic governors
and legislatures invited black belt whites to improve their children's
education at the expense of the Negroes. By providing state matching
grants for localities which voted to tax themselves more heavily and
by shifting the burden of educational expenditures to the counties and
municipalities, those who controlled state government added to the
differential between rich and poor areas.[5] The results of the combination of suffrage restriction and an educational "awakening," then,
were that schools for whites in urban and black belt areas improved
substantially, while schools for the Negroes and for hill country whites
deteriorated or at least lost ground relative to those in the wealthier
counties. Discrimination in voting, in other words, paralleled discrimination in government services, a condition unlikely to have been
coincidental.

PROGRESSIVISM FOR MIDDLE-CLASS WHITES ONLY

In such a restricted polity, the programs of the "Progressives"
could be little more than expressions of middle-class self-interest. The
benefits of the political system trickled down to the rest of the populace
only incidentally, if at all. Railroad regulation helped local commercial
shippers at the expense of national corporations, while "good roads"
(highway) campaigns assisted large merchants and industrialists as
well as railroads. Swamp drainage, the key reform of the Florida Progressives, subsidized the rich land speculators.[6] Warehousing laws in

5. Louis Harlan, *Separate and Unequal: Public School Campaigns and Racism in the Southern
Seaboard States, 1901–1915* (Chapel Hill, North Carolina: Univ. of North Carolina Press,
1958); Tinsley, "The Progressive Movement in Texas," pp. 181–183; Moore, *Alabama and
Her People*, 1: 826–827. According to Harlan's figures. South Carolina spent six times as much
for education per white as per Negro child in 1900, but eleven times as much in 1915. Moreover, the proportion of educational expenditures provided by local funds in Virginia, North
Carolina, South Carolina, and Georgia increased from 42.4 percent in 1900 to 72.4 percent
in 1915. This meant that white children in wealthy localities got an increasingly better education than whites in poor areas, assuming roughly equal tax rates.

6. On the shippers' leading role in railroad regulation, see Grantham, *Hoke Smith*, p. 132;
Steelman, "Progressive Era in North Carolina," pp. 542–562; Kathryn T. Abbey, "Florida
Versus the Principles of Populism," *Journal of Southern History* 4 (1938): 467–475; Moger,
Bourbonism to Byrd, pp. 101, 105; James F. Doster, *Railroads in Alabama Politics, 1875–1914*,
pp. 92–100, 112–113, 206. The "good roads" movement was an excellent example of

Texas benefited bankers and commercial warehouse men more than farmers. Such "good government" reforms as the establishment of city commissions and the elimination of patronage jobs cut taxes for the rich and employment for the poor. Progressive governors repeatedly broke strikes and passed laws allowing local business to regulate itself.[7] If Progressivism had a general theme in the South, it was hardly "democracy" or "the greatest good for the greatest number," but the stabilization of society, especially the economy, in the interests of the local established powers, at the expense of the lower strata of society in the South, and sometimes at the expense of out-of-state corporations.[8] After all, neither group voted in Dixie.

One important case may serve to illustrate these points. If any single election could be taken as typical of Southern Progressivism, it was the 1906 governor's race in Alabama. Son of a black belt plantation owner, the Progressive Braxton Bragg Comer was successively a plantation manager, wholesale grocer, and owner of a huge cotton mill. A large customer of railroad services, Comer became active in efforts to reduce charges to Birmingham shippers, and in 1904 was elected to the state railroad commission. He ran for governor two years later chiefly on his record of opposition to the Yankee-owned railroads. His opponent, Lieutenant-Governor Russell Cunningham, with whom

---

business-government cooperation in the interest of the former. The United States department of agriculture and J. P. Morgan's Southern Railroad co-sponsored a "good roads train" to publicize the need for more appropriations. See Steelman, "Progressive Era in North Carolina," pp. 581–585. On swamp drainage, see Proctor, *Napoleon Bonaparte Broward*, pp. 240–260, 292–295, especially on the role of Everglades speculator Richard J. Bolles.

7. On the warehousing laws and the "goo-goo" reforms, see Tinsley, "Progressive Movement in Texas," pp. 150–158, 202–212; James Weinstein, "Organized Business and the City Commission and Manager Movements," *Journal of Southern History* (1962): 161–182; Jackson, *New Orleans in the Gilded Age*, p. 45. On strikebreaking, see Wayne Flynt, "Pensacola Labor Problems and Political Radicalism, 1908," *Florida Historical Quarterly* 43 (1965): 315–332; Hackney, *Populism*, pp. 287, 307–310, 316–323. On the failure of labor unions to obtain any real legislative triumphs, see Tinsley, "Progressive Movement in Texas," pp. 135–149; Steelman, "Progressive Era in North Carolina," pp. 690–712. On the strong ties of prominent Progressive politicians with the corporations, often the ones they regulated, see Tinsley, "Progressive Movement in Texas," pp. 45–48, 305–306; Steelman, "Progressive Era in North Carolina, pp. 275–279.

8. For an interpretation of Southern Progressivism as an attempt to stabilize society, see Pulley, *Old Virginia Restored*. For the attack on out-of-state corporations, see Tinsley, "Progressive Movement in Texas," pp. 12, 75–90, 97, 98, 113–120; Kaufman, "Henry De La Warr Flood," pp. 141–143.

he differed only marginally on issues, represented most of the established county politicos.[9]

Only one man in five turned out to vote in the primary. Assuming no Negroes voted, the white turnout rate was only 34.8 percent. These gross turnout figures alone demonstrate that the election represented no massive popular revolt against the Louisville and Nashville Railroad's machine. Moreover, participation appears to have been confined primarily to the middle classes. Among whites, Comer's support correlated +.34 and Cunningham's +.58 with wealth (table 8.3).[10] Whites in the poorer counties did not vote in very large numbers, for the correlation between turnout and wealth was +.49. For every $1,000 rise in wealth across counties, Comer's vote increased 3.3 percent, Cunningham's 4.0 percent, and overall voting turnout increased 7.3 percent. If subcounty differences in wealth and in the class composition of turnout were fairly small, then these figures show that few poor whites voted. They apparently felt it not worth paying the poll tax in order to substitute a cotton mill boss for a railroad boss.

THE PRIMARY AND THE RISE OF THE "DEMAGOGUES"

From the time of the initiation of direct statewide primaries in the South, the voter found himself faced with a bewildering array of candidates, none easily distinguished from the others. Thus, South Carolinians had a choice of six candidates, all of whom polled respectable

Table 8.3. Progressivism for Middle-Class Whites Only:
Relations between Estimated White Wealth and Voting in the 1906
Gubernatorial Primary in Alabama.

Candidate	Correlation(r) between White Wealth and % of White Males in Primary	% Change in Voting per $1000 Increase in White Wealth
Comer	+.342	+3.30
Cunningham	+.577	+3.99
Turnout	+.489	+7.26

9. Doster, *Railroads in Alabama Politics*, pp. 92–100, 138–140, 148–153; Hackney, *Populism*, pp. 128–130, 255–287.

10. The election returns used here represent the percent of white adult males for each candidate and not voting. For the method of estimating white wealth per adult white male, see appendix A.

totals for a primary, in the 1902 race for the United States Senate, and five nominees in the contemporary race for governor. In 1906, eight hopefuls filed for governor; in 1908, seven for the Senate; in 1910, six for governor. Similarly, six men stayed in the race for governor of Mississippi in 1907, five for governor of Georgia in 1906, and five for governor of Texas in 1910. In such situations rational choice became well-nigh impossible for the voter and the frenetic reforging of coalitions the rule for the politician. Since, with so many candidates running, the voter had a difficult time telling the "ins" from the "outs," and therefore could not easily express dissatisfaction by ejecting the rascals, politicians had little reason to keep promises or exercise responsibility in office.[11]

The primary also fostered a politics of personality rather than issues. Historians have often speculated about why the early twentieth-century South witnessed the rise of so many "demagogues"—James K. Vardaman and Theodore G. Bilbo in Mississippi, Ben Tillman and Cole Blease in South Carolina, Tom Watson in Georgia, Jeff Davis in Arkansas, Tom Heflin in Alabama, Jim Ferguson in Texas. How did these men differ from earlier Southern politicians and contemporaries who escaped the label of demagogues? Not in class background, for most Southern politicians of whatever description came primarily from the moderately affluent and affluent classes. Ben Tillman's father and Tom Watson's grandfather were successful planters. Vardaman's father owned fourteen slaves at one time; Davis's had enough money to send him to aristocratic Vanderbilt. Not in the degree of their racism, for the leading antebellum Southerners had thought Negroes fit only for slavery; postwar politicians had actively organized such groups as the Klan and the Red Shirts to overthrow the Republican governments by force and had never hesitated to accuse opponents of racial treason; and more "enlightened" contemporary Southerners often backed the same extreme remedies for racial problems as the demagogues. Many Southern congressmen not usually described as demagogues openly favored repeal of the Fifteenth Amendment and sometimes the Four-

11. On the character of primaries and "nonpartisan" elections generally, and the South in particular, see V. O. Key, Jr., *Southern Politics in State and Nation* and *American State Politics*; Holmes, *White Chief*, p. 127; Boyce A. Drummond, "Arkansas Politics," pp. 177, 229–232; Charles E. Merriam, *Primary Elections*, pp. 112–132; Julius Turner, "Primary Elections as the Alternative," pp. 197–210; Allan P. Sindler, "Bifactional Rivalry," pp. 641–662; Charles R. Adrian, "Non-Partisan Elections," pp. 766–776.

teenth as well—Senators Bacon of Georgia, Williams of Mississippi, and Carmack of Tennessee, and Congressmen Underwood and Oates of Alabama and William Kitchin of North Carolina, to name a few.[12] Such Southern moderates as Professor R. H. Dabney of the University of Virginia, Florida muckraker Claude L'Engle, Senator Joseph W. Bailey of Texas, and Governor Robert B. Glenn of North Carolina approved withdrawing all white support for Negro education. At least three men with lengthy pedigrees—Virginia historian Philip A. Bruce, educational reformer J. L. M. Curry, and Senator Wade Hampton—endorsed the idea of sending the blacks back to Africa. Nor did most demagogues distinguish themselves by taking radical stands on nonracial issues during election campaigns or conducting their administrations in ways very different from other Southern politicians. Studies of three important canvasses involving Tillman, Davis, and Vardaman find them adopting almost identical stances as their opponents on all the important issues in each election.[13]

The question of whether the demagogues led an "uprising of the poor whites" is more complex. Table 8.4 examines the relationships between white wealth and voting in every primary election in South Carolina and Mississippi from 1902 to 1911 in which a demagogue or a candidate strongly identified with a demagogue ran. These two states were chosen because they allowed more white participation in

12. On the descent of demagogues, see Daniel M. Robison, "From Tillman to Long: Some Striking Leaders of the Rural South," *Journal of Southern History* 3 (1937): 299–310; Clark and Kirwin, *South since Appomattox*, pp. 120–122. On racial attitudes, consult *Atlanta Constitution*, August 12, 1906; George C. Osborn, *John Sharp Williams*, pp. 155–160; Guion Griffis Johnson, "The Ideology of White Supremacy, 1876–1910," in Green, *Essays in Southern History*, pp. 136, n. 40, 140; Thomas W. Hardwick, "Negro Suffrage: The Fourteenth and Fifteenth Amendments," pamphlet (Washington, D.C.: n.p., 1904), p. 4. The liberal aristocrat Edgar Gardner Murphy favored modification of the Fifteenth Amendment to make its execution local—i.e. nullification in the South; see Hugh C. Bailey, *Liberalism in the New South*, p. 122.

13. For the attitudes toward Negro education, see *Jacksonville Florida Times-Union*, December 6, 1888; *The Outlook* 69 (1901): 810–812; Tinsley, "Progressive Movement in Texas," p. 178; Joel Webb Eastman, "Claude L'Engle, Florida Muckraker," *Florida Historical Quarterly* 49 (1967): 250; Orr, *Charles Brantley Aycock*, pp. 256–257. For those favoring expatriation, see Wade Hampton, "The Race Problem," *The Arena* 2 (1890): 132–138; Daniel J. Crofts, "Blair Bill," p. 186. For an endorsement of deportation by conservative South Carolina governor, D. C. Heyward, see *New York Times*, November 13, 1906, p. 6. On the campaigns of Tillman, Davis, and Vardaman, see Simkins, *Pitchfork Ben Tillman*, pp. 264–272; Paige Mulhollan, "Davis-Berry Senatorial Campaign in 1906," pp. 118–125; Holmes, *White Chief*, p. 180.

Table 8.4 Did the "Demagogues" Represent Poor Whites? Relationships between Estimated White Wealth and White Voting in Elections Involving "Demagogues" in South Carolina and Mississippi, 1902–1911.

State	Election	Candidate	Correlation with white Wealth[a]	% Change in Voting per $1000 Increase[b]	% Change in Nonvoting per $1000 Increase[c]
So. Carolina	1902 Sen.	Evans[d]	+.445	+7.63	−5.09
So. Carolina	1906 Gov. (1st)	Blease	+.041	+0.74	+1.12
So. Carolina	1906 Sen.	Tillman	−.063	−1.52	+0.78
So. Carolina	1908 Gov.	Blease	+.149	+3.18	−5.24
So. Carolina	1908 Sen. (1st)	Evans	+.073	+1.17	−9.12
So. Carolina	1908 Sen. (2nd)	Evans	+.032	+0.55	+2.87
So. Carolina	1910 Gov. (1st)	Blease	−.142	−2.55	+0.07
So. Carolina	1910 Gov. (2nd)	Blease	+.279	+4.90	−1.44
Mississippi	1903 Gov. (1st)	Vardaman	−.013	−0.15	−1.04
Mississippi	1903 Gov. (2nd)	Vardaman	−.113	−1.07	+0.38
Mississippi	1907 Gov. (1st)	Scott[e]	+.719	+7.28	+1.71
Mississippi	1907 Sen.	Vardaman	−.607	−6.28	+1.25
Mississippi	1911 Sen	Vardaman	−.669	−7.46	+2.77

[a]Column gives the correlation coefficient (r) between the estimated white wealth, by county, and the percentage of white male adults voting for each "demagogue."

[b]Column gives the percentage change in voting for each "demagogue" for every $1000 increase in estimated white wealth when Negro wealth is estimated at $100 per Negro adult male.

[c]Column gives the percentage change in nonvoting among white adult males for every $1000 increase in estimated white wealth. Thus a positive figure implies that wealthier whites voted in smaller proportions than poorer whites.

[d]Evans was identified with the Tillman faction.

[e]Candidate endorsed by Vardaman.

the primaries than any other Southern states during this period. By law, the restrictions on voting did not apply in the white primaries in South Carolina, and in Mississippi they seem to have been informally relaxed to a greater extent than in other states. Turnout among whites surpassed 60 percent in each of the elections covered in the table. Moreover, these states produced three of the best-known demagogues, Tillman, Blease, and Vardaman, and these men were the chief demagogues who were candidates in primary elections during this period.[14]

14. The quoted phrase is taken from Grantham, *The Democratic South*, pp. 48–50. Of the best-known "demagogues," Tom Watson, Tom Heflin, and James Ferguson did not run for

South Carolina and Mississippi primaries, therefore, provide a good test for the thesis that demagogues attracted mostly lower-class followings.

The table shows that in eight of the thirteen contests there were only negligible correlations between wealth and support for the demagogues. In three others, their support correlated strongly and positively with wealth. In none of the elections did turnout increase very much from county to county as wealth fell, and in three, lower-class whites seem to have participated in considerably smaller proportions than the wealthier whites.

A closer look at a few of the elections demonstrates the propensity of intraparty politics to blur class lines in elections. From the first to the second primaries in 1910, for example, Cole Blease's support shifted from a grouping with a slightly lower-income tinge to one with a fairly heavy upper-income coloration, perhaps because the emphasis he put on his antiprohibition views attracted upper-class followers. In Mississippi, James K. Vardaman, who had fought the Populists and identified strongly with the conservative George-Walthall-Money faction of the Democrats during the nineties, ran as the Delta candidate for governor in 1903 with the support of such aristocratic planter-politicians as Leroy Percy and John Sharp Williams. Locked in conflicts with Williams in 1907 and Percy in 1911, Vardaman did seem to attract much more support from the "wool hat boys" of the hills than the rich Delta planters. Vardaman's faction was, however, much less cohesive and ideologically consistent than a party alignment. In 1907, for instance, Vardaman endorsed Charles Scott, a conservative corporation lawyer whose strength, table 8.4 shows, centered in the upper, not the lower strata. And Vardaman could not transfer his popularity to his chosen successor as governor. Only 15 percent of the electors who voted for Vardaman for governor in 1903 seem to have backed Scott for governor in 1907.[15]

---

statewide public office during the first decade of the century, and Jeff Davis ran in only one direct primary. The young Theodore G. Bilbo ran for his first statewide office, lieutenant governor, in 1911. His support appears to correlate strongly with Vardaman's in the same year.

15. On Blease in 1910, see Stark, *Damned Upcountryman*, pp. 62, 73. On Vardaman's 1907 and 1911 races, see Holmes, *White Chief*, pp. 46–53, 95, 112–115, 183. Holmes has laid to rest the conception that Vardaman was, as Jack Temple Kirby put it in *Darkness at the Dawning* (p. 28), "an implacable enemy of the Delta aristocracy." The fact that Vardaman did not

Francis Butler Simkins has remarked that Cole Blease's lack of upper-class reserve and his ability to speak in the accents of the common people "satisfied the ordinary man more completely than a program of social reform."[16] Such comments are beside the point. No program of real social reform is possible in an elective polity without the sustained support of a party or a very tightly knit faction, organizations which suffrage restriction and the primary had discouraged and, in most Southern states, destroyed. The reason Blease yelled so stridently was not to satisfy anyone, but to get the voters' attention, for otherwise, in a primary, he had no chance of winning.

What set the demagogues apart, then, was their style—the volume more than the content of their remarks, their characterization more than the character of their supporters. Most Southern Democratic politicians opposed Cleveland's deflationary schemes; Ben Tillman announced his intention to impale the president on a pitchfork. Most politicians in an agricultural region claimed to represent agrarian interests; Jeff Davis continually boasted about his followers' sunburnt necks. In a political system without parties, without a regular method of recruiting candidates and culling the competent from the incompetent, sensationalism was usually the shortest route to victory.

All in all, the post-1900 Southern political structure was markedly different from the post-Reconstruction order. In the eighties and nineties, turnout regularly exceeded 60 percent of all adult males, and sometimes reached 85 percent. By 1910, almost no Negroes and only about half of the whites bothered to vote in the most hotly contested elections. Party competition was almost nonexistent, particularly in the Deep South. Such extremely disorganized political systems generally reward elites, who can translate their superior social and economic positions into political power to gain what they desire or at least block

---

race-bait any more in 1907 than in 1903, and put relatively little emphasis on race questions in 1911 tends to show that lower-class whites did not back him and conservatives did not oppose him primarily because of his strong racism. The election returns indicate that class attitudes toward Vardaman varied, rather, because of his views on socio-economic subjects other than race. The statement about Scott is based on a table not given in the text.

16. Simkins, *Tillman*, p. 488. Simkins' evidence for the ordinary man's satisfaction consists of one reference from a newspaper extremely hostile to Blease, and the article Simkins quotes seems to have reflected postelection sour grapes after an election Blease won. Moreover, the fact that Blease attracted the support of only 35 percent of the white adult males in his third fling at the governor's mansion (he lost the first two) hardly justifies Simkins' view that "the inarticulate masses loved Blease."

what they strongly oppose; whereas, members of the lower strata, lacking comparable resources, require collective organization if they are to assert themselves.[17] Whether this generalization is universally true or not, rough measures of policy outputs during the "Progressive Era" in the South indicate that the combination of partyless politics and low participation levels among socioeconomically deprived groups did, indeed, produce a political system which for the most part assisted only those already privileged.[18] In addition, the new disorderly political system altered the rewards and punishments for certain kinds of behavior, making irresponsibility almost a virtue. Deprived of the normal party channels of rising to power and getting support in elections, politicians were practically forced to blare recklessly in an effort to become known to the amorphous public. Once elected, they had little reason to carry through their promises, for the political system was too unstructured for voters to punish their leaders systematically for poor performance.

17. Samuel P. Huntington, *Political Order in Changing Societies*, pp. 403–407; Key, *Southern Politics*, pp. 303–308.

18. There is good deal of political science literature on the relation between inputs and outputs. See, e.g., Richard E. Dawson and James A. Robinson, "Interparty Competition, Economic Variables, and Welfare Policies in the American States," in Charles Press and Oliver P. Williams, *Democracy in the Fifty States* (Chicago: Rand-McNally Pub. Co., 1966), pp. 193–212; Richard I. Hofferbert, "Socio-economic Dimensions of the American States, 1890–1960," *Midwest Journal of Political Science* 12 (1968): 401–418; and Thomas R. Dye, "Income Inequality and American State Politics," *American Political Science Review* 63 (1969): 157–162. I am presently engaged in a large-scale computerized study of the patterns of distribution, by race and class, of educational expenditures and services in the South from 1880 to 1910.

9

Why The Solid South?
Or, Suffrage Restriction and Its Results

The new political structure was not the product of accident or other impersonal forces, nor of decisions demanded by the masses, nor even the white masses. The system which insured the absolute control of predominantly black counties by upper-class whites, the elimination in most areas of parties as a means of organized competition between politicians, and, in general, the nonrepresentation of lower-class interests in political decision-making was shaped by those who stood to benefit most from it—Democrats, usually from the black belt and always socioeconomically privileged. As this chapter will demonstrate, the disfranchisers articulated consciously elitist theories about suffrage and wrote these theories into law in a successful effort to re-form the polity.

Table 9.1 summarizes the chronology of the passage of restrictive statutes detailed in chapters 4 through 7. Compared to previous pictures of disfranchisement, this table emphasizes the large number of statutes, the importance of legislative as well as constitutional restriction, and the gradual nature of the process of legal suffrage limitation. As tables throughout this book have shown, the solid South did not crystallize immediately after Reconstruction.[1] The electorate continued to be highly volatile in most Southern states for nearly two decades after Hayes withdrew the last troops. Disfranchisement, which finalized the transition from the Reconstruction to the one-party system, took more than three decades. It should also be noted, however, that the restrictive laws tended to come in waves. The high tides of the disfranchisement movements came in the years 1888 to 1893 and 1898 to 1902. The former period coincided with the threat of a Republican resurgence associated with the proposed Lodge Fair Elections Bill;

1. Cf., e.g., Hilary A. Herbert, et al., *Why the Solid South? Or, Reconstruction and Its Results.*

Table 9.1. Chronology of Passage of Major Restrictive Statutes in
All Southern States, 1870–1910.

Year	Poll Tax	Regis- tration	Multiple- Box	Secret Ballot	Literacy Test	Property Test	Under- standing Clause	Grand- father Clause
1871	Ga.							
1872								
1873								
1874								
1875	Va.							
1876								
1877	Ga.							
1878								
1879								
1880								
1881	Va. (repealed)							
1882		S.C.	S.C.					
1883								
1884								
1885								
1886								
1887								
1888								
1889	Fla.	Tenn.	Fla.	Tenn.				
1890	Miss. Tenn.			Miss.	Miss.		Miss.	
1891				Ark.				
1892	Ark.							
1893		Ala.		Ala.				
1894		S.C.		Va.				
1895	S.C.				S.C.		S.C.	
1896								
1897		La.		La.				
1898	La.				La.	La.		La.
1899		N.C.	N.C.					
1900	N.C.				N.C.	N.C.		N.C.
1901	Ala.				Ala.	Ala.		Ala.
1902	Va. Tex.				Va.	Va.	Va.	
1903				Tex.				
1904								
1905								
1906								
1907								
1908					Ga.	Ga.	Ga.	Ga.

the latter, with the ebbing of the Populist-Republican activities of the 1890s. The threats made restriction seem necessary for Democratic prosperity; the defeat of the Lodge bill and the decline of the insurgency of the nineties helped make restriction possible.

THE FAIT ACCOMPLI THESIS

Tables 9.2 and 9.3 are designed to measure the impact of suffrage restriction and to test Key's fait accompli thesis. Table 9.2 is based on comparisons of actual voting and estimated voting by race in the last election before the first restrictive law was passed in each state, with similar data for the first election after the last restrictive law went into effect. In Alabama, Georgia, and South Carolina, where two separate and effective laws were passed over the period of about a decade, two sets of election figures are provided.

The actual numbers given in table 9.2 are the proportionate reductions in overall turnout, estimated white turnout, etc. These figures are computed by dividing the decrease in voting from the first to the second election in each pair by the percentage voting in the first election. In Alabama, for example, 70.5 percent of the voters turned out in the 1892 governor's race, but only 57.0 percent in 1896—a decline of 13.5 percent. The proportionate reduction in turnout is equal to 13.5 divided by 70.5, or roughly 19 percent. The other figures are calculated analogously.[2]

Table 9.2 shows that there were massive declines in turnout and opposition party strength after suffrage restriction. The reduction in overall turnout ranged from 7 percent in the second Georgia case to 66 percent in Louisiana and averaged 37 percent.[3] The reductions in estimated white turnout ranged from 3 percent in the first Georgia case to 46 percent in Louisiana, averaging 26 percent. Likewise, the reductions in estimated black turnout and the percentages of adult males

2. The unweighted averages of these percentage declines are given in parentheses on the last lines of tables 9.2 and 9.3. For an explanation of why I used the proportionate reduction statistics to measure the impact of restriction, see appendix B.

3. The first pair of Georgia elections deviate from the general pattern partly because the non-cumulative poll tax went into effect in 1871. Turnout had already been cut before 1876. Moreover, the 1876 turnout figures, as calculated, are smaller than they should be, because they are computed on the basis of the 1880 population. The declines from 1876 to 1880 should actually be higher than those given in the table, but because of the deficiencies of the 1870 census, it is impossible to interpolate the correct figures.

The second pair deviates because disfranchisement had already been largely accomplished by 1908, as explained in chapter 7, above.

Table 9.2. Impact of Suffrage Restriction in the South: Proportionate
Reduction in Overall Turnout and Estimated Turnout by Race, and in
Percentage of Adult Males for Opposition Parties.

State	Elections	Percentage Reduction			
		Overall Turnout	Estimated White Turnout	Estimated Negro Turnout	% of Adult Males for Opposition Parties
Alabama	1892–1896 Gov.[a]	19	15	24	30
Alabama	1900–1904 Pres.	38	19	96	58
Arkansas	1890–1894 Gov.	39	26	69	72
Florida	1888–1892 Gov.	61	31	83	73
Georgia	1876–1880 Pres.	13	3	29	−7
Georgia	1904–1908 Pres.	7	23	−6	−16
Louisiana	1896–1900 Gov.	66	46	93	87
Mississippi	1888–1892 Pres.	57	34	69	60
No. Carolina	1896–1904 Pres.	46	23	100[b]	53
So. Carolina	1880–1884 Pres.	49	43	50	63
So. Carolina	1892–1896 Pres.	13	17	51	57
Tennessee	1888–1892 Gov.	19	4	68	13
Texas	1902–1904 Gov.	32	29	36	31
Virginia	1900–1904 Pres.	54	48	100[b]	61
Unweighted mean		37 (24)[c]	26 (19)	62 (32)	45 (12)

[a]The notation means that the elections compared are the 1892 and 1896 governor's races.

[b]In these two cases, Negro turnout after disfranchisement was estimated to be negative. I then set the percentage reduction at 100%.

[c]Figures in parentheses are the unweighted means of percentage decline in turnout, etc.

Table 9.3. Was There a Trend toward Declining Turnout and
Decreasing Party Competition before Legal Disfranchisement?

		Percentage Reduction			
State	Elections	Overall Turnout	Estimated White Turnout	Estimated Negro Turnout	% of Adult Males for Opposition Parties
Alabama	1888–1892 Gov.	−9[a]	−11	−11	−133
Alabama	1896–1900 Pres.	24	6	48	11
Arkansas	1886–1890 Gov.	−3	−7	5	−3
Florida	1884–1888 Gov.	6	−16	29	20
Georgia	1872–1876 Pres.	−30	_[b]	_[b]	19[c]
Georgia	1900–1904 Pres.	2	−12	52[c]	−6[c]
Louisiana	1892–1896 Gov.	−6	0	−10	−67
Mississippi	1884–1888 Pres.	10	5	15	37
No. Carolina	1888–1896 Pres.	0	2	−6	1
So. Carolina	1876–1880 Pres.	6	−32	28	37
So. Carolina	1888–1892 Pres.	17[c]	13	15	−5
Tennessee	1884–1888 Gov.	−1	−16	7	−8
Texas	1900–1902 Gov.	22	20	34	32[c]
Virginia	1896–1900 Pres.	16	11	23	20
Unweighted mean		4(2)[d]	−3(−2)	18(8)	−3(+1)

[a]A minus sign indicates a proportionate increase in turnout.

[b]I did not compute estimates for elections before 1876.

[c]Proportionate reductions greater than comparable figures in table 9.1.

[d]Figures in parentheses are the unweighted means of the percentage decline in turnout, etc.

voting for parties other than the Democrats averaged 62 percent and 45 percent, respectively.

Of course, correlation can never logically prove causation, and other things are never completely equal. But to prove that the relation between the restrictive laws and the declines in turnout and party competition is spurious, one would have to show that the relationships could occur by chance or specify other factors which could account for the connection.[4] Proponents and critics of the laws certainly believed

4. I computed "t" tests to determine whether the average declines and the proportionate reductions in turnout and opposition voting in table 9.2 were statistically significant. All were

the franchise limitations important. And reports of the pairs of elections disclose no changes in conditions which could explain such large declines. One could still reject the hypothesis of a causal relationship, however, if the decreases merely continued trends already begun. But the declines reflected ongoing trends in very few cases. In several states, in fact, the laws appear to have reversed tendencies toward greater participation and party competition, while in the rest, the statutes greatly intensified nascent proclivities among the voters or struck already declining segments of the electorate with coups de grace.

Table 9.3 shows the proportionate reduction in turnout and opposition voting for the pairs of elections before the passage of disfranchising laws. Each pair of elections is directly analogous to the pair given in table 9.2. For example, since 9.2 compared the 1890 and 1894 governors' races in Arkansas, 9.3 compares contests for the same position, the same interval apart, and ending with the first election in the 9.2 pair.

Forty-nine of the fifty-four cells show less proportionate reduction than the comparable cells in table 9.2. The differences in the deviant Texas and South Carolina cells are only 1 percent and 4 percent, respectively. The remaining deviant cells refer to elections in Georgia, a special case explained more fully in chapter 7 and footnote 3 of this chapter.

Table 9.3 does show that Negro voting usually fell off somewhat immediately preceding the enactment of disfranchisement laws. Since these reductions were reflected in changes in the composition of legislatures, they were often large enough to allow the restrictionists' bills to carry. It is in this weak sense that the fait accompli hypothesis is useful. It was not necessary for the disfranchisers to decimate the opposition and end Negro voting entirely before disfranchisement. Rather, they had somehow to reduce dissent to whatever point it took to push a law through the legislature, pass an amendment at a referendum, or call a constitutional convention. Sometimes violence and intimidation alone accomplished the necessary reduction of their adversaries, as in

---

significantly different from zero at the .0005 level—i.e. such declines would be likely to occur by chance only five times out of ten thousand. The same test for statistical significance gave the following results for table 9.3: the declines and proportionate reductions in Negro voting were statistically significant at the .025 and .01 levels, respectively. None of the rest of the averages were significantly different from zero.

Mississippi; sometimes, short-term but large-scale fraud sufficed, as in Tennessee; and sometimes, legislative restrictions added to coercion and apathy made disfranchisement possible, as in North Carolina. Such a reformulation of Key's contention preserves his insight into the necessity for a stage previous to disfranchisement in which political activity was muted, without disregarding the efficacy of the restrictive laws themselves.

Indeed, the strategic importance of the declines in Negro turnout before the passage of the restrictive laws should not obscure the actual size of those declines. The average decline in Negro turnout in the pre-disfranchisement elections was 8 percent, the proportionate reduction 18 percent. The decline and proportionate reduction figures for the elections immediately before and after disfranchisement were much more substantial—32 percent and 62 percent, respectively. Moreover, the death of opposition parties came *after*, not *before* disfranchisement. In several states, the opposition percentages were rising immediately before the Democrats enacted restrictive laws. Overall, the percentage change in the opposition totals in the elections preceding disfranchisement was very small (a 1 percent decline) compared to a 12 percent decline following disfranchisement. Further, average white turnout actually *rose* in the elections preceding enactment of franchise limitations; whereas, after the laws were put into effect, it immediately fell by 19 percent.

Table 9.4 may make the pattern of the relationships between opposition, participation, pre-disfranchisement actions, and disfranchisement clearer by reducing the data from tables 9.2 and 9.3 and chapters 4 through 7 to schematic form. The checks and letters in the boxes indicate the presence of the attributes named at the top of each column. In Alabama in 1893, for example, the opposition party percentage of the gubernatorial vote was high (i.e., over 40 percent), and that percentage, as well as the proportions of both Negro and white voting participation, increased over the 1888 percentage. Large-scale fraud probably occurred in the 1892 election. After the passage of the Sayre law in 1893, both opposition party and turnout percentages dropped. The rest of the cells in the table can be interpreted in a similar manner.

Small differences from state to state do not obscure the predominant pattern. White turnout and opposition to the Democrats were almost

Table 9.4. A Paradigm of the Transformation of Southern Politics: Patterns of
Opposition and Turnout before and after Passage of Chief
Disfranchisement Laws.

A. Before

State, Year of Passage	Opposition Threat	White Turnout Rising	Negro Turnout Declining	Widespread Violence or Intimidation	Probable Large-Scale Fraud	Antecedent Restrictive Law
Ala. 1893	HR	X			X	
Ala. 1901		X			X	
Ark. 1891–92	H	X	X		X	X
Fla. 1889–91	H	X	X		X	X
Ga. 1877		_b	_b			X
Ga. 1908		X	X	X	X	X
La. 1896–98	HR	0c			X	X
Miss. 1890	Rd		X	X		
N.C. 1899–1900	H			X	X	X
S.C. 1882	Hd	X	X		X	
S.C. 1895	R	X	X		X	X
Tenn. 1889–91	HR	X	X		X	
Tex. 1902			X	X	X	
Va. 1902	H	X				X
11-State Average	H	X	X		X	X

B. After

State, Year of Passage	Opposition Threat[a]	White Turnout Declining	Negro Turnout Declining
Ala. 1893	D	X	X
Ala. 1901	LD	X	X
Ark. 1891–92	D	X	X
Fla. 1889–91	D	X	X
Ga. 1877	L	X	X
Ga. 1908	L	X	X
La. 1896–98	D	X	X
Miss. 1890	LD	X	X
N.C. 1899–1900	D	X	X
S.C. 1882	D	X	X
S.C. 1895	LD	X	X
Tenn. 1889–91	D	X	X
Tex. 1902	LD	X	X
Va. 1902	D	X	X
11-State Average	LD	X	X

[a]H signifies high opposition threat, R rising threat; L signifies low opposition threat, D,

always high or rising, or both high and rising, before disfranchisement, but the opposition collapsed and the participation rates of whites and blacks both plummeted immediately after the institution of the new requirements. Extensive violence, intimidation, fraud, or a small but sufficient change in the election laws preceded passage of all major statutes and amendments. Although the relatively small declines in Negro voting previous to disfranchisement were enough to enable restrictive laws to pass, the laws did not simply mirror already established conditions. They had very large impacts on black and white turnout and voting for parties opposed to the Democrats.

WHO WERE THE DISFRANCHISERS?

If the laws and constitutional amendments making voting more difficult largely explain the declines in turnout and opposition to the Democrats, the important question becomes that of the identity and motivation of the disfranchisers and their enemies.

As chapters 4 through 7 showed, the proponents of disfranchisement were almost all Democrats; whereas, in state after state, the great majority of the Republicans and Populists opposed the bills in legislatures, conventions, and referenda. Only in North Carolina did large numbers of Populists back suffrage limitations, and even in that state, a majority of the People's Party men are estimated to have opposed the suffrage amendment.

Within the Democratic party, the chief impetus for restriction came from the black belt members. In the legislatures and conventions, the few men of real competence acquired positions of extraordinary importance. They drafted the bills, chaired the committees, corralled votes, gave the chief speeches, and directed strategy among the solons and propaganda among the masses. And in every state except Texas, the principal leaders in the fight for restriction came from counties with high proportions of Negroes. In Texas, two of the three key leaders

---

declining threat.

   [b]Not computed.

   [c]Zero signifies no change in turnout.

   [d]I designated the threat in Mississippi "rising" even though quick, renewed violence was sufficient to quash it before the 1890 election. In South Carolina, since the Republicans would have scored over 40 percent in the 1880 presidential contest with anything like a fair count, I designated the threat "high."

of the final push for the poll tax were aspiring Democratic politicians, probably concerned with furthering the interests of their party and, consequently, their own careers. Although the other important leader, Alexander W. Terrell, lived in a predominantly white county, he shared two traits with many black belt leaders: he was a plantation owner and virulent racist.

Not only did the vast majority of the leaders reside in the black belt, almost all of them were affluent and well-educated, and they often bore striking resemblances to antebellum "patricians." Indeed, almost every one was the son or grandson of a large planter, and several of the older chiefs had been slaveholders before the war. To trace a composite picture of these men is to discover the classic Southern politico—a leading landowner and member of the county clique who often doubled as a lawyer or local newspaper editor, a successful operator in the arena of the state legislature who sometimes graduated to higher office, often a flowery rhetorician with a courtly manner and a touch (and sometimes more) of the demagogue about him. Judges Thomas W. Coleman and A. D. Sayre of Alabama fit this pattern well, as did James P. Clarke and A. H. Sevier, Jr., of Arkansas, Samuel J. Turnbull and William Milton, Jr., of Florida, Governor Murphy J. Foster and Judge Thomas J. Semmes of Louisiana, Senator J. Z. George of Mississippi, Francis D. Winston and George Rountree of North Carolina, General Edward McCrady of South Carolina, J. H. Dortch of Tennessee, Senator John W. Daniel and Hal Flood of Virginia.[5]

In contrast, the principal white opponents of limitations on the electorate were so obscure that we know little of their lives. What information we have indicates that their common characteristics were (1) a willingness to affront the established powers by joining opposition parties and (2) residence in predominantly white counties, usually in the hills. Insofar as the Populists and Republicans represented the poorer whites, their leaders' position on the issue could be taken as evidence of poor white opposition to restriction.

But we also have more direct evidence of white class stands on

5. I have not been able to locate enough information on other key leaders to decide whether they run to type. Almost every one, however, did come from the black belt, and if the politics of their counties conformed to the usual pattern, their backgrounds probably resembled those of the men cited in the text. Of course, a few leaders—newspaper editors or publishers such as Carter Glass, Josephus Daniels, and Hoke Smith, and some city politicians such as Ernest Kruttschnitt of New Orleans—did not entirely fit the dominant pattern.

restriction. Table 9.5 presents the correlations between white wealth and votes on disfranchisement amendments for six of the seven states which held contended referenda on restriction.[6] In five of the states, pro-disfranchisement sentiment was positively correlated and opposition negatively correlated with wealth. Although both pro- and anti-restriction sentiments were negatively correlated with wealth in South Carolina, anti-disfranchisement voting there had a higher negative relation to wealth than pro-disfranchisement voting.

The regression coefficients in the second column of figures show just how strongly voting and wealth were related. In North Carolina, for instance, a county where the assessed wealth was $1,200 per white male could be expected, on the average, to vote for disfranchisement by a margin of about 48 percent to 28 percent, with 24 percent not voting. A county where the wealth averaged $200 could be expected to cast about 36 percent of its ballots for disfranchisement, 42 percent against, with 22 percent not voting. If wealth differences within counties were relatively small, on the average, then these figures show that poor whites were considerably less likely to favor and more likely to oppose suffrage restriction than more affluent whites. At the very least the figures demonstrate that whites in the richer counties of the black belt supported disfranchisement much more fervently than those in the small farming counties in the hills.

Moreover, contrary to the traditional view, opposition to restriction was not confined to Caucasians.[7] To be sure, there were Negroes who, tired of fighting Democratic violence and intimidation, angry at Republican failures to pass national legislation guaranteeing civil and political rights, and hopeless of ever getting a fair ballot count, dropped out of politics and counseled others to do likewise. A few blacks donned handkerchiefs and publicly acquiesced in the disfranchisement of their race. But many of their fellows fought valiantly against the new order.

In at least ten of the eleven ex-Confederate states, Negroes took

6. I have not been able to obtain wealth data for the seventh state, Georgia. Estimates of white wealth per capita were computed in the same manner as for table 8.3.

7. Statements in the next two paragraphs are based on a wide variety of sources—legislative and constitutional convention journals, contested election cases, the *Congressional Record*, U.S. Supreme Court cases, newspapers, contemporary journal articles, memoirs, dissertations, published monographs, and my own estimates of voting in referenda. The list of Negro activities is meant to be suggestive, not exhaustive. Further research would no doubt turn up other instances of Negro opposition to and acquiescence in disfranchisement. To avoid cluttering the text with lengthy documentation, I will not cite the exact sources for my statements, but I will be happy to supply more precise citations to interested readers upon request.

Table 9.5. Disfranchisement Was a Class Issue: The Relation of Estimated White Wealth to White Voting in Referenda on Suffrage Restriction.

State	Election	Position on Disfranchisement	Correlation between Wealth and Position on Disfranchisement	% Change in Voting for Every $1000 Increase in White Wealth
Alabama	Calling Convention 1901	For	.437	4.6
		Against	−.604	−6.8
		Not Voting	.154	2.3
Alabama	Ratifying Constitution 1901	For	.384	5.9
		Against	−.661	−9.5
		Not Voting	.251	3.6
Arkansas	Poll Tax 1892	For	.722	35.1
		Against	−.081	−2.1
		Not Voting	−.537	−33.0
Arkansas	Poll Tax 1908	For	.647	19.3
		Against	−.297	−3.1
		Not Voting	−.531	−16.4
No. Carolina	Suffrage Amendment 1900	For	.405	12.4
		Against	−.375	−14.4
		Not Voting	.063	1.8
So. Carolina	Calling Convention 1894	For	−.460	−4.3
		Against	−.730	−6.8
		Not Voting	not calculated	
Texas	Poll Tax 1902	For	.175	2.4
		Against	−.241	−2.3
		Not Voting	−.008	−0.1
Virginia	Calling Convention 1900	For	.251	4.3
		Against	−.233	−4.6
		Not Voting	.012	0.3

NOTE: In all these calculations I have assumed that no Negroes actually voted in the referendum, for the estimates of Negro voting indicate that none voted *against* the conventions and amendments. I therefore assumed that apparent Negro votes for disfranchisement in heavily Negro counties were fictitious, but do indicate greater support for disfranchisement by whites in the black belt.

There were two exceptions to this. In South Carolina, Negroes clearly controlled their votes in two rich counties, Beaufort and Georgetown, which voted heavily against the convention and sent all-Negro delegations to it. I therefore excluded these two counties in computing the correlations between voting and white wealth. In Virginia, Negroes in a good many counties seem to have voted freely, and I therefore subtracted from the voting totals estimated Negro voting. The percentages used in the subtractions were the estimates given in chapter 6 for Negro voting in the referendum (24 percent recorded for the convention, 16 percent against, 60 percent not voting).

public, legal action against disfranchisement. In four states blacks held meetings or conventions to protest suggested laws limiting the suffrage. In six, they organized election campaigns against proposed amendments in referenda. In seven, they spoke out against the intended changes in the legislatures or constitutional conventions, or, where they were not represented by men of their own race, sent protests or petitions. In four, they voted against restriction in referenda and managed to see that a large portion of their votes were counted. In five commonwealths, they brought suit to overturn the suffrage provisions of the new constitutions. Finally, Negroes from three states challenged the seating of several Democratic congressmen solely on the grounds of the unconstitutionality of the new Southern election codes.

Seventy years ago, a member of the Mississippi disfranchising convention, J. S. McNeilly, wrote that

The fact of disfranchisement was accepted by the masses of the sons of Ham without show of sorrow or sign of resentment. Suffrage had come to them unsolicited; it departed from them unregretted. As a demonstration of the Negro's incapacity and unworthiness for the equipment of political equality nothing more need be written.[8]

McNeilly's racist fantasy proved useful in justifying undemocratic practices to the tender consciences of contemporary white supremacists, but it was bad history, as even McNeilly ought to have known. The myth of Negro apathy in the face of disfranchisement must now be dropped along with the other dogmas of the religion of racial inferiority.[9] The blacks were disfranchised not because they surrendered, but because the Democrats overwhelmed them with superior physical and legal force.

THE "GROWING SENSE OF DISTRUST IN UNIVERSAL SUFFRAGE"

In identifying the disfranchisers and their opponents, we obtain clues to their motives. That suffrage restriction was aimed primarily at Negroes needs no further documentation at this point. Proponents

8. J. S. McNeilly, "History of the Measures," pp. 138–139.

9. The myth persists even in the writings of the most liberal historians. Thus, C. Vann Woodward states in *Origins of the New South*, p. 324, that, "with the white Republicans indifferent, the Populists divided, *and the Negro himself apathetic*, resistance to disfranchisement from within the South reached a low point by 1898" (my italics). Woodward did later implicitly qualify this statement by citing, on pp. 337–338, several of the protests of Negro leaders against disfranchisement.

in nearly every Southern state trumpeted their intent to disfranchise the vast majority of Negroes. Whether these men aimed to disfranchise whites, too, is a more complex problem. The fact that white turnout did drop, often dramatically, provides only circumstantial evidence, because that decline might have resulted from the decrease in party competition or might have represented merely an unintended consequence of regulations actually passed to cut down Negro voting which were phrased broadly in order to withstand constitutional challenges.

Perhaps the best way to answer this question is to view it as part of a more general inquiry: what theories of the suffrage underlay restriction? If those who favored limitation never put forward any theories, then the unintended consequence hypothesis will look stronger, and disfranchisement will merely confirm the belief that the "genius of American politics" is a paucity of abstract thought, that the fact that such movements existed does not indicate any break in the liberal American consensus. If, as some historians have claimed, the restrictionists extolled democracy in theory and extended it for whites in practice, and excluded Negroes out of simple racism, then disfranchisement reinforces the notion that the Progressives and others who backed the laws merely had a "blind spot" on the race question.[10] In fact, however, the late nineteenth century witnessed a recrudescence of antidemocratic theorizing on the question of who was entitled to vote.

American suffrage, in both theory and practice, had moved "from property to democracy" by 1860, at least for white males.[11] The phrase "the right to vote" became dogma, and few publicly adhered to Blackstone's dictum that the electorate should be confined to those who had "a will of their own," evidenced outwardly by property ownership. The franchise was extended to all black men during Reconstruction and to all women at the end of World War I. Nevertheless, "genteel reformers" in the North and Democrats throughout the

10. The best-known consensus interpretations of American history are Daniel Boorstin, *The Genius of American Politics* (Chicago: University of Chicago Press, 1953) and Louis Hartz, *The Liberal Tradition in America* (New York: Harcourt, Brace & World, 1955). The Progressive blind spot theory appears in David W. Southern, *The Malignant Heritage*, p. 85; Newby, *Jim Crow's Defense*, p. 153; Dewey W. Grantham, Jr., "The Progressive Movement and the Negro," in Wynes, ed., *Negro in the South*, pp. 77–78. Both Newby and Grantham realize that some Progressives and racists did challenge the democratic dogma, but they consider this challenge a very minor theme.

11. Willamson, *American Suffrage*; V. Jacque Voegeli, *Free But Not Equal*, p. 4.

country reacted strongly against the corruption, inefficiency, and unthinking partisanship which they believed characterized governments dependent on the votes of Negroes in the South and non–Anglo-Saxon immigrants in the North. To restore "good government," many of these upper-class reformers concluded, the power of Negro and immigrant votes had to be curbed. Since the most direct way to limit their power was to excise many of these "inferiors" from the electorate, the Mugwumps and their Southern counterparts were forced to question the doctrine of universal male suffrage.

The historian Francis Parkman, for instance, wrote that universal suffrage "gives power to the communistic attack on property." The only men who should be allowed to vote, that son of a distinguished Massachusetts family thought, were those who were members of groups with "hereditary traditions of self-government." Terming widespread suffrage "debased," and decrying "the monstrosities of Negro rule in South Carolina," the Beacon Hill Brahmin announced to his *North American Review* audience, "Good government is the end, and the ballot is worthless except so far as it helps to reach this end." Similarly, the popular spokesman for the social gospel, Washington Gladden, wrote in another leading Northern journal, *The Century*, that the idea of a natural right to vote was a mere "popular superstition." "[T]he paramount question in the bestowment of [the vote]," he went on, "is whether the persons receiving it are likely to use it to promote the public welfare. Those classes of whom this cannot be expected ought not to be intrusted with it." "There is not the slightest doubt in my own mind," remarked a leading Progressive political economist, John W. Burgess, "that our prodigality with the suffrage has been the chief source of corruption of our elections. We must begin with the cause if we would remove the effect."[12] Other writers wished to set qualifications for the suffrage based on education, intelligence, or even "wisdom" and "virtue," and most of these antidemocrats clearly directed

12. See Francis Parkman, "The Failure of Universal Suffrage," *North American Review* 127 (1878): 1–20. For similarly colorful statements, see William L. Scruggs, "Restriction of the Suffrage," in ibid. 139 (1884): 492–502; and Alexander Winchell, "The Experiment of Universal Suffrage," pp. 119–134. For a short biographical sketch of Parkman, see William R. Taylor, "Francis Parkman," in Marcus Cunliffe and Robin W. Winks, ed., *Pastmasters* (New York: Harper & Row, 1969), pp. 1–38. Washington Gladden, "Safeguards of the Suffrage," *The Century* 37 (1888–1889): 621–628. Burgess is quoted in Thomas F. Gossett, *Race: The History of an Idea in America* (Dallas, Texas: Southern Methodist Univ. Press, 1963), p. 112.

their tests at Negroes and recent immigrants.[13] Little wonder that two Yale historians surveying attitudes on voting in 1918 found that "the theory that every man has a natural right to vote no longer commands the support of students of political science." For themselves, these self-proclaimed "scientists" asserted that "if the state gives the vote to the ignorant, they will fall into anarchy to-day and into despotism to-morrow."[14]

Southern intellectuals and civic reformers joined the Yankee moss-backs in condemning suffrage so broad that it gave some power, in the words of the Southern "liberal" Edgar Gardner Murphy, to the "crudest" classes. Thomas Nelson Page, for example, believed that qualifications for voting for both whites and Negroes should be raised high enough to "leave the ballot only to those who have intelligence enough to use it as an instrument to secure good government rather than to destroy it." Newspaper editors seconded the intellectuals. The widely circulated *New Orleans Daily Picayune* denounced universal

13. Albert J. McCulloch, *Suffrage and Its Problems*, wanted a literacy test in order to elimi-nate "the two most dangerous classes of possible voters in America today . . . the Negroes and the foreigners" (p. 171). Similarly, see J. J. McCook, "Venal Voting," pp. 159–177; George H. Haynes, "Educational Qualifications for the Suffrage in the United States," *Political Science Quarterly* 13 (1898): 495–513; Thomas M. Cooley, *The General Principles of Constitutional Law in the United States of America* (Boston: Little Brown & Co., 1898), p. 292; J. B. Phillips, "Educational Qualifications of Voters," pp. 55–62; John R. Commons, *Races and Immigrants in America*, pp. 3–4, 11–12, 41–43, 52, 195; John J. Clancy, Jr., "A Mugwump on Minorities," pp. 178–182; John G. Sproat, *"The Best Men,"* pp. 253–254; James Bryce, "Thoughts on the Negro Problem," pp. 641–660; *The Outlook* 69 (1901): 751; 73 (1903): 950; 74 (1903): 339–340; 76 (1904): 632–634; and 79 (1905): 11–15; James Albert Hamilton, *Negro Suffrage and Congressional Representation*, pp. 17–18; Philadelphia *Times* (n.d.), quoted in Birmingham *Age-Herald*, January 3, 1893; and Tammany head Bourke Cochran, in The Southern Society for the Promotion of the Study of Race Conditions and Problems in the Society, *Race Problems in the South* (Richmond, Virginia: B. F. Johnson Publishing Co., 1900), pp. 206–207. Winchell, "Experiment of Universal Suffrage," p. 133, proposed the "wisdom" and "virtue" test, which he claimed would "secure the survival of the fittest."

14. Charles Seymour and Donald Paige Frary, *How the World Votes: The Story of Democratic Development in Elections*, 2 volumes (Springfield, Massachusetts: C.A. Nichols Co., 1918), 1:12–13, 2 : 320–321. Two other students of public affairs who agreed on little else joined in the view that Northern public opinion was increasingly against universal suffrage at the turn of the century. See Commons, *Races and Immigrants*, p. 4, and Archibald H. Grimke, "Why Disfranchisement is Bad," p. 10 of a reprint from the *Atlantic Monthly* (July, 1904). These attitudes persist even now. A majority of a national random sample in 1956 disagreed with the unfortunately rather ambiguous statement: "People ought to be allowed to vote even if they can't do so intelligently." Herbert McCloskey, "Consensus and Ideology in American Politics," in Edward C. Dreyer and Walter A. Rosenblum, *Political Opinion and Electoral Behavior*, p. 243.

manhood suffrage as "absolutely unnatural, unreasonable, and un-
sanctioned by any proper principle." A few days later the *Picayune*
declared that "the idea that a mere numerical majority of the people,
without regard to intelligence and other fitness, must rule the country
and make its laws is to argue [sic] in favor of a government of force."
The *Columbia* (South Carolina) *Daily Register* stigmatized manhood
suffrage as "a Yankee idea." The *Dallas* (Texas) *Morning News* favored
disfranchising all illiterates "without reference to the color or domicile
of the ignorant, North and South." Approving the "growing sense of
distrust in universal suffrage," *The Pine Bluff* (Arkansas) *Commercial*
disapproved of voting by white immigrants, as well as Negroes. "When
a native born citizen of the United States thinks of the fearful fact that
the offscouring of Europe, a people without homes, friends, or language; and in seventy-five percent of the cases only lacking a tail to complete the brute structure" could vote, "it makes one illy [*sic*] proud of
the boon of American citizenship." The paper favored limiting the
franchise to white males who had been in the United States for at
least 21 years.[15]

Many Southern politicians echoed the intelligentsia. United States
Senator Samuel D. McEnery told a Louisiana audience that the intent
of the proposed suffrage qualifications "is the exclusion of those only
who have no will of their own; that is, no personality. The government
is then founded in the strength of its intelligence, manhood, and in the
true will of the people, and not in the accidents of life, such as color or
race." "The bestowal of political power upon mere numbers—the

15. Murphy, quoted in Daniel Levine, "Edgar Gardner Murphy, Conservative Reformer,"
Alabama Review 15 (1962): 108–109. See also Murphy, *The Basis of Ascendency* (New York:
Longmans, Green & Co., 1909), pp. 235–236; J. L. M. Curry, speech to the Louisiana Con-
stitutional Convention of 1898, in its *Journal*, pp. 30–35; and J. Dickson Bruns, speech to New
Orleans Citizens League, in *New Orleans Picayune*, December 16, 1897. Thomas Nelson Page,
"A Southerner on the Negro Question," *North American Review* 154 (1892): 412. *New Orleans
Daily Picayune*, December 4, 1897, and January 4, 1898. The *Picayune* favored disfranchising
both blacks and whites. See, e.g., its editorial of March 23, 1898. For similarly antidemocratic
editorials, see *Baton Rouge* (Louisiana) *Daily Advocate*, January 18, 1896; *Columbia Daily
Register*, January 3, 1882; *Little Rock Arkansas Democrat*, quoted in *Pine Bluff Weekly Commercial*,
November 9, 1890; *Leighton* (Alabama) *News*, quoted in *Montgomery Daily Advertiser*, February
13, 1902; December 10, 1902. *Columbia Daily Register*, August 3, 1886, quoted in Cooper,
Conservative Regime, p. 75; *Dallas Morning News*, February 15, 1901, p. 6. Similarly, see *Jacksonville Florida Times-Union*, May 10, 1889, p. 4; *New Orleans Times*, December 24, 1866,
quoted in T. Harry Williams, "An Analysis of Some Reconstruction Attitudes," *Journal of
Southern History* 12 (1946): 477. *Pine Bluff* (Arkansas) *Commerical*, September 14, 1890.

impersonal mass—cannot be justified," McEnery announced in the United States Senate. "It is not the government of a free people. It will degenerate into absolutism. . . . Its inclusion in the electorate is the degradation of the whole." Edward McCrady, Jr., of South Carolina, favored disfranchising "the dense mass of ignorant voters of both colors." In an address to the Georgia legislature, Governor Allen D. Candler stated that a man who "failed to become a taxpayer contributing something to the support of his state, should have no voice in making its laws." Governor John Gary Evans urged the members of the South Carolina Constitutional Convention of 1895 to adopt a literacy test, "for only the intelligent are capable of governing." A delegate to the Virginia constitutional convention who openly endorsed disfranchising large numbers of whites as well as blacks, averred that "no man ought to be allowed to vote who has not sufficient intelligence to understand what he is doing, and besides has not some interest in the government which will induce him to vote aright."[16] Advocates of the poll tax tacitly accepted the Virginian's second criterion in their continually reiterated argument that no man unwilling or *unable* to pay a few dollars to vote should be allowed the franchise. Many other Southern politicians indicated their complete rejection of the idea of universal male suffrage either explicitly or implicitly, by denying that all whites should be allowed to vote.

Some Southern political activists integrated racism into a theory about the right to vote. Like Francis Parkman, they believed a group tradition of representative government created an inherent fitness to vote in members of that group.[17] A few devotees of this position, such as Birmingham corporation lawyer John B. Knox, suggested that

16. McEnery, quoted in *New Orleans Daily Picayune*, January 4, 1898, and *Congressional Record*, 56th Cong., 1 sess., 1064; Candler, quoted in Alton DuMar Jones, "Progressivism in Georgia," p. 137; Evans, quoted in S. C. Con. Con. *Journal* (1895), 12; McCrady, quoted in *Columbia* (South Carolina) *Daily Register*, Jan. 13, 1882; Richard McIlwaine, in Va. Con. Con., *Proceedings* (1901–02), 3001. See also the remarks of Goode, ibid., p. 20–21; Thom, ibid., pp. 2966–2967, 2977, 2988–2990.

17. Governor Charles B. Aycock of North Carolina, quoted in Hamilton, *Negro Suffrage*, pp. 32–33; Senator Furnifold Simmons of North Carolina, quoted in David Charles Roller, "The Republican Party in North Carolina," p. 21; Governor William A. MacCorkle of West Virginia, *Does the Experience of this Republic up to the Close of the Nineteenth Century Justify Universal Manhood Suffrage, or Should the Elective Franchise be Limited by Educational, Property, or Other Qualification?* (Cincinnati, Ohio: The Robert Clarke Co., 1901); John B. Knox, in Ala. Con. Con., *Proceedings* (1901), vol. 3, pp. 2922–2923; Tom Heflin, in ibid., 2844; Newby, *Jim Crow's Defense*, pp. 148–149.

members of groups lacking this tradition could remedy the fault quickly through education. Others, such as future demagogue Tom Heflin, held with Parkman that the defect was incurable. Far from ignoring the contradiction between universal white male suffrage and Negro disfranchisement, these men sought to justify their racism by encompassing it in a broader theoretical scheme. They recognized clearly the inconsistency between the democratic creed and the dogma of white supremacy, and sought to modify the first in order to enshrine the second.[18]

Like the proponents of disfranchisement, the movement's opponents expressed their views in terms of suffrage theory. Protesting against a clause which allowed the legislature to enact a poll tax, five Republican members of the Tennessee constitutional convention of 1870 stated:

Suffrage is a *right* and not a *privilege*—as much a right as life, liberty or property—a right not to be limited and not to be restricted; . . . and above all, a right not to be bestowed on the rich *in preference* to the poor. Suffrage is the political means of self-defense, and the disfranchised man is, or soon will be, a slave.[19]

Countering claims by elitists that honest government required a limited electorate, the egalitarian Southern intellectual George Washington Cable avowed that "not the banishment of all impure masses from the polls, but the equal and complete emancipation of all balloters from all impure temptations and constraints, is the key to the purification of the ballot. . . . So, first of all, free government; then pure govern-

18. The chief white defender of Negro rights after Reconstruction, Albion Tourgée, put forth the fascinating theory that once granted, suffrage "becomes a right." This view justified the actions of Northern states which withheld the suffrage from Negroes before 1870, while condemning Southern states which later tried to deprive blacks of the vote. See Tourgée, "Shall White Minorities Rule?" *The Forum* 7 (1889): 143–155. Tourgée's article further evidences the fact that concern about the proper extent of the electorate was so widespread in the late nineteenth century that virtually all articulate Southerners and many Northerners felt they had to relate their own political positions to a theory of the franchise.

19. Tenn. Con. Con. *Journal* (1870), pp. 179–181. For similar statements by Republicans and Populists, which often included specific approval for widespread Negro suffrage, see, e.g., Ala. Con. Con. *Proceedings* (1901), vol. 3, pp. 2971–2981, 3018–3019, 3285; Va. Con. Con. *Proceedings* (1901–02), pp. 3011, 3046–3047, 3056–3057; Governor John P. Buchanan, in Tenn. *House Journal* (1893), p. 58; 1890 Republican state platform in Tennessee, in Miller, *State of Tennessee*, p. 345; McKay, ed., *Texas Constitutional Convention*, pp. 170–177; J. E. Gore, quoted in Kirwin, *Revolt of the Rednecks*, p. 68; *Dallas Morning News*, October 25, 1902; Populist national platform, 1896, quoted in Grantham, "Progressive Movement and the Negro," p. 69.

ment." And the Southern Democrats had their Northern allies, just as the disfranchisers did. Congressman F. T. Greenhalge, a Massachusetts Republican, told his colleagues, "The theory of this government vests all sovereignty in the people. The only way the people can exercise that sovereignty is by means of the ballot. The ballot is the very breath of life of the body politic." "The ballot in the hand of the citizen is the badge of his sovereignty," added Republican Julius Caesar Burrows of Michigan. "Take that from him and he is a slave. Through the ballot, and that alone, he can make himself felt in the enactment of the laws and the administration of public affairs."[20]

Despite the Republicans' remarks, American government in the twentieth century was not based on the sovereignty of all the people. Political theorists throughout the country and practitioners at least in the South came to believe that mass suffrage and good government were inconsistent, and they eagerly chose the latter, to the detriment of the former. Another motive of the disfranchisers, then, was to limit the electorate to the "fit," most often defined as literate white men who owned at least some property. Critics of restriction defended the voting rights of all white men except criminals, and often all black men, too. But the critics, especially the Southern Republicans, were quickly forgotten, victims of the "Progressive Era's" revolt against democracy.

PARTISANSHIP, PROGRESSIVISM, AND SUFFRAGE RESTRICTION

In stating why some groups did not deserve to continue voting, of course, the restrictionists misrepresented the actions of these "unworthy classes." They claimed that the members of these groups had "no will of their own," or were mere "political automatons," or were "corruptible," when what they really meant was that those voters usually stubbornly refused to come over to the Democratic side.[21] As a con-

20. George Washington Cable, "The Southern Struggle for Pure Government" pamphlet (n. p., 1890, in Yale University Library), pp. 3–4. See the similar, perhaps even plagiarized statement by Louis E. McComas (R., Maryland) in *Congressional Record*, 51st Cong., 1st sess., p. 6678. Greenhalge's and Burrows's remarks appear in *Congressional Record*, 51st Cong., 1st sess., pp. 6694, 6786. See also similar remarks by Rep. Nils Haugen (R., Wisc.), in ibid., p. 6594; Senator Joseph N. Dolph (R. Oregon), in ibid., 2nd sess., pp. 365, 520; *New York Sun*, May 12, 1889, quoted in Evans, *Australian Ballot System*, p. 25.

21. Edward McCrady, Jr., quoted in *Columbia Daily Register*, January 13, 1882. *New Orleans Daily Picayune*, January 10, 1898; Senator James Z. George of Mississippi, in *Congressional Record*, 51st Cong., 2nd sess., p. 285; Rep. Thomas W. Hardwick, quoted in Newby, *Segregationist Thought*, pp. 98–105.

sequence of the lower strata's voting habits, Southern Democrats had
to stuff ballot boxes and try to bribe and intimidate voters in order to
win elections. This ironic inconsistency between rhetoric and reality
laid the Democrats open to the biting rebuke of a Virginia Republican:

> It is now proposed to right a wrong by punishing those who have been
> defrauded of their votes to the extent of destroying their right of suffrage;
> in other words the Negro vote of this Commonwealth must be destroyed to
> prevent the Democratic elections officers from stealing their votes.[22]

Direct Democratic assertions of the partisan purposes of restriction
were somewhat rare, since few Democrats dared to tempt the country's
Republican majority to return to its Reconstruction tactics. Privately,
a Chicago newspaper reported, Southern Democrats in Congress
freely admitted that "state constitutions were amended to perpetuate
Democratic control in state and municipal elections." And some
Democrats did make unguarded remarks. In the leadoff speech in the
Alabama constitutional convention's debate on suffrage, Judge Thomas W. Coleman emphasized that "this convention was called by the
Democratic party," and another delegate, George Harrison, capped
the convention whose chief work had been the suffrage article with the
observation that "upon the adoption of this Constitution whether right
or wrong, the very salvation and existence of the Democratic party in
Alabama depends." In the final speech before the vote on the Tennessee secret ballot act, J. H. Dortch "urged especially that [his bill]
was to the interest of the [D]emocratic party." E. B. Kruttschnitt
opened the Louisiana constitutional convention by noting, "I am called
upon to preside over what is little more than a family meeting of the
Democratic party."[23] In reaction to the threat posed by the Lodge
Elections Bill, the Mississippi constitutional convention put the literacy
test into effect immediately, according to the *Jackson Clarion-Ledger*,
because it "insured Democratic success in Mississippi." The purpose

22. Gillespie, in Va. Con. Con. *Proceedings* (1901–02), p. 3014.

23. *Chicago Chronicle* (n.d.), quoted in *Montgomery Daily Advertiser*, September 4, 1902.
That the *Advertiser* did not dispute the Chicago paper's report lends credibility to the contentions. For Coleman and Harrison, see Ala. Con. Con. *Proceedings* (1901), vol. 2, p. 2709,
and vol. 4, p. 4927. Dortch is quoted in *Nashville Banner*, April 2, 1889. Both the independent
Banner and the pro-Democratic *American* commented on the partisan purpose of the bill. See
ibid., April 3, 1889; Nashville *American*, March 27, April 3, 1889. For Kruttschnitt, see La.
Con. Con. *Journal* (1898), pp. 8–9. For other references to partisan motives, see above, chapters
4–7.

of that convention, according to Senator Hernando de Soto Money, had been "to maintain a civilization that is dependent very largely upon the Democratic party being in control." The chief author of Arkansas' secret ballot act told his colleagues that it had been "conceived in the interests of the Democratic party."[24]

The indirect evidence of a partisan intent is overwhelming. Every state except Texas passed a major restrictive law at a time of opposition upsurge or threat, or in the face of a grave, continuing challenge by the opposition. Texas disfranchisers pushed their bills at times of party crisis and finally succeeded only four years after the last serious campaign by the Populists. Moreover, the bills were perceived as partisan at the time, for the lineups on the proposals in legislatures, conventions, and referenda followed party lines extremely closely. Then, too, in legislatures and conventions where Populists or Republicans still held some power, the bills were drafted, debated, and voted on first in Democratic caucuses to insure that the opposition would not be able to water down or kill legislation so vital to party interests by playing off the Democrats against each other. Their sponsors also knew that the bills would disfranchise a larger proportion of potential opposition voters than of their own. Everyone realized that the severe decline in Negro voting would finish the Republicans, except in some upland areas, and the poll tax and literacy test could be expected to delete many of the mountain people from the electorate. The fact that opposition voting usually declined quite markedly after the suffrage changes, especially in black belt areas, in itself sets out a strong circumstantial case for partisan motivation. Could astute politicians who had usually spent the better parts of their lives combating insurgency have framed laws which did, in fact, so precisely accomplish party purposes with no awareness of their partisan consequences?[25]

24. *Clarion-Ledger*, September 25, 1890 is quoted in Mabry, "Disfranchisement of the Negro," p. 138; Money, in *Congressional Record*, 56th Cong., 1st sess., p. 1164; *Little Rock Arkansas Gazette*, February 26, 1891. For references to partisan motives in North Carolina, see Daniels, *Editor in Politics*, pp. 374–380.

25. The general point is also strengthened by the fact that partisanship was apparently the single most important reason for changes in election laws outside the ex-Confederate states. See Williams, *American Suffrage*, p. 272; Alan P. Grimes, *The Puritan Ethic and Woman Suffrage*, pp. 41–42, 46, 75, 96–97; Fredman, *The Australian Ballot*, pp. 42–43, 45; Lambert, *Arthur Pue Gorman*, pp. 286–287, 345–347; Richard P. McCormick, *The History of Voting in New Jersey*, pp. 124, 148–149, 163; Harold C. Livesay, "Delaware Negroes," pp. 95–97; Amy M. Hiller, "The Disfranchisement of Delaware Negroes in the Late Nineteenth Century," *Delaware*

It has often been noted that disfranchisement was concomitant with the rise of Progressivism. Virulent racism was the keynote of the campaigns of many Southern politicians usually characterized as "reformers." Ben Tillman of South Carolina and Hoke Smith of Georgia are only the best-known examples. Charles B. Aycock carried the main speaking load in the North Carolina "White Supremacy Campaign" of 1898 and race-baited his way to the governorship two years later. The threat of Negro domination was likewise A. J. Montague's chief theme in the 1901 general election for governor of Virginia. Murphy J. Foster, the Louisiana anti-Lotteryite, repeatedly played on fears of black power in the tough 1896 contest for that state's highest post.[26]

In fact, disfranchisement was a typically Progressive reform. The Redeemers had been content to allow a sort of political laissez-faire by blocking federal and state regulation of vote-counting. Good Social Darwinists, they realized that eventually the economically and socially powerful—nearly all of whom were Democrats—would control local politics.[27] The strategy contained some flaws. Just as the railroads had created enemies by purchasing state legislators and congressmen, and later by organizing private pooling agreements on rates and traffic, so those who killed and intimidated opponents and stuffed ballot boxes aroused antipathy. Moreover, such tactics stimulated rivals to counter-attack. Shippers and other consumers could demand railroad rate regulation; in the same manner, Republicans could attempt to regulate federal elections. To stop these attacks short of outright nationalization, Southern Democratic politicians as well as railroad magnates needed governmental sanction, even if the price of this sanction was some circumscription of their activities. But the most serious deficiency

---

History 13 (1968): 124–153.

26. Simkins, *Tillman,* pp. 393–407; Grantham, *Hoke Smith,* pp. 131–179; Orr, *Charles Brantley Aycock,* pp. 101, 118–132, 148, 186–187; William Larsen, *Montague of Virginia,* p. 111; Mabry, "Disfranchisement of the Negro," pp. 211–214.

27. This view of Progressive ideology and action draws heavily on Gabriel Kolko, *The Triumph of Conservation, 1900–1916* (New York: The Free Press of Glencoe, 1963), Kolko, *Railroads and Regulation, 1877–1916* (Princeton, New Jersey: Princeton Univ. Press, 1965), and Robert Wiebe, *The Search for Order, 1880–1920* (New York: Hill & Wang, 1967), which concentrate on the Progressives' industrial regulation policies. For evidence of the Redeemers' lassez-faire attitude toward politics, see Joseph M. Brittain, "Negro Suffrage and Politics in Alabama," p. 40; Wade Hampton, quoted in Paul Lewinson, *Race, Class, and Party,* p. 38; Charles Gayareé, "The Southern Question," *North American Review* 125 (1877): pp. 472–490.

of laissez-faire was its ineffectiveness. Private agreements could not prevent some railroads from breaking a pool or legislators from voting against those who bribed them. The Informal understandings among white men did not deter Populists or Republicans from electioneering and attempting to obtain fair counts. Again, the answer was government enforcement of both railroad rates and voting arrangements.

Like their counterparts in industry, the captains of Southern politics during most of the late nineteenth century had favored a policy of negative government. The Redeemers devoted their energies to stopping the federal government from regulating their bailiwicks with such measures as the Lodge Elections Bill. Southern Progressives, safe from national intervention, eagerly embraced public regulation (by the states) employing government to accomplish what they could not achieve privately.

Suffrage restriction was entirely consonant with the Progressive urge to rationalize the economic and political system, to substitute public for private agreements, to enact reforms which disarmed radical critics while actually strengthening the status quo.[28] In the last quarter of the nineteenth century, a third to a half of the Southern voters had been unreconstructed oppositionists. Despite ingenious gerrymandering, a few white Republicans, Independents, Populists, and even Negroes sat in nearly every session of every state legislature. Some non-Democrats filled congressional, gubernatorial, and senatorial seats.

How much more rationalized was the South after 1900! Virtually every elected officeholder was a white Democrat. For private agreements among white politicians not to bolt the party, Progressives substituted the publicly regulated white primary to insure regularity. Where the Redeemers had had to count out opponents during and after elections, Progressives stopped them from running at all by disfranchising their potential followers. And by doing so, they quieted Republican criticism of Southern fraud while avoiding the radical change—a change to a genuine two-party system with some semblance of political equality for blacks—which the GOP had favored.

A REACTIONARY REVOLUTION

In another sense, however, the new Southern political system, destined to last half a century, represented a fundamental change. Indeed,

28. See Pulley, *Old Virginia Restored.*

the restriction of the suffrage and elimination of opposition parties could be termed a reactionary revolution. The status quo of about 1890 tended toward segregation, single-party hegemony, a concentration of power in the hands of upper-class whites. By 1910, these tendencies were hardened into fundamental legal postulates of the society.[29] To put it differently, folkways became stateways, with all the psychological power of legality and the social power of enforceability now behind them. When the federal courts and Congress refused to overturn segregation and discriminatory voting laws, the new system gained the added buttress of constitutionality.

Seymour Martin Lipset has written that the state's legitimacy, which he defines as "a believed-in title to rule," has been most secure "where the society could admit the lower strata to full citizenship, to rights of participation in the economic and political systems, and at the same time allow the traditionally privileged strata to keep their status whilst yielding power." Such a solution to the problem of gaining legitimacy was impossible in the South, and perhaps elsewhere in fin-de-siècle America, for the elite denied the lower strata's moral right to take part in society's affairs. In fact, many believed that participation in politics by the "ignorant" and "unfit" eroded rather than strengthened public confidence in the government. According to the Virginia Progressive Carter Glass, "nothing can be more dangerous to our republican institutions than to see hordes of ignorant and worthless men marching to the polls and putting in their ballots against the intelligence and worth of the land."[30]

Other Southerners were more concerned about the decrease in respect for political institutions resulting from widespread election fraud. Again and again, advocates of disfranchisement argued that

29. The idea of a reactionary revolution was suggested by Governor Aycock of North Carolina, who coupled the Revolution of 1776 with that of 1900 in North Carolina three times in this inaugural address, printed in N. C. *Public Documents* (1901), pp. 1–13. On the hardening of Southern stateways, see John Hope, "Negro Vote," p. 55; Hackney, *Populism to Progressivism*, pp. 180–185.

30. Seymour Martin Lipset, "Party Systems and the Representation of Social Groups," in Marcridis, *Political Parties*, p. 44. See, similarly, Lipset and Rokkan, "Cleavage Structures, Party Systems, and Voter Alignments: An Introduction," in Lipset and Rokkan, *Party Systems and Voter Alignments*, p. 5; J. P. Nettl, *Political Mobilization, A Sociological Analysis of Methods and Concepts* (New York: Basic Books, 1967), p. 123. The Glass statement is from Lynchburg, Virginia *News*, September 8, 1892, quoted in Poindexter, "Carter Glass," p. 106.

substituting legal for extralegal methods of controlling politics would reinforce the Southern political system's legitimacy in the eyes of both Northerners and Southerners.[31] For example, a future governor of Alabama said during the disfranchising convention that the new constitution would "make permanent and secure honest and efficient government" and save the leaders of the state from having to resort to frauds "which have debased and lowered our moral tone." A prominent North Carolina politician who had led a mob in the bloody Wilmington race riot of 1898 felt that replacing violent with legal methods of suffrage restriction would "best conserve the commonwealth." Senator John W. Daniel of Virginia thought suffrage restriction would allow the white Southerner to rule with "decency and with the association of that law and order which will command the respect not only of himself but of the whole civilized world."[32] Southern political institutions, then, gained legitimacy not by expanding, but by contracting the electorate.

This legalized structure far surpassed the informal, customary arrangement in psychological strength. When segregation had been extralegal and ill-defined, Negroes could feel that the state laws and the federal Constitution upheld their right to be treated equally. When electoral machinations had withheld from dissenters, black and white, the right to vote or to have the votes honestly counted, these men could expect that rectification would follow simply from fair enforcement of the laws. A Republican Congress might pass a law guaranteeing fair elections or, as it did twenty-six times from 1880 to 1901, seat Southern Republican or Populist congressional candidates defeated by fraud.[33] After the revolutionary Southern legal changes, the segregated

31. This was often stated as a desire to restore the "purity of elections," or "good government." See, for example, Hilary A. Herbert, in Southern Society, *Race Problems in the South*, p. 37; MacCorkle, *Does the Experience of this Republic*, p. 25; Mr. Oates, in Ala. Con. Con. *Proceedings* (1901), vol. 3, pp. 2786–2789; Mr. Weatherby, in ibid., vol. 3, p. 2867; Mr. Martin, in ibid., vol. 3, p. 3009; *New Orleans Daily Picayune*, January 9, 10, 11, 1898; Judge Chrisman. in the Mississippi Constitutional Convention of 1890, quoted in Wharton, *Negro in Mississippi*, p. 206; Charles B. Aycock, quoted in Orr, *Aycock*, pp. 155–156; Edward McCrady, Jr., "The Registration of Electors," pp. 2–3.

32. Mr. O'Neal, in Ala. Con. Con. *Proceedings* (1901), vol. 3, p. 2780; Alfred Moore Waddell, in Southern Society, *Race Problems in the South*, p. 44; Daniel, quoted in Mabry, "Disfranchisement of the Negro," p. 422.

33. For Northern Republican claims that a national election law was necessary to prevent fraud and restore faith in the electoral process, see, e.g., Sen. William M. Evarts (R., New

and disfranchised retained no hope and no allies. Most, at that time, were excluded from the suffrage by the *enforcement*, not the nonenforcement of the laws. The statutes themselves proclaimed that the illiterate and the poor were inferior, pariahs, unfit to be citizens. Perhaps the psychological effect may best be illustrated by a description of voting registration in the Virginia mountains after the constitutional convention:

It was painful and pitiful to see the horror and dread visible on the faces of the illiterate poor white men who were waiting to take their turn before the inquisition. . . . This was horrible to behold, but it was still more horrible to see the marks of humiliation and despair that were stamped on the faces of honest but poor white men who had been refused registration and who had been robbed of their citizenship without cause. We saw them as they came from the presence of the registrars with bowed heads and agonized faces; and when they spoke, in many instances, there was a tear in the voice of the humiliated citizen.[34]

Undoubtedly Pendleton, a Republican, exaggerated a bit. But it must have been rather disheartening for a man living in a country which proclaimed itself democratic and egalitarian to be stripped suddenly of the right to participate in the basic act of citizenship. Those Populists and Republicans who had heard their opponents boast of stealing elections from them, who had often borne scorn and violence for their political beliefs, must have felt some disappointment when suffrage restriction dealt their parties a final blow. Rank-and-file voters of all parties, used to stiff battles over important issues with fairly well organized party opponents, must have been a bit bored by primary campaigns between candidates who usually differed on no vital issues. The Democratic leaders, then, replaced the often frantic activity of the late nineteenth century with the lassitude of the twentieth by teaching citizens that they were unworthy to vote, by legally and illegally bludgeoning down opposition, and by sterilizing the political system against the disease of conflict over real issues. Ending democracy was necessary to guarantee what John B. Knox, president of the Alabama

York), in *Congressional Record*, 51st Cong., 2nd sess., p. 1359, and Henry Cabot Lodge, "The Coming Congress," *North American Review* 149 (1889):pp. 297–299.Contested election statistics were computed from Rowell, *Contested Elections*.

34. William C. Pendleton, *Political History of Appalachian Virginia*, p. 459. Such experiences, of course, were much more common for black men.

constitutional convention, referred to as "the supremacy of virtue and intelligence in this State."[35]

35. Ala. Con. Con. *Proceedings* (1901), vol. 3, p. 2929.

Appendix A Estimation of White Wealth

Each of the Southern states in the early twentieth century published county-by-county statistics, sometimes segregated by race, on the assessed value of real and personal property or on the amount of taxes paid. If one assumes that the average Negro male adult owned, say, $100 in tax-assessed property, one can easily calculate the wealth per white male adult in each county from the overall wealth statistics. The formula for each county is:

$$\text{white wealth per white adult male} = \frac{\text{Total wealth} - (\text{number of Negro adult males}) \times \$100}{\text{number of white adult males}}$$

Two soluble problems are the validation of the estimate of Negro wealth and the assumption that Negro wealth was roughly constant across all the counties in a state. In 1908 in North Carolina, the average value of assessed property for Negroes was $137. Assuming Negro wealth to be $100 and $150, the correlations between the actual county-by-county figures on white property value—North Carolina conveniently separated the figures by race—and computed estimates of white property values are + .996 and + .997, respectively. This means that Negro poverty varied hardly at all from county to county. In Virginia a similar correlational analysis turned up a coefficient of + .982.

For the relevant tables in chapter 9, I assumed in every case that the average property value for Negroes was $100. I also computed the white wealth figures using estimates for Negro wealth varying from $50 to $300 in each state. Correlations between wealth and voting are virtually identical using any Negro wealth estimates in this range.

The chief difficulty with these estimates of white wealth per capita is that they are measured on the county, not the individual level. If subcounty differences in white wealth were consistently very large, correlations between these estimates and voting behavior would not be very meaningful. Unfortunately, I know of no very precise published information on subcounty differences in wealth among Southern whites.

While recognizing the imperfections in the estimates, we must also note that they are the best measures of white economic differences readily available. No other economic indexes for the postbellum South, so far as I know, expressly separate Negro from white wealth. Consequently, although one should not claim to "prove" propositions about individuals on the basis of aggregate data, correlations computed from these estimates of white wealth do have what Eric Allardt has referred to as "informative value" in making "causal interpretations."[1]

1. Eric Allardt, "Aggregate Analysis: The Problem of Its Informative Value," in Mattei Dogan and Stein Rokkan, eds., *Quantitative Ecological Analysis in the Social Sciences* (Cambridge, Massachusetts: MIT Press, 1969), pp. 41–52.

Appendix B The Use of Proportionate Reduction Statistics to Measure the Impact of Suffrage Restriction

One could assess the effect of the laws restricting the suffrage in several ways. The simplest method would be to subtract the proportion voting in each state in the first election after the restrictive law was passed from the proportion voting in the last election before passage. One could then use a "t" test to decide whether the declines in voting and in the percentages for opposition parties were significantly different from zero. In fact, the declines in overall turnout, in white and black turnout, and in opposition voting for the elections in table 9.2 are statistically significant at the .0005 level; i.e., the declines could be expected to occur by chance only five times out of ten thousand. Such tests, however, only tell us that, if there is no other explanation of the declines, the laws had *some* effect on voting. Significance tests do not measure *how much* impact the laws had.

To quantify the extent of the impact, we could present a table simply showing the percentage declines in turnout and opposition voting for each election pair. Although I did not include such tables in the text, I did give the unweighted means of these figures in parentheses on the last lines of tables 9.2 and 9.3.

Even though the percentage decline figures give us more information than mere tests of statistical significance, they are not by themselves adequate measures of the impact of the laws, for they include nothing about the conditions preceding disfranchisement. Consider two hypothetical states which passed new election laws; after the laws' passage both the overall turnout and the percentage of the population supporting the opposition fell 5 percent in each state. But suppose that in one state, the figures for the last election before the law was passed were: majority party, 50 percent; opposition party, 40 percent; not voting, 10 percent. Whereas in the other state, the figures were: majority party, 20 percent; opposition party, 10 percent; not voting, 70 percent.

I would argue that the laws would have different effects on the two political systems. Only one previously active voter in eighteen would have stopped voting in the first state, and the opposition, although damaged, would continue to be within striking distance of a majority if a small percentage of the dominant party's voters should, for some reason, defect. In that state, there

269

might still be a good deal of party competition within an essentially democratic framework. In the second state, however, one previously active voter
in six would have been disfranchised, the opposition would be a hopeless
minority, and party competition would be nonexistent. To take into account political conditions preceding the passage of the laws, I therefore
focused on the proportionate reduction in turnout and opposition strength.

The proportionate reduction figures, in effect, provide an answer to the
question, "What percent of those who, on the basis of past behavior, could
have been expected to vote in a given election, did not vote?" Other
things being equal, the best guess of how many people will turn out for an
election is the same as the number of voters who participated in the preceding election. Proportionate reduction measures the impact of events which
took place between the two elections not on the whole potential electorate
but only on those whose behavior might really have been changed by the
events. In this sense, proportionate reduction is superior to the simple decline
in turnout as an index of the effect of legal changes on the electorate.

Critical Bibliography

PRIMARY SOURCES

Election, Census, and Tax Records

County-level general election statistics for presidential and gubernatorial elections from 1880 to 1910 were supplied in machine-readable form by the Historical Archives of the Inter-University Consortium for Political Research at Ann Arbor, Michigan. The data provided was in partially proofed form, and the Consortium bears no responsibility for either the analyses or interpretations presented here. Computer analyses of the data were performed at Yale and Caltech. For a discussion of the methodology involved in the most important calculations and references to the methodological literature, see my article "Ecological Regression and the Analysis of Past Politics," in *Journal of Interdisciplinary History* 4 (1973): 237–262.

State-level presidential returns were taken from Walter Dean Burnham, *Presidential Ballots, 1836–1892* and Edgar E. Robinson, *The Presidential Vote, 1896–1932.* State-level gubernatorial and congressional returns were taken from contemporary almanacs—*The New York Tribune Almanac* (New York: Tribune Company, annually) and *The Chicago Daily News Almanac* (Chicago: Chicago Daily News Company, annually). Primary and referenda returns and registration statistics came from a variety of sources too lengthy to list here. For detailed citations, see my dissertation, "The Shaping of Southern Politics: Suffrage Restriction and the Establishment of the One-Party South" (Ph.D. diss., Yale University, 1971), pp. 427–429. Percentage figures for each election were calculated on the basis of straight-line interpolations from population data from the 1880–1910 censuses. From 1890 on, the census gave the numbers of adult males by race. The 1880 census did not give separate totals for white and black males over 21, so for that census I assumed the proportions were the same as the overall proportions of blacks and whites of all ages and of both sexes in each county.

County boundary changes often cut down the numbers of county units used as a basis for calculating the regression and correlation coefficients. Every Southern state created new counties during this period. To get correct turnout figures, I therefore had to consolidate population totals from the new counties with those from the old counties from which the new ones were drawn. Texas presented particular difficulties, since much of it was only

271

barely settled during this period. Many of the western counties had very small populations. To weight these counties equally with the more densely populated counties when computing voting estimates (as unweighted regression, in effect, would do) would make the estimates unreliable. To compute weighted regression coefficients or add together all the tiny counties would have increased by about a month the time it took to figure the Texas estimates. I therefore eliminated from the Texas calculations any country with an adult-male population under 500 in 1910. Since the resulting total number of Texas county-units used in the calculations after consolidations and deletions amounted to 195, the estimates based on them are probably very close to those I would have gotten had I included every tiny county and weighted the figures.

Statistics of taxes paid and assessed valuations of property were taken from published state documents. State librarians and archivists in ten of the eleven states were kind enough to supply me with copies of relevant tables, since I could not afford to travel to each state to examine the documents myself. I calculated regression values for each of the ten states, although I did not present all the data in the text. For the precise locations of the tax and wealth data, see my dissertation, pp. 431–432.

Legislative and Constitutional Convention Journals And Transcripts of Debates

The state legislative and convention journals are absolutely essential to a study of suffrage restriction, but often exasperating to use. Essentially they record bills introduced, motions made, and most important, roll calls on the motions. They may include petitions, biographical information, election returns, and complete texts of bills. Most are fairly well indexed. But it is obviously necessary to consider them in conjunction with contemporary newspapers to understand what each motion really meant, what caucuses or important politicians did behind the scenes, etc. The transcripts of debates are fuller and simpler to employ.

All the journals, records of debates, and compilations of statutes for each legislative session are available at the Sterling Library at Yale or at the Yale Law School Library, except the 1887 and 1889 Florida House and Senate journals, which I used at the Connecticut State Library, Hartford. Since they are generally available in the states of publication, in many state archives, and in large university libraries, I will not give exact citations for all the legislative journals and collections of laws. The somewhat less widely distributed stenographic records of constitutional convention debates which I used included: Seth Shepard McKay, ed., *Debates in the Texas Constitutional Convention of 1875*; Samuel W. Small, ed., *A Stenographic Re-*

port of the Proceedings of the Constitutional Convention Held in Atlanta, Georgia, 1877 (Atlanta: Constitution Publishing Co., 1877); *Official Proceedings of the Constitutional Convention of Alabama, 1901* (Wetumpka, Alabama: Wetumpka Printing Co., 1940); and *Report of the Proceedings and Debates of the Constitutional Convention, State of Virginia* (Richmond, Virginia: The Hermitage Press, Inc., 1906).

The journals and other documents described in this section are cited in abbreviated form in the footnotes.

Newspapers

During the nineteenth century, the newspapers covered state politics and the state legislatures in more depth than is usual today, although the extent and usefulness of the coverage varied widely from paper to paper. I made no attempt to read all the major Southern newspapers for the entire period but focused instead on a few newspapers during important sessions of legislatures and constitutional conventions.

The *Birmingham Age-Herald*, November 1892–March 1893, and October–November 1894, contained more information on the passage and effect of the Sayre law than did the *Mobile Daily Register*. The *Montgomery Daily Advertiser*, January–December 1902, was helpful for understanding the motives behind adoption of the white primary in Alabama. I supplemented the rather sparse treatment of the Arkansas secret ballot and poll tax acts in the *Little Rock Arkansas Gazette* with the biased, but informative *Pine Bluff Weekly Commercial*. The *Jacksonville Florida Times-Union*, November 1884, through August 1885, October–November 1886, and April–May 1887, had fair coverage of the 1885 and 1887 legislative sessions and the 1885 constitutional convention in Florida. The *Atlanta* (Georgia) *Constitution*, August–September 1906, covering the last days of the Smith–Howell campaign for the governorship, showed how racist the "conservative" Howell was, and helped me appreciate the importance of Tom Hardwick in the campaign for disfranchisement and, conversely, the relative unimportance of Tom Watson.

The *Baton Rouge* (Louisiana) *Daily Advocate*, January–July 1896, and November 1897–January 1898, provided complete and zestful comments on the 1896 Louisiana governor's race, the passage of the registration and secret ballot act, and the 1898 referendum on calling the constitutional convention. The most partisan of newspapers, it reflected the view of Governor Murphy J. Foster and the state Democratic machine. The *New Orleans Daily Picayune*, May–July 1894, January–July 1896, Novermber 1897–April 1898, covered the legislative sessions and the gubernatorial, senatorial, and constitutional convention campaigns in great depth. It reflected the views of the city reformer-conservatives, who wanted to disfranchise the entire lower class.

The *Raleigh* (North Carolina) *News and Observer*, January–April 1899, gave insightful and openly partisan coverage of the passage of the registration and multiple-box laws and the suffrage amendment in North Carolina. Edited by future "Progressive" Josephus Daniels, the paper spoke for the then-united Democratic party of Governor Charles B. Aycock and Senator Furnifold Simmons. The *Charleston* (South Carolina) *News and Courier*, November 1880–February 1882, and October–November 1894, reported the eight-box law and the referendum on the constitutional convention in South Carolina adequately. A "conservative" paper, it strongly favored the eight-box law, but weakly opposed the later constitutional convention on the grounds that the Tillmanites would control it. Though just as strongly Democratic, the *Columbia Daily Register*, which I also consulted for the 1880–1882 session, was frightened that the eight-box law would invite Northern intervention. Its coverage of the legislature was perhaps slightly better than the *News and Courier*'s.

The *Memphis* (Tennessee) *Daily Appeal* and the *Memphis Daily Avalanche* had the best reports on the passage and effect of the Dortch law and the 1888 frauds in West Tennessee. Rabidly racist, these papers openly exposed the motives of the disfranchisers; whereas, the partisan Democratic *Nashville Daily American* attempted to clothe the secret ballot and poll tax in bland "reform" togs. The politically neutral *Nashville Daily Banner* and the staunchly Republican *Knoxville Daily Journal* offered less complete, but more pro-Republican coverage. The *Journal* was perhaps more sympathetic toward Negroes in the early nineties than any other major white newspaper in the South. The *Dallas* (Texas) *Morning News*, January–March 1891, March–April 1892, January–February 1901, and October–November 1902, proved very sketchy on the Texas poll tax, as did the *Austin* (Texas) *Daily Statesman* for the same dates.

Published and Unpublished Secondary Works and Contemporary Magazine Articles[1]

Southern History from Reconstruction to the First World War

The literature on Southern history from the 1870s through the first decade of the twentieth century is large and diverse. The reader who wishes more comprehensive bibliographies of secondary sources should consult the

1. I include contemporary magazine articles under this rubric for the convenience of readers who may wish to use this bibliography as a guide to further study.

bibliography in C. Vann Woodward, *Origins of the New South, 1877–1913*; the historiographical essays by Paul M. Gaston, George B. Tindall, Allen J. Going, and Dewey W. Grantham, Jr., in Arthur S. Link and Rembert W. Patrick, eds., *Writing Southern History*; and, on Negroes, many of the sections in James M. McPherson, Laurence B. Holland, James M. Banner, Nancy J. Weiss, and Michael B. Bell, *Blacks in America, Bibliographical Essays*.

The starting points for any student of post-Reconstruction politics must be the works of C. Vann Woodward and V. O. Key, Jr., most notably Woodward's *Origins of the New South* and *The Strange Career of Jim Crow*, and Key's *Southern Politics in State and Nation*. Writing before the publication of many of the secondary accounts listed in this bibliography, Key tentatively put forth an argument—what I refer to in the text as the "fait accompli thesis"—which later and deeper research has shown to be essentially incorrect. In both *Origins* and *Jim Crow*, Woodward exaggerated the support which the Redeemers or "paternalists" gave to black suffrage. I have examined in detail the evidence Woodward and others have offered for this point of view in sections of my dissertation (pp. 35–43) not presented here. For short restatements of some of Woodward's views, see his "The Negro in American Life, 1865–1918," in John A. Garraty, *Interpreting American History* 2: 43–68; and "The Ghost of Populism Walks Again," *New York Times Magazine* (June 4, 1972). My disagreements with Woodward and Key have not diminished my respect for their tremendous scholarly achievements, a respect which has grown with every re-reading.

Of the general histories of the South, I found Francis Butler Simkins, *A History of the South*, most helpful. Thomas B. Clark and Albert D. Kirwan, *The South since Appomatox*; John Samuel Ezell, *The South since 1865*; and Monroe Lee Billington, *The American South* are occasionally misleading or contradictory on political changes. Two contemporary travellers' analyses reveal a good deal about the South in this period: "Studies in the South," written by Jonathan Baxter Harrison, but published anonymously, which appeared in several installments in *The Atlantic Monthly* 49 and 50 (1882), and Ray Stannard Baker's *Following the Colour Line*. The reader should be wary of the class bias resulting from most travelers' tendency to interview chiefly the articulate.

Paul M. Gaston found the era's ideology full of paradoxes and contradictions in his well-written *The New South Creed* by almost invariably taking his subjects' rhetoric seriously. On the issue of the New South's support for Negro voting, for instance, he counted as equally sincere statements made to rally support for the Democrats in local campaigns and those designed to reassure Yankees that they could, in good conscience, leave the Negro in white Southern hands. Like Woodward, Gaston read too much into the

remarks of Wade Hampton, Alexander Stephens, and L. Q. C. Lamar in
James G. Blaine, *et. al.*, "Ought the Negro to be Disfranchised? Ought He
to Have Been Enfranchised?" *North American Review* 128 (1879): 225–283, a
crucial symposium, in which all of these ex-rebels carefully avoided approving widespread Negro suffrage. Although George M. Frederickson, in his
thoughtful *The Black Image in the White Mind*, was somewhat harsher than
Gaston toward the paternalists and the "racist accommodationists" (his
rubric for a subgroup of the Southern Progressives), I believe even he was
too generous. My disagreements with these two scholars and others who
follow the same interpretative line result from differences of approach
rather than biases. Both Gaston and Frederickson concentrated on the
ideas of the paternalists and Progressives, while I try to test rhetoric against
actions. Moreover, they related the ideas of these groups primarily to Negro
rights, while I am concerned, as well, with their attitudes toward the rights
of lower-class whites. For example, Frederickson saw Edgar Gardner Murphy as a racial moderate because he opposed the escape clauses for whites
in the Southern constitutions; whereas I see Murphy as a reactionary on
the general question of suffrage rights, because he favored disfranchisement
of a large number of whites, along with virtually all the blacks.

Repelled by the uninformed Yankee view of white Southerners as either
firebrand Klansmen or julep-sipping aristocrats, a group of Southern
historians set out to prove that the South was just as liberal, just as "American" as the North. Applying this theme to the Progressive Era, they discovered a spirit of social, economic, and especially political reform which
indicated, in the words of Arthur S. Link, the great power of the Southern
"masses." Representative works of this school are Link, "The Progressive
Movement in the South, 1870–1914, " *North Carolina Historical Review* 23
(1946): 173–195; Dewey W. Grantham, Jr., *The Democratic South*, and "An
American Politics for the South, " in Charles Grier Sellers, Jr., ed., *The
Southerner As American*, pp. 148–179; and Hugh C. Bailey, *Liberalism in the
New South: Southern Social Reformers and the Progressive Movement*. It is now
apparent that Link and Grantham seriously exaggerated the liberality—
even for most white people—of the reforms they noted. Moreover, more
recent events such as the Northern response to racial integration and studies
such as I. A. Newby's *Jim Crow's Defense, Anti-Negro Thought in America,
1900–1930* have turned the question of Southern uniqueness upside down.
To oversimplify a bit, it is beginning to seem that America has been Southern
—basically racist, violent, and reactionary—rather than vice versa.

Of the works dealing with disfranchisement in the South as a whole,
Paul Lewinson's *Race, Class and Party* has less than 40 pages devoted to the
period from 1876 to 1908. In those pages, he telescoped events up to thirty

years apart, thereby confusing the timing of the laws, the various means of restriction, and the motives of the disfranchisers and their opponents. Misled by the biased and propagandistic monographs which dominated the secondary literature in 1932, Lewinson, while certainly no bigot himself, perpetuated several of the New South's myths about itself—for example, the illusion of white unity on suffrage restriction and the false conception that poor white leaders were the chief proponents of restriction.

William Alexander Mabry's "The Disfranchisement of the Negro in the South" (Ph.D. thesis, Duke Univ., 1933) is a much more solid piece of work based on extensive research in newspapers and other primary documents. Although Mabry's analysis of the events he covered was often prescient and comprehensive, he did not pay sufficient attention to the preconvention restrictions, to the issue of white disfranchisement, or to partisanship as a motivating force. And he did not generalize enough about the means of limitation, the motives of the disfranchisers, and the consequences of restriction. He also excluded from his analysis those states which did not enact broad, constitutional suffrage provisions. Some of his chapters have been published as "Disfranchisement of the Negro in Mississippi," *Journal of Southern History* 4 (1938): 318–333; "Ben Tillman Disfranchised the Negro," *South Atlantic Quarterly* 27 (1938): 170–183; and "Negro Suffrage and Fusion Rule in North Carolina," *North Carolina Historical Quarterly* 12 (1935): 79–102.

Stephen B. Weeks summarized the early restrictive laws in "The History of Negro Suffrage in the South," *Political Science Quarterly* 9 (1894): 670–703. His analysis and Kirk H. Porter's in *A History of Suffrage in the United States* are vitiated by exclusive concentration on Negro disfranchisement. The student can safely ignore Donald Norton Brown, "Southern Attitudes toward Negro Voting in the Bourbon Period, 1877–1890" (Ph.D. Thesis, Univ. of Oklahoma, 1960).

Frederic D. Ogden followed V. O. Key's thesis about the relative unimportance of the poll tax in *The Poll Tax in the South*. Ogden's monograph superseded Frank B. Williams' untrustworthy "The Poll Tax as a Suffrage Requirement in the South, 1870–1901" (Ph.D. Thesis, Vanderbilt Univ., 1950) and his article with the same title in *Journal of Southern History* 18 (1952): 469–496. H. Clarence Nixon's "Influences of the Past," in American Council on Public Affairs, *The Poll Tax*, may still be consulted with profit.

The growth of segregation in thought and practice is the subject of Franklin Johnson, *The Development of State Legislation Concerning the Free Negro*, which has little material on disfranchisement; Claude H. Nolen, *The Negro's Image in the South*; I. A. Newby, *The Development of Segregationist Thought*, a compendium of primary source readings; and two articles by Guion Griffis

Johnson, "The Ideology of White Supremacy, 1876–1910, " in Fletcher M. Green, ed., *Essays in Southern History*, pp. 124–156, and "Southern Paternalism toward Negroes after Emancipation, " in Charles E. Wynes, ed., *The Negro in the South since 1865*, pp. 103–134. Nolen and Johnson tended to treat white supremacist thought as if it emerged whole out of slavery and underwent no later development as conditions and institutions changed. Rayford W. Logan compiled a series of fascinating articles and editorials on later opinions in *The Attitude of the Southern White Press toward Negro Suffrage, 1932–1940*.

The bibliographies in Nolen, *Negro's Image*, and Newby, *Jim Crow's Defense* list contemporary articles and books which constituted the white South's propaganda on race and suffrage.

General analyses of Populist and Progressive attitudes toward black people include Jack Abramowitz, "The Negro in the Populist Movement," *Journal of Negro History* 38 (1953): 257–289; Robert Saunders, "Southern Populists and the Negro, 1893–1895," in ibid. 54 (1969): 240–261; C. Vann Woodward, "The Populist Heritage and the Intellectual," in *The Burden of Southern History*, pp. 141–166; and Dewey W. Grantham, Jr., "The Progressive Movement and the Negro," in Wynes, ed., *The Negro in the South since 1865*, pp. 62–82. Jack Temple Kirby's *Darkness at the Dawning*, an interpretative survey which attempts to specify the relationship of Southern Progressivism to racism, is internally contradictory and, at several crucial points, factually incorrect. Many of the documents in Norman Pollock's excellent collection, *The Populist Mind*, bear on white Populists' relations with Negroes. (See also the sections of this bibliography under individual states.)

To put the issue of Populist race relations in proper perspective, one must consult general works on Populism and party politics such as John D. Hicks' *The Populist Revolt*, and Theodore Saloutos' *Farmer Movements in the South, 1865–1933* which stressed economic conditions as an explanation for farmer agitation; and Robert F. Durden's *The Climax of Populism*, and Stanley L. Jones' *The Presidential Election of 1896*, which treated the difficulty of the decision to fuse or not to fuse with the Bryan Democrats. Daniel M. Robison defended the rural progressives from many attacks in his stimulating "From Tillman to Long: Some Striking Leaders of the Rural South," *Journal of Southern History* 3 (1937): 289–310.

Political Science

The general literature on political participation, party systems, and electoral laws is too vast to consider here, although much of it is relevant to the present work. For recent summaries and bibliographies, see Lester W.

Milbrath, *Political Participation*; Herbert McCloskey, "Political Participation," in David L. Sills, ed., *International Encyclopedia of the Social Sciences*, 12: 252–265; Donald E. Stokes, "Voting," in ibid., 16:387–395; Harry Eckstein, "Parties, Political: Party Systems, " in ibid., 11:436–452; Stein Rokkan, "The Comparative Study of Political Participation, " in Charles F. Cnudde and Deane E. Neubauer, eds., *Empirical Democratic Theory*, pp. 333–369; Rokkan, *Citizens, Elections, Parties*; Robert A. Dahl, *Polyarchy: Participation and Opposition* (New Haven: Yale Univ. Press, 1971); and my dissertation, pp. 476–484.

Political scientists have recently shown an increasing concern with historical changes in the way the American political system operates. Not yet well assimilated into the general literature on participation and parties, these works point toward the more comprehensive and sophisticated theory to be developed in the future: Walter Dean Burnham, "The Changing Shape of the American Political Universe, " *American Political Science Review* 59 (1965): 7–28, *Critical Elections and the Mainspring of American Politics*, and "Party Systems and the Political Process," in William N. Chambers and Walter Dean Burnham, eds., *The American Party Systems*, pp. 277–307; Donald E. Stokes, "Parties and the Nationalization of Electoral Forces," ibid., pp. 182–202; Angus Campbell, "Surge and Decline: A Study of Electoral Change," in Angus Campbell, Philip E. Converse, Warren E. Miller, Donald E. Stokes, *Elections and the Political Order*, and "Voters and Elections: Past and Present," in Edward C. Dreyer and Walter A. Rosenbaum, eds., *Political Opinion and Electoral Behavior*, pp. 354–365; Stanley Kelley, Jr., Richard E. Ayres, and William G. Bowen, "Registration and Voting: Putting First Things First," *American Political Science Review* 61 (1967): 359–379; and Jerrold G. Rusk, "The Effect of the Australian Ballot Reform on Split Ticket Voting, 1876–1908, " ibid. 64 (1970): 1220–1238; Philip E. Converse, "Change in the American Electorate," in Campbell and Converse, *The Human Meaning of Social Change*, pp. 263–338.

American historians have devoted some attention to the effects of electoral laws on politics in other periods and other areas. These works show that suffrage restriction was not limited to the South, and that electoral laws were often, probably almost always, framed for the purposes of partisan advantage. On the early nineteenth century, see Chilton Williamson, *American Suffrage from Property to Democracy, 1760–1860;* Roger W. Shugg, "Negro Voting in the Ante-Bellum South," *Journal of Negro History* 21(1936): 357–364; John L. Stanley, "Majority Tyranny in Tocqueville's America: The Failure of Negro Suffrage in 1846," *Political Science Quarterly* 84 (1969): 412–435; and V. Jacque Voegeli, *Free But Not Equal.* Literacy and property tests outside the South are listed, but not studied in depth, in George H.

Haynes, "Educational Qualifications for the Suffrage in the United States," *Political Science Quarterly* 13 (1898): 495–513; Albert J. McCulloch, *Suffrage and Its Problems*; and Dudley O. McGovney, *The American Suffrage Medley*. Richard P. McCormick stresses partisan haggling over election laws in *The History of Voting in New Jersey: A Study in the Development of Election Machinery, 1664–1911*. Suffrage laws in Maryland and Delaware provide close analogies to those in the states which seceded. See three excellent studies: Margaret Law Callcott, *The Negro in Maryland Politics, 1870–1912*; Harold C. Livesay, "Delaware Negroes, 1865–1915," *Delaware History* 13 (1968): 87–123; and Amy M. Hiller, "The Disfranchisement of Delaware Negroes in the Late Nineteenth Century," ibid. 13 (1968): 124–153. Alan P. Grimes indicated connections between the interests of various social and political groups and the enfranchisement of women in the plains states in *The Puritan Ethic and Woman Suffrage*.

Interesting also as comparisons with turn-of-the-century conditions are two works on attitudes toward Negro voting in the present-day South and the consequences of Negro re-enfranchisement. See Charles Francis Cnudde, "Consensus, Rules of the Game, and Democratic Politics: The Case of Race Politics in the South" (Ph.D. dissertation, University of North Carolina, 1967); and William R. Keech, *The Impact of Negro Voting*.

Intensive studies of electoral regulations have gone out of fashion in behavioristic political science, and were never in fashion in history. Contemporary views of the primary, such as Charles Edward Merriam's *Primary Elections*, and M. Ostrogorski, *Democracy and the Party System in the United States* were largely uncritical. By the 1950s, political scientists subjected that favorite Progressive reform to scathing scrutiny. The most important contribution to this viewpoint, V. O. Key, Jr.'s *American State Politics, An Introduction*, was a brilliant study of non-Southern politics. See also Julius Turner, "Primary Elections As the Alternative to Party Competition in 'Safe' Districts," *Journal of Politics* 15 (1953): 197–210; Charles R. Adrian, "Some General Characteristics of Non-partisan Elections," *American Political Science Review* 46 (1952) : 766–776; Allan P. Sindler, "Bifactional Rivalry as an Alternative to Two-Party Competition in Louisiana," ibid. 49 (1955): 641–662; and Austin Ranney, "The Representativeness of Primary Electorates," *Midwest Journal of Political Science* 12 (1968): 224–238. On registration and other facets of election administration, see Joseph P. Harris, *Registration of Voters in the United States*; and President's Commission on Registration and Voting Participation, *Report* (Washington, D.C.: G.P.O., 1963).

Northern Attitudes

Northern Republican, Democratic, and Mugwump attitudes and actions provided boundary lines within which the Southern Democrats had to work. The ex-rebels could not openly disfranchise blacks and other oppositionists until they felt sure the national GOP would not intervene in the South. Conversely, the growth of pro-Southern, racist, and elitist feelings in the North encouraged and justified antidemocratic actions in Dixie. The best single source for studying Northern Republican and Democratic attitudes on these topics in this period is the debate on the Lodge Fair Elections Bill in the *Congressional Record*, 51st Congress, and the debate on the Crumpacker and Olmstead Apportionment Bills in the 56th Congress. The most important published secondary works are Vincent P. DeSantis, *Republicans Face the Southern Question*; Stanley P. Hirshson, *Farewell to the Bloody Shirt*; and Rayford W. Logan, *The Betrayal of the Negro, from Rutherford B. Hayes to Woodrow Wilson*. Their excessive hostility to the Republicans made it difficult for these three writers to explain the change in the GOP attitude toward the South after 1892. For a guide to further books, articles, and unpublished theses on the subject as of 1962, see the bibliography in Hirshson's *Farewell to the Bloody Shirt*.

Of works since 1962, Daniel W. Crofts' "The Blair Bill and the Elections Bill: The Congressional Aftermath to Reconstruction" (Ph.D., diss., Yale Univ., 1968), and Richard E. Welch, Jr.'s "The Federal Elections Bill of 1890: Postscripts and Prelude," *Journal of American History* 52 (1965): 511–526, are good analyses, less hostile to the Republicans than DeSantis's and Hirshson's. In his insightful and scrupulously objective biography of one of the most important humanitarian Republicans, *George Frisbie Hoar and the Half-Breed Republicans*, Welch attempted unsuccessfully to carry the 1880 division of Republicans into "Stalwart" and "Half-Breed" factions through the next two decades. That fascinating scoundrel John J. Ingalls, an antireform, but "bloody shirt" Republican, fails to emerge very clearly in Burton J. Williams's *Senator John James Ingalls, Kansas' Iridescent Republican* (Lawrence, Kans.: Univ. Press of Kansas, 1972). Neither Harry J. Sievers's *Benjamin Harrison, Hoosier President* (Indianapolis, Indiana: Bobbs-Merrill Co., Inc., 1968) nor Kenneth E. Davison's *The Presidency of Rutherford B. Hayes* (Westport, Conn.: Greenwood Press, 1972), has much new information on their heroes' Southern policies.

A Northern group whose attitudes are often mistakenly represented as Republican received deserved treatment in John G. Sproat's "*The Best Men.*" William B. Hixson, Jr., failed to explain sufficiently the reasons for the changes in one of the most complex liberals, Moorfield Storey, probably because of inadaquacies in Storey's papers. A protégé of Charles Sumner, Storey turned into a fellow traveller of racists and then back into an anti-racist. See "Moorfield Storey and the Struggle for Equality," *Journal of American History* 55 (1968): 533–554; and *Moorfield Storey and the Abolitionist Tradition*.

For the period after 1897, David W. Southern's *The Malignant Heritage* is thin, but Horace S. and Marion G. Merrill's *The Republican Command, 1897–1913* is a balanced and thorough account. For further works on the era after 1900, see the Merrills' bibliography.

Blacks and Politics

Although black political power helped delay disfranchisement, and blacks initiated and fought out most of the challenges to restriction after it was accomplished, historians have paid too little attention to black political activism in the South after Reconstruction. In addition to the works cited below under "state politics and suffrage restriction," see August Meier's pathbreaking *Negro Thought in America, 1880–1915*, and Meier and Elliot Rudwick, "The Boycott Movement against Jim Crow Streetcars in the South, 1900–1906," *Journal of American History* 55 (1969): 756–775. Elsie M. Lewis concentrated on the 1860s in "The Political Mind of the Negro, 1865–1900," in Wynes, ed., *The Negro in the South since 1865*, pp. 22–38. Elliot Rudwick touched on the black response to restriction in "The Niagara Movement," in Meier and Rudwick, eds., *The Making of Black America*, 2:131–148.

Contemporary black men split on the question of what political strategy the race should adopt. T. Thomas Fortune advised a "balance of power" approach in *Black and White*. W. S. Scarborough called for a federal enforcement of voting rights in "The Future of the Negro," *The Forum* 7 (1889): 80–89, and "The Race Problem," *The Arena* 2 (1890): 560–567. As conditions worsened, some leaders turned to despair and unfair racial self-criticism—see, e.g., Jerome B. Riley, *The Philosophy of Negro Suffrage*, and William H. Councill, "The Future of the Negro," *The Forum* 27 (1899): 570–577. On the other hand, W. E. B. DuBois defended the Negro's political past in such essays as "The Freedman's Bureau," *The Atlantic Monthly* 87 (1901): 354–365, and "Reconstruction and Its Benefits," *American Historical Review* 15 (1909–1910): 781–799. Other important defenses included Richard P. Hallowell, "Negro Suffrage Justified," a pamphlet; Archibald H. Grimke, "Why Disfranchisement is Bad," reprint of an article from *Atlantic Monthly*, July 1904; and Thomas O. Fuller, *Twenty Years in Public Life, 1890–1910*. Samuel Denny Smith provided some information on prominent Negroes in *The Negro in Congress, 1870–1901*. Monroe N. Work listed many of the Negro state legislators in "Some Negro Members of Reconstruction Conventions and Legislatures and of Congress," *Journal of Negro History* 5 (1920) : 63–119. William J. Simmons's *Men of Mark* contains important biographical material on Negro politicians.

STATE POLITICS AND SUFFRAGE RESTRICTION

The analyst of Southern suffrage restriction must delve deeply into articles and monographs on each state's politics. The best way to group these works so as to provide an easy guide for future students is simply state by state. Such a division is not meant to imply that each commonwealth should be viewed altogether as a separate entity. On the contrary, comparisons of the politics and processes of restriction in several states ought to lead one to notice facts which might seem unimportant in a single state, and to formulate new general explanations of political events.

Alabama

Students looking into post-Reconstruction Southern political history often start with Alabama for more than alphabetic reasons. Well-kept document collections, several newspapers which covered politics thoroughly and from a variety of viewpoints, and starkly-drawn lines of cleavage among the whites between the black belt and the urban industrialists on the one hand, and hill country farmers on the other, have attracted numerous historians. Yet the very simplicity of its apparent structure and availability of primary source material have led students to base too many generalizations for the region as a whole primarily on the Alabama experience. The demography of other states was more complex, their political lineups less clearcut. Alabama is closer to being an "ideal-type" of Southern politics during this period than it is to representing the average state.

A person new to Alabama history should probably start with Albert B. Moore, *History of Alabama and Her People,* a careful and detailed narrative, fairly objective for the time it was written. Next, the student should turn to two newer works, Malcom Cook McMillan, *Constitutional Development in Alabama, 1798–1901,* and F. Sheldon Hackney, *Populism to Progressivism in Alabama.* McMillan's monograph covers much broader ground than its title suggests. Thorough and prescient, McMillan's work has had considerable influence on my own. Hackney's well-written and original book deserves the attention it has gotten from the profession. Nonetheless, I disagree with his unfavorable treatment of the Populists, whom he deprecated because they lost, and his charity toward the self-interested moderates called Progressives, whom he complimented because they won, even as he recognized that their voctories further submerged rather than uplifted the masses of Alabamians. Moreover, Hackney rested his overall thesis on a peculiar analysis of roll calls in the 1901 constitutional convention. The analysis is unusual, in that it does not adopt one of the standard procedures for determining clusters of issues or delegates, and faulty, in that it weighs all issues equally, when we know the delegates put much more emphasis on some subjects than others. As a consequence, Hackney got such anomalous results as placing former Governors Thomas G. Jones and William C. Oates in his "Progressive" bloc. If these black belt Gold Democrats were Progressives, then Alabama surrendered to Progressivism in 1890, rather than 1906, and the contemporaries and historians who almost unanimously considered Jones and Oates reactionaries must have been blind.

Other works on this period include William Warren Rogers' *The One-Gallused Rebellion*, which is thoroughly researched and full of information, but lacks on overarching synthesis of Alabama politics. David A. Harris's "Racists and Reformers: A Study of Progressivism in Alabama, 1896–1911" (Ph.D. diss., Univ. of North Carolina, 1967), mostly overlapped the superior monographs already cited. Horace Mann Bond's *Negro Education in Alabama* is brilliant and broader than its title, but sometimes careless about facts and contradictory. Allen Johnston Going's *Bourbon Democracy in Alabama, 1874–1890* is workmanlike, if now somewhat outmoded in its central theme. John B. Clark's *Populism in Alabama* has been rendered obsolescent by more recent works. Joseph Matt Brittain's "Negro Suffrage in Alabama since 1870" (Ph.D. thesis, Indiana Univ., 1958) is sketchy and rather unreliable.

More specialized works include James F. Doster, *Railroads in Alabama Politics, 1875–1914*, an excellent monograph. The incredible detail in Allen Woodrow Jones' "A History of the Direct Primary in Alabama" (Ph.D. thesis, Univ. of Alabama, 1964) provides a basis for interpretations different from the traditional one Jones offered. Joseph H. Taylor, in "Populism and Disfranchisement in Alabama," *Journal of Negro History* 34 (1949): 410–427, argued incorrectly that the Populists favored disfranchisement. Francis Roberts, "William Manning Lowe and the Greenback Party in Alabama," *The Alabama Review* 5 (1952): 100–121, treated the major "independent" leader in the state. Charles Grayson Summersell, "The Alabama Governor's Race in 1892," ibid. 8 (1955): 5–35, is the most thorough analysis of that campaign. Allen J. Going, "Critical Months in Alabama Politics, 1895–1896," in ibid. 5 (1952): 269–281, made sense out of a welter of cross-currents. Joseph F. Johnston's "Negro Suffrage in Alabama," *The Independent* 51 (1899): 1535–1537 showed how close the Alabama "liberals" and "conservatives" were on disfranchisement and explained Johnson's rather curious actions as governor. Nancy Milford's *Zelda, A Biography* contains some tantalyzing biographical data about Judge A. D. Sayre, who was F. Scott Fitzgerald's father-in-law. Wilford H. Smith's "Is the Negro Disfranchised?" *The Outlook* 79 (1905): 1047–1049, dealt with early attempts in Alabama to challenge the 1901 constitution in the courts. Smith, a Northern Negro lawyer, was employed by Booker T. Washington. Charles W. Smith, Jr., in *The Electorate in an Alabama Community*, demonstrated the effect of the poll tax and racial discrimination in the registration process in Tuscaloosa during the 1930s. Hallie Farmer's *Legislative Apportionment* showed how the 1901 constitution enthroned the black belt and left politics entirely in the hands of the governor and local elites.

Arkansas

Arkansas history during this period is a largely untilled but potentially fertile field. Home of the strongest independent farmers' political movement during the 1880s, this state also contained some of the most militant and articulate Negro political leaders in the South, who were able as late as 1912 to provide significant opposition to a proposed literacy test. The secondary literature on political events, however, is disappointingly thin.

David Y. Thomas' *Arkansas and Its People, A History, 1541–1930* provides a fairly good narrative of political events, but not so good as Moore's on Alabama. John Gould Fletcher's *Arkansas* is chatty. Francis Clay Elkins' "The Agricultural Wheel in Arkansas, 1882–1890" (Ph.D. thesis, Syracuse Univ., 1943) is a rather simplistic, pro-Wheel account of events. Clifton Paisley's "The Political Wheelers and Arkansas' Election of 1888," *Arkansas Historical Quarterly* 25 (1966): 3–21, is a straightforward account based on the newspapers. W. Scott Morgan's *History of the Wheel and Alliance and the Impending Revolution* is a reprint of a propagandistic 1891 book by a partisan of the Wheel.

The best work in Arkansas history in this period is by John W. Graves, "The Arkansas Negro and Segregation, 1890–1903" (M.A. thesis, Univ. of Arkansas, 1967) and his article, "Negro Disfranchisement in Arkansas," in *Arkansas Historical Quarterly* 26 (1967): 199–225. On the way to testing Woodward's Jim Crow thesis, which Graves' data supports, Graves uncovered mounds of fascinating information on suffrage restriction and Negro politicians. In "Political Disfranchisement of the Negro in Arkansas," (M.A. thesis, Univ. of Arkansas, 1961), James Harris Fain misconstrued the chief purpose and effect of the crucial 1891 secret ballot law, a failure which vitiates his analysis.

On post-disfranchisement politics, see Paige E. Mulhollan, "The Issues of the Davis-Berry Senatorial Campaign in 1906," in *Arkansas Historical Quarterly* 20 (1961): 118–125; and Stuart Towns, "Joseph T. Robinson and Arkansas Politics: 1912–1913," in ibid. 24 (1965): 291–307, both of which are reports of what the newspapers said. Boyce Alexander Drummond,

Jr., "Arkansas Politics: A Study of a One-Party System" (Ph.D. thesis, Univ. of Chicago, 1957) concentrated on the period after 1930 and offered few insights into the structure or reasons for development or continuation of the one-party system.

Florida

Although the Sunshine State has suffered less from neglect than Arkansas, we still badly need modern studies of the Populists and Progressives, adequate biographical articles on several key figures, and a study of the Negro leadership, particularly in Jacksonville. J. E. Dovell's *Florida: Historic, Dramatic, Contemporary*, 4 vols., sketched the political narrative as did Kathryn Trimmer Abbey, *Florida: Land of Change*. Both were pro-Democratic and did not depart from the traditional interpretations of contemporary newspapers. Charlton W. Tebeau's *A History of Florida* is an adequate narrative, more sympathetic than Dovell or Abbey toward Negroes, but weak on analysis.

Two articles by Jerrell H. Shofer, "The Constitution of 1868," *Florida Historical Quarterly* 41 (1963): 356–374, and "Political Reconstruction in Florida," in ibid. 45 (1966): 145–170, provide a good background for the 1885 constitutional convention and other political events. The *Report of the Republican State Executive Committee to the Republicans of the State upon the Election Held November 2, 1880* (Washington, D.C.: National Republican Publishing Co., 1881), a pamphlet in the Sterling library at Yale, is an exceptionally comprehensive report on Democratic election malpractices.

On the events of the 1880s and early 1890s, consult Edward C. Williamson, "Independentism, A Challenge to the Florida Democracy of 1884," in *Florida Historical Quarterly* 27 (1948): 131–156; "The Constitutional Convention of 1885," in ibid. 41 (1962): 116–126; "Black Belt Political Crisis: The Savage-James Lynching, 1882," in ibid. 45 (1967): 402–409; and "The Era of the Democratic County Leader: Florida Politics, 1877–1893" (Ph.D. thesis, Univ. of Pennsylvania, 1954). Although Williamson's articles and dissertation are the best source on Florida political history in this era, he paid insufficient attention to the blacks, the Populists, and changes in suffrage laws, and failed to relate Florida politics to the rapid socio-economic change taking place at the time.

On particular subjects, James Owen Knauss' "The Growth of Florida's Election Laws," *Florida Historical Quarterly* 5 (1926): 1–16, catalogued legal changes. Kathryn T. Abbey's "Florida Versus the Principles of Populism, 1896–1911," *Journal of Southern History* 4 (1938): 462–475, dealt primarily with railroad rate regulation. Samuel Proctor's *Napolean Bonaparte Broward*, was an unenlightening whitewash of the principal Florida Progressive. But in "Pensacola Labor Problems and Political Radicalism, 1908," in *Florida*

Historical Quarterly 18 (1965): 315–332, Wayne Flynt provided a corrective to Proctor by detailing Broward's strikebreaking activity. Flynt's *Duncan Upshaw Fletcher, Dixie's Reluctant Progressive* is a good biography of the public life of a reticent, private politician; it includes many fascinating details about Jacksonville politics during the eighties and nineties. Joel Webb Eastman treated a racist Progressive in "Claude L'Engle, Florida Muck-raker," ibid. 45 (1967): 243–252. Charles D. Farris has some material on the development of the white primary in "The Re-Enfranchisement of Negroes in Florida," *Journal of Negro History* 39 (1954): 259–283.

Georgia

Few corners of Georgia's political history in this period remain unexplored. Elisabeth Studley Nathans' *Losing the Peace* revised the picture of Georgia Reconstruction and her well-researched book largely superseded such earlier works as Alan Conway's *The Reconstruction of Georgia* and John Allen Meader, Jr.'s, "The Decline of the Two-Party System in Georgia" (M.A. thesis, Emory Univ., 1959), which dealt with the same period. Nevertheless, Nathans' moderate political viewpoint made her too anxious to condemn the Negro and white radicals for not compromising with the rich ex-Whig planters, and too willing to overlook violence, intimidation, and the im-position of the poll tax as key factors in stunting the growth of the Republi-cans.

Among the studies of Post-Reconstruction events is Judson Clements Ward, Jr.'s, excellent analysis, "The New Departure Democrats of Georgia: An Interpretation," *Georgia Historical Quarterly* 61 (1957): 227–236. Allie M. Allen Jackson's "The Georgia Constitutional Convention of 1877" (M.A. thesis, Atlanta Univ., 1936) supplements the printed convention debates. The Independent movement was treated by the perceptive wife of the chief Georgia Independent, in Rebecca Latimer Felton's *My Memoirs of Georgia Politics*. The prototypical representative of the Southern booster spirit was painted in undeservedly glowing colors by Raymond B. Nixon in his *Henry W. Grady, Spokesman of the New South*.

The Georgia Populists fared well at the hands of Alex Matthews Arnett, in *The Populist Movement in Georgia,* one of the best studies of Southern Populism. Where Arnett saw Populism as merely the farmer's natural response to poor economic conditions, C. Vann Woodward discovered a complex pattern of economics, politics, and psychology in his *Tom Watson: Agrarian Rebel*. Woodward's interpretation of Watson, and his and the Popu-list Movement's relationships with blacks has recently been stridently at-tacked in Charles Crowe's "Tom Watson, Populists and Blacks Recon-sidered," *Journal of Negro History* 55 (1970): 99–116, which I read only after forming most of my own views on the subject. Although too concerned with toppling idols—he came close to making the absurd charge that Woodward was a racist in 1938—Crowe did make a case for viewing Watson's whole career from the vantage point of his post-Populist rather than his Populist activities. For a much shriller attack, based less on hard evidence than on crude psychologizing, see Lawrence J. Friedman, *The White Savage, Racial Fantasies in the Postbellum South*, pp. 77–98.

Post-1900 reform politics and the 1908 suffrage amendment are covered in Woodward's *Watson* and in Dewey W. Grantham, Jr.'s *Hoke Smith and the Politics of the New South*; "Georgia Politics and the Disfranchisement of the Negro," *Georgia Historical Quarterly* 32 (1948): 1–21; and "Some Letters from Thomas W. Hardwick to Tom Watson Concerning the Georgia Gubernatorial Campaign of 1906," in ibid. 34 (1950): 328–340. Seeing the period essentially through Hoke Smith's eyes, Grantham found somewhat more to admire about Smith and his ilk and more to distinguish the "Progressives" from the "conservatives" than I do. Alton D. Jones accepted what the middle-class reformers said about themselves in his "Progressivism in Georgia, 1898–1918" (Ph.D. thesis, Emory Univ., 1963).

Clarence A. Bacote's "The Negro in Georgia Politics, 1880–1908" (Ph.D. thesis, Univ. of Chicago, 1955) is a mine of information on the subject. His articles based on that thesis include "Negro Proscriptions, Protests, and Proposed Solutions in Georgia, 1880–1908," in Wynes, ed., *The Negro in the South since 1865*, pp. 149–179; and "Negro Officeholders in Georgia Under President McKinley," *Journal of Negro History* 44 (1959): 217–239. Serious students should consult the dissertation. Bacote's work entirely superseded Ralph Wardlaw, "Negro Suffrage in Georgia, 1867–1930," *Bulletin of the University of Georgia* 33 (September, 1932), no. 2a, a superficial account.

On special topics, Lynwood Mathis Holland revealed little about a potentially interesting subject in "The Direct Primary in Georgia" (Ph.D. thesis, Univ. of Illinois, 1945). Olive Hall Shadgett chronicled patronage squabbles in *The Republican Party in Georgia, from Reconstruction through 1900*. Albert Berry Saye's *A Constitutional History of Georgia, 1732–1945* is biased and unimaginative.

Louisiana

Historians of Louisiana politics tend to focus on the revolts against the establishment—Populism, the New Orleans reformers, and Huey Long—instead of on the conservative establishment iteslf. But looking for faultlines draws attention away from more stable features of the geology. Thus, the best study of Louisiana politics in this period, William Ivy Hair's thorough and biting *Bourbonism and Agrarian Protest* saw the "Bourbons" only in the reflected glare of the farmer radicals. Hair's book superseded such earlier works as Melvin J. White's "Populism in Louisiana During the Nineties," *Mississippi Valley Historical Review* 5 (1918): 3–19; and Lucia E. Daniel's "The Louisiana People's Party," in *Louisiana Historical Quarterly* 26 (1943): 1055–1149. Hair's account of the important 1892 and 1896 elections may be supplemented by two good articles—Henry C. Dethloff's "The Alliance and the Lottery: Farmers Try for the Sweepstakes," *Louisiana History* 6 (1965) : 141–159; and Philip D. Uzee's "The Republican Party in the Louisiana Election of 1896," in ibid. 2 (1961): 332–344. Dethloff's interpretation of Louisiana politics offered in his "Populism and Reform in Louisiana" (Ph.D. diss., Univ. of Missouri, 1964), is almost entirely vitiated by his decision to consider all who claimed to be "reformers" as a unit. They had in common only an enemy, which was enough to unify them for a few short months, after which the widely divergent interests of sugar planters, urban businessmen and professionals, and upcountry Populists reemerged and shattered their temporary coalition. The Lottery Company, the chief issue in 1892, is covered in more detail in Berthold C. Alwes' "The History of the Louisiana State Lottery Company," in *Louisiana Historical Quarterly* 27 (1944): 946–1118. The horrifying story of the convict leasing system and the feeble attempts to end or reform it are detailed in Mark T. Carleton's excellent *Politics and Punishment: The History of the Lousiana Penal System* (Baton Rouge, La.: Louisiana State Univ. Press, 1971.)

Hair's work focused sympathetically on the small farmer independents, the Louisiana Farmers' Union and the Alliance, and the Populists. Two well-researched monographs that approach Louisiana politics from other perspectives and provide valuable insights into Negro political activity are Philip D. Uzee's "Republican Politics in Louisiana, 1877–1900" (Ph.D. thesis, Louisiana State Univ., 1950); and Edwin Aubera Ford's "Louisiana Politics and the Constitutional Convention of 1898" (M.A. thesis, Louisiana State Univ., 1955). There is important information on the convention in a contemporary article by J. L. Warren Woodville, "Suffrage Limitation in Louisiana," in *Political Science Quarterly* 21 (1906): 177–189. Anti-Italian feeling, which had a significant impact on the suffrage debate in Louisiana, is treated in George E. Cunningham's "The Italian, a Hindrance to White Solidarity in Louisiana," in *Journal of Negro History* 50 (1965): 22–36. Allie Bayne Windham Webb's "A History of Negro Voting in Louisiana, 1877–1906" (Ph.D. thesis, Louisiana State Univ., 1962) is sketchy and often unreliable.

Politics in the South's only real metropolis in this period is the subject of two complementary works, Joy J. Jackson's *New Orleans in the Gilded Age*, and George M. Reynolds' *Machine Politics in New Orleans, 1897–1926*.

Unfortunately, neither provides a very satisfactory explanation of the reasons why the reformers, victorious in 1896, lost out so quickly thereafter, or why the extremely competitive politics of the eighties and nineties gave way to an uninterrupted string of machine successes from 1898 on. Paul A. Kunkel, "Modifications in Louisiana Negro Legal Status under Louisiana Constitutions, 1812–1957," *Journal of Negro History* 54 (1959): 1–25, gives some information on the 1921 effort to insure that Louisiana Negroes remained voteless.

Mississippi

When they think of the South, too many Americans automatically think of Mississippi. It is hardly a typical state. More rural, less wealthy, and less industrialized than any other Southern state, it ranked second only to South Carolina in the proportion of Negroes in the late nineteenth century. Since 1874 it has had a stronger tradition of violence, especially racial violence, and a weaker political structure than any other Southern state. In the twentieth century, William Faulkner's novels and the media attention that violence brings have kept Mississippi in the spotlight. Students of disfranchisement and of post-Reconstruction Southern politics have over-emphasized Mississippi because of the plethora of excellent secondary works on the subject. The two best works. Vernon Lane Wharton's *The Negro in Mississippi, 1865–1890*, and Albert D. Kirwin's *Revolt of the Rednecks*, need no further praise from me. James Sharbrough Ferguson's "Agrarianism in Mississippi, 1871–1900: A Study in Nonconformity" (Ph.D. thesis, Univ. of North Carolina, 1952) supplements Kirwin on some subjects.

On the Independent movement and its effect on the Democratic and Republican parties, see Willie D. Halsell's three articles, "Democratic Dissensions in Mississippi, 1878–1882," *Journal of Mississippi History* 2 (1940): 123–136; "Republican Factionalism in Mississippi, 1882–1884," *Journal of Southern History* 7 (1941): 84–101; and "James R. Chalmers and 'Mahoneism' in Mississippi," ibid. 10 (1944): 37–58. Disregarding Halsell's warning that her articles were based primarily on the letters of white Republicans and did not attempt to present the views of Negro Republicans or conservative Democrats, many historians have made too much of her charges of collusion between the blacks and the "Bourbons," using it to support a general hypothesis that upper-class Southern politicians endorsed black suffrage because they found it easy to form alliances with Negroes. But white Republicans hunting federal patronage could be expected to accuse the dominant black faction of party disloyalty. Proof of a black–"Bourbon" entente awaits the discovery of public or private understandings of the part of Negroes and conservative Democrats and closer examinations of local election returns.

Interesting information on the 1890 constitutional convention and the effect of various provisions of the suffrage article appears in three contemporary articles and a pamphlet: Frank Johnston's "Suffrage and Reconstruction in Mississippi," in *Publications of the Mississippi Historical Society* 6 (1902): 141–244, and "The Public Services of Senator James Z. George," in ibid. 8 (1904): 201–226; J. S. McNeilly's "History of the Measures Submitted to the Committee on Elective Franchise, Apportionment, and Elections in the Constitutional Convention of 1890," in ibid. 6 (1902): 129–140; and the *Proceedings of a Reunion of the Surviving Members of the Constitutional Convention of 1890, Held November 1, 1927* (Jackson, Mississippi: Premier Printing Co., 1928), a pamphlet in the Sterling Library at Yale. There is not much material on the years after 1877 in the biography of the chief Republican who attended the 1890 convention, Lillian A. Pereyra's *James Lusk Alcorn, Persistent Whig*.

The two most important figures of early twentieth century Mississippi politics are the subjects of biographies. George Coleman Osborn's *John Sharp Williams, Planter-Statesman of the Deep South* gushes. In his definitive study, *The White Chief*, William F. Holmes failed to explain satisfactorily why Vardaman changed from a stalwart Delta conservative in the 1890s to the most left-wing Southern U.S. Senator from 1912 to 1918. Holmes' failure apparently reflected the scantiness of Vardaman's papers. A shorter synopsis of Holmes' views was given in his article, "James K. Vardaman: From Bourbon to Agrarian Reformer," *Journal of Mississippi History* 21 (1969): 97–115, which superseded an adulatory article by Ernest Ladner, "James Kimble Vardaman, Governor of Mississippi, 1904–1908," in ibid. 2 (1940): 175–205.

North Carolina

North Carolina's historians have assiduously uncovered the facts of that state's political history, but have been less successful in arranging them into patterns which advance our understanding of Southern history or institutions. Thus, Joseph Flake Steelman's massive "The Progressive Era in North Carolina, 1884–1917" (Ph.D. thesis, Univ. of North Carolina, 1955) seems authoritative on practically every major incident. Steelman, however, neglected broad analysis in favor of description, and failed to suggest overarching themes or even to justify treating the years he covered as an "era." And although the most complete published analysis of politics in the eighteen-nineties, Helen G. Edmonds' *The Negro and Fusion Politics in North Carolina, 1894–1901*, abounds in interesting data, too much of it is undigested.

Neither William A. Mabry's *The Negro in North Carolina Politics Since Reconstruction*, nor Frenise A. Logan's more liberal and detailed *The Negro in North Carolina, 1876–1894* is really about black people. Both, instead, largely describe white attitudes and actions towards the blacks. James A. Padgett's "From Slavery to Prominence in North Carolina," *Journal of Negro History* 22 (1937): 433–487, has some information about black state legislators.

The events of the nineties, from the point of view of the extremely racist and heatedly partisan Democratic editor of the *Raleigh News and Observer*, appear in Josephus Daniels' autobiographical volumes, *Tar Heel Editor* and *Editor in Politics*; and in the worshipful biography by Joseph L. Morrison, *Josephus Daniels Says* . . . . Daniels' inside account is often revealing, if not entirely trustworthy. Simeon Alexander Delap's "The Populist Party in North Carolina," in Trinity College Historical Society *Historical Papers*, series xiv, pp. 40–74, has been outmoded by more recent scholarship, but J. G. deRoulhac Hamilton's *North Carolina since 1860* is still worth consulting despite Hamilton's pro-Democratic and mildly racist biases.

Most of these works touch on the passage of the suffrage amendment. In addition, see J. O. Carr, "George Rountree," in Samuel A. Ashe, ed., *Biographical History of North Carolina*, 8:365–371; and Charles B. Aycock, "Francis D. Winston," in ibid. 2:475–480. These are good biographical sketches of the chief framers of the election law and suffrage amendment in the legislature. For excellent contemporary descriptions of the violence-and fraud-filled 1898 and 1900 elections, see A. J. McKelway, "The Cause of the Troubles in North Carolina," *The Independent* 50 (1898) : 1488–1492, and "The North Carolina Suffrage Amendment, " in ibid. 52 (1900) : 1955–1957; editorial, ibid. 52 (1900) :1874–1876; Marion Butler, "Election in North Carolina," ibid. 52 (1900) :1953–1955; and editorial *The Outlook* 55 (1900): 841–843.

If I were to recommend a single document to someone who wanted insights into Southern "Progressivism," it would be Governor Charles Brantley Aycock's inaugural address, contained in North Carolina Legislature, *Public Documents, 1901 Session* (Raleigh, North Carolina: n.p., n.d.), vol. I, Document la. Flaunting a rhetorical and empty paternalism toward black people, Aycock also openly avowed his firm disbelief in manhood suffrage and embraced violent revolution as a means of denying power to those he felt were enemies of his race, class, and party. Oliver H. Orr, Jr., idolized Aycock and berated the governor's critics in *Charles Brantley Aycock*, perhaps partly because Orr seems to have shared Aycock's racism (see p. 148 of Orr's book). For the period after disfranchisement, see David Charles Roller's "The Republican Party of North Carolina: 1900–1916" (Ph.D. thesis, Duke Univ. 1965). Although Roller set out to prove that the North Carolina GOP was more than a pack of patronage-hungry politicos in this period, he spent most of his time chronicling patronage squabbles.

South Carolina

White South Carolinians' well-known consciousness of history may explain why the quality of historians' writings about the Palmetto State in this period has been so high. David Duncan Wallace's *The History of South Carolina* ranks with Moore's volume on Alabama as the best of the Southern state histories. Despite his obvious biases, Wallace asked a great many important questions and knew his subject thoroughly enough that most of his answers have survived more recent scholarship. Ernest McPherson Lander, Jr.'s short *History of South Carolina, 1865–1960* summarized later research.

Hampton M. Jarrell's *Wade Hampton and the Negro* represented Hampton as one who favored the intimidation rather than the outright slaughter of Negroes in the 1870s and 1880s, and lauded him for this racial liberalism. Hampton's later antagonist, Ben Tillman, found a marvelous biographer, but no unthinking apologist, in Francis Butler Simkins, whose *Pitchfork Ben Tillman, South Carolinian* destroyed many myths about his subject. On the other hand, John D. Stark's *Damned Upcountryman*, is an uncritical view of a reactionary opponent of Tillman.

Several good studies focus more broadly on the post-Reconstruction period. George Brown Tindall's *South Carolina Negroes, 1877–1900* is comparable in content and quality with Wharton's *Negro in Mississippi*, though I believe that the Conservatives' racial policies were less well-intentioned than Tindall did. James Welch Patton has an excellent essay on "The Republican Party in South Carolina, 1876–1895," in Green, ed., *Essays in Southern History*, pp. 91–111. On that party after disfranchisement, see Willard B. Gatewood, "Theodore Roosevelt and Southern Republicans: The Case of South Carolina, 1901–1904," *South Carolina Historical Magazine* 70 (1969): 251–266, which also appears in Gatewood's *Theodore Roosevelt and the Art of Controversy*. Francis B. Simkins reviewed the state's laws on race in "Race Legislation in South Carolina since 1865," *South Atlantic Quarterly* 20 (1921): 165–177. In *The Conservative Regime* William J. Cooper, Jr., tried to picture the post-1865 "Bourbons" not as savvy operators willing to accommodate and eager to emulate their Yankee conquerors, but as romantics who not only fashioned the myth of an edenic antebellum South and a noble and united struggle against aggressive invaders during the Civil War and Reconstruction, but wholeheartedly believed their own fictions. Cooper's data does not support his generalizations.

Among the works absolutely crucial to an understanding of the theory and mechanics of suffrage restriction in the South are three speeches published in pamphlet form by the Southern Mugwump and chief author of the 1881 registration and eight-box law, Edward McCrady, Jr.: "The Registration of

Electors," "The Necessity of Education as the Basis of Our Political System," and "The Necessity of Raising the Standard of Citizenship and the Right of the General Assembly of the State of South Carolina to Impose Qualifications Upon Electors." There is some biographical data on McCrady, a fascinating case study for a student of Southern reform, in Yates Snowden, ed., *History of South Carolina*, 4:273–275. On the way the 1882 law worked in practice, see Robert Smalls, "Election Methods in the South," *North American Review* 151 (1890): 593–600.

On the campaign which led up to the 1895 constitutional convention, see George B. Tindall, "The Campaign for the Disfranchisement of Negroes in South Carolina," *Journal of Southern History* 15 (1949): 212–234. On the convention itself and the document it drafted, consult Tindall's *South Carolina Negroes*, Simkins' *Tillman*, and David Duncan Wallace's propagandistic, but still informative *The South Carolina Constitution of 1895*. Okon Edet Uya, *From Slavery to Public Service* contains all the available, but unfortunately scanty information on a leading South Carolina Negro politician.

Tennessee

There is as yet no adequate guide to the exceedingly complex politics of Tennessee during this period. Philip M. Hamer's *Tennessee, A History, 1673–1932*, is very sketchy on political affairs since 1870. Stanley Folmsbee, Robert E. Corlew, and Enoch L. Mitchell, *History of Tennessee* eschewed analysis and misrepresented the purpose of the secret ballot and poll tax acts. The pattern which Daniel Merritt Robison attempted to impose on the shifting coalitions within the Democratic party in his *Bob Taylor and Agrarian Revolt in Tennessee* falls apart on close examination. Robison barely mentioned suffrage restriction and had little to say about the potent Republican minority.

Outlines of a fuller portrait of Tennessee politics may be filled in with J. A. Sharp's "The Entrance of the Farmers' Alliance into Tennessee Politics," in the East Tennessee Historical Society's *Publications* 9 (1937): 77–92; and "The Farmers' Alliance and the People's Party in Tennessee," ibid. 10 (1938): 91–113. On a fascinating and paradoxical industrialist who sometimes ended up backing Populist candidates, consult Thomas Woodrow Davis, "Arthur S. Colyar and the New South, 1865–1905" (Ph.D. thesis, Univ. of Missouri, 1962). Robert E. Corlew's "The Negro in Tennessee, 1870–1900" (Ph.D. thesis, Univ. of Alabama, 1954) was biased, unreliable, and insubstantial, but the topic is potentially fruitful. Corlew's underestimate of anti-Negro violence was corrected in Richard O. Curry, "Introduction," in Curry, ed., *Radicalism, Racism and Party Realignment*.

On the 1870 constitutional convention which authorized the poll tax, and later battles over enacting the tax, see Joshua W. Caldwell, *Studies in the Constitutional History of Tennessee*, and Wallace McClure, *State Constitution-Making, With Especial Reference to Tennessee*. Charles A. Miller, ed., *The Official and Political Manual of the State of Tennessee* has information on the 1890 gubernatorial campaign, which was fought partially on the issue of the recently passed election laws. For the period after the restriction of the suffrage, see Verton M. Queener's "The East Tennessee Republican Party, 1900–1914," the East Tennessee Historical Society's *Publications* 22 (1950): 94–127, an article based mostly on the *Knoxville Journal*. Gary W. Reichard showed that some Negroes still voted in the four major cities in 1920 in his "The Aberration of 1920: An Analysis of Harding's Victory in Tennessee," *Journal of Southern History* 36 (1970): 33–49.

Texas

Much of Texas was a frontier area in the late nineteenth century, and much of late nineteenth century Texas history is still a frontier. We finally have an adequate narrative of post-Reconstruction politics in Chester Alwyn Barr, Jr., *Reconstruction to Reform*. Frank W. Johnson, *A History of Texas and Texans*, ed. by Eugene C. Barker, with chapters on the period after statehood written by Ernest William Winkler, also provides some information. Winkler, the state librarian at the time, also edited *Platforms of Political Parties in Texas*, a book useful in identifying the multiferous parties and recording issue shifts and party splits. Seth Shepard McKay made the 1875 constitutional convention one of the best documented events in Texas history after the Republic with his earlier cited *Debates*, and his two studies *Making the Texas Constitution of 1876* and *Seven Decades of the Texas Constitution of 1876*.

On the period after 1876, Roscoe C. Martin's *The People's Party in Texas* was in many ways an exemplary state study of Populism. The other principal study of Texas politics before 1920 is James Aubrey Tinsley's well-researched "The Progressive Movement in Texas" (Ph.D. thesis, Univ. of Wisconsin, 1953). Although he illuminated many topics, Tinsley tended to take Progressive rhetoric too much at face value. For instance, he seems to have put some credence in the disfranchisers' claims that they acted only in the interest of "purity and honesty in elections." Lawrence C. Goodwyn showed how much an imaginative historian can do with oral history in "Populist Dreams and Negro Rights: East Texas as a Case Study," *American Historical Review* 76 (1971): 1435–1456. Paul Casdorph's *A History of the Republican Party in Texas, 1865–1965*, is uninformative on this period. Ben H. Proctor failed to puncture the surface of a complex and interesting figure in *Not Without Honor*. Robert C. Cotner's adulatory *James Stephen Hogg, A Biography* has disappointingly little material on the poll tax or other election laws. Neither does George Portal Huckaby's apologetic "Oscar Branch Colquitt: A Political Biography" (Ph.D. diss., Univ. of Texas, 1946), a study of a conservative Texas governor.

In *The Negro in Texas, 1874–1900*, Lawrence Delbert Rice presented a thorough overview of his subject, but failed to clarify the identity of the suffrage restrictionists and the reasons why numerous efforts to enact restrictions were defeated. Rice did successfully refute the hypothesis that the poll tax was aimed chiefly at the poor whites, a hypothesis put forward by Donald S. Strong, "The Poll Tax: The Case of Texas," *American Political Science Review* 38 (1944): 693–709, and followed by W. E. Benton, *Suffrage and Elections*, and Dick Smith, "Texas and the Poll Tax," *Southwestern Social Science Quarterly* 45 (1964): 167–173. Charles K. Chamberlain's biography of the chief agitator for the poll tax, "Alexander Watkins Terrell, Citizen, Statesman" (Ph.D. thesis, Univ. of Texas, 1956), is an uncritical celebration. Information on others who backed the tax is scarce, but Seth S. McKay and Odie B. Faulk gave some facts about Pat Neff, poll-taxer in 1901 and progressive governor from 1920 to 1924, in *Texas After Spindletop*. The effect of the repeal of the poll tax is the subject of an interesting article by Don Nimmo and Clifton McCleskey, "Impact of the Poll Tax on Voter Participation: The Houston Metropolitan Area in 1966," *Journal of Politics* 31 (1969): 682–699.

Virginia

The student of post-Reconstruction Virginia politics can choose among pro- and anti-Democratic accounts, pro- and anti-Progressive interpretations, racist and anti-racist versions of history. Biographies of even minor figures abound. Monographs on politics do not slight economic or social factors. In the Old Dominion, the analyst of Southern politics enjoys the rare luxury of having to decide which of several well-argued views of the period is correct.

Allen W. Moger's *Virginia, Bourbonism to Byrd, 1870–1925* provides a good overview of the whole period and an especially revealing look at covert corporate machinations. On the 1870s and 1880s, both Charles Chilton Pearson's *The Readjuster Movement in Virginia* and Nelson M. Blake's *William Mahone of Virginia, Soldier and Political Insurgent* are thorough studies. Pearson's slight hostility to Mahoneism was more than balanced by Blake's admiration for his subject. Jack P. Maddex, Jr., painted the pre-1879 Conservatives as young, Whiggish, and pro-business in his well-written *The Virginia Conservatives, 1867–1879: A Study in Reconstruction Politics*, one of several recent works demonstrating the inappropriateness of the title "Bourbon" for the post-Reconstruction Democrats. Robert R. Jones attempted a slight refurbishment of the reputation of one Redeemer in "James L. Kemper and the Virginia Redeemers Face the Race Question: A Reconsideration," *Journal of Southern History* 38 (1972): 393–414, but the effort is not wholly convincing. The memoir of a Readjuster-Republican editor, William C. Pendleton's *Political History of Appalachian Virginia*, provides insights into the motivations of mountain nonconformists. Walter T. Calhoun has an excellent account of the climactic event in the Readjuster downfall in "The Danville Riot and Its Repercussions on the Virginia Election of 1883," *Studies in the History of the South, 1875–1922*, pp. 25–51.

Virginia Negroes fare poorly in a Dunningesque monograph by Richard L. Morton, *The Negro in Virginia Politics, 1865–1902*. Works by three Negro scholars provide a useful corrective to Morton's racist view: Alrutheus Ambush Taylor, *The Negro in the Reconstruction of Virginia*; Robert E. Martin, "Negro Disfranchisement in Virginia," in *Howard University Studies in the Social Sciences*, vol. 1, no. 1 (Washington, D. C.: Howard University, 1938); and Luther Porter Jackson, *Negro Officeholders in Virginia, 1865–1895*. These works should be supplemented by Charles E. Wynes' *Race Relations in Virginia 1870–1902*, which generally confirmed Woodward's Jim Crow thesis; and the first four chapters of Andrew Buni's solid *The Negro in Virginia Politics, 1902–1965*. Populism was only a minor eddy in Virginia, and William DuBose Sheldon gave it about all the attention it deserves in *Populism in the Old Dominion*. The close 1896 presidential race is the subject of Allen W. Moger's "The Rift in Virginia Democracy in 1896," *Journal of Southern History* 4 (1938): 295–317.

Virginia scholars seem readier than historians of other Southern states to question the traditional view of the Progressives as simply altruistic liberal reformers. Even the most pro-Progressive studies, such as William E. Larsen's *Montague of Virginia*, turned up little to differentiate the "independent" reformers from the "machine" conservatives. In *Old Virginia Restored*, Raymond H. Pulley saw the Progressives as men who sought to impose controls on what they perceived as the social and political chaos of Reconstruction, Readjusterism, and Populism, and thereby to return the state to an idealized, aristocratic past. Pulley's analysis rested on a series of recent biographies of Virginia political figures, of which three were important to a study of suffrage restriction. Richard Burke Doss, "John Warwick Daniel, A Study in the Virginia Democracy" (Ph.D. thesis, Univ. of Virginia, 1955) deals with a politician outstanding even in his profession for his vacuous magniloquence. Harry Edward Poindexter gave ample proof in "From Copy Desk to Congress: The Pre-Congressional Career of Carter Glass" (Ph.D. thesis, Univ. of Virginia, 1966) that his subject was an unblemished reactionary. On the other hand, in "Henry De La Warr Flood: A Case Study of Organization

Politics in an Era of Reform" (Ph.D. thesis, Rice Univ. 1966) Burton Ira Kaufman depicted a conservative machine politician as a man who often at least sounded like a liberal reformer.

The disfranchising convention, a central event in the interpretation of Virginia Progressivism, may most easily be approached through Wythe W. Holt, Jr.'s "The Virginia Constitutional Convention of 1901–1902: A Reform Movement Which Lacked Substance," *Virginia Magazine of History and Biography* 76 (1968): 67–102. It is not clear what of substance Holt expected to find, or why. Holt's and the other works previously cited largely replace Ralph Clipman McDanel's *The Virginia Constitutional Convention of 1901–1902*, which had already superseded J. A. C. Chandler's racially biased "History of Suffrage in Virginia," in *Johns Hopkins University Studies in Historical and Political Science*, (Baltimore, Maryland, 1901), pp. 279–352. Three contemporary articles by prominent delegates also help explain the convention's actions and the politicians' motives: William A. Anderson, "Virginia Constitutions," in *Report of the 12th Annual Meeting of the Virginia State Bar Association* (Richmond, Virginia: John T. West, 1900), pp. 145–178; John W. Daniel, "The Work of the Constitutional Convention," in *Report of the 14th Annual Meeting of the Virginia State Bar Association* (Richmond, Virginia: Everett Waddey Co., 1902), pp. 257–294; and A. Caperton Braxton, "The Fifteenth Amendment—An Account of Its Enactment," in *Report of the 15th Annual Meeting of the Virginia State Bar Association* (Richmond, Virginia: Everett Waddey, Co., 1903), pp. 243–308.

The consequences of the narrowing of the suffrage and the perfecting of the Democratic organization were detailed in Herman L. Horn's "The Growth and Development of the Democratic Party in Virginia since 1890" (Ph.D. thesis, Duke Univ., 1949), a fine thesis which also stressed the partisan motives for disfranchisement. In "The Political Career of C. Bascom Slemp" (Ph.D. thesis, Duke Univ., 1950), Guy B. Hathorn treated the chief Southern Republican after 1900, a dull racist millionaire who had as little in common with the party of Radical Reconstruction as more recent Southern Republicans do.

Partial Alphabetical List of Frequently Quoted Books

Abbey, Kathryn Trimmer. *Florida: Land of Change.* Chapel Hill, North Carolina: University of North Carolina Press, 1941.

Albright, Spencer D. *The American Ballot.* Washington, D.C.: American Council on Public Affairs, 1942.

Arnett, Alex Matthews. *The Populist Movement in Georgia.* New York: Columbia University Press, 1922.

Ashe, Samuel A., ed. *Biographical History of North Carolina.* 8 vols. Greensboro, North Carolina: Charles L. Van Noppen, 1903–1908.

Bailey, Hugh C. *Liberalism in the New South: Southern Social Reformers and the Progressive Movement.* Coral Gables, Florida: University of Miami, 1969.

Baker, Ray Stannard. *Following the Colour Line: An Account of Negro Citizenship in the American Democracy.* New York: Doubleday, Page & Co., 1908.

Barr, Chester Alwyn, Jr. *Reconstruction to Reform: Texas Politics, 1876–1906.* Austin, Texas: University of Texas Press, 1971.

Barrows, Isabel C., ed. *First Mohonk Conference on the Negro Question.* June 4, 5, 6, 1890. Reprint ed. New York: Negro Universities Press, 1969.

Bendix, Reinhard, ed. *Nation-Building and Citizenship.* New York: John Wiley & Sons, 1964.

Benton, W. E. *Suffrage and Elections.* Dallas, Texas: The Arnold Foundation of Southern Methodist University, 1960.

Beth, Loren P. *The Development of the American Constitution, 1877–1917.* New York: Harper & Row, 1971.

Billington, Monroe Lee. *The American South.* New York: Charles Scribner's Sons, 1971.

Blaine, James G. *Twenty Years of Congress.* 2 vols. Norwich, Connecticut: Henry Bill Publishing Co., 1884–1886.

Blake, Nelson M. *William Mahone of Virginia, Soldier and Political Insurgent.* Richmond, Virginia: Garrett and Massie, 1935.

Bond, Horace Mann. *Negro Education in Alabama: A Study in Cotton and Steel.* Washington, D.C.: Associated Publishers, 1939.

Buni, Andrew. *The Negro in Virginia Politics, 1902–1965.* Charlottesville, Virginia: University Press of Virginia, 1967.

Burnham, Walter Dean. *Critical Elections and the Mainsprings of American Politics.* New York: W. W. Norton, 1970.

Burnham, Walter Dean. *Presidential Ballots, 1836–1892.* Baltimore, Maryland: Johns Hopkins University Press, 1955.

Caldwell, Joshua W. *Studies in the Constitutional History of Tennessee.* Second edition. Cincinatti, Ohio: The Robert Clarke Co., 1907.

Calhoun, Walter T. *Studies in the History of the South, 1875–1922.* Greenville, North Carolina: East Carolina College, 1966.

Callcott, Margaret Law. *The Negro in Maryland Politics, 1870–1912.* Baltimore, Maryland: The Johns Hopkins University Press, 1969.

Campbell, Angus, and Converse, Philip E., eds. *The Human Meaning of Social Change.* New York: Russel Sage Foundation, 1972.

Casdorph, Paul. *A History of the Republican Party in Texas, 1865–1965.* Austin, Texas: The Pemberton Press, 1965.

Chambers, William N., and Burnham, Walter Dean, eds. *The American Party Systems.* New York: Oxford University Press, 1967.

Clark, John B. *Populism in Alabama.* Auburn, Alabama: Auburn Printing Co., 1927.

Clark, Thomas B., and Kirwin, Albert D. *The South since Appomatox: A Century of Regional Change.* New York: Oxford, 1967.

Claude, Richard. *The Supreme Court and the Electoral Process.* Baltimore: Johns Hopkins University Press, 1970.

Cnudde, Charles F., and Neubauer, Deane E., eds. *Empirical Democratic Theory.* Chicago: Markham Publ., 1969.

Commons, John R. *Races and Immigrants in America.* New York: The Macmillan Co., 1920.

Conway, Alan. *The Reconstruction of Georgia.* Minneapolis, Minnesota: University of Minnesota Press, 1966.

Cooper, William J., Jr. *The Conservative Regime: South Carolina, 1877–1890.* Baltimore, Maryland: Johns Hopkins University Press, 1968.

Cotner, Robert C. *James Stephen Hogg, A Biography.* Austin, Texas: University of Texas Press, 1959.

Current, Richard M.; Williams, T. Harry; and Freidel, Frank. *American History.* Rev. ed. New York: Alfred A. Knopf, 1966.

Curry, Richard O., ed. *Radicalism, Racism and Party Realignment: The Border States during Reconstruction.* Baltimore, Maryland: Johns Hopkins University Press, 1969.

Daniels, Josephus. *Editor in Politics.* Chapel Hill, North Carolina: University of North Carolina Press, 1941.

——— *Tar Heel Editor.* Chapel Hill, North Carolina: University of North Carolina Press, 1939.

DeSantis, Vincent P. *Republicans Face the Southern Question: The New Departure Years, 1877–1897.* Baltimore, Maryland: Johns Hopkins University Press, 1959.

Di Palma, Guiseppe. *Apathy and Participation: Mass Politics in Western Societies.* New York: The Free Press, 1970.

Doster, James F. *Railroads in Alabama Politics, 1875–1914.* University, Alabama: University of Alabama Press, 1957.

Dovell, J. E. *Florida: Historic, Dramatic, Contemporary.* 4 vols. New York: The Lewis Historical Pub. Co., 1952.

Dreyer, Edward C., and Rosenbaum, Walter A., eds. *Political Opinion and Electoral Behavior.* Belmont, California: Wadsworth Pub., 1966.

Durden, Robert F. *The Climax of Populism: The Election of 1896.* Lexington, Kentucky: University Press of Kentucky, 1965.

Edmonds, Helen G. *The Negro and Fusion Politics in North Carolina, 1894–1901.* Chapel Hill, North Carolina: University of North Carolina Press, 1951.

Evans, Eldon C. *A History of the Australian Ballot System in the United States.* Chicago: University of Chicago Press, 1917.

Ezell, John Samuel. *The South since 1865.* New York: Macmillan Co., 1963.

Farmer, Hallie. *Legislative Apportionment.* University, Alabama: University of Alabama Press, 1949.

Felton, Rebecca Latimer. *My Memoirs of Georgia Politics.* Atlanta, Georgia: Index Printing Co., 1911.

Ferguson, John L. "Arkansas Governors and United States Senators." A pamphlet. Little Rock, Arkansas: Arkansas Historical Commission, 1970.

Fletcher, John Gould. *Arkansas.* Chapel Hill, North Carolina: University of North Carolina Press, 1947.

Flynt, Wayne H. *Duncan Upshaw Fletcher: Dixie's Reluctant Progressive.* Tallahassee, Fla.: Florida State University Press, 1971.

Folmsbee, Stanley; Corlew, Robert E.; and Mitchell, Enoch L. *History of Tennessee.* New York: Lewis Historical Pub., 1960.

Fortune, T. Thomas. *Black and White: Land, Labor and Politics in the South.* Reprint. ed. of the 1884 ed. New York: Arno Press, 1968.

Frederickson, George M. *The Black Image in the White Mind: The Debate on Afro-American Character and Destiny, 1817–1914.* New York: Harper & Row, 1971.

Fredman, L. E. *The Australian Ballot: The Story of an American Reform.* East Lansing, Michigan: Michigan State University Press, 1969.

Friedman, Lawrence J. *The White Savage, Racial Fantasies in the Postbellum South.* Englewood Cliffs, New Jersey: Prentice-Hall, 1970.

Fowler, Dorothy Ganfield. *John Coit Spooner, Defender of Presidents.* New York: University Publishers, 1961.

Fuller, Thomas O. *Twenty Years in Public Life, 1890–1910.* Nashville, Tennessee: National Baptist Publishing Board, 1910.

Garraty, John A. *Interpreting American History: Conversations with Historians.* 2 vols. New York: Macmillan Co., 1970.

Gaston, Paul M. *The New South Creed.* New York: Alfred A. Knopf, 1970.

Gatewood, Willard B. *Theodore Roosevelt and the Art of Controversy: Episodes of the White House Years.* Baton Rouge, Louisiana: Louisiana State University Press, 1970.

Gillett, Frederick H. *George Frisbie Hoar.* Boston, Mass.: Houghton Mifflin Co., 1934.

Going, Allen Johnston. *Bourbon Democracy in Alabama, 1874–1890.* University, Alabama: University of Alabama Press, 1951.

Grantham, Dewey W., Jr., *The Democratic South.* Athens, Georgia: University, of Georgia Press, 1963.

————. *Hoke Smith and the Politics of the New South.* Baton Rouge, Louisiana: Louisiana State University Press, 1958.

Green, Fletcher M., ed. *Essays in Southern History.* Chapel Hill, North Carolina: University of North Carolina Press, 1949.

Grimes, Alan P. *The Puritan Ethic and Woman Suffrage.* New York: Oxford University Press, 1967.

Hackney, F. Sheldon. *Populism to Progressivism in Alabama.* Princeton, New Jersey: Princeton University Press, 1969.

Hair, William Ivy. *Bourbonism and Agrarian Protest: Louisiana Politics, 1877–1900.* Baton Rouge, Louisiana: Louisiana State University Press, 1969.

Hallowell, Richard P. "Negro Suffrage Justified." A pamphlet. Boston, Massachusetts: George H. Ellis, Co., 1903.

Hamer, Philip M. *Tennessee, A History, 1673–1932.* 4 vols. Chicago and New York: The American Historical Society, 1933.

Hamilton, J. G. deRoulhac. *North Carolina since 1860.* Chicago and New York: The Lewis Pub. Co., 1919.

Hamilton, James Albert. *Negro Suffrage and Congressional Representation.* New York: The Winthrop Press, 1910.

Handlin, Oscar. *The History of the United States.* New York: Holt, Rinehart & Winston, 1967.

Harris, Joseph P. *Registration of Voters in the United States.* Washington, D.C.: The Brookings Institution, 1929.

Herbert, Hilary A., et al. *Why the Solid South? Or Reconstruction and Its Results.* Baltimore: R. H. Woodward and Co., 1890.

Hicks, John D. *The Populist Revolt.* Minneapolis, Minnesota: University of Minnesota Press, 1931.

Higham, John. *Strangers in the Land: Patterns of American Nativism, 1860–1925.* New York: Athenaeum, 1963.

Hirshson, Stanley P. *Farewell to the Bloody Shirt: Northern Republicans and the Southern Negro, 1877–1893.* Bloomington, Indiana: Indiana University Press, 1962.

Hixson, William B., Jr. *Moorfield Storey and the Abolitionist Tradition.* New York: Oxford University Press, 1972.

Hoar, George Frisbie. *Autobiography of Seventy Years.* New York: Charles Scribner's Sons, 1903.

Holmes, William F. *The White Chief: James Kimble Vardaman.* Baton Rouge, Louisiana: Louisiana State University Press, 1970.

Huntington, Samuel P. *Political Order in Changing Societies.* New Haven: Yale University Press, 1968.

Jackson, Joy J. *New Orleans in the Gilded Age: Politics and Urban Progress, 1880–1896.* Baton Rouge, Louisiana: Louisiana State University Press, 1969.

Jackson, Luther Porter. *Negro Officeholders in Virginia, 1865–1895.* Norfolk, Virginia: Guide Quality Press, 1945.

Jarrell, Hampton M. *Wade Hampton and the Negro: The Road Not Taken.* Columbia, South Carolina: University of South Carolina Press, 1950.

Johnson, Frank W. *A History of Texas and Texans*, edited by Eugene C. Barker. Chicago and New York: The American Historical Society, 1916.

Johnson, Franklin. *The Development of State Legisilaton Concerning the Free Negro.* New York: The Arbor Press, 1919.

Jones, Stanley L. *The Presidential Election of 1896.* Madison, Wisconsin: University of Wisconsin Press, 1964.

Keech, William R. *The Impact of Negro Voting: The Role of the Vote in the Quest for Equality.* Chicago: Rand, McNally, 1968.

Key, V. O., Jr. *American State Politics, An Introduction.* New York: Alfred A. Knopf, 1956.

———. *Politics, Parties, and Pressure Groups.* 5th ed. New York: Thomas Y. Crowell, 1964.

———. *Southern Politics in State and Nation.* New York: Alfred A. Knopf, 1949.

Kirby, Jack Temple. *Darkness at the Dawning: Race and Reform in the Progressive South.* Philadelphia: J. B. Lippincott Co., 1972.

Kirwin, Albert D. *Revolt of the Rednecks: Mississippi Politics, 1876–1925.* Lexington, Kentucky: University Press of Kentucky, 1951.

Knoles, George Harrison. *The Presidential Campaign and Election of 1892.* Stanford, California: Stanford University Press, 1942.

Lambert, John R. *Arthur Pue Gorman.* Baton Rouge, Louisiana: Louisiana State University Press, 1953.

Lander, Ernest McPherson, Jr. *History of South Carolina, 1865–1960.* Chapel

Hill, North Carolina: University of North Carolina Press, 1960.

Lang, Louis J., comp. and ed. *The Autobiography of Thomas Collier Platt.* New York: B. W. Dodge and Co., 1910.

LaPalombara, Joseph, and Weiner, Myron, eds. *Political Parties and Political Development.* Princeton, New Jersey: Princeton University Press, 1966.

Larsen, William E. *Montague of Virginia: The Making of a Southern Progressive.* Baton Rouge, Louisiana: Louisiana State University Press, 1965.

Lewinson, Paul. *Race, Class, and Party: A History of Negro Suffrage and White Politics in the South.* Paperback reprint of 1932 edition. New York: Grosset & Dunlap, 1965.

Link, Arthur S., and Patrick, Rembert W., eds. *Writing Southern History: Essays in Historiography in Honor of Fletcher M. Green.* Baton Rouge, Louisiana: Louisiana State University Press, 1965.

Lipset, Seymour Martin. *Political Man.* Garden City, New Jersey: Doubleday & Co., 1960.

Lipset, Seymour Martin, and Rokkan, Stein, eds. *Party Systems and Voter Alignments.* New York: Free Press, 1967.

Logan, Frenise A. *The Negro in North Carolina, 1876–1894.* Chapel Hill, North Carolina: University of North Carolina Press, 1964.

Logan, Rayford W. *The Attitude of the Southern White Press toward Negro Suffrage, 1932–1940.* Washington, D.C.: The Foundation Publishers, 1940.

——*The Betrayal of the Negro, from Rutherford B. Hayes to Woodrow Wilson.* New York: Collier Books, 1965.

Lynd, Staughton, ed. *Reconstruction.* New York: Harper & Row, 1967.

Mabry, William A. *The Negro in North Carolina Politics since Reconstruction.* Durham, North Carolina: Duke University Press, 1940.

McClure, Wallace. *State Constitution-Making, with Especial Reference to Tennessee.* Nashville, Tennessee: Marshall and Bruce Co., 1916.

McCormick, Richard P. *The History of Voting in New Jersey: A Study in the Development of Election Machinery, 1664–1911.* New Brunswick, New Jersey: Rutgers University Press, 1953.

McCrady, Edward, Jr. "The Necessity of Education as the Basis of Our Political System." A pamphlet in the Columbia University Library. Charleston, South Carolina: Walker, Evans, and Cogswell, 1880.

——. "The Necessity of Raising the Standard of Citizenship and the Right of the General Assembly of the State of South Carolina to Impose Qualifications upon Electors." A pamphlet in the Columbia University Library. Charleston, South Carolina: Walker, Evans, and Cogswell, 1881.

——. "The Registration of Electors." A pamphlet in the Charleston Library Society. Charleston, South Carolina: Walker, Evans, and Cogswell, 1879(?).

Macridis, Roy C., ed. *Political Parties*. New York: Harper and Row, 1967.

McCulloch, Albert J. *Suffrage and its Problems*. Baltimore, Maryland: Warwick and York, 1929.

McDanel, Ralph Clipman. *The Virginia Constitutional Convention of 1901–1902*. Baltimore, Maryland: Johns Hopkins University Press, 1928.

McGovney, Dudley O. *The American Suffrage Medley: The Need for a National Uniform Suffrage*. Chicago: University of Chicago Press, 1949.

McKay, Seth Shepard. *Making the Texas Constitution of 1876*. Philadelphia: University of Pennsylvania Press, 1924.

———. *Seven Decades of the Texas Constitution of 1876*. No city or publisher, 1942.

McKay, Seth Shepard, ed. *Debates in the Texas Constitutional Convention of 1875*. Austin, Texas: University of Texas Press, 1930.

McKay, Seth Shepard, and Faulk, Odie B. *Texas after Spindletop*. Austin, Texas: Stack-Vaughn Co., 1965.

McMillan, Malcom Cook. *Constitutional Development in Alabama, 1798–1901: A Study in Politics, the Negro, and Sectionalism*. Chapel Hill, North Carolina: University of North Carolina Press, 1955.

Maddex, Jack P., Jr. *The Virginia Conservatives, 1867–1879: A Study in Reconstruction Politics*. Chapel Hill, North Carolina: University of North Carolina Press, 1970.

Martin, Roscoe C. *The People's Party in Texas*. Austin, Texas: University of Texas Press, 1933.

Mayer, George H. *The Republican Party, 1854–1964*. New York: Oxford University Press, 1964.

Meier, August. *Negro Thought in America, 1880–1915*. Ann Arbor, Michigan: University of Michigan Press, 1963.

Meier, August, and Rudwick, Elliot, eds. *The Making of Black America*. New York: Atheneum, 1969.

Merriam, Charles Edward. *Primary Elections: A Study of the History and Tendencies of Primary Election Legislation*. Chicago: University of Chicago Press, 1908.

Merrill, Horace S., and Merrill, Marion G. *The Republican Command, 1897–1913*. Lexington, Kentucky: University Press of Kentucky, 1971.

Milbrath, Lester W. *Political Participation: How and Why Do People Get Involved in Politics?* Chicago: Rand, McNally, 1965.

Milford, Nancy. *Zelda, A Biography*. New York: Harper & Row, 1970.

Miller, Charles A., ed. *The Official and Political Manual of the State of Tennessee*. Nashville, Tennessee: Marshall and Bruce Co., 1890.

Moger, Allen W. *Virginia, Bourbonism to Byrd, 1870–1925.* Charlottesville, Virginia: University Press of Virginia, 1968.

Moore, Albert B. *History of Alabama and Her People.* Chicago and New York: The American Historical Society, 1927.

Morgan, W. Scott. *History of the Wheel and Alliance and the Impending Revolution.* Reprint. ed. of 1891 ed. New York: Burt Franklin, 1968.

Morison, Samuel Eliot, and Commager, Henry Steele. *Growth of the American Republic.* 5th ed. New York: Oxford University Press, 1962.

Morris, Richard B., and Greenleaf, William, *U.S.A.: The History of a Nation.* Chicago, Rand, McNally, 1969.

Morrison, Joseph L. *Josephus Daniels Says . . . .* Chapel Hill, North Carolina: University of North Carolina Press, 1962.

Morton, Richard L. *The Negro in Virginia Politics, 1865–1902.* Charlottesville, Virginia: University of Virginia Press, 1919.

Nathans, Elisabeth Studley. *Losing the Peace: Georgia Republicans and Reconstruction, 1865–1871.* Baton Rouge, Louisiana: Louisiana State University Press, 1969.

Newby, I. A. *The Development of Segregationist Thought.* Homewood, Illinois: Dorsey Press, 1968.

———. *Jim Crow's Defense: Anti-Negro Thought in America, 1900–1930.* Baton Rouge, Louisiana: Louisiana State University, 1965.

Nixon, H. Clarence. "Influences of the Past." In American Council on Public Affairs, *The Poll Tax.* Washington, D.C.: American Council on Public Affairs, 1940.

Nixon, Raymond B. *Henry W. Grady, Spokesman of the New South.* New York: Alfred A. Knopf, 1943.

Nolen, Claude H. *The Negro's Image in the South: The Anatomy of White Supremacy.* Lexington, Kentucky: University Press of Kentucky, 1968.

Nordlinger, Eric, ed. *Politics and Society.* Englewood Cliffs, New Jersey: Prentice-Hall, 1970.

Ogden, Frederic D. *The Poll Tax in the South.* University, Alabama: University of Alabama Press, 1958.

Orr, Oliver H., Jr. *Charles Brantley Aycock.* Chapel Hill, North Carolina: University of North Carolina Press, 1961.

Osborn, George Coleman. *John Sharp Williams, Planter-Statesman of the Deep South.* Baton Rouge, Louisiana: Louisiana State University Press, 1943.

Ostrogorski, M. *Democracy and the Party System in the United States.* New York: Macmillan Co., 1910.

Pearson, Charles Chilton, *The Readjuster Movement in Virginia.* New Haven, Connecticut: Yale University Press, 1917.

Pendleton, William C. *Political History of Appalachian Virginia.* Dayton, Virginia: The Shenandoah Press, 1927.

Pereyra, Lillian A. *James Lusk Alcorn, Persistent Whig.* Baton Rouge, Louisiana: Louisiana State University Press, 1966.

Pollock, Norman. *The Populist Mind.* Indianapolis, Indiana: Bobbs-Merrill, Co., 1967.

Porter, Kirk H. *A History of Suffrage in the United States.* Chicago: University of Chicago Press, 1918.

Proctor, Ben H. *Not Without Honor: The Life of John H. Reagan.* Austin, Texas: University of Texas Press, 1962.

Proctor, Samuel. *Napolean Bonaparte Broward: Florida's Fighting Democrat.* Gainesville, Florida: University of Florida Press, 1950.

Pulley, Raymond H. *Old Virginia Restored: An Interpretation of the Progressive Impulse, 1870–1930.* Charlottesville, Virginia: University Press of Virginia, 1968.

Pye, Lucian W. and Verba, Sidney, eds. *Political Culture and Political Development.* Princeton, New Jersey: Princeton University Press, 1965.

Reynolds, George M. *Machine Politics in New Orleans, 1897–1926.* New York: Columbia University Press, 1936.

Rice, Lawrence Delbert. *The Negro in Texas, 1874–1900.* Baton Rouge, Louisiana: Louisiana State University Press, 1971.

Richardson, James D. *A Compilation of the Messages and Papers of the Presidents, 1789–1897.* Washington, D.C.: G.P.O., 1900.

Richardson, Leon Burr. *William E. Chandler, Republican.* New York: Dodd, Mead and Co., 1940.

Riley, Jerome B. *The Philosophy of Negro Suffrage.* Washington, D.C.: The Author, 1897.

Robison, Daniel Merritt. *Bob Taylor and the Agrarian Revolt in Tennessee.* Chapel Hill, North Carolina: University of North Carolina Press, 1935.

Robinson, Edgar E. *The Presidential Vote, 1896–1932.* Stanford, California: Stanford University Press, 1934.

Rogers, William Warren. *The One-Gallused Rebellion: Agrarianism in Alabama, 1865–1896.* Baton Rouge, Louisiana: Louisiana State University Press, 1970.

Rokkan, Stein. *Citizens, Elections, Parties: Approaches to the Comparative Study of the Processes of Development.* New York: David McKay Co., 1970.

Rowell, Chester H., compiler, *Digest of Contested Election Cases, 1789–1901.* Washington, D.C.: G.P.O., 1901.

Saloutos, Theodore. *Farmer Movements in the South, 1865–1933.* Berkeley, California: University of California Press, 1960.

Saye, Albert Berry. *A Constitutional History of Georgia, 1732–1945.* Athens, Georgia: University of Georgia Press, 1948.

Sellers, Charles Grier, Jr., ed. *The Southerner as American.* Chapel Hill, North Carolina: University of North Carolina Press, 1960.

Shadgett, Olive Hall. *The Republican Party in Georgia, from Reconstruction through 1900.* Athens, Georgia: University of Georgia Press, 1964.

Sheldon, William DuBose, *Populism in the Old Dominion.* Princeton, New Jersey: Princeton University Press, 1935.

Sievers, Harry J. *Benjamin Harrison, Hoosier President.* Indianapolis, Indiana: Bobbs-Merrill Co., 1968.

Sills, David L., ed. *International Encyclopedia of the Social Sciences.* 12 vols. New York: Macmillan Co. and The Free Press, 1968.

Simkins, Francis Butler. *A History of the South.* New York: Alfred A. Knopf, 1963.

———. *Pitchfork Ben Tillman, South Carolinian.* Baton Rouge, Louisiana: Louisiana State University Press, 1944.

Simmons, William J. *Men of Mark: Eminent, Progressive and Rising.* Reprint ed. of 1887 ed. New York: Arno Press, 1968.

Skaggs, William H. *The Southern Oligarchy.* New York: The Devin-Adair Co., 1924.

Smith, Charles W., Jr. *The Electorate in an Alabama Community.* University, Alabama: University of Alabama Press, 1942.

Smith, Samuel Denny. *The Negro in Congress, 1870–1901.* Chapel Hill, North Carolina: University of North Carolina Press, 1940.

Snowden, Yates, ed. *History of South Carolina,* 5 vols. Chicago and New York: The Lewis Pub. Co., 1920.

Southern, David W. *The Malignant Heritage: Yankee Progressives and the Negro Question, 1900–1914.* Chicago: Loyola University Press, 1968.

Sproat, John G. *"The Best Men": Liberal Reformers in the Gilded Age.* New York: Oxford University Press, 1968.

Stark, John D. *Damned Upcountryman: William Watts Ball, a Study in American Conservatism.* Durham, North Carolina: Duke University Press, 1968.

Stone, Alfred Holt. *Studies in the American Race Problem.* New York: Doubleday, Page, & Co., 1908.

Taylor, Alrutheus Ambush. *The Negro in the Reconstruction of Virginia.* Washington, D.C.: Association for the Study of Negro Life and History, 1926.

Tebeau, Charlton W. *A History of Florida.* Coral Gables, Florida: University of Miami Press, 1971.

Thomas, David Y. *Arkansas and Its People, A History, 1541–1930.* 4 vols. Chicago and New York: The American Historical Society, 1930.

Tindall, George Brown. *South Carolina Negroes, 1877–1900.* Columbia, South Carolina: University of South Carolina Press, 1952.

Trelease, Allen W. *White Terror: The Ku Klux Klan Conspiracy and Southern Reconstruction.* New York: Harper & Row, 1971.

Uya, Okon Edet. *From Slavery to Public Service: Robert Smalls, 1839–1915.* New York: Oxford University Press, 1971.

Voegeli, V. Jacque. *Free But Not Equal: The Midwest and the Negro during the Civil War.* Chicago: University of Chicago Press, 1967.

Wallace, David Duncan. *The History of South Carolina.* 4 vols. Chicago and New York: The American Historical Society, 1934.

———. *The South Carolina Constitution of 1895.* Columbia, South Carolina: University of South Carolina Press, 1927(?).

Welch, Richard E., Jr. *George Frisbie Hoar and the Half-Breed Republicans.* Cambridge, Mass.: Harvard University Press, 1971.

Wharton, Vernon Lane. *The Negro in Mississippi, 1865–1890.* Chapel Hill, North Carolina: University of North Carolina Press, 1947.

Williamson, Chilton. *American Suffrage from Property to Democracy, 1760–1860.* Princeton, New Jersey: Princeton University Press, 1960.

Winkler, Ernest William, ed. *Platforms of Political Parties in Texas.* Austin, Texas: University of Texas Press, 1916.

Woodward, C. Vann. *The Burden of Southern History.* Rev. ed. Baton Rouge, Louisiana: Louisiana State University Press, 1968.

———. *Origins of the New South, 1877–1913.* Baton Rouge, Louisiana: Louisiana State University Press, 1971.

———. *The Strange Career of Jim Crow,* 2nd rev. ed. New York: Oxford University Press, 1966.

———. *Tom Watson: Agrarian Rebel.* New York: Oxford University Press, 1938.

Wynes, Charles E. *Race Relations in Virginia, 1870–1902.* Charlottesville, Virginia: University of Virginia Press, 1961.

Wynes, Charles E., ed. *The Negro in the South since 1865.* University, Alabama: University of Alabama Press, 1965.

Index

Alabama: Independents, 25, 130; violence and fraud, 27, 41, 43, 47, 131–32, 134, 138, 166–67, 170–71; Jeffersonian Democrats, 34, 131, 134, 136, 137; Democratic party, 38n, 130–38 passim, 168, 170–71; registration laws, 48, 55n, 59, 61, 135–36; illiteracy figures, 55; literacy test, 60, 70 165, 169; poll tax, 63–71 passim, 165, 169; Populist party, 75–77, 130–38, 167–68, 170, 198n; white primary, 76–77; Republican party, 77, 130, 133n, 135–38, 170, 213; suffrage restriction in, 130–38; Alliance party, 131; black belt leadership, 132–33, 167–69, 196; Independent Democrats, 136; property test, 165, 169; residency laws, 169; Progressivism in, 230–31
—Voting patterns: figures, 15, 25, 27, 41, 67, 137, 166, 168, 226, 227, 240–42, 245–46; white, 28, 42, 55, 137, 226, 227, 231, 240–42, 249; Negro, 28, 42, 55, 137, 240–42, 245–46
—Secret ballot law: Sayre, 32, 40, 53, 55–56, 132–37, 165, 167, 244; Lawson, 132n
—Constitutional convention: attempt to call (1889–1900), 46n, 132, 133, 134, 165–66; of 1901, 66–67, 70, 166–71, 221, 258
—Negroes: registration of, 61; as political activists, 130, 131; disfranchisement of, 134–38, 169–71
—Whites: registration of, 61; disfranchisement of, 135, 137, 169, 170
Alcorn, James L., 142–43
Aldrich, Nelson W., 31
Allain, Theophile T., 153
Allison, William B., 31
Anderson, William A., 47, 70
Anti-Saloon League, 227
Arkansas: Agricultural Wheel, 25, 33, 123; Independents, 25, 43; poll tax, 32, 37, 40, 70, 124, 125–27, 129; secret ballot law, 32, 55–56, 124–30 passim, 259;

Brothers of Freedom, 33, 123; Populist party, 43, 123, 126–29; illiteracy figures, 55; registration laws, 55n; Union Labor party, 123, 124, 125; Republican party, 123, 126–30; Democratic party, 123–30 passim; suffrage restriction in, 123–30; violence and fraud, 129
—Voting patterns: figures, 15, 25, 27, 41, 67, 129, 226, 227, 240–42, 245–46; white, 28, 42, 55, 126, 128, 130, 222, 227, 240–42, 245–46, 249; Negro, 28, 42, 55, 126, 128, 130, 240–42, 245–46
—Constitutional convention: of 1874, 46n; attempts to call (1888, 1891), 125, 126
Arthur, Chester A., 24–25, 93
Australian ballot. See Secret ballot
Aycock, Charles B., 72, 78, 188, 189, 192, 193, 260, 262n

Bacon, A. O., 220n, 233
Bailey, Joseph W., 233
Ballot, secret. See Secret ballot
Barnett, J. W., 201
Baskin, A. P., 99–100, 101
Bilbo, Theodore G., 232, 235n
Binford, H. C., 130
Black belt: voting patterns, xiii, xv, 16–17, 36; thesis, 6–7; and disfranchisement, 16–17, 36, 43, 67, 246–48, 259; and Negro education, 229 See also under specific states
Blaine, James G., 23, 31
Blair, Henry W., 31
Blanchard, Newton C., 152, 158, 159
Blease, Coleman, 232, 234, 235–36
Blodgett, Foster, 213
Bloxham, William D., 93
Boatner, Charles J., 46n
Bowers, Eaton J., 144
Bragg, Walter L., 73
Brian, Hardy, 158
Brosius, Marriott, 21–22
Broward, Napoleon Bonaparte, 97